BURT FRANKLIN: BIBLIOGRAPHY & REFERENCE SERIES 447

A GENERAL HISTORY OF PRINTING

A GENERAL
HISTORY
OF
PRINTING

FROM

The firſt INVENTION of it

IN THE

CITY of *MENTZ*

TO ITS

PROPAGATION and PROGRESS

Thro' moſt of the

KINGDOMS in *EUROPE*

PARTICULARLY

The INTRODUCTION and SUCCESS of it here in
ENGLAND

WITH THE

CHARACTERS of the moſt celebrated PRINTERS

From the firſt INVENTORS of this ART to the Years 1520 and 1550

ALSO

An ACCOUNT of their WORKS

And of the conſiderable IMPROVEMENTS which they made during that Time

---

By *S. PALMER*, PRINTER.

Burt Franklin
New York

Published by LENOX HILL Pub. & Dist. Co. (Burt Franklin)
235 East 44th St., New York, N.Y. 10017
Originally Published: 1733
Reprinted: 1972
Printed in the U.S.A.

S.B.N.: 8337-26625
Library of Congress Card Catalog No.: 75-80258
Burt Franklin: Bibliography and Reference Series 447

PREFACE.

*A*S it is very natural and commendable for every man to be ever inquiring after any discovery or improvement that may be useful to his profession, and to communicate it to the *publick*, I am willing to hope that the care and pains, the time and expence I have bestow'd on the following *History*, will be approv'd by every one who considers the nature, use and extent of it; and the rather, because nothing has been yet publish'd, at least in English, on the subject of PRINTING, so methodical and comprehensive either in the Historical or Practical *part of it*. As to the *History*, I could not, without some regret, observe that we had nothing in our own language but some few fragments dispers'd in several *Authors*, who only spoke of it occasionally, whilst so many Italians, Germans and French had wrote so copiously upon it, and ex professo. *Tho'* even these seem rather to have had a view to the introduction and progress of the Art in their respective countries, than to the displaying of its excellency and improvements. Neither did I find that any of them had given so particular a History of the Invention and Inventors, or so general a one of its progress and promulgation through Europe, and beyond it, as I could have wish'd, or as I thought might be compiled.

A 2

How-

However, neither these considerations, nor the discoveries I had made from some ancient and valuable editions I met with in some of our noble libraries, nor even the examples of several men of my profession abroad, who have writ largely on both the subjects, could have prevail'd upon me to have undertaken this Historical *part, which I knew deserved a much better pen. The* Practical *being more within my province, my ambition reached no higher than to have published such a compleat system of it, from the helps I had received from Mr.* Fertel *and Mr.* Jn. Andr. Endters, (*two eminent* Printers, *the first at* St. Omer's, *and the other at* Nuremberg, *who have published two curious treatises of it*) *and from my own observations and improvements on them; as few of my profession would have fail'd of being the better for in some branch or other of the Art. And I could with the utmost pleasure have communicated all the other discoveries which I had occasionally made, to any person that would have been at the pains of writing this History. But when I discover'd my design, I found, to my surprise, that the* Practical *part would not meet with that encouragement and approbation I expected, particularly from those for whose benefit and improvement I had chiefly design'd it, tho' the publick could not but have been the better for it, by having much better and neater impressions than are generally done.*

Upon this account my friends and patrons persuaded me to alter my Design, and to suspend the Practical *part, till the* Historical, *which they press'd me also to undertake, had in some measure made way for it. Pursuant therefore to this new plan, I resolved to spare neither cost nor pains to get a sight, or at least a certain intelligence of all the Old editions that were valuable either for their antiquity, elegancy, or for any light they could give me into this History, and to add my own*

ob-

obſervatious upon them, not only as an hiſtorian, but more eſpe-cially as a PRINTER. *The Reader will find, by the ſequel, that none but one of that profeſſion, and one that is well vers'd in thoſe old ancient works can form a right judgment of them; and this is the reaſon that ſo many of them have been miſtaken for Manuſcripts, or have been ſuppoſed to have been printed upon wooden blocks, even by perſons otherwiſe very learned and judi-cious, whereas it is even demonſtrable that they were done by ſeparate metal types.*

My next care was to read over all that has been writ hitherto upon the ſubject, eſpecially by the judicious Malinkrot, *by* De la Caille, Chevilier, Endters, P. Pater, Orlandi, *and by the learned Mr.* Maittaire, *from all whom the Reader will find I have re-ceived no ſmall helps, and which I do here gladly acknowledge; and if I have at any time ventured to diſſent from them, I hope he will find my opinion back'd with ſufficient authority; but where that could not be obtained, I have contented myſelf with leading the Reader to the moſt probable ſide. And it is with no ſmall pleaſure that I have found one or two of my conjectures ſince confirm'd by the diſcovery of ſome latent pieces, which were not known to them. They had indeed acceſs to the moſt cele-brated Libraries of their own countries, but this Hiſtory will convince them that all that is valuable and curious is not con-fined to them, and that we have many as nobly and richly furniſh'd in our own as any in theirs.*

And here I ſhould be extremely ungrateful, if I did not take this opportunity of acknowledging the great helps and curious in-formations I have been favour'd with by ſeveral of the Patrons and Encouragers of this work, as well as my great obligations to the Right Honourable the Earls of Pembroke *and* Oxford, *to whom I am proud to own myſelf beholden (but more eſpecially*

to

to the former,) for all the discoveries which this History has above any other extant. My free access to those two Libraries, as well as to those of my very good friends Dr. Mead, Dr. Rawlinson, Mr. Richardson, and others, besides some of our publick ones, such as those of Oxford, Cambridge, and of the Middle Temple, have afforded me the satisfaction of seeing many of those scarce editions, which have been mention'd by most Annalists, if we except Mr. Maittaire, either from Catalogues or hear-say. And here I gladly take this opportunity of returning my thanks to these learned Correspondents, who have favour'd me with any curious intelligence from those Libraries, which my Business and the bad state of health, would not permit me to visit.

The order of this History is as follows.

The first book contains an account of the Discovery and Inventors of the Art, whether really such, or only pretended, with remarks on their first tryals upon Blocks, and their first editions.

The second book treats of the promulgation of PRINTING into all the several cities and places in Europe, and the improvements made to it by the most eminent Printers down to An. 1520.

The third gives an account of its first introduction into England, its rise and progress in several cities, towns and monasteries; with the characters and works of the most famous English Printers to an. 1550, a fuller account of all which may be seen in the following Table of CONTENTS.

This Performance I entirely submit to the approbation or censure of the curious and candid, as it shall deserve. And I shall gain the main end I propos'd, if what I have done shall contribute to some more full and elaborate productions of this nature.

Thus

PREFACE.

Thus far Mr. PALMER's *Preface* to the Hiſtorical part, as to what relates to the Practical, we need not trouble the Reader with it here. What the Author defign'd to treat of in it, may be feen by the *Table of Contents* prefix'd to the firſt Number of this work. In this Table he will likewife find feveral particulars which were promis'd to be added to this Hiſtory, but which we have been obliged to omit, either for want of materials, or becaufe they were not thought fo neceſſary to this work by the promoters of it. Of the firſt fort was the *Hiſtory of Printing* in *Scotland* and *Ireland*; concerning the former of which we can add nothing to the ſhort account which was printed at *Edenburgh* by Mr. *Watfon* the King's Printer there; and as for *Ireland* we are ſtill more in the dark for want of Memoirs. Mr. PALMER had likewife promis'd the Prints of the *Rebus's* of all the foreign eminent PRINTERS, but, as he had not got them cut before his death, and has given an account of them at the end of their works, it was thought that charge might as well be ſpared; ſo that we have only added thofe which were ufed by the moft confiderable ones of our own nation. His liſt of the moft excellent PRINTERS from 1500 to this time; the feveral acts for regulating the Prefs, and for fecuring the property of Copies, being left very imperfect, the charge of finiſhing them was likewife thought unneceſſary; for which reafon they are alfo omitted.

All that needs be added with regard to his Practical part, is, that, as it was intended to have been printed firſt, the Author has left it in ſuch perfect order, that, if the Publick will be pleafed to encourage it, an Edition may be eafily printed from his Manufcript. 'Twere needlefs to tell the world how fit he was for ſuch a work, what pains he has taken, and what improvements he made to it; thofe who knew Mr. PALMER will think it fufficient to fay that the fubject is the *Art of Printing*, and he the Author of it.

THE

THE

C O N T E N T S.

BOOK I.

BOOK

The CONTENTS.

BOOK II.

AP‑

The CONTENTS.

CHAP.

The CONTENTS.

A

The CONTENTS.

A lift of XVI volumes of Drawings and Prints relating to the fame fubject, and taken from the Manufcript-titles of the books themfelves in the fame library.

A chronological and alphabetical Table of all the cities and places in which the Art of Printing began to be exercis'd before *an.* 1500, and in *England* to *an.* 1550.

ERRATA.

PAGE 2. Note † *l.* 8. *for* fciae *r.* fcire. p. 22. *l.* 28. *r.* Regio monte. p. 93. *l.* 2. *dele* of. p. 150. *l.* 6. *r.* BACTIBOVIUS. p. 151. *l.* 23. *r.* VITALIS. p. 173. *l. ult.* marg. *for* fient *r.* tient. p. 178. *for* CHAP. V. *r.* CHAP. VI. p. 182. *l.* 15. *r.* SCINZENZELER. Ibid. *l.* 27. *r.* Montegatiis. p. 190. *l.* 3. *r.* BERNARDIN. p. 190. *l. penult. dele* 15. p. 193. *l.* 22. *r.* L'Aquila. p. 196. *l.* 2 *r.* dei. Ibid. *l.* 30. *r.* Tanaidis. p. 198. *l. ult. r.* Tradidit, *and Ferrarienfis.* p. 208. *l.* 19. *r.* 1472. p. 210. CHAP. IX. *for* CHAP. VIII. *and all that follow are wrong,* &c. p. 224. *l.* 4. *from the bottom* dele , p. 236. *l.* 8. *r.* ENGELHARD. Ibid. *l.* 13. *r.* Afc. p. 249. *l.* 3. *r.* MINCHAR *Happenim.* Ibid. *l.* 5. *r.* BECHINATH. Ibid. Not. 1. *l.* 6. *r.* נכה. p. 250. *l. ult. r.* Verdnfen. p. 252. *l.* 6 *from the bottom, r.* edition. p. 253. *l.* 4. *r.* ROUEN. Ibid. *l.* 6 *from the bottom, r.* Rotomaginm. p. 255. *l.* 6. *r.* Hebraice. Ibid. *l.* 4. *fiom the bottom, r.* Epidemiæ. p. 256. *l.* 12. *r.* ABARBANEL. Ibid. *l.* 14. *r.* Jofuæ. p. 258. *l. ult. joyn the laft word with the firft in the next page.* Ibid. *l.* 13. *r.* ALBUMAZAR. Ibid. *l.* 22. *r.* Hypnerotomachia. Ibid. *l.* 5. *from the bottom, r.* Montegna. p. 260. *l.* 28. *r.* 1516. p. 266. *l.* 19. *r.* 1514. p. 270. *l.* 17. *dele* in. p. 271. Not. 2. *l.* 6. *r.* aptandos. p. 281. *l.* 26. *r.* bought. p. 283. *l.* 4. *r. propaganda.* p. 285. *r.* CHAP. XIV. p. 290. *l.* 8. *r. Chapuis.* Ibid. *l.* 12. *r. creditnr. Ex De,* &c. Ibid. *l.* 18. *r. puro* p. 294. Not. *l. penult. r.* literaria. Ibid. *ult. r.* luat. p. 295. Not. *l.* 3. *r.* aberratum p. 345. *l.* 7. *r. heraldica.* p. 356. *l.* 15. *r.* Poete. p. 364. *l.* 12. *r.* cum. p. 365. *l.* 20. *r.* Mufter. p. 367. *l.* 3. *from the bottom, r.* MDXXXVII. p. 372. *l.* 4. *r.* 1539. p. 375, 376, 377 & 378, *in the Printers dates, dele the redundant* I *between the* XX. p. 380. *l.* 16. *r.* Retractation.

A

A GENERAL
Hiſtory of Printing:

BOOK I.

Of its Origin, Improvement and Progreſs by JOHN FAUST from 1440. to 1462.

CHAP. I.
An Enquiry into the Riſe of Printing.

Y deſign is to give an hiſtorical account of the authors, diſcovery, improvement and progreſs of the Art of Printing ; an Art ſo highly beneficial to mankind, by preſerving and tranſmitting to poſterity the treaſures of antient and modern learning, that its original has been eſteem'd divine. I ſhall begin with a previous enquiry into the cauſes and concurrent circumſtances, which excited the inventors of it to a diſcovery, that might anſwer this end, with more expedition and exactneſs, than *Tranſcribing*, the only method known before.

B   THE

T H E world at this time began to recover from a ftate of ignorance, under which it had labour'd many centuries ; learning reviv'd, and was patroniz'd in almoft every country of *Europe* ; its votaries exerted a laudable zeal in fearching the libraries for thofe valuable books, which had lain buried in obfcurity, and were become extremely fcarce, great numbers being loft in the times of ignorance. Manufcripts were procur'd and multiplied ; but the price of them was fuch, that none but men of fortune could purchafe them : 120 crowns for a *Livy*, and 80 crowns for three volumes of *Plutarch*'s Lives *, was then a moderate price : a few manufcripts were thought a portion worthy a nobleman's daughter ; and one or two intitled the donor and his pofterity to the perpetual prayers of a monaftery : nay kings themfelves difdain'd not the office of procuring them for their learned friends, as appears from a letter of *Antoninus Bocatellus*, firnam'd *Panormus*, to *Alphonfus* king of *Naples* and *Sicily* † ; and an old *manufcript hebrew bible* was a prefent from the Emperor *Frederick* III. to *Reuchlin*, who was fent embaffador to him. *Paulus Jovius* relates a pleafant ftory of one *Jafon Mainus*, a ftudent of *Pavia*, whofe extravagance having brought him to a goal was oblig'd to depofit a manufcript *Codex Juris* on parchment, into the hands of an ufurer, in order to procure his enlargement : *Petrarch*'s rhetoric mafter likewife, by pledging two volumes of *Cicero*'s works, fav'd himfelf from a prifon.

A s this exceffive price tempted fome to purchafe eftates by the fale of their books, and exchange learning for money ; fo the learned at that time freely parted with their wealth to procure thofe invaluable remains of antiquity, out of a generous defign to communicate them to the world.

T H E Tranfcribers now had a favourable opportunity of enriching themfelves, which they might have enjoy'd much longer, had not they (poffefs'd with the moft mercenary views) done an incredible, and in fome cafes ir-

---

* De trib.s voluminibus P L U T A R C H I in quibus parallela viginti quatuor continentur, titulos fumpfit, ut mones ; pretium minus LXXX aureis effe non poteft, &c. *Papiens.* p 114. vet. edit.

† Significafti mihi nuper ex Florentia extare T I T I L I V I I opera vænalia, libros pulcherrimos; libro pretium effe CXX aureos. Quare majeftatem tuam oro, ut L I V I U M, quem regem librorum appellare confuevimus, emi no-

mine meo, ac venire ad nos facias ; interim ego pecuniam procurabo, quam pro libri pretio tradam, Sed illud a prudentia tua fciae defidero, uter ego an Pegnius melius fecerit; is, ut villam Florentiæ emeret, L I V I U M vendidit, quem fua manu pulcherrime fcripferat ; ego, ut L I V I U M emam, fundum profcripfi. Hæc ut familiariter a te peterem, fuafit humanitas & modeftia tua. Vale & triumpha. *Epiftl.* lib. 5.

recoverable

recoverable damage to learning, by mutilating and corrupting the beſt authors : hence ariſe thoſe frequent complaints againſt their negligence and ignorance, which have coſt the learned an infinite deal of labour to remedy : to evince this the following inſtance will ſuffice.

JOHN ANDREAS, biſhop of *Aleria*, one of the greateſt criticks of that age, tells Pope *Paul* II. in his dedication prefix'd to *Pliny's Natural Hiſtory**, printed at *Rome* in the houſe of the *Maximis* by *Panaratz* and *Sweyn-heim, anno* 1470, that tho' he had ſpent nine whole years in cor-recting that author ; yet ninety more would not compleat a correct edi-tion. This demonſtrates what difficulties the republick of learning en-counter'd with at it's revival ; namely, the ſcarcity and exceſſive price of books, and the ſordidneſs of the Tranſcribers, from whoſe hands they came ſo maim'd and incorrect, that the great Printer *Stephens* truly ſaid, *they were a plague to the purchaſer.* Theſe were motives ſufficient to ex-cite the Inventors of this Art to a diſcovery ſo beneficial to the world, and of ſuch honour and advantage to themſelves : who thoſe excellent perſons were, and where it was made, will come under our enquiry in its proper place. And here the reader will find juſt cauſe of wonder, that this Art, which has been ſtiled the nurſe and preſerver of arts and ſciences, ſhould (if I may uſe the expreſſion) be ſo forgetful of itſelf, as not to leave us the leaſt ſketch of its own hiſtory, the inventors being *more ambitious of deſerving, than of purchaſing praiſe.* Some light indeed we receive in this affair from a few inſcriptions uſed by *Fauſt* at the end of his firſt prin-ted books, to this purpoſe. *This preſent work, with all its embelliſhments,* &c. *was done, not with pen and ink,* &c. *but by a new invented Art of caſt-ing Letters, Printing,* &c. *by me* John Fauſt *and my ſon-in-law* Peter Schoeffer *in the famous city of* Mentz *upon the* Rhine, *anno* —— : but re-courſe muſt be had to the writers of thoſe times for the hiſtory of this In-vention. Many cities have contended for the glory of it, and engaged the learned in defence of their claim ; but thoſe on the ſide of *Harlem* have manag'd the controverſy with great warmth, and charged *Fauſt* the Inven-tor with robbing his ſuppoſed maſter *Laurence John Coſter* of many thou-ſand weight of his materials, on Chriſtmas-Eve, when the whole family and city were in prayer at church ; with other ſuch ridiculous ſtories, in-vented meerly to deprive this *Great Man* of the honour, which he had ſo

---

* In nonum annum premi non potuit emendatio, ne futura quidem exacta poſt nonageſimum.

long

long inconteftably enjoy'd. Had this been publifh'd in his life-time, when he might have defended himfelf, or prefently after his death, when his fon-in-law or fome of his friends might have done it for him, he had undoubtedly been clear'd ; but fuch an accufation was not hinted till 125 years after, and then grounded only on fufpicion, as Dr. *Junius* owns *, who was the firft that attempted to transfer this Difcovery from *Mentz* to *Harlem*. However *Fauft*'s name died not with him, tho' fome *Dutch* writers made ufe of *his art* to afperfe his memory : and others of feveral nations rofe immediately in his defence ; in particular the learned *Malincrot*, dean of *Munfter*, in his treatife *De Ortu & Progreffu Artis Typographicæ*, has not only refuted what was advanc'd on the other fide, but made fuch refearches after the old monuments of the Art, and collected fo great a variety of teftimonies, fupported by undeniable facts, as feem at once to determine the controverfy. *Boxhorn* indeed attempted an anfwer ; but whoever reads it over, cannot but be convinc'd, that an over-fondnefs for his country's honour has made him deaf to the moft evident demonftrations of his antagonift. However as he and his followers, have given up the point as to feparate Metal Types in favour of *John Fauft*, and lay claim only to the invention of *Printing on Blocks of Wood*, which they affirm to have been ftoln from *Cofter* by *Fauft*, whofe next invention they would have to be only an improvement of the former ; I fhall give the reader an idea of both, and fhew the difference between thofe firft effays of Printing, and that perfect one, which fucceeded and continues to this day.

C H A P. II.

An Account of the different Manners of Printing by Blocks of Wood, *and* feparate Metal Types.

TIS agreed by moft writers on this fubject, that about the year 1440, feveral attempts were made by fome perfons, with vaft expence and labour, which prov'd abortive ; but that the difcovery of feparate Metal Types was not brought to perfection till about the year 1450. We find that their firft effays were by carving or cutting letters with a fharp-pointed knife upon Blocks of Wood, each Block containing a page or one fide of a leaf ; that inftead of the common

---

* Ut fert fufpicio.

Ink,

Ink, which is the fort they firft us'd, they invented a more glutinous one which fucceeded better, being lefs apt to fpread ; that they pafted the two white fides of each leaf together, to make them look like fingle leaves : but of this I fhall have occafion to fpeak more particularly in fome of the following chapters. In the mean time I fhall endeavour to demonftrate that this invention has not that merit for ingenuity, ufefulnefs, or novelty, which the *Dutch* writers boaft of.

W I T H refpect to the firft, the only requifites are a tolerable genius, fharp tools, and a good copy : as to its ufefulnefs, the only advantage refulting from it, is, that whatever the book be, the forms remain intire, fo that as many editions as the author pleafes may be printed without the expence of a new compofition ; but on the other hand, if we confider that thofe forms are of no ufe to any other work, and the time and expence in cutting them very great, with the great fpace fo many Pages of Wood muft take up, we fhall perceive the neceffity of inventing moveable Metal Types : But farther, this method of Printing was far from being novel, it is even demonftrable from authentick teftimonies to have been practis'd in *China* and *Japan*, above four centuries before it was known in *Europe* : it is not eafy, I grant, to prove that we receiv'd it from them, becaufe of their vaft diftance, and the little commerce between us before the year 1440 : yet there is no impoffibility, but that it might have been brought us by fome merchant either by the way of *Mufcovy* or the *Red-Sea*, the *Perfian Gulph* or *Arabia* : of which opinion I could mention many authors. *Gonzala de Mendofa*, in his hiftory of the *Marvels of China*, written in Spanifh, Book III. Chap. 16 ; and *Martin Martini* in his *Atlas Sinenfis*, tell us, that they could prove by good arguments, that the Invention of *Guns*, of the *Loadftone* and *Printing* was known to us by their means. What adds to the probability of my conjecture is, that the *Chinefe* to this day fend with their goods, printed papers in the manner of our fhop-keepers hand-bills, feveral of which I have feen ; and 'tis not impoffible but the hint of Printing on Blocks of Wood might have been taken this way.

W H O E V E R has a juft idea of the genius of the *Chinefe* and *Japonefe*, will own their capacity to have invented the method of Printing with feparate types, if their manner of writing had admitted it ; but as they are known to write, not with letters, as other nations, but with characters, each of

which

which ftands for a whole word ; and that the number of thofe charaƈters a-
mount at leaft to 10,000, (tho' fome authors reckon above 40,000) ; it
would be impoffible to have cafes large enough to contain 'em, befides
the infuperable difficulty of diftinguifhing and retaining them in memory.   To return from this digreffion, let us now take a fhort view of the
other new and more expeditious method.

I f we duely confider it in all its branches, it will evidently appear the
refult of no fmall ftudy, time and coft.   The cutting the counter-punches
and punches and finking them into the matrices, the adjufting them to the
mould,   that curious piece of mechanifm, for cafting fingle letters ; the
difficulty of the whole manual operation of Letter-founding: in the Printing, the difpofition of the cafes, the curious contrivance of the feveral
parts of the work between the compofitors, correƈtors and prefs-men, &c.
add to all this the fine invention of the Printing-prefs, fo admirable for its
mechanical fabrick,   together with the curious apparatus neceffary for
a Printing-houfe, for an explication of whofe terms we muft refer to the
fecond volume of this work : thefe are things which require a genius vaftly fuperior to devife, better hands to execute, greater forecaft to obviate,
and readinefs to remedy all unexpeƈted defeƈts, more time and patience to
go thro' all its various parts, more refolution to overcome all difficulties,
and laftly the expences neceffary to this invention vaftly larger than thofe
of the former ; and confequently we fhall be far from thinking an interval
of ten years too long, but rather admire that fuch a prodigious defign
could be contriv'd and perfeƈted in fo fhort a time.

W h a t has been faid on this head, will fufficiently demonftrate the dif-
parity between thefe two methods, and convince the reader how much the
former is inferior in every refpeƈt to the latter ; nay, if we dare rely on
the judgment of the learned, we fhould fcarce think it worthy the name
of Printing, fince it has nothing common with it except the ink ; and even
a rowler, cover'd with cloath, would fupply the place of a prefs to print
their Pages of Wood.

N o w whether it be *Fauft* or *Cofter*, who praƈtis'd this method on wood
firft, whether *Mentz, Harlem*, or any other city, gave it firft encouragement ; whether the afore-nam'd perfons had the hint from *China*, or happen'd on it accidentally, (tho' if we admit of the latter fuppofition, *Fauft*
and *Mentz* have the better title) ; this muft be granted from what has
been

been faid, that by Printing we do not underftand the method of Printing on Blocks of Wood claim'd by *Harlem*, but the prefent Art of Printing by feparate Metal Types, which is fo juftly admir'd for its expeditious and correct way of preferving and propagating knowledge; and to which we owe the improvements made in moft arts and fciences for near three centuries paft.

HENCE it appears how little reafon the *Dutch* writers have to value themfelves upon an imaginary victory, which, were it granted in its fulleft extent, would be defpicable in comparifon of the other. Yet *Boxhorn* in his *Theatrum Hollandiæ*, page 142, places his hero *Cofter* in a kind of triumphal chariot, dragging his vanquifh'd enemies the *Germans* and *French* after him, with a pompous infcription, which I think worthy the curious readers notice ✱. He exults as if every fentence in that book was demonftration, and impofes an eternal filence on all thofe nations, which have appear'd in defence of *Mentz*, in a ftanza of fhort verfes after the manner of *Claudian*, which for its fingularity is likewife here quoted †. However, I perfwade my felf that two or three of the following chapters will convince us of the vanity of thefe triumphs, unlefs this piece of divinity and poetry compos'd by *Scriverius* fhall alter our fentiments; it contains four verfes, to be plac'd under *Cofter*'s ftatue, and cited in the *Theatrum Holland.* abovementioned p.156 ✱. I fhall only inform the *Englifh* reader, that the author of them pronounces it as rank atheifm to deny *Cofter* the glory of this invention, as to deny God that of the creation. I fhall now leave *Harlem* and the *Dutch* writers, and pafs over to the city

---

✱ Quem
Flos urbium,
HARLEMUM
Patritia familia edidit,
LAURENTIO COSTERO,
Qui incredibili & prope inhumana
Ingenii felicitate,
Moguntinis ne quidquam negantibus
&
Gallis fruftra obftrepentibus,
ARTEM TYPOGRAPHICAM
Primus invenit,
MONUMENTUM
hoc
L. M. P. Q.
Typis
Pofuimus.

† Serrarii libelli,
Streperi tacete Galli;
Taceat fonourus autor.
Solus ovantem Batavus
Emeditatus artem.
Hæc vox ætheriis infonet axibus,
Hæc vox per populos, per mare tranfeat;
HARLEMUS Typicam prodidit artifex.

✱ Vana quid archetypos & præla *Moguntia*
jactas?
Harlemi archetypos prælaque nata fcias.
Extulit hic, monftrante deo, *Laurentius* artem.
Diffimulare virum hunc, diffimulare deum
eft.

of

of *Mentz*, to examine the teſtimonies brought in favour of her, after having return'd *Boxhorn* four lines from a learned *Italian* poet, who may be ſuppos'd a more impartial witneſs in this controverſy *.

C H A P. III.

Teſtimonies of writers from the middle of the 15th century in favour of John Fauſt.

MALINCROT hath collected the teſtimonies of writers on either ſide of the controverſy, from the promulgation of the art to the time in which he wrote. *viz. ann.* 1640. and rang'd them in the beginning of his book in the following order.

Thoſe who declar'd for *Mentz*, before the diſpute was ſtarted by } 62
    Dr. *Junius*, and quoted by him in that work
Thoſe, who have written on the ſame ſide ſince *Junius*   47
                                                 109

Thoſe who have written in favour of *Harlem*   13
Thoſe who are neuters   11

BY this liſt 'tis manifeſt where the advantage lies as to numbers, but leſt ſo many teſtimonies ſhould be thought tedious, it will not we hope be improper to ſelect the moſt conſiderable, eſpecially from thoſe authors, who wrote ſoon after the diſcovery, and were better acquainted with this matter, than thoſe who liv'd any time after it, and may be juſtly ſuppos'd to have follow'd their predeceſſors. But I would therefore avoid, as much as poſſible, clogging or interrupting the thread of this hiſtory. I ſhall only extract the moſt material authorities out of them, and in ſuch a manner as ſhall be conſiſtent with it, by inſerting the paſſages themſelves in the notes, that the reader may uſe his pleaſure either in reading or omitting them.

---

* Abſtulerat *Latio* multos *Germaniæ* libros;   Et quod vix toto quiſquam perſcriberet anno,
  Nunc multo plures reddidit ingenio: Munere *Germanico* conficit una dies.
                                             Laur. Valla.

HOWEVER

B U T before I proceed any farther, it will be neceſſary to obviate an ob-jection, that will infallibly occur to the reader's mind; which is, that in mentioning the firſt inventors of printing in the two preceding chapters, I have not ſo much as nam'd *John Guttenbergh* : whereas the greateſt part of the authors, whom we are about to quote, place him in the firſt rank, and mention only the other two as co-adjutors to him. In anſwer to this it will be ſufficient for the preſent to ſay, that the ſequel of this Hiſtory will ſhew that *Guttenbergh* had no other ſhare in this invention, than by fur-niſhing the other two with neceſſary ſupplies to defray the great charges of it; and that the authors of the *Mentz* and *Cologn* Chronicle, whom the reſt ſeem to have follow'd in this, as alſo the learned antiquary *Tri-themius*, have certainly confounded *Guttenbergh* with *Fauſt*, that is, mi-ſtook the one for the other, as will hereafter appear in its proper place.

O F all the authors, to whom the world is indebted for a particular ac-count of this Diſcovery, Abbot *Trithemius* juſtly claims the pre-eminence, both upon the account of his living neareſt the time of this diſcovery, which he tells us happen'd in his younger years [1], as well as for his care to derive his intelligence from its origin. We have two noble teſtimo-nies out of his Chronicle ; the one from the firſt part, intitled *Chronicon Spanheimenſe*, where [2] ſpeaking of the year 1450 he ſays ; ,, That about ,, this time the Art of Printing and Caſting Single Types was found out ,, *a-new* in the city of *Mentz* by one *John Guttenberg*, who having ſpent ,, his whole eſtate in this difficult diſcovery, by the aſſiſtance and advice ,, of ſome honeſt men, *John Fauſt* and others, brought his undertaking ,, at length to perfection : that the firſt Improver of this Art, after the In-,, ventor, was *Peter Schoeffer* (in Latin *Opilio*) *de Gernſheim*, who after-,, wards printed a great many volumes : that the ſaid *Guttenberg* liv'd ,, at *Mentz* in a houſe call'd then 𝔷𝔲𝔪=𝔧𝔲𝔫𝔤𝔥𝔢𝔫, but afterward known ,, by the name of the *Printing Houſe*. " But leſt the reader ſhould be

[1] Tempore infantiæ meæ apud *Moguntiam,* &c. *Trith. Epiſt. Fam. Epiſt.* 48.

[2] His quoque temporibus ars imprimendi & characterizandi libros, de novo reperta eſt in ci-vitate *Moguntina* per quendam civem , qui *Jo-hannes Guttenberg* dicebatur : qui cum omnem ſubſtantiam propter nimiam difficultatem in-ventionis novæ in eam perficiendam expoſuiſſet, conſilio & auxilio bonorum virorum *Johannis*

Fuſt & aliorum adjutus, rem inceptam perfecit. Primus autem hujus artis dilator fuit, poſt ip-ſum inventorem, *Petrus Opilio de Gernſheim,* qui multa volumina ſuo tempore impreſſit. Morabatur autem præfatus *J. Guttenberg Mo-guntiæ* in domo 𝔷𝔲𝔦𝔫𝔧𝔲𝔫𝔤𝔥𝔢𝔫, quæ domus uſ-que in præſentem diem illius novæ artis nomi-ne noſcitur inſignita. *Chronic. Spanheim.* ad ann. 1450.

C			ſtartled

ſtartled at the word *a-new (de novo)* it will be requiſite to acquaint him that *Trithemius* was in all probability of the ſame opinion with ſome other writers, who from a paſſage of St. *Cyprian* miſunderſtood, wherein the invention of Printing (by which is meant no more than that of ſtamping of Letters and Hieroglyphicks upon Medals, Coins, &c.) is attributed to *Saturn*, took occaſion to reckon it among the *artes perditæ*, and conſequently eſteem'd this rather a revival of the art than a new diſcovery ; but he ſufficiently retracts that error in the next paſſage we ſhall quote from him, which was not wrote till many years after, and that from a more diligent enquiry into the diſcovery and merit of this new, and *till then unheard of, Art* ; for this will appear from his words as you will ſee immediately.

T h i s next paſſage, which is fuller, and for its ſingularity and deciſiveneſs deſerves to be ſet down at length, is taken out of the ſecond part of *Trithemius*'s Chronicle, intitled *Chronicon Hirſaugienſe*. This book was unknown to the learned till the year 1690. when the *Benedictins* of the monaſtery of St. *Gall* in *Switzerland* beg'd leave to publiſh it from the original manuſcript, which had lain hid all that time. The Abbot wrote this towards the cloſe of his life, after he had been inform'd of many particulars, relating to this invention, from the mouth of *Peter Schoeffer* (in *Engliſh, Shepherd*) ſirnam'd *de Gernſheim*, to whom *Fauſt*, for the many helps he had receiv'd from him, namely, in deviſing Punches, Matrices, and Moulds for caſting their Metal Types (in which the main perfection of the Art conſiſted) gave his only daughter *Chriſtina* in marriage, and from a ſervant took him into partnerſhip with him, as appears by the inſcriptions to the firſt books publiſh'd by them, of which we have given a ſketch already. The paſſage is as follows [1] . ,, About this time (*ann.*

---

[1] His temporibus in civitate *Moguntina Germaniæ* prope *Rhenum*, & non in *Italia*, ut quidam falſo ſcripſerant, inventa & excogitata eſt ars illa mirabilis, & prius inaudita imprimendi & characterizandi libros, per *Johannem Guttenberg* civem Moguntinum, qui cum omnem pene ſubſtantiam ſuam pro inventione hujus artis expoſuiſſet, & nimia difficultate laborans, jam in iſto, jam in illo deficeret, jamque prope eſſet ut deſperatus negotium intermitteret, conſilio tandem & impenſis *Johannis Fuſt* æque civis Moguntini, rem perfecit incœptam. Imprimis igitur characteribus literarum in tabulis ligneis per ordinem ſcriptis, formiſque compoſitis, vocabularium, *Catholicon* nuncupatum, impreſſerunt ; ſed cum iiſdem formis nihil aliud potuerunt imprimere, eo quod characteres non fuerunt amovibiles de tabulis, ſed inſculpti, ſicut diximus. Poſt hæc inventis ſucceſſerunt ſubtiliora, inveneruntque modum fundendi formas omnium *Latini* Alphabeti literarum, quas ipſi matrices nominabant ; ex quibus rurſum æneos ſive ſtanneos characteres fundebant ad omnem preſſuram ſufficientes, quos prius manibus ſculpebant : & revera, ſi uti ante triginta ferme annos ex ore *Petri Opilionis de Gernſheim* civis Moguntini, *qui gener erat primi artis inventoris*, audivi, magnam a primo inventionis ,, 1450.)

„ 1450.) in the city of *Mentz* in *Germany* upon the *Rhine*, and not in
„ *Italy*, as ſome writers falſly affirm'd, the wonderful and *till then un-*
„ *known Art* of Printing Books by Metal Types [*charaƈterizandi*] was in-
„ vented and devis'd by *John Guttenberg*, citizen of *Mentz*; who having
„ almoſt exhauſted his whole eſtate in contriving of this new Method, and
„ labouring under ſuch inſuperable difficulties, in one reſpeƈt or other,
„ that he began to deſpair of, and to throw up the whole deſign; was
„ at length aſſiſted with the advice and purſe of *John Fauſt*, another ci-
„ tizen of *Mentz*, and happily brought it to perfeƈtion. Having there-
„ fore begun with cutting charaƈters of the letters upon wooden planks,
„ in their right order, and compleated their forms, they printed the vo-
„ cabulary intitled *Catholicon*; but could make no farther uſe of thoſe
„ forms, becauſe there was no poſſibility of ſeparating the letters, which
„ were engraven on the planks, as we hinted before. To this ſucceeded
„ a more ingenious invention; for they found out a way of ſtamping the
„ ſhapes of every letter of the *Latin* Alphabet, in what they call Matri-
„ ces, from which they afterwards caſt their letters, either in copper or
„ tin, hard enough to be printed upon, which they firſt cut with their
„ own hands. It is certain this art met with no ſmall difficulties from
„ the beginning of its invention, as I heard 30 years ago from the mouth
„ of *Peter Schoeffer de Gernſheim*, citizen of *Mentz*, and *Son-in-law to the*
„ *firſt Inventor of the Art*. For when they went about printing the Bible,
„ before they had work'd off the third quire, it had coſt them already
„ above 4000 florins. But the afore-mention'd *Peter Schoeffer*, then ſer-
„ vant and afterwards *Son-in-law to the firſt Inventor* John Fauſt, as we
„ hinted before, being a perſon of great ingenuity, diſcover'd an eaſier
„ method of caſting letters, and perfeƈted the art as we now have it.
„ Theſe three kept this manner of printing very ſecret for ſome time,

ſuæ hæc Ars impreſſoria habuit difficultatem; impreſſuri namque Bibliam, priuſquam tertiam compleſſent in opere quaternionem, pluſquam 4000 florenorum expoſuerunt. *Petrus* autem memoratus *Opilio* tunc famulus, *poſtea gener*, ſicut diximus, *Inventoris primi Johannis Fuſt*, homo ingenioſus & prudens, faciliorem modum fundendi Charaƈteres, & artem, ut nunc eſt, complevit. Et hi tres imprimendi modum a-liquandiu tenuerunt occultum, quouſque per fa-mulos ſine quorum miniſterio artem ipſam ex-

ercere non poterant, divulgatus fuit in Argenti-nenſes primo, & paulatim in omnes nationes. —— Et hæc de impreſſoria mira ſubtilitate diƈta ſufficiant, cujus inventores primi cives *Moguntini* fuerunt —— Habitabant autem primi tres artis impreſſoriæ inventores, *Johan-nes* videlicet *Guttenber*, *Johannes Fuſt* & *Petrus Opilio*, gener ejus *Moguntiæ* in domo Jum-junghen diƈta, quæ deinceps uſque in præſens *Impreſſoria* nuncupatur. *Chronic. Hirſaugienſe* ad ann. 1450.

C 2

„ until

,, until it was divulg'd by their ſervants, without whoſe help it was im-
,, poſſible to manage the buſineſs, who carry'd it firſt to *Straſburg*, and
,, by degrees all over *Europe.* ———— Thus much will ſuffice concerning
,, the diſcovery of this wonderful art, the firſt inventors of which were
,, citizens of *Mentz.* ———— Theſe three firſt diſcoverers of printing,
,, *viz. John Guttenberg, John Fauſt* and *Peter Schoeffer* his Son-in-law, liv'd
,, at *Mentz*, in a houſe then call'd 𝖅𝖚𝖒-𝖏𝖚𝖓𝖌𝖍𝖊𝖓, but ever ſince known
,, by the name of the *Printing-houſe.* ,,

FROM this authentick teſtimony, I ſhall beg leave to make the following obſervations, *viz.* 1. That when the author concluded his Chronicle,
ann. 1514. two years before his death, and above 64 years after the diſcovery, this invention was indiſputably aſcrib'd to *Mentz* ; he ſays indeed
that ſome writers had attributed it to *Italy*, but without any foundation ;
and therefore he rejects this notion as abſolutely falſe. Yet *Junius*, as
has been already hinted, firſt ſtarted a diſpute in favour of *Harlem*, almoſt
130 years after the art became known ; and after him Dr. *Mentel* began
another in favour of *Strasburgh, ann.* 1650, both which ſhall be anſwer'd
in their places.

THE next obſervation is, that tho' the paſſage quoted out of his firſt
Chronicle ſeems to be taken, if not copy'd out of that of *Mentz*, which
is likewiſe a very antient and authentick monument, yet our author ſeems
not to have been ſatisfy'd with it, till he had it confirm'd by ſurer hands.
Other authors indeed have written concerning the origin of this art, according to the beſt memoirs they could procure, whether true or falſe ;
but our author alone has been at the pains to fetch his information from
the fountain head, and deliver'd the particulars of it, as he receiv'd 'em
from the principal agent in the invention, in the quotation from his ſecond
Chronicle : ſo that his teſtimony, were it the only one we could produce for *Mentz*, ought ſtill to be eſteem'd unqueſtionable and de-
ciſive.

ANOTHER particular worth our obſervation is, that tho' he mentions
two books as printed immediately upon the diſcovery, *viz.* the *Catholicon*
and the *Bible*, yet he ſufficiently ſhews the difference between the methods
of their impreſſion ; the former being done upon wooden planks, cut with
a knife after the *Chineſe* manner, as our wooden cutts are done now ;
whereas the *Bible* was printed with ſeparate types, which, as we ſhew'd in
the

the preceding chapter, is the only way that merits the name of *Printing.* This ſeems plainly intimated by the words in the citation before-mentioned, *When they came to print the Bible; and by the vaſt expence they had been at before they finiſh'd the third quire of it:* from which it is evident, that this ſacred book was the firſt work of conſequence which the authors of this art made choice of to ſignalize the firſt-fruits of their invention.

T H E laſt thing I would obſerve is, that tho' *Trithemius* gives the precedency of this diſcovery to *John Guttenbergh,* in the beginning of this paſſage, yet within a few lines after, he twice gives the title of *The firſt inventor of Printing* to *John Fauſt;* which contradiction cannot be well reconcil'd otherwiſe, than by ſuppoſing that he, thro' inadvertency, wrote the name of *John Guttenberg* inſtead of *John Fauſt* and this is far from being improbable, ſince their chriſtian names are the ſame: and tho' he again puts *Guttenbergh* firſt, when he ſpeaks of the houſe in which they liv'd, yet this might be done only out of reſpect to him, either as being a knight (according to the writers of that time), or becauſe he was the moſt opulent of the three, and had contributed moſt to the charges of the invention.

T H I S muſt be allow'd, unleſs we could ſuppoſe that the editor having compar'd the two paſſages together, namely, that out of the firſt, and this out of the ſecond Chronicle, had corrected, as he imagin'd, the latter by the former, upon a ſuſpicion, that the author writing the laſt almoſt 30 years after he had receiv'd the account from *Schoeffer,* might have miſtaken one name for the other; but to be certain of this, it would be neceſſary to conſult the original. However, what confirms me in my conjecture is, that the author or his editor have committed a miſtake, and that *Guttenberg* had no other intereſt in the diſcovery than by aſſiſting them with money to promote the deſign, is, the law-ſuit which he commenc'd againſt *Fauſt* at *Mentz* about the money expended, and the judgment of the court thereupon; of which the learned *Salmuth* has given the following account in his appendix to *Pancirol*'s commentaries [1]; and this may

---

[1] Eodem tempore *Moguntiæ* commorebatur *Johannes Guttenbergius,* honeſtis parentibus natus, qui proxime *Fauſti* ædibus habitabat. Hic cum animadvertiſſet inſignem hanc artem Typographicam, non ſolum omnium ore paſſim celebrari, ſed etiam admodum lucroſam eſſe, familiaritatem cum *Fauſto* contraxit; & quia opulentus erat, pecuniam ei ad ſumptus neceſſarios obtulit; quod *Fauſto* minime ingratum fuit, quandoquidem comperiebat ſumptus, quos in artem faciebat, quotidie creſcere, & tunc opus chartæ pergamenæ imprimendum ſub manibus habebat: quapropter cum *Guttenbergio* convenit & pactus eſt, ut quic-

be

be eſteem'd another pregnant teſtimony for *Fauſt*, ſince 'tis extracted from an original record of the law-ſuit. The narrative as related by our author is as follows.

,, A B O U T this time there liv'd at *Mentz* one *John Guttenbergh*, born
,, of honeſt parents, who dwelt next door to *John Fauſt*: he obſerving
,, this famous art of Printing was not only cry'd up every where, but
,, alſo very gainful, contracted a friendſhip with *Fauſt*; and being ex-
,, ceeding rich, offer'd to ſupply him with money to defray the charges
,, of it, which was gladly accepted by *Fauſt*, who began to find the ex-
,, pence grow too faſt upon him, and wanted *vellum* to print a work then in
,, hand. Upon this he agrees and covenants with *Guttenbergh*, that whatever
,, ſums were laid out in the work, ſhould turn to their common profit
,, or loſs. But becauſe *Fauſt* had diſpos'd of more money then *Guttenbergh*
,, imagin'd the buſineſs would require, he refuſed to pay his moiety;
,, upon which a diſſenſion aroſe between them, and they ſummon'd each
,, other before the judges at *Mentz*. The parties being heard, it was
,, decreed, that if *Fauſt* would make oath, that all the money which he
,, had borrow'd, had been expended in carrying on the common buſi-
,, neſs, and that he had converted no part thereof to his own private uſes;
,, *Guttenbergh* ſhould be oblig'd to pay him. *Fauſt* ſubmitted to this de-
,, cree; as may evidently be prov'd from an original inſtrument ſtill
,, extant, which was drawn *Nov. 6. ann.* 1455. by *Uldric Helmoſperger*,

quid in illud opus impenderetur, communi utri- uſque lucro vel damno cederet. Quoniam ve- ro *Fauſtus* plus inſumpſerat, quam *Guttenbergius* neceſſitatem poſtulaſſe arbitrabatur: hic dimi- diam ſuam partem exſolvere detrectavit; qua ex re cum lis orta eſſet, alter alterum *Maguntiæ* in jus vocavit, ubi, partibus auditis, pronunci- atum fuit; ſi *Johannes Fauſtus* interpoſito jura- mento affirmare poſſet, omnem pecuniam, quam mutuam ſumpſiſſet in commune opus e- rogatam, non autem in proprios uſus conver- ſam fuiſſe, *Guttenbergium* ad ſolvendum obliga- tum eſſe. Cui ſententiæ *Fauſtus* paruit, ſicut ex archetypo inſtrumenti, quod etiamnum ſu- pereſt, anno 1455 ſexto novembris a *Johanne Ulrico Helmoſpergero* notario de ea re confectum fuit, liquido demonſtrari poteſt. Unde eviden- ter apparet *Guttenbergium* nequaquam artis ty- pographicæ inventorem & primum authorem eſſe, ſed aliquot annis poſtquam ea inventa fu-

iſſet, a *Johanne Fauſto* in conſortium adſcitum, pecuniam ei ſuppeditaſſe —— Cum igitur *Guttenbergius* ad ſumptus refundendos damna- tus fuiſſet, & ex eo ſimultates inter illum & *Fauſtum* magis exarſiſſent, ille autem interea ar- tem vidiſſet & didiciſſet, ſiquidem inter tot operas, quæ ad illam excudendam requiruntur, fieri non potuit, ut ea diutius occultaretur, quod etiam Deus proculdubio noluit, *Moguntia Argentinam* ſe contulit, quo aliquot ex operis ſecum attraxit. Poſt illud diſſidium alii quo- que, qui apud *Fauſtum* artem illam didicerant, eum deſeruerunt, & *Francofurtum* atque in alia loca ſe receperunt; cum præſertim anno 1462 *Moguntia* capta, & priſtina ſua libertate privata fuiſſet, quo factum eſt, ut hæc præclara ars omnibus innoteſceret, & publici juris fieret. *Appendic. ad Commentar. Pancirol. ad titul.* 12, *qui eſt de Typographia.*

,, a

„ a notary publick, purſuant to the ſaid ſentence. Hence it manifeſtly
„ follows that *Guttenbergh* was in no wiſe the inventor or firſt author of
„ Printing; but that he had been admitted by *Fauſt* into partnerſhip
„ with him ſome few years after the diſcovery of the art, and had lent
„ him money to proſecute the deſign. —— *Guttenbergh* being caſt, and
„ oblig'd to pay coſt and charges, and new quarrels ariſing daily be-
„ tween *Fauſt* and him, and he having ſeen and learn'd the buſineſs, as
„ it was impoſſible that among ſo many hands requiſite to the carrying
„ on of the art, it ſhould continue longer a ſecret, which probably
„ God would not ſuffer it to be, he [*Guttenbergh*] went off to *Strasburg*,
„ taking ſome of the workmen along with him. After this breach, o-
„ thers having learn'd the art from *Fauſt*, left him, and ſettled ſome at
„ *Frankfort*, and others elſewhere; eſpecially when the city of *Mentz*,
„ was taken [1] *ann*. 1462. and depriv'd of all its former liberties, where-
„ by this excellent art became more publick and univerſally known. „
Thus far *Salmuth*, whoſe account is confirm'd by the author of the *En-comium Chalcographiæ*[2]. *J. Arnold Bergellanus* (who wrote an elegy upon
the diſſenſion between thoſe two perſons, in which he ſeems to favour
Guttenbergh more than *Fauſt*, and to have follow'd *Wimpheling*; who out
of love to his fellow-citizen, for he repreſents *Guttenbergh* as born at
Strasburgh, and not to have remov'd to *Mentz*, till he had almoſt perfected the art) makes him the chief perſon in this diſcovery; yet mentions both the law-ſuit and the decree, as well as the deed before mention'd; but differs from *Salmuth* in affirming that the law-ſuit was not
yet ended when he wrote his book, which might ariſe from *Guttenbergh's*
hanging it upon the hooks, and eſcaping to *Strasburgh*, as *Salmuth* obſerves, or to *Harlem*, as others believe. However, this is evident, and a-
greed on by all hands, that there was an end at once to all their partnerſhip, into which he was only admitted for the ſake of his purſe,
which was abſolutely neceſſary to *Fauſt*.

FROM all theſe teſtimonies, which are not only quoted, but ſtrongly
aſſented to by the judicious *Malincrot*[3], I ſhall make one or two remarks
in favour of *Mentz* and *Fauſt*, which are; 1. that among all the learn-

---

[1] The city of *Mentz* formerly a very wealthy city of the Empire, was taken thro' a
ſtrategem, by the Archbiſhop *Adolph*, in the
night preceding St. *Simon* and *Jude* in the year
1462, and plunder'd and depriv'd of its freedom.
[2] Vid Malinkrot. p. 77.
[3] Vid. Malinkrot. c. 9.

ed

ed I have convers'd with, whose curiosity hath lead them to search into the rise and progress of Printing, and all the writers upon this subject I could ever meet with, not one has pretended to have seen any book printed in *John Guttenbergh*'s name, even in the oldest monuments remaining of the infancy of this art, whether printed upon wood, or by separate metal types: 2. That on the contrary, where there is any mention made of either printer or place, it is still in *Faust*'s and *Schoeffer*'s name.

THEREFORE until there is some better proof of *Guttenbergh*'s name, either jointly with the other two, or separately, or some book produc'd with it, it seems evident beyond contradiction, that the glory of this invention is wholly due to *John Faust*, and the improving and perfecting it to his son-in-law *Peter Schoeffer*, exclusive of *John Guttenbergh*: this I hope, will suffice to justify my conjecture, that either *Trithemius* mistook the names, or the editor of his second chronicle chang'd them, to make it agree with his first, and to satisfy the reader, that I had good reasons and authority to forbear mentioning *Guttenbergh* among the first inventors : I shall only add with respect to the learned *Salmuth* that he prefaces this account with a succinct relation of the improvements which the ingenious *Peter Schoeffer* made to the art, as the invention of Punches, Matrices, &c. as likewise of the difficulties which they met afresh, by reason of the softness of the metal in which they had cast their first types, and of his finding out a new mixture which fully answer'd the design : lastly that *Faust* was so pleas'd with his servants ingenuity, that he made him his son-in-law. This passage which I have here subjoin'd[1] is so exactly like that out of *Trithemius*'s second Chronicle that one might easily be induc'd to think he had copy'd it from him, were it not that this letter was neither printed or indeed known, till almost a whole cen-

---

[1] Cæterum in exercenda hac nova arte, operis qui_ _sdam usus est *Faustus*, in quibus fuit *Petrus Schoeffer Gernsheimensis*, qui cum heri sui institutum percepisset, magno illius artis studio incensus est & quia ingenio valebat, animum ad illam amplificandam adjecit, ac singulari Dei instinctu, rationem inivit, qua Characteres Matrici, ut vocant, inciderentur & ex ea funderentur. Alphabeto hoc modo inciso, characteres inde fusos, *Fausto* hero suo ostendit, quibus ille usque adeo exhilaratus est, ut ei protinus filiam suam unicam desponderet, ac paulo post in uxorem daret : quamvis autem in hoc genere Characterum aliqua difficultas suborta esset, propterea quod materia mollior esset quam ut pressuræ resistere posset, tamen mox ejusmodi mixtura inventa fuit quæ vim præli aliquandiu sustinere potuit. *Appen. ad tit. de Typogr.* p. 312.

tury

tury after *Salmuth* wrote, as appears by *Camerarius*'s letter prefix'd to his book, and dated from *Nuremberg ann.* 1596.

T H E learned *Wimpheling* claims the next rank, as being contemporary with *Trithemius,* and a no leſs diligent ſearcher after the memorable things of his own country. He wrote his book *ann.* 1502 or 1504, wherein is the following account, *viz.* ,, That in the year 1440, when ,, *Ferdinand* was *Emperor* of the *Romans,* that great and almoſt divine ,, gift, the diſcovery of a new way of writing, was beſtow'd upon man- ,, kind by *John Guttenbergh* ; who having firſt invented the art of Print- ,, ing, went afterwards to *Mentz,* where he perfected it. ,, ——— The reſt of the paſſage, which relates chiefly to the promulgation of the art, and the Printers who enrich'd and ſignaliz'd themſelves by it, we ſhall refer to the ſecond book, to which it properly belongs.

I have already remark'd ſomething of *Wimpheling*'s partiality to his own city *Strasburg :* and indeed 'tis what the reader may obſerve in all authors, whoſe country laid the leaſt claim to this invention ; *Fauſt* for having carry'd on the buſineſs with all poſſible ſecreſy, and ſcarce being known out of his own city till the diſperſion of his workmen ; they, wherever they ſettled, challeng'd to themſelves the honour of this diſcovery, or at leaſt of being co-adjutors to the inventor, as we ſhall ſhew in its proper place. However the reader will ſee with pleaſure how our author retracts his too great liberality to his fellow-citizen, in another work, *viz.* his catalogue of the Biſhops of *Strasburg,* wherein he expreſſes himſelf thus : ,, Under that Biſhop *Robert* of *Bavaria* was the no- ,, ble art of Printing found out by a certain *Strasburgher,* tho' in an ,, imperfect manner ; but upon his going to *Mentz* unto other practiti- ,, oners of that art, by the directions of one *John Gensfleich,* an old gen- ,, tleman blind with age, the art was perfected, in the houſe call'd *Gut-* ,, *tenbergh* in [Engliſh *Good-hill*] where the College of Lawyers now ,, ſtands, to the eternal honour of the *German* nation.

T H E R E is no need to obſerve to the reader, the difference between this paſſage and the former ; nor to inquire whether it was out of remorſe, or upon better information, that the author gave this latter account ; but it will be proper to remark, that *Gensfleich* is another name given by ſeveral writers to *Fauſt,* or perhaps a nick-name which he was known by, it ſignifying gooſe-fleſh : ſo that our author has attributed to

D

him

him at leaſt the glory of having practis'd the art at *Mentz* before *Gutten-bergh* came, and to have directed him in perfecting what he had in vain attempted at *Straſburg*. The reader may likewiſe obſerve that *Gutten-bergh* ſeems to have been thus denominated from the houſe ſo call'd, in which *Fauſt* and he carried on the buſineſs, till their mutual diſcords parted them.

JOHN NAUCLERUS author of the univerſal hiſtory, which is divided into generations,[1] tells us, that this art of Printing with metal types was diſcover'd at *Mentz* under the Emperor *Ferdinand* III. *ann.* 1440; and extols the genius of *Germany,* as for other glorious inventions, ſuch as Guns, &c. ſo more particularly for this of Printing, which he makes a large encomium upon. He liv'd near the times of this invention, *viz. ann.* 1450, and tho' he mentions not the authors of it, yet ſince he ſays it was diſcover'd at *Mentz ann.* 1440, it is plain he could mean none but *Fauſt,* ſeeing no books were printed there for many years after, but by him and his ſon-in-law.

NEITHER have the poets of thoſe times been wanting in celebrating this invention, from which alone they and their works could expect that immortality, which they confer upon the *Great* and *Good.* We have quoted ſome of them in the preceding chapter, as *Laurentius Valla* an *Italian,* and *Sebaſtian Brand* a *German* ; tho' this laſt being a native of *Straſburgh,* and afterwards Mayor of that city, we will not pretend to de-termine whether what he ſings of the *Rheniſh* nation and the *German* ge-nius be meant of *Mentz* or his own city : however 'tis evident that he ne-ver dreamt of *Holland* or *Harlem.* But let us now hear *Conrad Celt,* the firſt *German* Poet-Laureat, who ſpeaking of the river *Rhine* has the follow-ing Tetraſtich upon the city of *Mentz* [2];

Jamque Moguntiacam *vaſtus te flectis in urbem,*
   Quæ prima impreſſas tradidit ære notas ;
Qualem ego te memorem ? talem qui invenerit artem,
   Italicis, Graiis *plus memorande viris.*

IN another elegy [3] he expreſſes his deſire of viſiting that famous city, which had taught the *Germans* this excellent method of writing without

---

[1] Hiſtor. Univer. Gen. 49.   [2] Amor. lib. 3. Eleg. 13.   [3] Ibid. Eleg. 1.

pen, &c. I hope to be excus'd the pains of a larger collection of this nature ; the reader may find plenty of ſuch poetical encomiums upon this art in *Malinkrot's* hiſtory, chap. 2. and elſewhere. But I cannot omit in-ſerting a ſhort paſſage out of the famous *Swediſh* poet *Nicodemus Friſchlin*, who in his *Julius Redivivus*, a comedy in praiſe of *Germany* and the Art of Printing, has theſe lines,

> —— *primus Inventor* [*Typographiæ*] Moguntiæ
> *Vixit, fatale nomen adeptus* Fauſti. ——

ſoon after which he gives an elegant deſcription of the wonderful change produc'd by this art: which render'd the *Germans,* (before a rude and il-literate people) able to teach the moſt polite nations of *Europe,* by its ad-mirable quickneſs in multiplying of books, which is elegantly expreſs'd by *Campanus* biſhop of *Aleria* in this verſe,

> *Imprimit illa die quantum non ſcribitur anno.*

To return to the hiſtorians of later date ; *Peter Apian,* who for his in-comparable skill in mathematicks had the honour to be tutor to the Em-peror *Charles* V. aſſures us [1] that *Mentz,* a frontier town between high and low *Germany,* was the place where Printing was diſcover'd by *John Fauſt,* ann. 1453. *Sebaſtian Munſter,* another Coſmographer, gives a larger account of this invention [2], tho' he ſeems to follow *Trithemius* and thoſe who place *Guttenbergh* at the head of the triumvirate: his words are theſe, ,, From the year 1440 to the year 1450 the noble Art of Printing was ,, diſcover'd at *Mentz*; thence it was carry'd to *Cologn,* then to *Stras-* ,, *burgh, Baſil,* and at laſt to *Venice.* Its firſt author and inventor was ,, *John Guttenbergh,* otherwiſe call'd 𝔃𝔲𝔫𝔧𝔲𝔫𝔤𝔢𝔫, who had two other ,, citizens for aſſiſtants, viz. *John Fauſt* and *John Medimbach,* who kept ,, this art very ſecret, having ſworn their ſervants not to divulge it. ,,

[1] *Coſmograph. lib.* 2.
[2] Ab anno 1440 uſque ad ann. 1450 nobilis ars imprimendi *Moguntiæ* reperta eſt ; ea *Mo-guntia Coloniam,* deinde *Argentinam.* & *Baſileam,* tandem *Venetias* delata eſt. Primus ejus author & inventor *Johannes Guttenbergius,* qui *Zunjungen* dicebatur, iſque cives alios duos *Mo-guntinos* adjutores habuit : *Johannem Fauſtum* & *Johannem Medimbachium,* qui artem hanc in ſecreto tenuerunt, famulis de ea non propa-landa jurejurando conſtrictis, *Munſter. Coſmo-graph. lib.* 5. *c* 159. *apud Malinkrot c.* 2. *p.* 14.

Mutius, who wrote his *German* Chronicle *ann.* 1539 attributes the invention of Guns, and soon after that of Printing, to *Mentz*. But the most illustrious testimony in favour of *Faust*, is that of the great collector of *German* antiquities *John Aventine*, to this purpose : [1] ,, In the year
,, 1450 *John Faust*, citizen of *Mentz* in *Germany*, confer'd on man-
,, kind a great and truly divine gift, *viz.* a new method of writing,
,, undoubtedly reveal'd to him from heaven, commonly call'd *Chalco-*
,, *graphy* or Printing, which he invented and perfected within the space
,, of two years. This gentleman, like an indulgent father, study'd how
,, to preserve learning and excellent Books to posterity, which must o-
,, therwise have perish'd, thro' the carelesness and indolence of these
,, times; had not this art (by which one man can print as many pages
,, in a day, as several hands can write in a year,) quoted before, given
,, new vigour to men's genius, made learning flourish, render'd books
,, so cheap as to be a purchase for students of the lowest fortunes, and
,, excited men to the study of arts and sciences by the plenty of learned
,, works which it hath afforded us. This divine invention was kept pri-
,, vate by *John Faust* and *Peter Schoeffer de Gernsheim*, to whom he had
,, given his only daughter *Christina* in marriage ; and all their workmen
,, were bound by an oath not to disclose it. Ten years after this, *John*
,, *Guttenbergh* of *Strasburgh*, one of *Faust*'s servants, divulg'd it in *Ger-*
,, *many*. *Ulric Han* a fellow-citizen of his, and *Xyxtus Resius* brought it
,, to *Rome* and *Italy* ; where, within my memory, *Aldus Manutius*, a
,, person design'd for the restoration of learning, signaliz'd himself, &c.

[1] Hoc anno 1450. magnum ac vere divinum beneficium *Johannes Faustus Germanus*, civis *Moguntinus*, generi humano contulit, novum scribendi genus haud dubie cœlitus revelatum (quod chalcographiam, excusoriam, impressoriamque vocare solent) invenit & biennio complevit. Consuluit pater indulgentissimus honestis literis, autoribus præclaris, de quibus actum fuisset; ita torpore languescimus, adeo delicatuli sumus, fugitantesque laborum; tantum literarum uno mense ab uno homine imprimitur, quantum uno anno a pluribus scriberetur; quod *Campanus Aprutinus* pontifex uno versu elegantissime scribit.

Imprimit illa die &c. ut supra.

Hinc indies magis ingenia vigent, studia literarum florescunt, copia librorum parvo ære egenis suppetit, omnes ad capessendas præclaras artes tantum librorum commoditate alliciuntur. Hoc cœlestissimum munus a *Fausto* & *Petro Schoeffer* de *Gernsheim* genero suo, cui unicam filiam *Christinam* desponderat, inter secreta, adactis omnibus sociis ad fidem jurisjurandi religione habitam- Decimo post anno *Fausti* minister *Johannes Guttenbergius Argentoratensis* in *Germania* vulgavit. Municeps hujus *Ulricus Han*, hoc est *Gallus*, & *Xystus Resius Roma*, *Italiaque* intulere; ubi hoc artificio, mea memoria, *Aldus* ille *Manutius*, vir ad instaurandas literas natus, claruit. —— *Annal. Boicor. lib.* 7. *de Typographia.*

The

The remainder of this paſſage chiefly relates to the diſperſion and promulgation of the art; and therefore is unneceſſary to be ſet down here.
There is but one thing in this quotation that can puzzle the reader;
which is, that the author makes *Guttenbergh* to have been one of *Fauſt*'s
ſervants, inſtead of his partner and uſurer as has been ſhewed already; in
the reſt he exactly agrees with the writers quoted before. With reſpect
to the diſagreement among authors concerning the names of the firſt
inventors, if we remember that *Guttenbergh*, to evade the ſentence pronounc'd againſt him at *Mentz*, departed with ſome of *Fauſt*'s workmen
to *Strasburgh*, it will not appear improbable that ſome, who wrote at a
diſtance, might confound him with thoſe ſervants, eſpecially conſidering
that his name was never in any Book printed at *Mentz*. However 'tis
plain that a place of one writer miſtaken by another, has been the occaſion of leading many more, who have follow'd him implicitely, into the
ſame error. An inſtance of this, which will be no digreſſion from our
hiſtory, is as follows.

THE authors who have follow'd *Peter Ramus*, from *Sabellicus*, *Zurin-
ger*, &c. down to *Paul Pater*, author of the treatiſe *De Germaniæ Mira-
culo* [the Art of Printing] publiſh'd *ann.* 1709 have aſcrib'd this invention to *J. Regiomontanus*, and thought they did the Art no ſmall honour,
in making ſo great a Mathematician its author. What ſeem'd to confirm their opinion was, that *Fauſt*, *Guttenbergh* and he were contemporaries, and 'tis probable, liv'd near each other; tho' he afterwards remov'd to *Nurembergh*. What made this ſtill more probable was, that
Regiomontanus perfectly underſtood Mechanicks, ſo that, as it is ſaid, he
made an iron Flyſpring from under his hand, fly round the room with
a humming noiſe, and return back under his hand; he is likewiſe reported to have made a wooden Eagle, which flew from *Nurembergh* to meet
the Emperor, hover'd over his head in a tonick motion, and went back
the ſame way with him. It would be dangerous now to aſſert the truth
of theſe ſtories, ſince ſuch flights of ingenuity have been ſo long diſcou-
rag'd, to make way for more uſeful inventions; yet *Jul. Scaliger* was ſo
far from doubting of them, that he pretends to have found out the Art,
and bragg'd that he could perform the like with a wet finger. However this was ſufficient to perſuade our authors that *Regiomontanus*, repu-
ted ſo univerſal an artiſt, was moſt probably the perſon who invented
the

the method of Printing, and communicated it to *Fauſt* and *Guttenbergh*; in conſequence of which they have plac'd him at the head of the other two. Neverthelefs this notion feems to take its rife from a paffage in *Purbach*'s tables, wherein 'tis faid that the difcovery of Printing is to be refer'd to the times of *Regiomontanus*, as *Malinkrot* has fully prov'd. This ſtory, I hope, will both convince the reader of the danger of following an author too implicitely, and juſtify my differing from the generality of thofe who attribute the difcovery to *John Guttenbergh*, whofe opinion I apprehend to be fufficiently confuted. Setting afide this miſtake of *P. Ramus* with refpect to *Regiomontanus*, he agrees with the reſt of our other teſtimonies in favour of *Fauſt*; and I conceive it to be not in the leaſt improbable, that the inventors might, in fuch a variety of tools, implements, and other things neceffary to the perfecting this Art, have recourfe to him or fome other ingenious perfon, for advice and affiftance.

H o w e v e r it is certain that *Regiomontanus* was a very early printer, tho' not taken notice of as fuch by any writer I have met with. I did indeed believe him to have been an affiſtant in perfecting of the Art, but never could meet with any fufficient authority to fix the honour upon him, till I was admitted into the Library of the Right Hon. the Earl of *Pembroke*, whom I beg leave to take this firſt opportunity of mentioning with honour and gratitude, not only for his great condefcenfion in allowing me a free accefs to his noble Collections of antient Editions, but likewife for feveral very curious hints upon this fubject, which fhall be mention'd in their proper places; here it was that his Lordfhip was pleas'd to fhew me the following great curiofity, viz. *Manilius* in 4to. with thefe words at the end.

Ex Officina Johannis de Regiomente *in Nuremberg.*

T h e antiquity of this curious Edition fhews it felf at firſt fight, tho' there be no date to it, a circumſtance much to be lamented, tho' too common to many of thofe antient monuments in the infancy of the Art. I muſt therefore be oblig'd to rank it with the reſt of thefe datelefs works, of which I fhall have occafion to fpeak in the fequel of this hiſtory: it is evident this is an older edition than that mention'd by *Fabricius* of 1474,

which

which 'tis reaſonable to ſuppoſe, not only by his being contemporary with, but aſſiſtant to, *Fauſt* in perfecting this art: however as *Regiomontanus* was a man of ſuch profound ſkill in aſtronomy, mechanicks, and ſeveral other branches of learning, I am willing to hope time will bring forth ſome further teſtimonies concerning him.

But what convinces me that he had no ſhare in the firſt diſcovery of the Art, is that in his long dedication prefix'd to his *Aſtronomical Tables*, the firſt piece he ever publiſh'd, which I have ſeen, and which is dedicated to the Primate of *Hungary*, he doth not make the leaſt mention of his having been concern'd in ſuch a noble diſcovery, which it is reaſonable to ſuppoſe he would have done, could he have claim'd ſuch a ſingular piece of merit to have recommended him to ſo great a patron; eſpecially when he expatiates ſo much upon the difficulties that attended the work he dedicates to him: but to return.

I apprehend a probable objection againſt the teſtimonies before quoted (which are ſcarce a fourth part of thoſe collected by *Malinkrot,*) that they are taken from *Germans*, who may be reaſonably ſuppos'd too partial to their country, and conſequently leſs to be relied on than foreign writers, whoſe authority would be of far greater weight in this caſe. This I ſhall obviate by ſhewing, that learned authors of other nations are conſiſtent with the *Germans* in this particular. I have already cited two poets, the one an *Italian*, the other a *Swede*; the former of whom aſcribes this diſcovery to *Germany*, and the latter to *John Fauſt* of *Mentz*. My next deſign is to produce ſome of thoſe, who are eminent for their enquiries into the antiquities of their own and other countries. At the head of theſe ſtands *Polydore Vergil*, an *Italian*, who in his Book *de Rerum Inventoribus*, after an elegant encomium upon the Art, and a deſcription of its important benefits to mankind, proceeds thus [1] „ Wherefore that the author of ſuch a diſcovery may not be depriv'd „ of his due praiſe, and that poſterity may know to whom we are in-

[1] Quare tantæ rei author non eſt ſua laude fraudandus, præſertim ut poſteritas ſciat, cui divinum acceptum beneficium referre debeat. Itaque *Johannes Guttenbergius* natione *Teutonicus*, equeſtri vir dignitate, ut ab ejus civibus accepimus, primus omnium in oppido *Germaniæ*, quam *Moguntiam* vocant, hanc imprimendarum literarum artem excogitavit, primumque in ea exercere cœpit; non minore induſtria reperto ab eodem, prout ferunt, authore, novo atramenti genere, quo nunc literarum impreſſores utuntur. Decimo ſexto deinde anno, qui fuit ſalutis humanæ M CCCC L VIII. quidam nomine *Conradus*, homo itidem *Germanus*, primum in *Italiam* attulit, &c. *lib.* 2. *cap* 7.

debted

,, debted for this divine gift; it was *John Guttenbergh*, by nation a *Ger-*
,, *man*, and a Knight, who firſt devis'd this Art of Printing Books in
,, the city of *Mentz*, and began to practiſe it there, as we have been
,, inform'd by the citizens themſelves; he is reported likewiſe to have
,, made another diſcovery, *viz.* of a new kind of Ink, us'd now by
,, all printers. Sixteen years after this, *ann.* 1457, one *Conrad* a *Ger-*
,, *man*, brought it firſt to *Rome*, &c. ,, —— Our author makes no mention of any but *Guttenbergh*; yet as he ſays the Art was firſt practis'd at
Mentz, 'tis plain from what has been ſaid before, that he deſerv'd not
the firſt name in this invention. The citizens who gave this account,
were certainly thoſe that diſpers'd themſelves from *Fauſt*; who, though
they learn'd the Art of him, yet might eſteem *Guttenbergh* the firſt author, becauſe he was moſt conſiderable; and not unlikely lorded it over
the reſt, who he knew, could not carry on the buſineſs without his purſe;
whilſt *Fauſt*, whoſe chief care was to conceal the Art, till he had reimburs'd himſelf ſo far as to be able to carry it on without his help, might
let him enjoy the honour of the diſcovery in the mean time. What
confirms my conjecture is, that if *Conrad* arriv'd at *Rome* in the year
1457 he muſt have left *Mentz* before *Fauſt* and *Schoeffer* had printed a-
ny Books with their names. However in this caſe *Fauſt* would not be
the only man, whoſe indigence and honeſty have been inducements to
part with the credit of a beneficial diſcovery to a perſon of leſs merit,
rather than to let it die with him, for want of means to carry it on.

THE following author *Jacobus Philippus Bergomenſis*, who is doubtful
concerning the genuine inventor, may eaſily be ſet right, from what
has been already ſaid. He tells us, ,, that the Art of Printing was
,, firſt brought to light in *Germany*, about the year 1457; that the diſ-
,, covery was by ſome attributed to *Guttenbergh* of *Strasburgh*, by others
,, to one *Fauſt*, and by a third ſort to *Nicholas Genſon* or *Jenſon*, that
,, the authors of it got immenſe riches, &c. ,, With relation to this *Jen-*
ſon, it will appear by the ſequel of this hiſtory, that he was only one of
thoſe who firſt carry'd the Art into *Italy*, where he diſtinguiſh'd himſelf

---

¹ *Jacob. Philip. Bergomenſ lib.* 15. *ſupplem. Chronic. ad ann.* 1458. Ars imprimendi libros his temporibus in *Germania* primum enata eſt, quam alii repertam eſſe aſſeverant a *Cuthimber-*gio *Argentino*: alii a quodam alio, nomine *Fauſ-to*; alii a *Nicolao Genſon* prædicant; pro qua innumerabiles authores ipſi congregarunt divitias, &c.

by

by his fine impreſſions, &c. but never made the leaſt pretences to the invention. There is no neceſſity of repeating what has ſo often been ſaid concerning *Guttenbergh*, whom *Palmerius* of *Piſa* aſſerts to have been the author of this diſcovery about the year 1440; his words are as follow:
„ [1] What obligations the learned world hath to the *German* nation, can-
„ not be ſufficiently expreſs'd; for the Art of Printing, which had been
„ invented by *John Guttenbergh* Zum-jungen, a knight of *Mentz* upon
„ the *Rhine*, about the year 1440, is at this time (*viz. ann.* 1457) di-
„ vulg'd almoſt throughout the world; by which the works of the antients
„ may be purchas'd at a ſmall price, and be read in an infinite number of
„ volumes ſince printed. „ There are a prodigious many more authors,
who, tho' they do not mention either the names of the inventors, or the
place of the diſcovery, yet unanimouſly give the honour of it to *Germany*; and even *Paulus Jovius*, who aſcribes the invention of wooden planks
to the *Chineſe*, from whom it was brought into *Europe*, by the way of
Scythia and *Muſcovy*, when he ſpeaks of the other method of Printing,
ſays, it is no wonder that ſeveral arts and ſciences owe their birth to the
Germans, ſince the noble diſcovery, of metal types, as well as that of braſs
cannons, was found out by them [2].

M y next teſtimony is that of the celebrated politician *John Ruterus*,
who not only in his hiſtorical relations attributes the invention of Guns
and Printing to the *German* nation, but confirms it more fully in his
book *de fortuna illuſtrium virorum*, &c. where he ſays, [3] „ That he will
„ not contend about the author of Printing; but gratefully acknow-
„ ledge the ſingular gift of God in it, ſeeing one man can print as much
„ in one day, as the beſt hand can write in a whole year; for there is
„ ſcarce (continues he) a Preſs, eſpecially in the *German* Printing

[1] Quantum literarum ſtudioſi *Germanis* de beant nullo ſatis dicendi genere exprimi poteſt: namque a *Johanne Guttenberg* Zum-jungen, equite *Moguntiæ*, *Rheni*, ſolerti ingenio librorum imprimendorum ratio anno 1440 inventa, hoc tempore in omnes fere orbis partes propagatur, qua omnis antiquitas parvo ære comparata poſterioribus infinitis voluminibus legitur. *Chronic. ad ann.* 1457.

[2] Lib. 14. Hiſtor.

[3] *Ruterus*'s his words, as I find them tranſlated by *Gaſpard Euſus* in *Malinkrot*, p 19. are theſe. " De Authore artis impreſſoriæ hic " non digladiabor: ſummum id Dei beneficium " grato animo nos ſedulo decet agnoſcere; ab " uno enim homine uno die tantum literarum " imprimitur, quantum vix toto anno ſcribi poſ- " ſet; ſingulis enim diebus in quolibet prelo in " *Germanorum* typographiis ter mille ſexcentæ " chartæ, nonnunquam etiam quater mille, in- " terdum ultra, &c. "

E　　　　　　　　„ houſes.

,, houſes, which doth not print off 3600 ſheets *per diem*, nay ſome
,, 4000, and others exceed even that number. ,,

I ſhall conclude this chapter with a paſſage out of the great Monſieur
Thevet, coſmographer to the king of *France*, not only becauſe his authority will eaſily out-balance that of all the *Dutch* writers, but likewiſe becauſe there are ſome particulars in it which will be acceptable to the reader. As it is ſomething prolix, I ſhall only extract the moſt remarkable
part, as follows:[1] ,, This art [of Printing] is believ'd to have been firſt
,, invented at *Mentz* in *Germany*, about the year 1442. by *John Gutten-*
,, *bergh*, a *German* knight ; who began his firſt eſſays of it there, and
,, found out a new ſort of ink, now us'd by the Printers : but there are
,, ſome writers of opinion that this honour rather belong'd to *John Fauſt*
,, and *Ives* [in latin *Ivo*] *Schoeffer* two years before that time, and affirm
,, that *Guttenbergh*, *John Mentel* and others [whoſe names our author
,, quotes out of *Pantaleon*] all *Germans*, improv'd afterwards the art, and
,, divulg'd it in ſeveral parts of *Germany* ; and at length carry'd it to fo-
,, reign nations. Others write that this art came originally from *China*
,, and *Cathai* ; but this aſſertion is without any foundation, ſeeing the
,, *Eaſt-Indies* were not diſcover'd by the *Portugeſe* till about 65 years ago ;
,, whereas Printing has been invented and practis'd ever ſince 1442.
,, *Paul* the *Venetian* indeed gave the firſt deſcription of that country about
,, 400 years ago, but made not the leaſt mention of Printing being us'd
,, there. A confirmation of my opinion is, that the *Greeks*, *Mingrelians*,
,, *Abyſſines*, *Turks*, *Perſians*, *Moors*, *Arabs* and *Tartars* write all their
,, books by hand, this method was ordain'd in *Turky* by an edict of *Ba-*
,, *jazet* II. who prohibited the uſe of printed books under pain of death
,, *ann.* 1483 ; which edict was confirm'd by *Selim* I. *Bajazet*'s ſon *ann.*
,, 1515. Beſides this, whilſt I was in *Egypt*, I ſaw ſeveral books ſo neat-
,, ly written on the bark of palm-trees, that they might be taken for
,, printed ones. The merchants, which bring their wares from *India*
,, through the *Red-ſea*, make uſe of the ſame ſort of written books, ſome
,, of which are now to be ſeen at the library of the Queen dowager at
,, St. *German*'s in the fields near *Paris*. Others pretend that this art of
,, Printing has been carry'd as far as *Mexico*, which kingdom is directly

[1] *Thevet*'s Lives and Pictures of Illuſtrious Perſons, *ch.* 97.

,, oppoſite

,, oppoſite to *Cathai*, the one being in *Aſia* towards the ſouth, and the
,, other in *America* towards the north-pole.   However it muſt be own'd
,, that the *Americans* write with characters, repreſenting ſeveral kinds of
,, beaſts, fiſh, fowl, the different parts of human bodies, and the like ;
,, by which they expreſs their mind, as the *Egyptians* did formerly. —— I
,, have two of thoſe books by me, with an interpretation of their hiero-
,, glyphicks.   The goddeſs *Minerva* is ſaid to have been the inventreſs
,, of learning and war ; and the *Germans* have imitated her in both theſe
,, reſpects, by the invention of bombs and printing, which were certain-
,, ly diſcover'd by them.   One fault however that nation labours under,
,, which ſomewhat eclipſes their glory, which is, that they know not how,
,, or at leaſt neglect to improve thoſe inventions, that were ſo eaſily
,, found out by them. ,, —— The author proceeds in an encomium upon the art and thoſe who raiſ'd it to greater perfection ; but that belongs
to another chapter.

I hope that the teſtimonies produc'd hitherto will be more than ſufficient to fix the palm upon *Fauſt* and the city of *Mentz* ; and that the reader
will follow me with pleaſure to the next chapter, where they will be confirm'd by inconteſtable matters of fact.

C H A P. IV.

Authentick Facts in favour of Fauſt *and* Mentz.

IF the teſtimonies alledg'd in the preceding chapter are inſufficient to
   convince any perſon that this invention is due to *Fauſt* ; what follows
in this will, I conceive, put it quite out of doubt, unleſs he be more in-
credulous in this caſe than a *Dutchman* : for the great *Eraſmus* has not only own'd himſelf convinc'd of this truth by one ſingle fact, but even
tranſmitted it to poſterity.   I ſhall therefore begin with that noble teſtimony, which is a privilege granted by the Emperor *Maximilian* to *John
Schoeffer*, grand-ſon of *John Fauſt*, not only for the ſole printing the
works of *T. Livy* (at the end of which, the privilege is annex'd, printed by
the ſaid *John Schoeffer* at *Mentz, ann.* 1499), but likewiſe prohibiting all
perſons to reprint either the ſaid book, or any other which ſhould be af-

terwards printed by him, in confideration of his being grand-fon to the firft Inventor of the art of Printing : concerning whom *Erafmus*, who firft publifh'd that work, fpeaks in his preface to it as follows : ,, If thofe, ,, who furnifh'd *Origen* and St. *Jerom* with writers and parchments, have ,, merited the higheft commendation ; what praife is due to Printers and ,, Bookfellers, who fupply us with whole volumes for a fmall price ? If ,, *Ptolemy Philadelphus* acquir'd fuch reputation, for collecting fo great ,, a library ; what recompence can be made to thofe, who furnifh us ,, daily with books in all languages ? But amongft all thefe, to whom ,, we are fo much oblig'd, we muft gratefully remember the firft inven- ,, tor of this divine fecret ; *John Fauft* grand father to *John Schoeffer*. ,, Thus far *Erafmus*, without the leaft mention of his countryman *Cofter*. With refpect to the Emperor's priviledge, it could not be fufpected of any partiality to *Fauft* rather than to *Guttenbergh*, or to *Mentz* rather than *Strasburg*, &c. fince they were equally under his dominion.

THE next fact to be related, is that of the tools, old types, *&c.* of the inventors, preferv'd in *Mentz*, above 130 years at leaft after the fack- ing of that city *ann.* 1462, and view'd before that time by fome eminent perfons, as curious relicks of the art: among others, *John Arnold Ber- gellanus* [1] affures us, that he had feen them there ; and *Nic. Serrarius* [2] fays, they were then kept at *Mentz* in a houfe in the ftreet call'd *Keyfer*'s *garden*, and fhewn to him by one *Albinus* a Printer. We need not bring a greater number of authors to atteft this, feeing it may likely be efteem'd but a weak proof by fome of our readers ; but if they will confider what noife *Junius* and *Scriverius* have made about fome trifles (compar'd to thefe) preferv'd at *Harlem* in memory of *Cofter*, according to a tradi- tion of two or three old gentlemen ; they will not wonder that I lay fome ftrefs upon this, and choofe fometimes to make ufe of their own wea- pons againft them. I fhall therefore fubjoin another fact, which is the infcription fet up at *Mentz* by *Ives* of *Witigen* or *Venza*, doctor of laws, and profeffor in that univerfity, in the inner court of the college of law-

---

[1] Hodie vetuftiffima quædam in eum (impri- mendi fc.) ufum ab authoribus comparata, quæ vidi, inftrumenta extant Moguntiæ. *Bergellan. in præfat. E.com. fui Typograph.*

[2] —— adjiciantur primi denique artis hu- jus modioli, quos antiqua hic (*Moguntia enim fcribebat*) domus in *Cæfarii* horti platea cufto- dit, quofque mihi infuper *Albinus* typographus, monftrabat. *Nichol. Scrrarius de Rebus Mogun- tin. l. 1. c. 37.*

yers.

yers. Johanni Guttenbergenſi Moguntino, *qui primus omnium literas ære imprimendas invenit, hac arte de toto orbe bene merenti,* Ivo Witigenſis *hoc ſaxum pro monumento poſuit,* anno 1508. This inſcription tho' it favours *Guttenbergh* more than *Fauſt,* is more authentick than any of thoſe three brought by *Junius* for *Coſter,* the laſt of which as *Malinkrot* obſerves, is either written or at leaſt publiſh'd by him ; the ſecond is but a few years older, and the firſt not plac'd over *Coſter's* door 'till after *Junius* had publiſh'd his deſcription of *Holland.*

A proof ſtill ſtronger is the inſcriptions found in the oldeſt books printed at *Mentz,* wherein that city is ſtyl'd the mother and inventreſs of printing. If *Harlem* or any other city could have ſhewn a juſter title to this honour, it is ſurprizing that this place ſhould have enjoy'd it for above 125 years without the leaſt contradiction, and that no *Dutch* writer did ſo much as attempt, in all that long interval, to confute thoſe known and remarkable *colophons* or inſcriptions, which *Fauſt* began to print at the end of his books, when he could no longer conceal his diſcovery ; and in which he gives an account of the inventors and manner in which the books were done, firſt negatively, viz. *not with pen and ink or any other writing inſtruments,* and then affirmatively, *but by a new art of caſting types and printing;* to which he adds the city of *Mentz* as the place where they were printed ; and concludes with the date of the month and year when they were finiſh'd. We ſhall only ſubjoin ſome of the oldeſt and moſt remarkable of them for the preſent.

I begin with that which is at the end of the *Codex Pſalmorum,* printed *an.* 1457, and conſequently the oldeſt book known to be printed with a date or inſcription. It is in the Emperor's library at *Vienna ;* and *Peter Lambec* who was library keeper, gives this account of it [1] ; that he met with one of them there printed on vellum, at the end of which was this remarkable account of the origin of printing, viz. *This preſent Book of Pſalms, embelliſh'd with beautiful capitals, and illuminated with all neceſſary*

---

[1] Reperi interea unum impreſſum in membrana, in cujus fine de origine artis typographicæ hoc legitur teſtimonium. „ Præſens „ pſalmorum codex, venuſtate capitalium de„ coratus, rubricationibusque ſufficienter di„ ſtinctus, ac inventione artificioſa imprimen„ di ac characteriſandi, abſque calami exaratio „ ne ſic effigiatus, ad euſebiam Dei induſtrie eſt „ conſummatus per *Johannem Fuſt* civem *M)*„ *guntinum* & *Petrum Schoeffer de Gernſheim,* „ anno Domini Milleſſimo CCCCLVII in vi„ gilia aſſumptionis. „ *L'b.* 2. *Bibliothec. Vindobon. pag.* 989.

rubricks

rubricks, was thus form'd by an ingenious invention of printing by separate Types, *without pen or wrinting, and finiſh'd with great care, for the ſervice of God, by* John Fauſt, *citizen of* Mentz, *and* Peter Schoeffer de Gernſheim, *in the year of our Lord* One Thouſand CCCCLVII, *on the eve of the aſſumption,* i. e. Aug. 14.

THE next impreſſion is the *Rationale Divinorum Officiorum* of *William Durand,* printed at *Mentz* an. 1459. in *fol.* *Malinkrot* has it, and tells us that it had been formerly bequeath'd to the monaſtery of *Galilea* near *Zutphen* (a place afterwards deſtroy'd in the civil wars,) to be kept chain'd in the library ; and for which the donors were to be pray'd for, together with their whole generation. The inſcription at the end of it being exactly the ſame with that of the Book of Pſalms, needs not be repeated here. It is likewiſe mention'd by *Hoffman* in the ſecond volume of his *Lexicon Univerſale* printed at *Baſil* ann. 1677, who ſays he ſaw it in the library of that univerſity, bearing date 1459, he calls it *Officiale Durandi,* p. 508, and gives this inſcription at the end, *præſens hoc,* &c. as before.

THE next in date is the *Catholicon,* a *latin* vocabulary, the ſame which is affirm'd by *Trithemius* to have been printed in wood ſome time before 1450, and which was reprinted at *Mentz* ann. 1460. I have ſeen two of theſe books, one in the Earl of *Pembroke's* library, and the other in the learned Dr. *Mead's,* with this very remarkable colophon at the end ; [1] ,, By the aſſiſtance of the moſt high God, at whoſe nod ,, the tongues of infants become eloquent, and who often reveals that ,, to babes which he conceals from the wiſe, this excellent book, the ,, *Catholicon* was finiſh'd in the year of our Lord's incarnation 1460, in ,, the city of *Mentz* belonging to the noble *German* nation (which God ,, of his goodneſs has vouchſaf'd to prefer to other nations, and of his ,, free gift to make conſpicuous by this glorious invention) this work was ,, done, not by the help of quil, pencil or any writing inſtrument, but

---

[1] Altiſſimi præſidio, cujus nutu infantium linguæ fiunt diſertæ, quique nimio ſæpe parvulis revelat, quod ſapientes celat ; hic liber egregius *Catholicon,* Dominicæ incarnationis anno MCCCCLX, alma in urbe *Moguntina,* nationis inclytæ *Germanicæ* (quam Dei clementia tam alto ingenii lumine, donoque gratuito, cæteris nationibus præferre illuſtrareque dignatus eſt) non calami, ſtyli, aut pennæ ſuffragio, ſed mi-ra patronarum formarumque concordia, proportione & modulo impreſſus atque confectus eſt

Hinc tibi, ſancte Pater, Nato, cum Flamine ſacro

Laus & honor, Domino trino tribuatur & uno ; Eccleſiæ laude libro hoc Catholice plaude ; Qui laudare piam ſemper non linque *Mariam.*
Deo gratias.

,, by

,, by the agreement, ſymmetry, and proportion of the printing-preſs. ,,
then follows a doxology in four *latin* verſes to this purpoſe;

To thee Father, Son and Holy Ghoſt, three in one, be honour and praiſe : O
*Catholick reader give thanks for this book in the church, and never ceaſe
to praiſe the bleſſed Virgin* Mary.

Thanks be to God.

THIS book, tho' it mentions not the printers, yet is eaſily known
to have been done by *Fauſt* and *Schoeffer* from the likeneſs of the types,
and becauſe at that time there were no other printers at *Mentz*, or any
where elſe.

TWO years after this came out the great *Latin Bible* in *folio*, which I
alſo ſaw in Dr. *Mead*'s library, which according to *Trithemius* and the
Cologn chronicle muſt be the ſecond edition of it, the firſt having been
printed ſoon after the year 1450, tho' without any colophon, whereas
this has the following; [1] ,, This preſent work was finiſh'd and compleated,
,, deſignedly for the ſervice of God, in the city of *Mentz*, by *John Fauſt*
,, citizen of it, and *Peter Schoeffer de Gernſheim* clerk of the ſaid dioceſs
,, in the year of our Lord's incarnation 1462, on the vigil of the aſ-
,, ſumption of the glorious virgin *Mary*. ,,

IT is unneceſſary to remark that the word *Clerk* [*Clericus*] doth not here
ſignify a clergyman, for 'tis plain that *Schoeffer* was not ſo by his mar-
rying *Fauſt*'s daughter, and leaving a ſon to ſucceed him; but it was
uſual then to give that title to men of moderate literature. Father *le
Long* in his *Bibliotheca ſacra* gives us the colophon of this Bible ſomething
different from ours, tho' of the ſame date, the reader may ſee it at full
length in the ingenious Mr. *Mattair*'s Annals *page* 60, *not.* 6.

CONCERNING this bible ſome writers give us the following account,
which is not a little in favour of *Fauſt*; that it was ſo like hand-writing,
and the titles and capitals ſo finely painted on vellum, that *Fauſt* ſold
ſome of them at *Paris* for a prodigious price: but the buyers finding a
greater number upon him, than it was poſſible for ſeveral men to tran-

---

[1] Præſens hoc opus finitum ac completum
& ad euſebiam Dei induſtrie in civitate *Moguntina* per *Johannem Fuſt* civem, & *Petrum Schoeffer* de *Gernſheim* clericum dioceſis ejuſdem,
eſt conſummatum anno incarnationis dominicæ
1462, in vigilia aſſumptionis glorioſæ virginis
Mariæ.

ſcribe

fcribe in their whole life, and the pages of each copy fo exactly alike, that he was feiz'd, try'd and condemn'd for 𝔐𝔞𝔤𝔦𝔠𝔨 and 𝔖𝔬𝔯𝔠𝔢𝔯𝔭, and was accordingly drag'd to the ftake to be burnt ; but upon difcovering his Art, the parliament of *Paris* made an act to difcharge him from all profecution, in confideration of his admirable invention.   However 'tis not amifs to inform the reader, that his 𝔅𝔩𝔞𝔠𝔨 𝔄𝔯𝔱, for which he was fo roughly treated, was printing his Bible on the 𝔅𝔩𝔞𝔠𝔨 𝔏𝔢𝔱𝔱𝔢𝔯. I fhall in its proper place give my reafons for my opinion, that the bible, which *Fauft* fold for MS. was the firft printed by him ; in the mean time this procefs againft him, and his difcharge from it by order of that Parliament, being matter of fact, it was not foreign to our purpofe to mention it here.

T H E laft book which we fhall fpeak of, is, *Tully's Offices* printed *ann.* 1465, at the end of which are thefe words [1] ,, *John Fauft,* citizen of Mentz, *happily perfected this famous Work of* Marcus Tullius, *not with pen and ink,* &c. *but by a* new beautiful Art, *by the affiftance of my Boy* Peter de Gernfheim, Feb. 4. ann. 1465, the edition at *Oxford* is dated 1466, tho' generally thought to be the fame. This infcription I faw in the book which that great Lover of the antiquities of the Art of Printing, and Promoter of learning, the Right Honourable the Earl of *Oxford,* fhew'd me the firft time I had the honour to wait on his Lordfhip, and to whofe kind reception and information I ftand greatly indebted.

T H E next infcriptions I fhall mention, are thofe in *Peter Schoeffer's* name alone, in which there is a conftant and remarkable ftrain of gratitude and refpect for the city of *Mentz,* from which, befides other ample encouragements, he had receiv'd his freedom as a reward for his improvements in the art. As every one of them has an encomium upon that city, I fhall content my felf with abridging fome of the firft, and giving the laft, which has fomething fingular in it, at full length ; and conclude this head with a remarkable one us'd by his fon *John Schoeffer* at the end of fome of his books.

I N the book call'd the *decifions of the Rota* printed *ann.* 1477, and faid to be ftill extant in the library of *Franckfort,* he ftyles the city of *Mentz* the inventrefs and protectrefs of printing ; in fome other books,

---

[1] Præfens *Marci Tullii* clariffimum opus *Johannes Fuft Moguntius* civis, non atramento plumali, canna, neque ærea, fed arte quadam perpulchra manu *Petri de Gernfheim,* pueri mei, feliciter effeci, finitum *an.* MCCCCLXV die IV *Februarii.*

viz.

viz. Juſtinian's Inſtitutions, printed *ann.* 1468 and 1477, *&c.* he calls her
the noble city which God has prefer'd to all others, and ſignaliz'd with
ſuch ſuperior gifts, *&c.* the like is alſo to be ſeen at the end of *Harpia-*
nus's Speculum decem præceptorum, printed, *ann.* 1474.

T H E laſt is at the end of St. *Jerom's Epiſtles* in *Latin*, printed in
folio upon vellum *ann.* 1470, one of which is in the library of St.
Victor, and another at the College of *Sorbon* at *Paris*, [1] and runs in
Engliſh thus;

> *Now it behoves us to conclude as we began,*
> *The honour be to him, who was with us at the beginning;*
> *And alſo honour to him, who hath been with us to the concluſion:*
> *'Tis the churches honour to preſerve ſo many writings of her champion,*
> *If you deſign them for any, let it be for the churches honour.*

„ T H I S book therefore of *Sophronius Euſebius Jerom* and [worthy its
„ author] a moſt eminent defender of the orthodox church of Chriſt; or,
„ if you rather chooſe to call it with me, the book of his epiſtles is fi-
„ niſh'd, that the honour of *Jerom's* name may be preſerv'd, which is
„ owing to the excellent *John Andreas*, who mov'd with a devout zeal
„ towards that holy man, formerly publiſh'd this work to the world.
„ This book was happily finiſh'd by the art of Printing by *Peter Schoef-*
„ *fer de Gernſheim* in the city of *Mentz*, to the honour of which city the

---

[1] Vide *de la Caille's hiſtory of Printing*, Paris 1689 pag. 13

Jam decet ut noſtris concordent ultima primis
Sit Decus illi qui dedit hoc opus initiare;
Et qui finire dedit ipſum, ſit decus illi.
Eſt decus eccleſiæ pugilis tot ſcripta tenere:
Si quibus intendas eſt decus eccleſiæ.

Igitur *Sophronii Euſebii Ieronymi*, orthodoxæ
eccleſiæ Chriſti propugnatoris clariſſimi liber
Hieronianus, aut ſi mavis, quod & ipſe velim, liber epiſtolaris explicit, ut dignitas nominis *Ieronimi* egregio viro *Joh. Andreæ*
permaneat, qui hoc ipſum, zelo devotionis erga
virum ſanctum affectus, tempore priſco vulga-

vit in orbem. Eſt autem opus præſens arte
impreſſoria feliciter conſummatum per *Pe-*
trum Schoeffer de Gernſheim in civitate *Mogun-*
tina, cujus nobilitati vir beatus *Ieronymus* ſcri-
bens ad *Ageruntiam* de monogamia, teſtimonium perhibet ſempiternum, multis millibus in-
colarum ejuſdem in eccleſia pro fide Catholica
ſanguine proprio laureatis.

Huic Laudatori reddit Moguntia *vicem,*
Tot ſua ſcripta parans uſibus eccleſia.

Anno Domini MCCCCLXX,
ſeptima menſis *Septembris,*
quæ eſt vigilia Nativitatis *Mariæ.*
Da gloriam Deo.

F   „ bleſſed

,, bleſſed St. *Jerom*, writing to *Ageruntia* concerning monogamy (or mar-
,, rying but once,) has given this laſting teſtimony, that many thou-
,, ſands of its inhabitants are honour'd in the church, for having ſuffer'd
,, martyrdom in defence of the catholick faith. ,,

> *Mentz now returns him (* Jerom *) praiſe for praiſe,*
> *by publiſhing ſo many of his writings for the ſervice of the church.*

in the year of our Lord 1470, *the ſeventh day of* September, *which is the*
eve of the nativity of the Virgin Mary.   *Give glory to God.*

T H I S is an inſtance how ready *Schoeffer* was to take all opportunities of
expreſſing his love and gratitude to that city, and rendering her praiſe as
laſting as his own works.

T HE laſt inſcription which gives a ſuccinct account of the diſcovery,
is at the end of *Trithemius*'s breviary of hiſtory, and is as follows[1] : ,, This
,, preſent chronological work was printed and finiſh'd *an.* 1515, on the
,, eve of St. *Margaret* Virgin, in the noble and famous city of *Mentz,*
,, firſt inventreſs of this art of Printing, by *John Schoeffer* grand-ſon of
,, the worthy *John Fuſt* citizen of *Mentz,* the firſt author of this art, who
,, found it out at length by his own ingenuity, and began to practiſe it
,, *anno* 1450, in the time of the thirteenth indiction, *Frederic* III be-
,, ing then Emperor, and the moſt reverend father in God *Theodorick*
,, *Pincerna de Erbach* being Prince-Elector and Arch-biſhop of *Mentz*.

---

[1] Impreſſum & completum eſt præſens Chro-
nicorum opus *Anno Domini* MDXV, in vigilia
Margaretæ virginis, in nobili famoſaque urbe
Moguntina, hujus artis impreſſoriæ inventrice
prima, per *Joannem Schoeffer* nepotem quondam
honeſti viri *Johan. Fuſt* civis *Moguntini,* memo-
ratæ artis primarii auctoris ; qui tandem imprimendi artem proprio ingenio excogitare ſpe-
cularique cœpit *ann. Dom.* nativitatis MCCCCL
indictione xiii regnante illuſtriſſimo Romano
imperatore *Federico* III, præſidente ſanctæ *Mo-
guntinæ ſedi* Reverendiſſimo in Chriſto patre
Domino *Theodorico Pincerna de Erbach* principe
Electore; *anno* autem MCCCCLII perfecit, de-
duxitque eam (Divina favente gratia) in opus
imprimendi (opera tamen ac multis neceſſariis

adinventionibus *Petri Schoeffer de Gernſheim* mi-
niſtri ſuique filii adoptivi) cui etiam filiam ſuam
Chriſtinam Fuſti pro digna laborum multarum-
que adinventionum remuneratione nuptui dedit. Retinuerunt autem hi duo jam prænun-
ciati, *Johan. Fuſt* & *Petrus Schoeffer,* hanc artem
in ſecreto (omnibus miniſtris ac familiaribus
eorum, ne illam quoquo modo manifeſtarent, jurejurando adſtrictis,) quæ tandem *anno Domini* MCCCCLXII per eoſdem familiares in di-
verſas terrarum provincias divulgata, haud pa-
rum ſumpſit incrementum, Cum Gratia &
Privilegio Cæſariæ Majeſtatis, juſſu & impenſis
honeſti *Joannis Haſſelperg* ex Aſia Majore Conſtant. dioceſis. *Breviar. Trithemian.* Part. I.

,, *anne*

,, *anno* 1452. he perfected this art under God, and began to put it in
,, practice, with the affiſtance of *Peter Schoeffer de Gernſheim*, firſt a
,, fervant, and then his ſon-in-law ; who having made many neceſſary in-
,, ventions in it, had his Daughter *Chriſtina Fuſt* in marriage, as a juſt
,, recompence for his labour, and uſeful diſcoveries. Theſe two above-
,, nam'd, *viz. John Fuſt* and *Peter Schoeffer* kept this art ſecret, having
,, taken an oath of all their workmen and ſervants not to divulge it
,, in any manner whatſoever : but afterwards it was divulg'd by thoſe
,, very workmen *anno* 1462, and ſpread it ſelf over ſeveral provinces of
,, *Europe*, &c. ,,

THE like inſcription is at the end of the *Breviarum Mindenſe*, printed
anno 1516, by the ſame perſon : In both which the reader will be pleas'd
to obſerve, that there is not a word mention'd of *John Guttenbergh*.

UPON the whole 'tis my opinion, that were there no other evidence
but theſe inſcriptions, they would be ſufficient to determine this controverſy, ſeeing neither *Harlem, Strasburgh*, nor any other place can produce any thing equivalent. Had *Harlem*, for inſtance, any ſuch authentick impreſſions in favour of *Coſter*, all other teſtimonies of the beſt writers for *Mentz* would have been rejected as inconſiderable : or if Dr. *Mentel* could have produc'd any ſingle book printed by his progenitor, of
older or even equal date with the oldeſt of theſe, he would infallibly have
triumph'd over all his antagoniſts. 'Tis certain that there is no book
known to be printed at *Harlem* or any other place, of equal date with
the laſt which were done by *Fauſt*, tho' it has been prov'd, that he continu'd printing near ten years before he put his name to his impreſſions :
whence it follows, that he was not only the firſt Printer with fuſile metal types, but likewiſe the firſt inventor of them, according to the teſtimonies quoted in the preceding chapter.

I doubt not but the reader is now willing to hear what methods the
competitors with *Fauſt* take, in order to evade ſuch a cloud of authentick
teſtimonies ; and what arguments they can allege in defence of their
claim : in ſhort, what grounds they have of triumphing in ſuch an extraordinary manner. But I muſt here acquaint him, that if he expects evidence anſwerable to thoſe clamours, he will be extremely diſappointed in
the two next chapters. However, ſince a controverſy cannot be fairly

decided,

decided, unlefs both parties be heard in their turn ; I fhall not defire the reader to believe me implicitly, but propofe their pretenfions in as juft a light, and brief a manner as poffible, together with the anfwers of *Malinkrot* and others to them ; to which I fhall take the liberty to add my own thoughts and obfervations, whether they chance to illuftrate and confirm, or to contradict the concurrent teftimony of the early, and the eftablifh'd notion, of the modern writers, upon the fubject, and leave it to him to judge of the merit of the caufe.

I hope what I faid laft will not be look'd upon as either a piece of prefumption or oftentation in me : no man can be more ready, than I am, to own the great helps I have receiv'd from thefe great men, efpecially from *Malinkrot, Chevalier, Mattaire, Orlandi* and fome others of lefs note, or my own infufficiency for fuch a work as this, without fuch an affiftance ; but tho' they are all great and learned men in their way, yet for want of a fufficient acquaintance with the bufinefs of Printing, it was impoffible for them not to overlook fome things of moment, which a printer would eafily difcover at firft fight, *viz.* Whether a book be MS. or printed ; whether printed from pages of wood or with feparate types, in both which refpects, many of them have been either puzled or miftaken : I fhall add but one inftance more, not foreign to our purpofe ; the famous Monf. *Naudé* directed his readers how to know the books printed by *Fauft* by the mark in the paper, which he calls the *Heifer's Horns* ; Mr. *Mattaire*, who has been as curious and diligent as any one, tells us he could never obferve that mark or any thing like it, whereas the very firft book the Earl of *Pembroke* fhew'd me of *Fauft's* printing, by holding a leaf againft the light, the mark appear'd very plain ; I fhall beg leave to add, that the hints and helps I have had from the curious and learned, and my accefs to feveral noble libraries, have moreover enabled me to make many more curious obfervations, on this fubject, than I could otherwife have done. Let this be faid once for all.

C H A P.

CHAP. V.

The Pretenſions of Harlem *examin'd and con-fut ed.*

I Have more than once hinted, that this controverſy in favour of *Harlem* was not ſtarted till above 125 years after the diſcovery of the art, when *Hadrian Junius*, M.D. began the diſpute. During that long interval, the invention was univerſally aſcribed to the city of *Mentz*, tho' the names of the inventors were ſometimes confounded ; and what ought to ſurprife us moſt of all is, that not one *Dutch* writer, during that time, ever offer'd to contradict the received opinion concerning *Fauſt* and *Mentz* ; tho' many of them were men of great learning, and ſome either natives of *Harlem*, or had been educated in that univerſity. 'Tis really wonderful, that neither regard to truth, or their country's honour, nor the common ambition of being the author of a new diſcovery, ſhould have inſpir'd ſome of them to undeceive the world in this point, if they had the leaſt grounds of ſuſpicion. But whatever be the reaſon of this unpardonable ſupinenefs in them, Dr. *Junius*, rather than fall under ſuch a charge, undertook a task, as difficult as that *Egyptian* one, of making brick without ſtraw. For from a collection of old traditions, wooden types, and two or three books, printed on wood, without name, date, or any other mark (by which it might be gueſs'd when, where, and by whom they were done), with ſome other tranſ-muted relicks of the firſt eſſays of the art, he has form'd a ſtory, which he thinks will baffle all the teſtimonies urg'd on the other ſide, and turn the panegyricks, beſtow'd by the learned on the noble inventor, into the vileſt calumnies. As his ſtory is very prolix, and unneceſſary to be ſet down at length, the following abſtract may ſuffice.

,, T H o' the glory of this art is entirely due to the city of *Harlem* ;
,, yet I am ſenſible how deep the contrary notion in favour of *Mentz* is
,, rooted in the minds of men. —— Were I bleſt with that eloquence which
,, *Carneades* is ſo fam'd for, who never affirm'd any thing but what he ful-
,, ly

,, ly prov'd, nor oppos'd any error, but what he clearly confuted; I
,, might have just hopes to reduce this stol'n glory to its owner, and
,, bring to light the truth, which has so long lain hid in *Democritus*'s
,, well. —— For if those antients, who contended for the invention of
,, letters, in behalf of their favourite heroes, have merited such ap-
,, plause ; what hinders but that I, influenc'd neither by partiality to
,, one place, nor envy towards another, but with a sincere love to truth,
,, should appear in so just a cause, which has been suffer'd to sink for want
,, of advocates? —— And if *Plutarch* esteems him the best evidence,
,, who is not byass'd by favour or affection ; I have a sufficient claim to
,, it, since none of *Coster*'s posterity can reward me for my performance.
,, I shall therefore relate what has been told me by some grave and
,, worthy old *Gentlemen*, who have fill'd the best offices in the city, and
,, heard it from others of equal weight and authority ; *viz.* That about
,, 128 years ago, there liv'd at a noted house, standing to this day,
,, over against the Royal Palace, one *Laurence John*, sirnam'd *Coster*,
,, (which word signifies a sexton or church-warden ; or, in the *Romish*
,, sense one who is intrusted with all the rich plate, sumptuous robes, *&c.*
,, belonging to the parish church ; a place hereditary in his family,)
,, who was the person to whom the Art of Printing owes its original,
,, tho' he has been unjustly depriv'd of that honour. —— That walking
,, by chance in an adjacent wood, according to custom, after a full meal,
,, or on holy-days, he cut some letters out of the bark of beech-trees ;
,, which being inverted and joyn'd together, he began to print some
,, words, and then whole lines, in hopes that this might turn to the
,, advantage of his grand-children : that the success of this prompted
,, him to greater discoveries, he being a man of an extraordinary geni-
,, us : that he with *Thomas Peter* his son-in-law, finding the common ink
,, apt to spread, invented a more glutinous sort, and began to print
,, whole pages ; of which kind I saw some essays in an anonymous
,, work, printed only on one side, and entitled the *Mirour of our Salvati-*
,, *on*, written in *Low Dutch*, the white sides of the paper being glew'd
,, together to hide the chasms : that after this he chang'd his wooden let-
,, ters into lead ; and then into tin, which was still harder and more du-
,, rable : some of these old types being cast into drinking-cups are still

,, to

„ to be feen at the aforefaid houfe, out of which *Gerard Thomas, Cofter's*
„ great-grand-fon, dy'd a few years ago.   But as all new inventions
„ meet with encouragement, this art began to require a greater number
„ of hands, which prov'd the firft caufe of mifchief to this family : for
„ one of his fervants nam'd *John* (but whether *Fauft* or not I fhall not
„ now enquire) being employ'd in this bufinefs, after having taken an
„ oath of fecrecy, had no fooner learn'd, as he thought, the method
„ of cafting and joining the fufile types, &c. but he took the next op-
„ portunity of robbing his mafter of all his printing-tools, together with
„ his art :   to which end he chofe the night before *Chriftmafs*, as the
„ moft proper for his defign, when the whole family, with the reft of
„ the city were at church at midnight-mafs.   Thence he efcap'd to
„ *Amfterdam*, next to *Cologn*, and at laft fettled at *Mentz* ; where the
„ year following, viz. *ann.* 1442 he printed *Alexandri Galli doctrinale*, a
„ grammar much in vogue at that time, with thofe very types that his
„ mafter *Cofter* had us'd before.

„ THIS is the fubftance of what I had from thofe gentlemen of vera-
„ city, who told me they had it handed down by tradition ;   and this
„ has been likewife confirm'd to me by others of equal repute.   I re-
„ member to have heard my tutor *Nich. Gallius*, an old gentleman of a
„ very tenacious memory, fay, that when he was a boy, he heard one
„ *Cornelius* a printer, an old man, who had been one of *Cofter's* workmen,
„ mention the ftory of the firft trials of printing, with a great deal
„ of vehemence, and even with tears, efpecially when he came to the
„ thievifh part of it ; protefting he could execute the rogue himfelf with
„ the utmoft pleafure, if he had been alive then ; curfing thofe nights,
„ in which, for near three months together, he had lain with fo vile a
„ mifcreant.   A ftory like this one *Quirinus Talefius* reports that he had
„ heard from the fame Printer.

„ THIS is what my fincere love of truth oblig'd me to publifh, what-
„ ever the confequence be,——— but I am fearful that prejudice in this
„ cafe will out-balance reafon and authority.   The paffing of this in-
„ vention into *Germany* in a lawful way had been no harm ; nay, I be-
„ lieve that it pleafed God to make it the means of perfecting and di-
„ vulging fo ufeful an art, &c. „

HERE

HERE is all that our author could collect in defence of his cause, which he has made the best of after his way: it were indeed to be wish'd, the Doctor had rather imitated the modesty of *Carneades*, than wish'd for his eloquence; since that great philosopher (however he seems to forget it) never was known to affirm any thing. Convinc'd as he was of the weakness of human understanding, and of the power of prejudice; he always contented himself with confuting the opinions of others, without ever shewing that he held any of his own: but such an excellent talent would have spoil'd his design, and condemn'd both his book and his old men's fables to obscurity and oblivion, and saved some other authors the trouble of writing in the vindication of either; but tho' he has been follow'd by about a dozen of his country-men, yet no additional testimonies are to be expected from any of them: for even *Boxhorn*, who wrote with the greatest vehemence and spleen against *Malinkrot*, has been oblig'd to content himself with palliating the account of *Junius*, and endeavouring to shew, that it is not quite so improbable as his antagonist hath represented it. However it must be owned, that except the two last nam'd authors, and one or two more, *viz. Berchius* and *Scriverius*, the first of whom has been confuted by *Nicholas Serrarius* a Jesuit in his book *de rebus Moguntinis, lib.* I. *Cap.* 36, 37, 38, and 39; and the later by the learned Monf. *Naudé, George Draude* and others; I say except these, all the rest write more moderately, without invectives or ill language, and some of them even with doubt; whilst others modestly contend only for the invention of printing on wooden-planks, leaving that of metal types to *Faust:* but even this is inconsistent with the story of *Junius*, who asserts *Coster* to be the inventor of them both, and *Faust* the thief. It would be superfluous to multiply quotations out of the writers on the side of *Harlem*, since they follow *Junius* upon his bare testimony; and a confutation of him will easily dispatch all the rest. I shall therefore examine the probability of his account, and see how far it outweighs the testimonies and authorities alleg'd on the other side: in the execution of this, the best method will be to follow the steps of the learned *Malinkrot*, who has sufficiently expos'd the numerous absurdities, which this story is attended with. Setting aside therefore the oddness of *Coster*'s fancy, in chusing to make his first letters of the bark of beech, which

which will bend whilft green, and break when dry ; whilft the wood it˜
felf would have been much more proper to bear the weight of the prefs; ;
and the improbability of his changing them into metal ones, which is
barely afferted by *Junius*, and contradicted by *Berkius*, *Boxborn*, and other
Dutch writers, as we hinted before : nothing can be more ridiculous than
the converting thofe types into drinking cups to perpetuate the memory
of their difcovery ; they had certainly been more authentick in their former ftate ; at leaft, if fome notable work or infcription had been printed with them : or would it not have been a better method to celebrate
the name of the inventor, to have diftributed annually a portion of wine
out of them, in order to infpire their poets with fongs in his honour and
Fauft's fhame ; or to have hang'd them up, as trophies, in the town-hall
or great church, *&c.* with refpect to the ftolen types, (which were turn'd
to a better purpofe by the thief, who the next year printed with them
Alexandri doctrinale, and the works of *Petrus Hifpanus*, if *Junius* may be
credited, who was the firft that faid or thought of this ;) well might *Serrarius* fay after the Emperor *Julian*, *Who will be found innocent, if one accufation makes a man guilty?* One would naturally think that this ftory was
devis'd in the woods and walks about *Harlem*; for feveral of the writers
before mention'd, and particularly the *Colognian Chronicle* alleg'd by *Boxborn*, agree that the *Latin* bible was the firft book printed by *Fauft* at
Mentz. 'Tis furprizing that thefe gentlemen of *Harlem* fhould pretend
to tell us what was done with their types in the very heart of *Germany*,
and yet be entirely ignorant of what was done in their own city : befides
at that time it is certain, as we have already fhewn, that feparate types
of any fort of metal were unknown —- But to proceed ; this treacherous fervant, it feems, went off at 12 a-clock at night, when the whole
family was at church. — It is highly improbable, that a *Dutchman* fhould
leave his fhop fo open and expos'd at that time of night, when it was
fill'd with all the tools and apparatus of an invention fo important, and
known only to himfelf and his man : for it is downright abfurdity to think,
that he might depend on the oath, with which he had engaged the latter to fecrecy. Such a night as that, wherein the inhabitants of the city were going to or coming from mafs, was by no means proper for fuch
a defign ; and fuppofing he might have pafs'd undifturb'd with his ftoller

G treafure,

treafure, yet he could not with the fame facility pafs thro' the gates, or leap over the walls, with at leaft a thoufand weight of letters on his back : or if his booty was thofe wooden planks, with which the two large books mention'd before were printed, as fome of the *Dutch* writers feem to hint againft *Junius,* it was fufficient to load two or three carts : that he fhould go with them to *Amfterdam,* then to *Cologn,* and at laft to *Mentz,* without being taken notice of, is no lefs aftonifhing.   I fhall not infift upon his rafhnefs in chufing to go thro' fuch publick roads and noted cities,   and thereby running the danger of being feized ;   the confequence of which would have been capital punifhment : nor upon the unaccountable fupinenefs of his mafter in not purfuing nor caufing him to be apprehended,   when he open'd fhop at *Mentz,*   where he could eafily have reach'd him : nor yet upon the probability, that the publick muft have been obliged,   by this daring attempt of robbing the country of fuch a glorious difcovery,   to profecute the robber with the utmoft feverity where ever he could be found.

In the next place fhould we grant that *Fauft,* or fome other fervants had ftollen the types ; does it neceffarily follow that he carry'd away the art with them ?   Could neither *Cofter,* nor his fon-in-law and affiftant *Tho. Peter,* nor any of his grand-children, recover a new prefs, caft new types,   and publifh fomething that might expofe the thief, and fhew to whom the world was indebted for this invention ?   Befides, it appears from *Junius* that fome of the types were left behind,   which were afterwards transformed into drinking-veffels : if thefe were not fufficient to fet them to work again, the interval of ten years, *viz.* from the pretended robbery *anno* 1441, to the divulging of the art *anno* 1452, was more than enough to have compleated a new fet ; feeing the firft inventors devis'd, try'd, and perfected this method in lefs time.   But 'tis urg'd that *Cofter* dy'd either of grief or otherwife before he had brought the art to any perfection ;   fo that *Harlem* was anticipated by *Mentz.*   This is affirmed by *Majolus* and *Quadi,* tho' without grounds ; for *Junius* tells us, that he invented the feparate metal types, as well as wooden-blocks ;   and met with fuch encouragement that people came far and near to purchafe his books, tho' at very dear rates :   now if he was alive, as *he* and *Berkius* relate, *anno* 1447, fix years after this pretended flight ; during that interval
terval

terval he might have renew'd his works, there being no want of buyers, and infcrib'd his books after this or fome fuch manner; *This work was done at* Harlem *by* L. J. Cofter, *the inventor of this art of printing,* &c. *and not by that notorious pretender* John Fauft, *who ftole my art and inftruments, and is fet up at* Mentz, *&c.* But nothing of this nature was ever done by *Cofter* or his pofterity; which is a plain indication that this whole ftory is, what *Salmuth* and other learned writers affirm it to be, a mere old wife's fable without foundation or even probability. How the devifers and publifhers of it can maintain it with fo much pofitivenefs and vehemence, with fuch calumnies, invectives and ill language, againft perfons of incomparable learning, who could not give into fuch an abfurd and legendary account, is not my bufinefs to enquire. I fhall only obferve, that their charge upon a man of fuch confpicuous merit as *John Fauft* recoils with double force and fhame upon themfelves; for it proves them guilty of a crime more flagrant than what they accufe him of, in endeavouring to deprive him not only of the glory of that invention, in order to fix it upon an imaginary country-man of theirs; but even of what is moft valuable in the world, his reputation, upon the bare teftimony and tradition of three old citizens, whofe memory is as juftly queftionable, as their and *Junius's* impartiality, in a cafe wherein the honour of their city and fellow-citizens is concern'd; and what is ftill a greater aggravation of their unjuft calumny, to make ufe of *Fauft's* noble difcovery to publifh and perpetuate his fhame, whofe honour and memory ought rather to have been celebrated by it: little did that good man think, that his art would ever be put to fo vile a ufe againft himfelf.

In the mean time, I muft not omit to remark, that of all the writers, whom we have quoted for *Mentz,* and of many more collected by the diligent *Malinkrot* in his *Hiftory of Printing,* there is not one native of that city. *Munfter* indeed was born near it, but educated at a greater diftance; and *Serrarius,* tho' he liv'd fometime there, was born in *Lorain;* yet if fuch an objection had been juft againft ten or twelve of 'em, there remains enough to fix the laurel on *Fauft's* head. But with refpect to the old evidences of *Harlem,* we only know what *Junius* is pleas'd to tell us of them, that they were perfons who ferv'd feveral confiderable offices in the city. However *Malinkrot* makes a very fhrewd remark upon one of

them,

them, *viz.* *Cornelius* the Printer, who in a fally of paffion wifh'd *Fauft* had been then alive, that he might have executed him with his own hands; and was at that time, as *Junius* relates, above eighty years old : now as this theft is pretended to have been committed *anno* 1441, and it appears from an edition of *Tully's offices* that *Fauft* was living *anno* 1466; it is plain that in this fpace of 25 years *Cornelius* might have had an opportunity of gratifying his revenge upon him if he had thought fit. This circumftance therefore, which was contriv'd to add weight to the ftory, ferves only to burlefque and overthrow it.

I fear the reader is more weary of this argument than I could wifh; fince there are two or three new allegations out of thofe who followed *Junius*, which tho' of fmall weight, I would willingly examine before I difmifs this chapter; tho' it were only to fhew what fhifts they are driven to, who undertake to fupport the credit of *Junius's* legend; and to let the world judge whether fuch arguments are not more likely to overthrow than maintain this caufe. I fhall here propofe 'em with the utmoft brevity.

B O X H O R N, in his *Theatrum Hollandiæ*, triumphs upon the evidence of two eminent writers, whom he has violently wrefted to fpeak in defence of his claim. One is the author of the *Cologn Chronicle*; the other *Mariangelus Accurfius*, a learned man, who flourifh'd in *Italy* about the beginning of the fixteenth century. The former writes to this purpofe [1], that ,, altho' the Art of Printing had been found out at *Mentz*, in the man-,, ner we now have it, yet the firft hints or pattern was taken from the ,, *Donatus* of *Holland*, which had been printed there; that the aforefaid ,, art took its origin from them, tho' the latter invention is much fu-,, perior in contrivance and ingenuity. ,, 'Tis to be obferv'd by the bye, that this author wrote in the year 1499, almoft 50 years after the difcovery, and had thefe particulars from *Ulric Zel* an old bookfeller then living at *Cologn.* The next teftimony is a paffage written by *Accurfius* upon the

---

[1] *Chronic. Colonienf.* Quamvis autem, ut præmittitur, *Moguntia* ars hæc inventa fuerit, eo modo quo nunc temporis communiter ufurpatur; prima tamen ejus præfiguratio, feu fimulacrum ex *Donatis Hollandiæ* reperta & defumpta fuit, qui ibi ante id tempus excufi fuerunt; e quo illis principium artis depromptum eft: at pofterior hæc inventio priore, quoad artificium & fubtilitatem, longe præftantior fuit.

N. B. The author wrote this *chronicle* in *High Dutch*, but I could never procure the original, and have been oblig'd to make ufe of *Malinkrot's* tranflation of it.

firft

firſt leaf of a *Donatus* printed at *Mentz* by *John Fauſt*, as follows[1].
,, *John Fauſt* citizen of *Mentz*, grand-father by mother's ſide of *John*
,, *Shepherd*, was the firſt that devis'd this Art of Printing with braſs types,
,, which he afterwards chang'd for leaden ones : his ſon *Peter Schoeffer*
,, added many other improvements to the art : this *Donatus* and the
,, *Confeſſionalia* were firſt printed in the year 1450. He certainly took
,, the hint from the *Donatus* printed before in *Holland* upon wooden
,, planks. ,, What this *Donatus* and other books of that ſort were, and
whether really done in wood or otherwiſe, with ſome other particularities relating to them, ſhall be conſider'd in a diſtinct chapter : our preſent enquiry is how far they make for the cauſe of the *Dutch* writers.

We will ſuppoſe that *Ulric Zel* was a man of as good a memory as thoſe
mention'd by *Junius* ; and that the ſecond paſſage quoted was actually
written by *Accurſius*, which is far from being certain : let us now examine what both theſe writers do, and what they do not, affirm. They
affirm, 1. that this method of printing by fuſile types was found out at
Mentz by *John Fauſt*, and improv'd by his ſon-in-law *Peter Schoeffer* : 2.
that they printed ſome books in the year 1450 : 3. that there was a *Donatus* printed before that time upon wooden planks in *Holland* : and 4.
that from the hint, or, as the chronicler terms it, the model or pattern
[**vorbilding**] of thoſe wooden planks, *Fauſt* began the new way of
printing by fuſile types ; tho' this laſt article ſeems only a conjecture of
theirs.

They do not affirm, 1. that the old method of printing on wood
was the foundation of the new one : 2. that this *Donatus* was printed at
Harlem rather than at any other place, or by *Coſter* than any other perſon : tho' if they had aſſerted this, it ought to be examin'd how they got
that intelligence ; ſeeing it was not known in *Holland ann.* 1575. in which
year *Junius* dy'd, that any ſuch book had been printed there ; for that
author, who was indefatigable in collecting whatever favour'd his cauſe,
would never have fail'd to mention it ; and *Joſ. Scaliger*, tho' he ſince de-

---

[1] *Joannes Fauſt* civis *Moguntinus*, avus ma-
ternus *Joannis Schoeffer*, primus excogitavit imprimendi artem typis æreis, quos deinde plumbeos invenit; multaque ad poliendam artem ad-
didit ejus filius *Schoeffer:* impreſſus eſt autem
hic *Donatus* & *Confeſſionalia* primo omnium *anno* 1450, admonitus certe fuit ex *Donato Hollan-
dia* prius impreſſo in tabula inciſa. *Theatr.
Holland.* p. 138.

clar'd

clar'd himself for *Harlem*, formerly attributed this rude invention to the city of *Dort*: 3. they don't affirm that this *Donatus* was printed before the *Catholicon* of *Mentz*, wherein lies the main point ; for tho' they say it was done before *Fauſt* had perfected his invention, yet it does not follow that it was before he had begun to print with wooden planks. Nothing therefore can be gather'd from these authors, even with respect to this invention in wood, that favours *Coſter* or *Harlem* more than *Fauſt* or *Mentz*.

I have already obſerv'd that some of the *Dutch* writers are for dividing the glory between those two corrivals, and particularly *Peter Berchius:* in this he is follow'd by no less an author than *Boxhorn*, so often mention'd for his zeal in this diſpute. He finding the impoſſibility of defending all the aſſertions of *Junius*, is willing to come to a compoſition. His words are theſe: [1] ,, It will be no difficulty to reconcile this ,, great and weighty controverſy, which has exercis'd the greateſt wits of ,, the age, if we will, as indeed we ought, yield the honour of the old ,, wooden invention to *Coſter* of *Harlem*, and that of metal types to *John* ,, *Fauſt* citizen of *Mentz*. ,, But this accommodation is attended with this diſadvantage, that it will ſet the *Dutch* writers at variance not only with one another, but alſo with themſelves ; whereas 'tis much better in my opinion, to continue in war with the whole world, than to bring a domeſtick one into their own bowels. A conſequence ſtill worſe is inevitable ; for what will become of the pompous ſtory of *Fauſt*'s robbery ? And of thoſe creditable evidences mention'd by *Junius?* Would not they with the utmoſt vehemence proteſt againſt ſuch a partition treaty ? And old *Cornelius* the falſe accuſer, deſerve the moſt ſanguinary treatment to be retaliated on him from ſome angry *Moguntine?* Will not the drinking cups, thoſe noble relicks of *Coſter*'s metal types, run the riſque of being turn'd into veſſels of diſhonour? And all the inſcriptions in his praiſe, his ſtatues, and even his houſe at *Harlem*, be liable to ſome ſuch diſmal fate. — If we ſhould yield them this invention of wooden planks, so

[1] Sed non difficile eſt hanc tam gravem ac tam nobilem controverſiam, & quæ clariſſima noſtri ævi ingenia exercuit, componere, nempe, ſi vel id, quod res eſt, concedamus, typos quidem ligneos a *Laurentio Harlemenſi* primum fuiſſe inventos, typos vero ſtanneos, æreos, & plumbeos ad horum exemplar efformatos eſſe a *Joanne Fauſto* cive *Moguntino.* Boxhorn *Ib. at. Holland.*

eagerly

eagerly contended for; or agree with the more moderate of their writers that *Fauſt* and *Coſter*, tho' at ſo great a diſtance, happen'd upon it together ; or grant to *Boxborn*, that *Harlem* was the mother, and *Mentz* the nurſe of theſe two diſcoveries ; and that the one is but an improvement of the other : yet *Coſter* would not have deſerv'd half of the incenſe beſtow'd on him ; nor *Fauſt* the leaſt part of the calumnies which he has ſuffer'd. In vain were ſuch ſhifts and forgeries uſed to deprive him of ſo ſmall and inconſiderable ſhare of his glory ; whilſt the far greateſt part of it, which could not be touch'd, was more than ſufficient to make him outſhine and even eclipſe his rival, for whoſe ſake he was ſo ungratefully treated. Had not he been bleſs'd with a genius vaſtly ſuperior to that of his ſuppoſ'd competitor, or contented himſelf without aiming at a more uſeful and expeditious method than the firſt ; the common wealth of letters had receiv'd as little advantage from his diſcovery, as his own name and memory from thoſe *Dutch* writers, were they the only perſons to tranſmit them to poſterity. However if their partiality, and adherence to *Junius,* have influenc'd them ſo far as to make ſuch returns for thoſe improvements, which they are oblig'd to acknowledge that he made ; common juſtice will oblige me to acquaint the reader, that other writers of that country, of equal learning, and a more generous nature, have been ſo far from joyning with them, that they have aſcrib'd the invention to *Fauſt* alone. I have before quoted an encomium of the great *Eraſmus* upon him and his art, and ſhall cloſe this chapter with another out of the learned *Opmer* of *Amſterdam,* who dy'd about the year 1595, *i. e.* 20 years after *Junius,* and has left us the following teſtimony in his poſthumous book of *Chronography* : [1] — ,, This year 1440 the art of printing
began

Etenim hoc anno *Moguntiæ* a *Joanne Fauſto* ars imprimendi exerceri coepta eſt, fuerat is avus *Joannis Shoefferi* chalcographi noſtræ ætatis, vir dignus ut celebretur.——

Quid? quod ſub mundi veſperam, inſtante ſupremo jam die, inter caliginoſas impiorum atque diſcordiarum feralium procellas raræ pietatis, ſummæque doctrinæ non pauci inſtar micantium ſyderum emicaſſe cernuntur ; ut crederes orbem a graviore morbo convaluiſſe, atque amiſſas eloquentiæ artiumque vires ſenſim recollegiſſe ; opitulante diſciplinis arte illa, qua plumbeis literarum characteribus ingenioſe fuſis, atque ſcribendi ratione optime compoſitis, atramentoque madefactis convenienter ac prælo compreſſis, diverſarum linguarum libri numeroſo quaſi partu in quamplurima exemplaria in lucem producuntur : *Typographiæ* arti nomen dedere, ac per *Joannem Fauſtum* anno 1440 excogitatam in lucem produxiſſe certiſſime conſtat. Mirum tanti artificii repertorem, & divinarum humanarumque diſciplinarum generoſum adminiſtrum a *Germanicarum* rerum ſcriptore indigno plane ornari elogio : fuit certe vir ille immortalis memoriæ digniſſimus, & acutiſſimis ingeniis annumerandus. *Opmer. op. poſth, p.* 703. *edit. Colon.*

,, began to be exercis'd at *Mentz* by *John Fauft*, who was the grandfa-
,, ther of *John Schoeffer* (a printer of this age,) and worthy the higheft
,, encomiums. ,, In another place (in the beginning of the 4th book) there
is the following elegant panegyrick upon the art and inventor : — ,, that
,, at the decline of the world, when the laft day feem'd to approach, fo
,, many men of accomplifh'd learning and fingular piety fhould break
,, forth, like bright ftars, with unufual luftre thro' the tempeftuous clouds
,, of deadly difcord ; fo that you would have thought the world had been
,, recover'd from a long difeafe, and gradually reaffumed its loft ftrength,
,, the arts and fciences : this was effected by the affiftance of that art,
,, which from metal characters of letters ingenioufly caft, difpos'd in the
,, order in which we write, fpread over with a convenient quantity of
,, ink, and put under the prefs, has ufher'd into the world, books in all
,, languages, and multiplied their copies like a numerous off-fpring,
,, and has obtain'd the name of Typography. This *art of Printing* was
,, moft certainly invented and brought to light by *John Fauft* in the year
,, 1440. It is amazing that the author of fo important a difcovery, and
,, fo generous a promoter of divine and human learning, fhould be un-
,, worthily traduc'd by a writer of the *German* affairs: furely fuch a per-
,, fon deferves eternal remembrance, and a place amongft men of the
,, brighteft genius. ,, —— Who this *German* writer was our author no
where tells us ; but it feems as if his unnatural ufage of his own countryman had taken off *Opmer*'s wonder at the like treatment from the *Dutch*
writers. If it fhould be asked what converts thefe laft have made among
other nations, I can only anfwer, that I know of none.

THE generality of writers have efteem'd *Junius*'s ftory unworthy of
either credit or confutation ; and if any of the moderns feem neuter or
doubtful in this cafe, it is more owing to a peculiar affectation of modefty, than either to any defign of complimenting the *Dutch*, or fear of
being miftaken in fo evident a matter.

C H A P.

C H A P. VI.

An Enquiry into the firſt Books *printed on* Blocks *of* Wood, *viz. the* Donatus, Speculum, *&c.*

AS the reader may reaſonably think, there is ſomething excellent in theſe Books, either for beauty of impreſſion, learning, correct-neſs, *&c.* from the great noiſe which they have made among the writers of this controverſy ; I muſt begin with acquainting him that their whole merit conſiſts only in their being look'd upon by them as the very firſt eſſays of the art of printing, even before the invention of fuſile types. This is ſo far from admitting of any controverſy, however ſome of them may have been miſled into a contrary opinion, that their being print-ed only on one ſide of the paper, and afterwards glew'd together, on the blank ſide, from which they were call'd *paginæ conglutinatæ,* is a very pregnant proof of their being done after the firſt method, *viz.* upon wood-en blocks ; tho' we ſhall not only corroborate the fact by many other un-deniable arguments in the ſequel of this chapter, but even lead the rea-der into ſo plain a method of judging of thoſe works, from thoſe printed by fuſile types, that he will not have the leaſt room left to doubt of it.

A s for the *Donatus,* ſo ſtrenuouſly inſiſted upon, by *Bertius* and others, in favour of *Harlem,* it is a queſtion whether there be one copy of it ex-tant, ſeeing 'tis not to be met with in any of thoſe curious libraries I have either ſeen or heard of, nor could ever be procured by any of our ſearch-ers into theſe antient monuments, tho' they have ſpar'd neither pains nor coſt to have it ſought for far and near : to which let me add, that no au-thor I am acquainted with, has pretended to have ſeen it, if we except *Angel Rocha,* who in his *Bibliotheca Vaticana,* printed at *Rome* in the year 1591, 4*to.* pag. 411, tells us, that *Aldus Manutius, jun*. ſhew'd him a grammar of *Donatus* printed on vellum, upon one of the firſt white leaves of which *Mariangelus Accurſius,* a learned author living in *Italy* about the year 1500 had wrote, as he ſuppos'd, with his own hand, the following words in latin, ,, that this *Donatus,* and another book entitled *Confeſſio-*

nalia

nalia were the firſt printed books, and that *John Fauſt* citizen of *Mentz*
and firſt inventor of the Art of Printing, had printed them *ann.* 1450, a
has been ſaid in the laſt chapter.

F R O M this account of *Accurſius* it is plain : *firſt*, that this *Donatus* bor
neither date nor name of place or printer, otherwiſe he need not to have
been at the trouble of gueſſing at them. *Secondly*, That *Donatus* is the
name of the author, not of the book ; and that it was only a grammar
for boys, for ſo *Rocha* calls it in the place before quoted ; to which we
may add, that in the laſt liſt which the firſt Printers at *Rome* gave of their
works to the Pope, they call it *Donatus pro pueris* ; ſo that it could not
be ſuch a trifling thing as ſome authors have thought it, who only call it
a Primer. The *third* thing I would obſerve from this paſſage is, that
John Fauſt, who is here call'd the firſt inventor of printing, is affirm'd
to have printed it at *Mentz :* but what has puzled the world is, what the
ſame author adds at the end of the paſſage, *viz. that* Fauſt *did certainly
take the hint from the* Donatus *in* Holland, *firſt printed on Blocks of wood ;*
which for that very reaſon, thoſe authors who have follow'd him, have
thought fit to make 10 years older, and have ſuppos'd them printed about
the year 1440. I might indeed have omitted this paſſage, ſeeing *Accurſius*
ſeems to hint that this book of his was printed by fuſile types ; but as
it was the only one that has been ſeen by any author, and confirms ſome
of our former aſſertions, I thought it would not be amiſs to inſert it, eſpecially conſidering that it was not impoſſible for *Accurſius* to be miſtaken
in his judgment, of its being printed after the new method of ſeparate types,
as many other learned men have been in the like caſe. The merit of this
quotation has been examin'd in the laſt chapter, and it is plain that all
the authors that have mention'd the date of this book, ſuch as *Beughen,*
Boxhorn, Bertius, and others have taken it upon truſt, as well as what
they affirm of its being done upon wooden blocks, ſince none of them pretend either to have ſeen it, or to have taken it from any author that had :
and if we ſhould admit what *Accurſius* affirms, that thoſe ſuppos'd *dutch
ones* were older than this he wrote upon, it will make it ſtill plainer that
they had neither date, printer, nor place's name ; ſince this, which is ſuppos'd ten years younger, is without any of them. The ſame may be
ſaid of the other books I am now going to give an account of, *viz.* the

Speculum,

Speculum, Ars moriendi, &c. which are in the Earl of *Pembroke's* curious collection, none of which, tho' they seem to be improvements of one another, has the least mention of time, place, or printer.

However, as to their being engraven upon wooden blocks, and consequently being the first essays, or as some antiquaries call them, the first *Maculatures* of the art, I am fully convinc'd, both by the ink with which they are printed, *viz.* the common writing ink, and by some undoubted trials I have made of them. I shall therefore lay down the following rules to distinguish between books printed on blocks of wood and separate metal types.

First, Let an m, w, or any other remarkable letter, be curiously examin'd both as to its length, breadth and shape, and compare it with the same letter in another word, if they vary either in similitude or size, you may be assur'd they are not metal types, since the most curious letter-cutter, writing-master, or engraver, cannot make any two letters so alike, but a nice observer will distinguish one from the other : on the contrary, in separate metal types each letter being cast in the same matrice, it is impossible there should be the least difference either in shape or size.

Secondly, Another way is by choosing any word, the longer the better, take the length of it with the points of the compass, and compare it with the same word in another place, and if you find them both of the same length, you may depend upon their being printed with separate metal types; for as each letter is cast in the same mould, it is impossible that their length should vary : but in writing and engraving there will be a visible difference in the same word in various places.

Thirdly, Measure the length of a page ; tell the number of lines in a full one, and take the white spaces between each line, and by comparing them to any other full page in the book, if they are printed with metal types there can be no variation in any of these respects : whereas, if they were done in wood it would be as impossible for them to agree in any one instance, as it would be to engrave or write any two pages wherein there should be no visible variation in some one or more of the foremention'd particulars. It was by these methods that I distinguish'd, in the *five* books in the Earl of *Pembroke's Library,* what was done on wood, and what by separate metal types.   H 2   *Melchior*

MELCHIOR ADAMUS, and after him the learned *Malinkrot* and ſome others, tell us of ſeparate wooden types cut with a knife, which were us'd by the firſt Printers, before the diſcovery of caſting them into metal ; but beſides that this ſeems inconſiſtent with the moſt authentick teſtimonies we have quoted hitherto concerning this invention: whoever conſiders the vaſt time and trouble it would require to cut ſuch a quantity of them as is neceſſary to print any moderate work, the great difficulty of making them ſtand exactly upright and even in line and body, how liable they would be to ſplit, break, warp, ſhrink and ſwell with continual wetting and the weight of the preſs, with many more ſuch like inconveniences and difficulties, will eaſily judge, not only of the abſurdity of this notion, but alſo of the impoſſibility of any of thoſe old books being printed by any ſuch types ; ſince it is obvious to every eye, that no one ſingle work could have come perfect out of their hands for the reaſons abovemention'd.

BEFORE I diſmiſs this point, I muſt not omit acquainting the Reader with a miſtake into which *Chevillier* has been unwarily drawn, even when he took the ſureſt method of coming at the truth, concerning one of theſe books in queſtion, *viz.* the *Speculum Salutis*, he tells us, *pag.* 281 and 282 of his *Origin of Printing*, that having one of them in his own poſſeſſion, and having met with another in the library of the *Celeſtin* Monks at *Paris*, he had the curioſity to have them examined by a Printer, a Founder, and an Engraver, who judg'd them to be printed with ſeparate-metal-types ; ſo that thoſe who have read his book, have thought it a ſufficient ground to alter their opinion of their being done on wooden blocks. But this miſtake of *Chevillier*'s proceeded from his not examining the whole book, becauſe as I ſhall ſhew anon, there were many leaves ſupply'd afterwards by ſeparate metal types, one of which he had the misfortune to light upon, otherwiſe they muſt have manifeſtly ſeen the difference

I come now to give the reader an account of the other *five* books, *viz. Ars Moriendi*, the *Hiſtory of the Apocalypſe*, the *Hiſtory of the Bible*, the *Speculum Salutis*, and the *Spiegel* or *Speculum* tranſlated into *Low Dutch*. That theſe however are not all that was done upon wooden planks, is plain, becauſe *Trithemius* tells us of the *Catholicon*, firſt printed upon wood,

Scaliger

Scaliger fpeaks of a *Pfalter* of the fame ftamp, which his grand-mother had, and other antiquaries mention feveral others not worth inferting here, all which are either perifh'd, or are as yet undifcover'd : however I cannot omit the *Speculum,* and fome others feen by *Saubert* in the *Nuremberg* library, of which he was keeper ; and mention'd by him in the catalogue of that library, call'd in latin *Bibliotheca Norica,* which books were printed in *High Dutch,* and may juftly be fuppos'd fome of *Fauftus's* firft *Tentamina* or effays from *ann.* 1440 to 1450 : but as that author has only given us the names, without any further account of them ; I fhall pafs them by, and return to the *five* abovementioned ; which are no where to be met with together, but in that noble Collection of the Right Hon. the Earl of *Pembroke:* and as no one befides my felf has defcrib'd them all, I hope the reader will not be difpleas'd, if I give him a more particular account of them, than any but a Printer could poffibly have done : They are all *five* printed on a very fmall *Folio.*

I. *ARS MORIENDI*; or, *SPECULUM MORIENTIUM.*

I t is a moral treatife upon the fubject of dying well, with wooden cuts fuited to the tafte of the Romifh church ; a fick man is figur'd lying in his bed with angels and devils attending him, the one to tempt, the other to ftrengthen him ; to which end the defigner has made labels from their mouths, to exprefs the intention of each : the defigns of this firft book are fomewhat better drawn than thofe of the reft ; for in that age, as well as ours, there were good and bad painters or defigners, but the prefs-work is the worft of the *five:* this induces me to think this piece to be the oldeft, and its wanting the feveral improvements which we find in the others, does not a little confirm me in my conjecture : for *firft,* it is printed with common writing ink without any gum, which is plain from its fpreading it felf, and foaking into the paper, fo that in many places it is fcarce legible ; and the ink is grown withall fo pale by length of time, that it doth but juft fhow it felf at the beft : *fecondly,* it feems to have received feveral degrees of improvement as the work went on, and is better printed, and with better ink, the nearer it draws to the end : the *third* circumftance that proves its priority to the reft, is, that it hath

neither

neither the capitals A, B, C, &c. (which are now call'd Signatures) at the bottom of the firſt pages of each ſheet, nor any direction word at the end of each page ; which is a guide to the book-binder how to place the ſheets, this improvement we find in the two next books.

II. *The* HISTORY *of the* APOCALYPSE.

THIS book, which I venture to give the ſecond rank to, hath the advantage of being printed with better ink than the former, which makes it much more legible ; it appears to have ſome gum diſſolv'd with the ink, which was one of the firſt improvements that was made to the common ſort of ink ; it has likewiſe the ſignatures at the top of each page of the ſheet : This piece contains the hiſtory of St. *John* the *Evangeliſt* in forty ſix pages, each having ſome figures ill cut, repreſenting ſome part of that ſaint's life ; the cuts are interſpers'd with ſhort ſentences, arguments and explications, in Monkiſh latin proſe ; likewiſe cut in wood after an indifferent manner ; the paper has the mark of the *heiffer's head and horns,* which is allowed to be the mark in the paper *Fauſt* uſed.

III. *The* HISTORY *of the* BIBLE.

THIS contains only hiſtories out of the Old and New Teſtament, promiſcuouſly blended together, with wooden cutts better perform'd, tho' worſe drawn, than any of the two foregoing ; it has likewiſe the arguments and explanations of each cut, and the paper ſeems to be the ſame with that of the *Apocalypſe* ; it has alſo the improvements of ink and ſignatures [1].

IV. *The* SPECULUM HUMANÆ SALVATIONIS.

IT is commonly called *Speculum Salutis* ; or, the *Mirrour of our Salvation* ; and is a comparative hiſtory of the old and new teſtament it is writ-

---

[1] Theſe were in all probability the firſt SIGNATURES, the 4th and 5th here have them not, nor the books with *Fauſt*'s name. And tho' the Terence printed at *Milan* 1470 has them, yet *Spira* and *Jenſon* printed afterwards without ; nor have they us'd them in *France* in 1468, yet in the ſame year they were us'd at *Oxford*.

ten

ten in Monkifh latin verfe rhim'd. This is by far the moft perfect of the two I have feen, *that* which *Dr. Mead* fhew'd me wanted many leaves, but *this* only two : it confifts of fifty fix pages, and each page has two columns of verfes, which are fo well cut, that were it not for fome differences in the magnitude and fhape of the fame letters, one might eafily be induc'd to think them printed with metal types; and I believe this is the reafon, that made fome authors fuppofe them to be done with feparate wooden types. I have already taken notice of the improbability of that notion.

V. *De SPIEGHEL.*

THIS is only a tranflation of the *Speculum Salutis* into *Flemifh:* it was upon this book that Dr. *Junius* and the other *dutch* writers, who have followed him, lay fo great a ftrefs ; and upon whofe antiquity, preferable to all others, they ground their claim to the invention of printing in favour of *Cofter*. However it is very plain that the *Latin* one is prior to this, and that *this* is only a tranflation of *that*, becaufe the wooden cuts are the fame in both, the latin explanations at the bottom are left untranflated, and the cuts are printed with the fame pale gum'd writing ink as in the *Latin* one, rather brown than black ; whereas the body of this work is compos'd with feparate metal types, and printed with an ink as remarkable for its blacknefs as any fort fince made ufe of: it has alfo in feveral places the fame mark in the paper, *viz.* the *heiffer's head and horns,* acknowledg'd by Monf. *Naudé* to be the mark in *Fauft's* paper. In the *Latin Speculum* a great many pages are fupply'd with the fame feparate metal types, prefs-work and ink as the body of this whole *Flemifh* one ; and has all the appearances fufficient to convince any one, of its being done at the fame time, and by the fame hand ; one of which *fupply'd* pages of the latin *Speculum*, *Chevillier* happen'd to pitch upon, when he fhew'd it to the Printer, Founder and Engraver before mention'd. There is one circumftance worth noting, which is, that the *Speculum falutis,* tho' cut on wood, each page confifts of two diftinct pieces, the head piece is the draught or reprefentation of the hiftory, the lower piece is the hiftory itfelf in two columns, and if I may venture to account for this motled

work

work, it muft be by fuppofing, that after they had cut the defign, they might print feveral proof fheets, as is ufual now, to fee if it needed any amendment; which proof fheets of the draughts only, together with a compleat book of the latin *Speculum,* might afterwards fall into the hands of fome *dutch Printer,* who got it tranflated into *low dutch* and printed it with feparte metal types upon the fame proof fheets under the defigns which were before printed at the head of the page; and this will evidently appear from the manifeft difference of the ink, as before mention'd.

T H E R E remain ftill two points to be examin'd with relation to the *Donatus*; 1. whether it be the firft book printed with wooden planks; 2. whether it was done by *L. Cofter* at *Harlem.* To the firft there is only the teftimonies of *Ulric Zel* citizen of *Cologn,* who relates what was done almoft fifty years ago, and of *Mar. Accurfius,* who wrote in *Italy* what he heard was done at, a ftill, greater diftance from him. To thefe, who could not poffibly be acquainted with every circumftance of this difcovery, we may reafonably oppofe the authority of *Trithemius*; for he learn'd what he tells us, not from report and uncertain tradition, but from the mouth of *Peter Schoeffer,* who related nothing but what he was an eye-witnefs of, or rather particularly interefted in. Now *Trithemius* afcribes the invention of wooden blocks to *J. Fauft*; and afferts that the *Catholicon* was the firft book (of any confequence) printed in that manner; and that his next ftep was the more ingenious invention of feparate metal types.

L E T the world judge whether his teftimony be not far preferable to that of the two former. *Scriverius* indeed, and after him Mr. *Beughen,* affirm the *Donatus* to have been printed *anno* 1440; but give no reafon for their fixing on that year rather than any other; and it is manifeft from what they fay before, that they only proceed upon a fuppofition, that this method being difcovered about that time; this book (which is perhaps the leaft confiderable of thofe which were printed then) might be one of the firft effays of it. However let the *Catholicon,* the *Donatus* or any other, be the firft book printed in *Europe* with wooden planks, yet there is no ground of boafting it to be the firft in the world; fince the *Chinefe* practis'd that way of Printing at leaft 300 years before either *Fauft* or *Cofter* were born.

T H E

THE next confideration is, where and by whom it was printed. The *Dutch* attempt two ways of proving it was done by *Cofter* at *Harlem*: the firft is that of *Junius*, who pretends that it was one of the firft tryals of *Cofter*'s metal types; but this has been fo fully confuted, that they have been oblig'd to recur to another fhift; which is, that *Cofter* invented the engraven planks, and with thefe printed the *Donatus* and *Speculum Salutis*; and that from this *Fauft* took the hint of inventing metal types, an improvement of the former method[1]: As the latter part of this affertion has receiv'd a fufficient anfwer in the fecond chapter and elfewhere, fo I need not infift long upon a confutation of the former part, *i. e.* the books themfelves; fince they carry no evident charaƈteriftick, nor are affirm'd with certainty by any author to have been done in *Holland*. No doubt the *Latin Speculum* is the original, and the *Dutch* only a tranflation; fince as I obferv'd before, the latin arguments under the figures are left untranflated. The learned *Saubert* likewife tells us in his *Hiftory of the* Norimbergh *library*, that he hath feen feveral books there printed in *high dutch* after this manner, one of which is the *Speculum*[2]. Who can therefore determine which is the moft antient, or where they were printed? If the *Dutch* one could be done no where but in *Holland*, becaufe it is in *low dutch*; by parity of reafon the *high dutch* muft have been printed in *Germany*; and as to the *Latin*, it will remain ftill undetermin'd, whether it was done in the one or the other, and nothing will be certain concerning it, except that it muft have been printed before the tranflations. From the whole of what has been faid, it is apparent, that all the proofs which the *Dutch* bring either from faƈts or authentick writers, confute, rather than fupport, their pretenfions: and I hope by this time the reputation of *Fauft* is fufficiently clear'd from the two fold wrong done it by thofe, who endeavour to deprive him of his due honour, and afperfe him with the vileft accufations of treachery and theft: and that the rea-

---

[1] Alibi enim ars, alibi ornamenta artis inventa; illa inter *Hollandos*, hæc inter *Germaniæ Moguntinos*. ——— *Harlemum Typographiæ* velut matrem, *Moguntiam* autem nutricem fuiffe & alumnam; ibi fuperatum quicquid in novæ rei exordiis impeditum, hic additam majorem arti fpeciem & facilitatem. *Boxhorn de Art. Typogr invent.* p 38, 39.

[2] Quæ ligno incifa funt, huc non refero, v. g. libellum fabularum & fimilitudinum, qualis eft *D. Hartliebii* libellus *Germanicus*, itemque *Speculum Morientium, Speculum Salutis*, & id genus alia, *Saubert. Hiftor. Biblioth. Norimberg.* p. 116.

I   der

der not only eſteems him acquitted of both, but is ſatisfy'd that neither *Coſter* nor *Harlem* have the leaſt ſhare in this diſcovery.

B E F O R E I conclude this chapter, I cannot omit a conjecture of the in‑genious Mr. *Mattaire*, which will be a conſiderable confirmation of what has been ſaid before. He tells us [1], that he is inclin'd to think the books beforemention'd were printed at *Harlem*, rather than at *Mentz* or *Straſ‑burgh*, becauſe tho' *Guttenbergh* remov'd at firſt to the latter, ſoon after the ſentence pronounc'd againſt him by the judges of *Mentz*; yet it appears from ſeveral authors even of our own nation, that he either ſuſpecting his ſafety there, and a farther proſecution from *Fauſt* for the money ad‑judg'd to him by the decree and deed mention'd in a former chapter, or upon ſome other reaſon, came afterwards to *Harlem*: in this city he is ſuppos'd by our author to have taught the art to *Coſter*, and practis'd it with him about the year 1459. If this be admitted, which has all the air of probability to recommend it, *Coſter* will be left entirely deſtitute of his former glory. The reader will find Mr. *Mattaire*'s proofs for what he advanceth concerning *Guttenbergh*'s printing at *Harlem*, in his book before quoted [2]; which I refer to, rather than to thoſe old and ſcarce authors, from whom he has extracted them. I ſhall cloſe this contro‑verſy of *Harlem* with the words of *Malinkrot*: [3] ,, 'Tis not the ſpacious

De loco & opifice incertiora adhuc ſunt omnia. Si pro *Mguntia* pronuncietur, non multum hærendum erit de opificibus, tribus ſcilicet antea celebratis; aut tempore, quod an‑no 1457, (quo primum, juxta receptam hacte‑nus a pleriſque opinionem, integræ Typogra‑phiæ opus per *Johannem Fuſt* & *Petrum Schoef‑fer* elaboratum prodiit) fuerit forte vetuſtius; opus enim minus perfectum oportet perfectiori præiviſſe, ſin autem cui *Argentina* plus placeat, aut (quam cur duarum malim, poſtea aperiam) *Harlemum*; *Guttenbergius*, quem quidam *Ar‑gentinam* migraſſe, potior vero (de qua dein‑ceps diſſeram, authoritas *Harlemi* confediſſe af‑firmat, hæc primæ ſuæ artis molitus eſt rudi‑menta; non qui ern ante annum 1455, quo ac‑cidiſſe fertur inter ipſum *Fauſtumque* diſſidium (quæ ipſi fuit migrandi cauſa) neque forſan multo poſt 1457 quo perfectior innotuerat im‑primendi ratio. *Annal Typ graph.* p. 17.

[2] *Ibid a* pag 25, ad 30.

Quæ ex *Lambethano* MS. deſcripſit, de eo rum veritati cur dubitemus non video: ex iis itaque pauca mecum colliget lector alibi forſan non ediſcenda.

1. *Johannes Guttenbergus*, quem, exorta in‑ter ipſum & *Fauſtum* contentione, *Argentinam* migraſſe ſcribit *Henricus Salmuth*, *Harl mum* inde aliquando profectus eſt, ibique primus ar‑tem Typographicam a ſe inventam n onſtravit, & ipſe anno 1459 exercuit: quod ſi admitta‑tur, contra *Laurentium Coſterum*, cui inventionis palma a *Belgis* tribuitur, manifeſte faciet, *&c.* *ib.* p. 31.

[3] Non hercle *Harlemica* ſilvæ ſpatiis, non *Ba‑tavicis* deambulationibus, non *Hollandico* otio tam laborioſæ artis anxium & difficilem partum debemus; ſed *Moguntinis* potius ſudoribus *Rhe‑ninæ* induſtriæ & difficilibus nixibus, *Germanica* aſſiduitatis indefeſſæ operationi, continuæ multo‑rum annorum inſtantiæ illum acceptum ferre te‑nemur. *Typograph. cap.* 8. *pag.* 69.

,, woods

,, woods of *Harlem,* nor the fine walks of *Holland,* nor the fupinenefs of
,, its inhabitants that could produce an art fo difficult and laborious ; but
,, 'tis to the ftrenuous endeavours of the city of *Mentz,* and the affidu-
,, ous and indefatigable induftry of the *Rhenifh* nation for many years
,, together, that we are indebted for it. ,,

C H A P. VII.

The Pretenfions of Strasburgh *confuted.*

IN the two former chapters, the falfity of the charge againft *John
Fauft* has been fo fully demonftrated, that one would have reafonably expected the ill fuccefs of this accufation, and the many learned advocates that appear'd in his defence, might have been fufficient to deter
the moft fanguine of mortals from a fecond attempt upon fo great a
man. Neverthelefs the reader muft have patience to hear him arraigned
at another bar for the like crimes, committed about the fame time, tho'
upon another perfon, and at another place diftant feveral hundred miles
from the former.

FOUR years after the publication of *Boxhorn's Differtatio de Typographiæ inventione & inventoribus,* printed at *Leyden* 1640; there ftarted up
another, who in a fmall treatife intitled, *Brevis de loco, tempore & authore Typographiæ excurfus,* pretended to prove that *Fauft* ftole the art of
Printing from *John Mentel* at *Strasburgh.* 'Tis true, this author was
afham'd to fet his name to it ; but neither that, nor the meannefs of his
performance hinder'd the diligent *Malinkrot,* who was then writing his
treatife *de ortu & progreffu artis Typographicæ* againft *Junius* and his followers, from confuting it. Hereupon *James Mentel* doctor of phyfick at
Paris, a man of learning, and great grand-fon of *Mentel,* the firft *Straf-
burg* Printer of that name, publifh'd a book call'd *Parænefis de vera Typographiæ origine* at *Paris anno* 1650; wherein he undertook to make good
the charge, which the anonymous author had laid againft *Fauft,* and challeng'd the glory of the invention in favour of his anceftor. Tho' no particular anfwer to this book has been publifh'd, yet there is not one writer

upon

upon this subject, that I know of, that has not taken occasion to confute, or at least to say something to discountenance it. I should therefore
esteem my self, wanting to this art and its inventor, should I omit giving
a short account of this controversy, and expose the vanity of such an attempt; especially because it may be thought, that Dr. *Mentel* would not
have troubled the world with it so soon after the other, unless he had
had something more weighty to alledge in favour of *Strasburgh*, than the
Dutch had for *Harlem*.

I hope to propose the arguments on both sides so fairly, that the reader
will easily judge of the pretensions and merit of this new competitor;
and with such brevity, that he will not be tired with it, by referring
still to the quotations in the margin without interruption to the story.

THE first evidence alledg'd by Dr. *Mentel*, is an old *Strasburgh* chronicle, of equal authority with the *Harlem* tradition, to this purpose[1]:
„ that *anno* 1440 *Nich. Schantlitt* being consul, *&c.* the excellent and tru-
„ ly useful art of Printing was invented at *Strasburgh* by the incompara-
„ ble *John Mentel,* who dwelt in the *Fronhoff* market, and at the house
„ commonly called **Diergarten** *(brothel-house* ;) which divine invention he
„ communicated to a servant of his of great ingenuity and dexterity, by
„ name *John Gensfleich*, a native of *Mentz*, that he might be assisting to
„ him in the business. But this treacherous fellow had no sooner learn'd
„ the mystery, but he serv'd his master a base trick, by associating him-
„ self with his counrryman *J. Guttenberg*, a wealthy silver-smith, who
„ began to smell out something of the art (having been employed by
„ *Mentel* to make some necessary tools ;) and discovering to him the se-

---

[1] Anno millesimo quadringentesimo quadra-
gesimo als zum Drittenmahl, &c. quæ Latine
sic sonant : cum e tribu Victorum tertius in
consulem esset electus Dominus *Nicholaus Schantlitt*, & prætura urbana fungeretur *Walterus
Spiegel*, &c. eximia illa & mire utilis *Typographia Strasburgi* inventa est, ab incomparabili viro *Johanne Mentlio* habitante in foro *Fronhoff*,
in ædibus vero *Diergarten*, hoc est lustri, vulgo
nuncupatis: quod divinissimum opus non cela-
vit unum ex famulis suis, sibi dexteritate ingenii atque acumine notum, *Johannem Gensfleich*
vocatum, & illum *Moguntinensem*, ut abs illo in
ea re juvaretur: Sed male feriatus is servus,
ubi quadamtenus industriæ istius fuisset consci-
us, nequissime cum hero se gessit. Nam cum
Johanne Gutembergio, populare suo, pinguis
census homine, ac vitæ forte aurifice, se soci-
ans; qui jam de arte quidpiam subodorabatur
(*ut meritoria cujus opera fabricardis ad id in-
strumentis usus antea fuisset Mentelius*) secreta
quæ a patrono fuerat expiscatus, detexit. Ac
sic utrique cum nova & illustria per ipsam nomina comparandi spes foret; nec tamen impune id *Argentorati*, ubi esset inventor possent
consequi, illac egredi apud se constituerunt, ac
Moguntiam profecti sunt. *Mentel.* p. 6, 7.

,, cret, which he had been intrusted with by his master. These two ho-
,, ping to make themselves famous by this art, but being fearful of di-
,, vulging it at *Strasburgh* where the inventor liv'd, resolv'd to remove
,, thence, and settle at *Mentz.* ,,

WITH respect to this chronicle and the writer of it, we only know what our author tells us in his translation inserted at the bottom of the page, for the chronicle is written in *high dutch.* As it wants therefore some better authority for its support, Dr. *Mentel* brings, as a confirmation of it, the testimonies of the writers quoted in our third chapter, who make mention of *Guttenberg*'s carrying the art from *Strasburgh* to *Mentz,* where he perfected it by the assistance of *John Faust* alias *Gensfleich* ; whose words are not therefore necessary to be repeated here. In the next place he alledges an inscription, which with *Mentel*'s coat of arms was put at the beginning of *Otho Brunsfield*'s *Onomasticon* printed at *Strasburgh* by *John Schott anno* 1543, importing [1], that these arms of *Schott*'s family had been given to *John Mentelin,* first inventor of the art of Printing, and to his posterity by the Emperor *Frederic* III. *anno* 1466. After this he gives us a *latin* epigram written by *Erhard Windsberg* and inscrib'd to the three famous *Germans,* who set up the first Printing-press at *Paris.* In the first verse of this he has thought fit to change the word *Alemannia (Germany)* for these of *tu Argentina (thou Strasburgh)* as more proper for his purpose.

THE book, at the end of which are these verses, is the *Epistles of* Crates *the Cynick,* printed by *Martin Crantz* and his two partners beforemention'd *anno* 1470, not at *Strasburgh,* as our author would fain insinuate to his readers, but at *Paris* ; where it is still extant in the library of the *Sorbon,* and was seen among others by *Chevillier,* who has occasionally confuted *Mentel*'s supposition, and expos'd his unfair quotation of the epigram, pag. 31. of his *History of Printing* ; as we shall shew in its proper place.

THIS is all that I can find in *Mentel*'s book, which has the appearance of argument: the rest consists chiefly in digressions, and quotations in praise of the art, and of the *German* nation ; which are entirely foreign

---

1 Insigne *Schotterum* familiæ ab *Frederico Romanorum* III imperatore *Joanni Mentelin* primo Typographiæ inventori, ac suis concessam anno 1466. p. 104.

to this controverſy. In ſhort our author ſhews himſelf more deſirous of appearing zealous for his anceſtor's honour, than ſolicitous what credit his work will merit among the learned: I ſhall give an inſtance or two of this, and proceed to the confutation of his main arguments.

In page 31, he gives us a piece of a comedy written by the famous *Swe-diſh* poet *Nicodemus Friſchlin* ; but is pleas'd to overlook the lines quoted by us before at p. 19, in which he affirms, *John Fauſt* citizen of *Mentz* to have been the inventor of the art ; tho' they are at a very ſmall diſtance from the paſſage quoted by him ; what is ſtill more remarkable is, that *Mentel* affirms that our *Swediſh* poet dedicated this dramatic piece to the ſenate of *Strasburgh* ; which he would ſcarce have done, had he dreamt any thing of that city's claiming the glory of this invention againſt his Hero *John Fauſt*, or heard any thing of the charge of theft alledg'd againſt him by the *Strasburgers.* The other inſtance of his unfairneſs is no leſs conſiderable at *p.* 67 ; where having ſuppos'd that the *Rationale Durandi* was not printed 'till after the falling out of *Fauſt* and *Guttenbergh,* viz. *ann.* 1461, to evade the force of the real date 1459, he ſays with a very ſerious air, that he had credible information from men of great learning, both Printers and others, that it was wrong printed, and that the figure I, which is put before, ſhould have been after the X, that in-ſtead of MCCCCLIX, it ſhould have been MCCCCLXI : wheieas Mr. *Mattaire* aſſures us [1], that the year is not printed with numeral letters, but in words at length, *one thouſand four hundred fifty nine* ; I can hardly ſuppoſe Dr. *Mentel* could be miſtaken for want of an opportunity of con-ſulting the book itſelf, ſeeing it is to be ſo eaſily met with in ſeveral libraries of *Paris*, which ſtand always open to the learned and curious ; and I don't find he has been wanting in ranſacking them to find out any thing to his purpoſe : tho' ſhould even this ſuppoſition about the date be allow'd, it would not therefore follow, that no books were printed before the year 1460 with *Fauſt's* and *Schoeffer's* names, excluſive of *Guttenbergh's,* as Dr. *Mentel* attempts to perſuade his readers ; for the *Pſalmorum codex* printed *ann.* 1457 mentions only the names of the two former ; and the

---

[1] Vide quæſo *Mentelii* in opinione falſa ob-ſtinati, ipſiuſque hominum ornatiſſimorum hal-lucinationem manifeſtam; annus enim illius li-bri exprimitur non numeralibus litteris, ſed diſertis verbis. *Milleſime quadringenteſime quinquageſimo nono. Annal. Typograph. p.* 11 *annot. col* 1.

latter

latter was never printed in any book that could yet be produc'd. What is ſaid will ſuffice, I hope, to give an idea of this author's ſincerity, whoſe three principal authorities I ſhall now examine.

First, as to the *Strasburgh* chronicle, we may reaſonably be excus'd for not laying the ſame ſtreſs upon it, that our author doth; ſince the obſcurity of the writer, a ſuſpicion of his partiality for his country's honour, and a difficulty of believing a perſon in his own cauſe in oppoſition to a great number of more credible witneſſes, are obſtacles almoſt invincible. I am therefore inclin'd to think, that the bare oppoſing of the chronicle of *Cologne* and *Trithemius*, who aſſert that the art was firſt brought from *Mentz* to *Strasburgh*, will be a ſufficient confutation of it, tho' there were no other authorities for the one, nor arguments againſt the other. However we have an unexceptionable witneſs to produce againſt this chronicle, *viz.* the learned *Wimpheling*, who was not only an eminent citizen of *Strasburgh*, and almoſt contemporary with the diſcovery of the art, but is likewiſe quoted by Dr. *Mentel*, tho' his teſtimony be diametrically oppoſite to his purpoſe: the firſt part of the paſſage is ſet down at length in *pag.* 15, wherein he attributes the whole invention to *John Guttenbergh*; and tells us that he did not perfect it 'till he had been ſometime at *Mentz*; whilſt *John Mentel* undertaking the ſame buſineſs, printed a great many volumes very neat and correct, and grew exceeding rich in a ſhort time [1]. This is all that *Wimpheling* ſays of *Mentel*; nor has any author, except that of this *Strasburg* chronicle, mention'd or ſuppos'd him to be the inventor, but only one of the firſt that practis'd that art at *Strasburgh*: and if the reader will recollect what moſt of the writers, quoted in the *third* chapter of this book, have ſaid concerning *Guttenbergh*'s leaving *Mentz* and returning to *Strasburg*, where ſome of them affirm him to have taught *Mentel* the art; we ſhall not wonder that *Wimpheling* makes him the firſt inventor of it, ſeeing he practis'd it there ſometime before it was known that *Fauſt* had done the like at *Mentz*; and was conſequently the firſt Printer, that *Wimpheling* might know of: nor is it reaſonable to ſuppoſe that *Guttenbergh* could have been weak enough to ſay any thing

---

[1] Interea *Joannes Mentel* id opificii genus incœptans, multa volumina caſtigate & polite imprimendo factus eſt brevi opulentiſſimus. *Wimphel. loco citat.*

of

of what had pass'd at *Mentz* between *Fauſt* and himſelf, it being ſo little to his credit.

MENTEL's next authority is taken from the coat of arms given to the family by the Emperor *Frederick* III; for which there is no other teſtimony but the firſt leaf of the *Onomaſticon.* However ſuppoſing it to be authentick, may we not with the greateſt reaſon oppoſe to it the patent or privilege granted by the Emperor *Maximilian* to *John Schoeffer,* in conſideration of his being the grand-ſon of *John Fauſt* the firſt inventor of the art of Printing? this privilege being of much later date than the other, may be reaſonably enough ſuppos'd a retractation of the former, which might have been ſurreptitiouſly obtain'd; eſpecially conſidering that *Fauſt* has the concurrent teſtimonies of writers and inconteſtable facts, but *Mentel* only brings an old chronicle and the moſt precarious grounds to ſupport his pretenſions. However the authenticknefs of this grant is not only much queſtion'd by the generality of writers, but has one material objection againſt it, which is, that the perſon to whom it was given, never made any mention or ſhew of it in all the books printed by him at *Strasburgh,* which, according to *Wimpheling*'s account, were very numerous. It ſeems to me ſurprizing, that if he had really obtain'd ſuch a noble teſtimony of his being the firſt inventor of Printing, and had been ſo treacherouſly robb'd both of the ſecret and the glory of it by a faithlefs ſervant, he had not made uſe of his Imperial Majeſty's authority (whoſe ſubject he was as well as *Fauſt,*) to confirm the honour of the invention upon himſelf, and the ſhame of the theft upon the other. But on the contrary, there is not one book to be met with, (tho' we may reaſonably think Dr. *Mentel* was not negligent in ſuch a ſearch,) that was printed by *John Mentel* before the year 1473, and even this was without any mention of the place where it was printed; as appears from the *Speculum morale* of *Vincentius* in folio, which is the oldeſt book known to bear his name: whereas *Fauſt* and his ſon-in-law put their names to their impreſſions almoſt ſixteen years before that time, as is plain from the *Pſalmorum Codex* printed *ann.* 1457. What is ſtill more wonderful, is, that *John Mentel* never plac'd this coat of arms in any of his books as we can find; for the oldeſt edition that hath it, is the *Geographical work of Ptolemy* printed by his nieces ſon MDXX, that is, 70 years after the invention

vention, 64 years after the grant, and 63 after *Fauſt* had begun to print in his own name, even by *Mentel's* own confeſſion.

I come now to conſider the epigram, and Dr. *Mentel's* wild inferences from it, (which he grounds upon a ſuppoſition, that the *epiſtles,* at the end of which it is printed, were done at *Strasburgh,*) from which he would conclude, that from this city, not only the three firſt Printers of *Paris,* to whom they are inſcrib'd, but alſo the moſt celebrated ones of *Europe* came. His words are theſe [1]: ,, So truly may it be affirm'd, that this ,, art at firſt flow'd from *Strasburgh,* as from its fountain-head, whence ,, it diſpers'd it ſelf abroad : to that city therefore, and to the greateſt ,, part of her firſt Printers mention'd by *Wimpheling,* is that epigram of ,, *Erhard Windsbergh* directed, which is at the end of *Crates's Epiſtles* ; ,, whereſoever theſe are printed, (for there is no place nam'd, tho' I ,, ſhou'd rather think at *Strasburgh,*) they being done with ſome of the ,, firſt types, whoſe rudeneſs plainly ſhews the infancy of the art. ,, All this is ſaid without any foundation, and would ſcarce have deſerv'd to be inſerted here, but that it afforded me an opportunity of ſhewing the reverſe from the teſtimony of *Chevillier,* who examin'd and compar'd the the edition of *Crates's Epiſtles* with the firſt impreſſions of theſe three Printers of *Paris,* which are given under the firſt liſt, and found them exactly alike : they are all done upon the ſame paper, with the ſame types, ink, &c. and demonſtrate the infancy of the art. He adds farther, that there is a greater probability that theſe three partners came from *Mentz* than from *Strasburgh,* tho' there is no record left of the particular place, but of *Germany* in general ; becauſe he finds a great conformity between their characters and impreſſions, and thoſe of *Peter Schoeffer* ; thus he tells us *p.* 51 of his *Hiſtory of Printing,* that the *Speculum* of *Zamora* printed by them at *Paris ann.* 1475, bears a very great likeneſs with St. *Jerom's Epiſtles* printed at *Mentz* 1470 ; their *Rationale Durandi* of 1475 with *Scheoffer's Speculum Harpianum* X *Præceptorum* ;

[1] Ut ita conſentaneum ſit aſſeverare, ab *Argentorato* velut a capite hoc artificium primo fluxiſſe atque dimanaſſe. Hinc ad eam ſuoſque magnam partem *Typographos* primores illos quorum meminit *Wimphilingus Erhardi Windsberg* cujuſdam *epigramma,* quod habetur in calce *Epiſtolarum Cratetis,* ubi ubi-vis gentium (nam locus non ponitur, quanquam putem *Strasburgi*, at certe novellis, & artis infantiam plane redolentibus literarum characteribus impreſſarum, &c. p. 15.

K

their

their edition of *Utinus's lenten Sermons* of 1477, with the *Scrutinium Scripturarum Pauli Burgenfis* printed at *Mentz* 1478 ; from which the author reafonably concludes, that it is more likely they came from the city of *Mentz* than from that of *Strasburgh.* I fhall now fubjoin at the bottom of the page the epigram, both as it is printed in the genuine edition of the *Epiftles,* and as *Mentel* has alter'd it [1] : I need not, I believe, point out to the reader the material difference between *Alemannia* and *tu Argentina* ; the latter of which, were it authentick, would undoubtedly determine the difpute on the fide of *Strasburgh:* but as the former is exactly according to the edition preferv'd in the *Sorbon* library, ever fince it was printed ; 'tis plain that author of the epigram, who was probably a country-man and intimate acquaintance of the three Printers, and corrected their editions, adding fometimes a copy of verfes in their praife, did not defign to particularife any city, but to give the honour of the art to the *German* nation in general. It is likewife probable enough, that they might not come all three from one and the fame city, but perhaps each of them from a diftinct one ; in which cafe the poet muft have been forc'd, either to name them all, or difobliged one or two of them, or fpoil a good epigram; and therefore rather chofe to compliment them under the name of *Germans* without regard to the place of their birth.

T H o' I have now done with Dr. *Mentel,* yet before I clofe this controverfy it will not be improper to obferve that there are two cities more of *Germany,* which have laid claim to this invention, *viz. Ausburgh* and *Ruffenburgh* in *Alface.* The firft of thefe owes its original to a paffage mifunderftood in the fupplement to *Polydore Vergil De rerum inventoribus,* attributed by *Irenicus* to *Gilbert Cognatus,* and printed *ann.* 1604 in 16°, it runs thus : ,, The art of Printing is reported to have been difco-
,, ver'd by the induftry of *Peter Schoeffer* of *Ausburgh,* or invented by
,, fome of his relations, and cultivated by him. ,, 'Tis plain here, that

---

[1] *Erhardi Windsbergh epigramma ad Germanos librarios egregios, Micha lem, Martinum & Uldaricum.*

Genuine Edition.
Plura licet fummæ dederis, *Alemannia,* laudi,

M E N T E L.
Plura licet fumma dederis, tu Argentina, *laudi,*

At reor hoc majus te genuiffe nihil;
Quod prope divinam fumma ex induftria fingis
Scribendi hanc artem, multiplicans ftudia.
Felices igitur, *Michael Martineque* femper
Vivite, & *Ulrice,* ho queis opus imprimitur;
Erhardum veftro & non dedignemini amore,
Cui fido femper pectore claufi eritis.

the

the author doth not say that the art was invented at *Ausburgh*, but that the inventor was a native of the place ; in which he was certainly mistaken, seeing *Schoeffer*, who best knew the place of his own birth, declares himself in all his inscriptions a native of *Gernsheim*, a small town upon the *Rhine*, a little below *Worms*.   Besides we have no books extant, which are printed before the year 1471 at *Ausburgh*, when *John Schuster* gave an edition of *Paul Orosius*'s *Chronography* in *folio*.   The other town, *viz. Russenburgh* is likewise said by the same *Irenicus* to have been esteem'd by some writers, the inventress of the art of Printing ; and that it receiv'd its name from the noise of the many Printing-presses at work in it : but this name seems to be more antient than that art ; and no book printed there has been ever produc'd, nor any author of antiquity mention'd it ; so that this was only a mistake in *Cognatus*, if he was the writer of the book beforemention'd.   I hope, that by this time enough has been said, to satisfy the reader, that all which hath been urg'd in favour of *Harlem, Strasburgh*, or these two last cities, is unworthy to come into competition with these noble testimonies and facts we have alleg'd on the side of *Mentz*.   I shall therefore with the greatest pleasure dismiss this rough and tedious path of controversy, and resume the thread of our history.

C H A P. VIII.

The Time of the Discovery of Printing.

THE difficulty of fixing the exact time of the discovery arises from these two reasons : 1. Because the inventors made many fruitless tryals, and a great number of maculatures, before they could bring the art to any tolerable degree of perfection : 2. Because the vast expences of such a discovery oblig'd them to keep it secret as long as possible, or at least 'till they had reimburs'd themselves in some measure, by finishing the *latin bible*, which tho' a great and expensive work, was most likely to compensate their pains and cost when finish'd. This is the foundation of the disagreement between writers upon the subject ; which may how-

ever

ever be easily reconcil'd by attending to the different epocha's, from which they date the discovery. Some of them, as *Wimpheling, Palmerus, Althamerus,* &c. date it from the infancy of the invention of wooden blocks, and assign the year 1440. Others, as the author of the chronicle of *Cologn, Trithemius, Aventine,* and many more, from the invention of fusile types *ann.* 1450. *Andrew Thevet, Angel Rocha,* &c. fix the discovery of the former method in 1442; whilst others place the time of the second invention in 1453 or 1454, among whom are *Apianus* and *P. Langius.* Lastly, *Philip Bergomensis* and *Peter Ramus* assign the year 1458 for the perfection of it. To accommodate this discrepancy among all these authors, it will be sufficient to say with relation to the first, that they take their date from the time in which the invention of wooden blocks was perfected, rather than from its infancy: with respect to the last, that they thought a ten years interval much too short for the transition from the infancy of the former to the perfection of the latter method, and therefore allow'd a few years more than their predecessors had done. As for those who fix the latter invention in 1458, they were such as esteem'd the first printed book to have been the *Catholicon* printed *ann.* 1460, or perhaps the second impression of the *bible ann.* 1462, or *Tully's offices an.* 1466, as *Zwinger* and others suppos'd; and allow'd some years more for the invention and perfection of the art. Now 'tis plain that before the *Psalmorum Codex,* as we have hinted, there is not any book known to have been printed with an *imprimatur* at the end; and it is equally certain, that the learned knew nothing of this last book 'till the year 1669, in which *Peter Lambeck* publish'd the second part of his catalogue of the *imperial library,* where this noble monument is preserv'd; which is the reason that it is omitted in all the lists of the first printed books. 'Tis not strange therefore that these writers, for want of dates and facts, should be oblig'd to guess, as well as they could, at the time of the discovery. However we find that the chronicler of *Cologn, Serrarius, Sebast. Munster,* and others after them, well enough reconcile this diversity of opinions, by assigning the year 1440 for the former invention, and 1450 for the latter. To these if we add the authority of *Trithemius,* who certainly had the best information in this matter, from *Peter Schoeffer* a principal person in the invention, it will be evident, that about the year 1440 they began to ap-

ply

ply themselves to cutting or engraving upon wooden blocks, after the *Chinese* manner, and printed some books with them ; but that after the year 1450 they found out a more excellent way, for these are *Trithemius*'s words in the famous passage quoted in *chap.* 3 [1], *viz.* of casting separate metal types : this method they might have been devising and trying before that time, *i. e.* during some part of the first ten years ; tho' they continued still printing after the old way, 'till they had quite perfected the new one ; either to bring in a continual supply of money necessary, or perhaps to keep the world from prying into the new discovery wherein they were engag'd.

I have said nothing hitherto of the *dutch* writers, who to make the time of this invention agree with *Junius*'s story of *Faust*'s pretended theft, have put it back, some above ten, others twenty years: how little credit they merit in this particular is already shewn ; and the reader will be still more convinc'd of it, when he sees what shifts they are reduc'd to, for want of authorities to oppose to the vast number of writers quoted on *Faust*'s side, not one of whom ever thought of fixing this remarkable epocha beyond the year 1440.

Their first authority is the inscription set over *Laurence Coster*'s door by one of the citizens of *Harlem*, which is mention'd by all the *dutch* writers, and says that he found out this art *ann.* 1430 : but this is of too recent a date to be of any weight.

Scriverius in his *apology against Naudé* makes the discovery two years older, and gives us a *Chronographic* verse [2], whose numerical letters make up the date of MCCCCXXVIII, *Boxhorn* carries it still farther back, *viz.* to the year 1420.

But as the two former dates were affirm'd without any foundation, this author has endeavour'd to confirm his own with something, that might bear the appearance of authority ; and to reconcile it with the other two, by affirming that *Coster* began to lay the foundation of this art *ann.* 1420, tho' he did not perfect it 'till ten years after. The author, upon whose testimony he would have us believe it, is one *Joseph Karro*, a *Jewish*

---

[1] Post hæc inventis successerunt subtiliora, inveneruntq e modum fundendi formas omnium Latini alphabeti literarum, &c.

[2] hIC sago eXfCVLptas LaVrentI CVspIde forMas.
Scriver. Apolog. pro patr. contra Naudæum.

Rabbi

Rabbi, who in a book intitled *Shulkan Aruch* or *Menfa inftructa*, extracted by him out of another Jewifh book call'd *Arbagh Thurim*, i. e. *quatuor ordines*, tells us of an old chronicle printed at *Venice A. M.* 5188, which anfwers to our year MCCCCXXVIII. This book of *Rabbi Jofeph* he owns that he could never meet with ; yet he infers from what is faid there, that there could be no printing at *Venice* at that time, unlefs *Harlem* had it fome years before. I fhall content my felf with giving *Boxhorn*'s words in the margin [1]; efpecially fince neither his *Rabbi* nor himfelf have gain'd any credit in this particular ; as it would indeed be wonderful, if a *Jew* fhould be believ'd before the concurrent teftimonies of all the learned men in *Europe*. If he wrote what *Boxhorn* quotes out of him, he either was prodigioufly miftaken, or affirm'd it (as is too common with his nation) contrary to his knowledge : tho' if we fhould deny that he ever wrote thus, I can't fee with what reafon *Boxhorn* could refent it ; fince he neither faw the book himfelf, nor gives the author's name from whom he took it. However leaving him and the reft of the *Dutch* writers to fearch for more authentick proofs than what they have hitherto alleg'd, let us return to our own , which if we dare rely upon, as we have the greateft reafon to do, it will be plain, that this art was firft attempted about the year 1440, and about ten years after happily perfected by *John Fauft* and *Peter Schoeffer* in the city of *Mentz* ; that tho' the former imperfect method was known in *China* fome hundred years before we had it, yet this latter, the only one which deferves the name of printing, was neither known nor practis'd 'till thofe two perfons had communicated it to fome of their fervants, by whom it was divulg'd and difpers'd over *Europe* and even beyond it. This will appear more evident in the next and fubfequent chapters.

[1] Circa annum 1420 prima nobiliffimæ artis Typographicæ fundamenta a *Laurentio Coftero Harlemi* poni cœpta. Quod in annum hujus fæculi vigefimum, non tricefimum, aut quadragefimum, ut fit vulgo, hanc artem periclitatam velim, fuadet *Rabbi Jofephus*, qui in chronico fuo exemplar omnium vetuftiffimum *Venetiis* excufum refert anno Judaico 5188, Chrifti anno MCCCCXXVIII. Jofephum iftum diu quæfitum videre non licuit : Chronicon haud dubie illud eft quod *Menfa inftructa* infcribitur ; liber eft ex *Arba Turim* excerptus per *Rabbi Jofeph Carro*, & in formam thefium & conclufionum redactus ; adjectæ funt novellæ gloffæ & obfervationes de jure, ritibus & confuetudine horum temporum per *Mofem Iferles* : tertium impreffus *Cracoviæ* anno Chrifti 1594 indicante in *Bibliotheca Rabbinica* rerum & fcriptorum orientalium peritiffimo *Johanne Buxtorfio*. Locum hunc certe velim accuratius afpiciant, qui habent.

C H A P.

C H A P. IX.

Of the first books printed by Fauſt *and* Schoeffer.

THERE has been frequent occaſion of mentioning the *Catholicon*, as the firſt tryal of the art of Printing, according to *Trithemius*'s teſtimony; but as it is our deſign to ſpeak of thoſe only, which are done with ſeparate metal types, and bear ſome certain date or mark of the Printer; I ſhall ſuſpend the account of it, 'till I come to treat of its ſecond impreſſion by the ſame *Fauſt* and *Schoeffer ann.* 1460.

'Tis certain that if only that book, which bears the oldeſt date, is to be eſteem'd the firſt printed; the *book of pſalms* ſo often mention'd will bid the faireſt for the firſt rank. Nevertheleſs I can ſee no reaſon to depart ſo far from the teſtimonies of *Trithemius* and the *Chronicle* of *Cologn*, as not to allow the preference to the *Latin Bible*, which, as they tell us, was the firſt book, to which the pious authors of this art thought fit to conſecrate their labours. In this opinion they have been follow'd by many learned and judicious writers both antient and modern; particularly *Malincrot, Chevillier, de la Caille, Paul Pater* and *Watſon*. I ſhall therefore ſelect the ſtrongeſt of their reaſons, add a few remarks of my own upon them, and leave the deciſion to the reader.

FIRST with reſpect to *Trithemius*'s teſtimony; which, I think, is unexceptionable, ſeeing he affirms nothing but what he had from *Peter Schoeffer*'s mouth: He plainly enough intimates, that the *Bible* was their firſt work, when he ſays that the art was found out by degrees: that after they had finiſh'd the diſcovery in ſpeculation, and came to put it in practice, they were involv'd in many difficulties: that[1] *ſoon after or from the beginning of this invention, when they went about printing the Bible,* before they had finiſh'd the third quaternion (or quire of four ſheets,) the charges amounted already to four thouſand *florins*, a prodigious ſum in thoſe days. If we duly conſider theſe words, we cannot but conclude the *Bi-*

---

[1] A primo inventionis ſuæ, *&c.* impreſſuri namque Bibliam. *Trithem. loco ſupra citato.*

b.t.

ble to have been the firſt book they engaged in. Our author indeed mentions not the year in which it was printed ; but this might proceed from
forgetfulneſs or want of information.   However ſince ſuch a work could
not be finiſh'd in a ſhort time, when the art was in its infancy, the hands
but few and unacquainted with the ſeveral branches of compoſition, impoſition, correction, diſtribution, &c. we may ſuppoſe the invention to
have been perfected in ſpeculation about the year 1450, and yet to have
required ſome time before it could be put in practice, by reaſon of the
difficulties ariſing in it ; ſo that it will be reaſonable to allow a year or
two more, before the impreſſion of the *bible* could be compleated.   This
may in all probability be the reaſon why *Trithemius,* who is always very exact in his *chronicles,* and mentions the year of any fact, when he is
ſure of it, rather chooſes to make uſe of a more general expreſſion in this
caſe, *viz. his temporibus* about this time, when he ſpeaks of the year 1450:
if we recollect that he expreſſes himſelf in the ſame words in his firſt *Chro-*
nicle, we ſhall be oblig'd either to allow a larger ſcope to them ; or
elſe ſuppoſe that the *Catholicon,* which was done in wood, and the *Bible*
printed with metal types, were finiſh'd at the ſame time, which would be
abſurd.

    The *Manuſcript Cologn Chronicle* tells us, that it was printed in the *Ju-*
bile year 1450, in a large character, ſuch as is us'd in the impreſſions
of *Miſſals* or *Maſs books,* which anſwers to our *Double Pica.*   This *Chro-*
nicle was written in *high dutch ann.* 1499 ; the author of which acquaints
us, that he had the particulars of this invention from *Ulric Zel,* an old
bookſeller then living at *Cologn.* As the original is not ſo well underſtood
here, I ſhall ſubjoin at the bottom of the page, the whole paſſage in latin, as I find it tranſlated by *Malinkrot* [1]: the words are to this purpoſe,
,, that the art of Printing was found out at *Mentz* —— *ann.* 1440: that
,, from that time to 1450 they were employ'd in perfecting it: that they

---

[1] Ars primum inventa in *Germania* urbe *Vo-*
guntina ad *Rhenum* circa annum 1440 ; & ab eo
donec ſcriberetur 1450, inventioni ejus eorum-
que quæ ad illam pertinent, opera impenſa fuit ;
eoque anno, qui *Jubilæus* fuit, cœptum fuit primum libros imprimere ; primuſque qui excu-
deretur liber *Biblia* fuere *Latina,* impreſſaque

ea ſunt ſcriptura grandiori, quali hodie *Miſſalia*
imprimi ſolent. —— initium & progreſſum me-
morati artificii ex honorabilis magiſtri *Ulric Zel*
Hanovienſis narrantis ore cognovi, qui etiam
nunc hoc anno 1499 *Colonia* Typographum
agit. V.d. *Malinkrot de arte Typog.* p. 37.

,, were

„ began to print books in the *Jubile* year: and that the firſt that was
„ printed was the *Latin Bible*, in a large character, *&c.* „ Here *Ulric
Zel's* words are to be taken in a lax ſenſe; for he is far from ſaying that
any thing in this kind, much leſs the *bible*, was finiſh'd in the year 1450;
but only that they began then to ſet about printing it: how long it was
before they compleated it, or what date it bore, is what he neither doth,
nor perhaps could ſo well inform us of. However, tho' we cannot be
certain either from him, or *Trithemius*, when this noble work was perfected; yet it is manifeſt from their teſtimony, that, except ſome maculatures and ſmall tryals, the *Bible* was the firſt conſiderable piece printed by
Fauſt.

I am not ignorant that Mr. *Mattaire* in his *Annals* has declar'd himſelf
of the contrary opinion; but as he has not confuted any of the abovemention'd teſtimonies, tho' he muſt have read them in the authors before
quoted, nor given any reaſon for his departing from them; I have given preference to the judgment of ſo many learned writers confirm'd
by two ſuch conſiderable teſtimonies, to his ſingle opinion. I apprehend
but two tolerable objections againſt this; the *firſt* is, that not one of
theſe *bibles* is known to be extant: The *ſecond* is, that *Fauſt* cannot probably be ſuppos'd to have begun with ſo large and expenſive a volume,
when a ſmaller would have been more proper for an eſſay, and brought
him a more ſpeedy gain. To the *firſt* I anſwer, 1. That this *bible* being ſo full of abbreviations, *&c.* in imitation of the old way of writing,
and difficult to be read, might undergo the ſame fate with many other
books both MS. and others, to be thrown by and deſtroy'd, when the
fairer and more legible impreſſions came in vogue: 2. The learned *Saubert* in his *Oration de Bibliotheca Reipublicæ Noribergenſis* tells us, that he
had ſeen no leſs than eight copies of them in the *Norican* library, without
date, colophon, or any other mark of their being printed by *Fauſt*. As
I have not been able to procure *Saubert's* book, I muſt content my ſelf
with giving the reader the paſſage out of *Paul Pater*, in which this is
mention'd: it is as follows, ¹ „ The *Latin Bible*, commonly ſuppos'd to

---

¹ *Biblia Latina*, quorum tranſlatio *Divo Hi-
ero ymo* vulgo tribuitur, circa 1450 & ſequen-
tem *Moguntia* in membrana impreſſa, quorum

Fauſtus exemplar nummis uncialibus ſeu thale-
ris ſeptingentis quinquaginta *Pariſis* venum de-
derat, ut ſupra ex *Abbate Spanhemenſi* narravi-

L „ have

,, have been tranflated by St. *Jerom*, printed at *Mentz* upon vellum about
,, 1450 or the following year, a copy of which *Fauftus* fold at *Paris* for
,, 750 crowns, as we related out of *Trithemius*, is juftly reckon'd among
,, the firft beginnings of this art by *Corn. Beughen* (in his *Incunab. Ty-*
,, *pograph. Amfterd. ann.* 1688.) *Henry Salmuth* likewife mentions ano-
,, ther Bible publifh'd *ann.* 1459, at the end of which are thefe words ;
,, *This prefent Rationale,* &c. *was finifh'd at* Mentz *by* John Fauft, *&c.*
,, but *Salmuth* is doubtlefs miftaken in taking this book for the Bible, of
,, which it was only a fhort explanation. A copy of this *Bern. Malin-*
,, *krot* tells us that he had by him. I would not however be too po-
,, fitive that there was not a *Latin Bible* printed in the fame year, fee-
,, ing *John Saubert* owns that he had feen eight copies of it in the *Nori-*
,, *can* library, without *Fauftus*'s colophon, undoubtedly for the reafon
,, beforemention'd, (*viz.* in order to fell 'em for Manufcripts.) ,, From
this paffage it appears, that there are eight bibles without *Fauft*'s mark
preferv'd in that library, and feen by *Saubert* ; tho' both he and *P. Pa-*
ter took them for the fecond impreffion, in which they are certainly miftaken : 1. Becaufe this was printed *ann.* 1462, and not *ann.* 1459 : 2. Becaufe it is fo far from having been printed without a *colophon,* that it
has one of the fulleft and plaineft that *Fauft* ever us'd at the end of any
of his books : the reader will fee it, when we come to the edition itfelf.
But 3. 'tis not impoffible but that there may be ftill more of thefe copies
in fome other libraries, as yet undifcover'd. The only intelligence
which we had concerning thefe eight, is owing to *Saubert* ; neither would
thefe gentlemen have believ'd that there had been a *Pfalmorum Codex* printed
at *Mentz ann.* 1457, tho' affur'd of it by *Trithemius* and *Zel,* had not *Pe-*
ter Lambeck the Emperor's library-keeper 28 years ago told us, that he

mus, inter primordia merito numerari *Corneli-*
us Beughen memorat (*Incunab. Tyopgraph. Am-*
fterd. ann. 1688 *editis.*) fimiliter *Henricus Sal-*
muth alium Bibliorum codicem ibidem lucem
vidiffe denarrat, cui hæc in fine verba erant ap-
pofita : *Præfens rationalis Divinorum codex con-*
fummatus eft per Johannem Fauft *civem* Mo-
gunt. *& Petrum Gernfheim, &c. ann.* 1459,
&c. Sed errare hac parte *Salmuthum,* quod
rationale illud facrum fcripturam effe putet,

cum tantum breve aliquod *Guillelmi Duranti*
fcriptum fit, quod fe quoque poffidere *Bern. a*
Malinkrot refert. Neque tamen prorfus nega-
verim *Biblia Latina* hoc ipfo anno vulgata typis denuo fuiffe, quandoquidem *Joh. Saubertus*
fatetur fe in bibliotheca *Norica* octo exemplaria vidiffe, ac fubfcriptionis *Fuftiniana* notis ca-
ruiffe haud dubie ob caufam paulo ante a nobis
adductam. *P Pater de German. Mirac. Lipfia*
ann. 1710. *pag.* 75.

met

met with it in that famous library. I have been likewiſe aſſur'd from the mouth of a gentleman of credit, that a friend of his had ſeen one abroad with the date of 1457, and farther that 'twas his opinion 'twould be brought to *England*. How many authors have had a notion that *Tully's Offices* was the firſt printed book? yet time has produc'd no leſs than four printed before it, excluſive of the *bible* now in queſtion; and may yet diſcover more concerning this.

I come now to the *ſecond* objection ſo much inſiſted upon by ſome; *viz.* that 'tis improbable *Fauſt* would begin his firſt eſſays with a volume ſo large and expenſive, when a ſmaller would have anſwer'd his purpoſe much better, and brought an immediate gain. My reply is, 1. That the great expence at firſt conſiſted in purchaſing ſuch a quantity of materials as the buſineſs requir'd, and not in printing of the firſt book, which was inconſiderable compar'd with that; conſequently a ſmaller volume would have been too ſlender a reimburſement for ſuch great ſums expended: Beſides we have ſhewn that they took up money of *Guttenbergh* for buying of parchment, *&c.* and were not ſo ſtraitned as before. 2. As *Fauſt* deſign'd to ſell as many of his firſt printed books as he could for manuſcripts, in order to make up the coſt which he had been at; 'tis obvious that he muſt pitch upon ſome conſiderable and valuable book, before his art was diſcover'd, and where could he fix upon one more adapted to his purpoſe than this? I will not inſiſt upon the piety of the perſons ſo conſpicuous in all their inſcriptions, (tho' our age may call it ſuperſtition,) which might have a great ſhare in determining their choice. I ſhall only add, that as it was by no means adviſeable for him to ſell any of his firſt eſſays, leſt they ſhould betray his invention; ſo it was moſt prudent to make them upon the firſt leaves of the Bible, which if they ſucceeded, would in time make him ample amends; and if they did not, the loſs was no greater than if they had been try'd upon a *Donatus* or a *Primer*. Beſides none of our authors have affirm'd that he began to print the *bible* before he had perfected the art both in theory and practice; and made a ſufficient number of maculatures and other tryals, which it was the moſt prudent way to burn as ſoon as printed off. I ſhall leave this diſcourſe of the firſt *bible* to the reader's choice, either to cloſe in with, or diſſent from us in allowing it the firſt rank; and proceed now to the

remainder

remainder of our propos'd liſt.   It will be neceſſary however to acquaint him, altho' we have given the preference to that ſacred book upon the teſtimonies of ſo many antient and modern writers, tho' it bears no date, yet in the following liſt I am about to give him of theſe firſt impreſſions of *Fauſt*, we chiefly inquire after ſuch as carry either date or ſome other certain mark of the year in which they were printed : for as to thoſe that do not, I ſhall ſpeak of them afterwards, and ſhew that thoſe authors who thought to have found out their date, have prov'd to have been in an error ; which will be a ſufficient reaſon for us not to depend upon any others of the like nature.

N E x t to the *Bible* we find *five* ſeveral impreſſions, which have certainly been made between the years 1457 and 1466.   The firſt of theſe, which as we hinted, is omitted in all the liſts of the firſt books that have been printed before *Lambeck's* catalogue of the *Vienna* library, is the *Pſalmorum Codex* printed at *Mentz* upon Vellum *anno* 1457 ; concerning this, what has been ſaid already will ſuffice, the colophon of it is in the *fourth* chapter, p. 29.

T H E *ſecond* is the *Rationale Divinorum Officiorum*, written by *William Durand*, printed at *Mentz* upon Vellum two Years after the *Pſalter*, viz. *anno* 1459 by *John Fauſt* and *Peter de Gernſheim* or *Schoeffer* ; *Malinkrot*, who knew nothing of the *Pſalter*, reckons it the firſt printed Book next to the *Bible* ; and tells us that he purchas'd one of them, which had formerly belong'd to a Monaſtery of *Franciſcan* Monks, deſtroy'd by the civil Wars, the inſcription of which is very near the ſame with that of the *Pſalter*.   This *Rationale* is likewiſe in the Earl of *Pembroke's* Library, where I ſaw it ; it is beautifully printed in Folio, upon Vellum, and is a ſingular Beauty as to Preſs-work.

T H E Suppoſition of *Malinkrot* and others that this was the firſt printed Book, was the reaſon that *Father L'Abbé* a learned *Jeſuit* began his Liſt of printed Books from the Years of its date, viz. 1459 to 1500. and the author of the Supplement to *Bellarmin's Eccleſiaſtical* Writers makes this remark upon it, That *Anno* 1459, *John Fauſtus* having diſcovered the art of Printing, firſt printed the Book of *Guill. Durand de Officiis Eccleſiaſticis* in the city of *Mentz*.   Theſe authors were certainly

in

in the right, feeing no book was then known of an older date : but fince the fecond part of *Trithemius's Chronicle*, and the fecond volume of the *Imperial-library* have been publifh'd, we muſt look fome years back for the firſt impreſſion, and give that rank to a more noble work.

THE *Third* is the *Catholicon*, a *Latin* vocabulary, printed at *Mentz anno* 1460. the fecond time ; for the firſt impreſſion was done upon wood. This Book is likewife in the Earl of *Pembroke's* library, where I faw it, it is in a large folio, and beautifully printed. We have given the in-fcription of it in the fourth *chap*. p. 30, in which tho' the printer's name is not expreſs'd, yet it was done by *Fauſt* and *Schoeffer*, both from the fimilitude of its charaᐸter, paper, *&c.* with that of their other works, and becaufe there were at that time no other printers either at *Mentz* or any where elfe. This *Catholicon* is a kind of *Grammar*, compil'd by *John* of *Genoa* a *Dominican Fryar anno* 1286. It is divided into four parts, the laſt of which contains a diᐸtionary of *Latin* words digeſted alphabetically. There have been feveral editions of it in *folio*, as *Chevillier* tells us, who faw two of them ; one, very old and without date ; the other printed at *Paris anno* 1506. by *Jodocus Badius*. Another im-preſſion of it is done at *Lyons* by *Antony Du Ry anno* 1520, and aug-mented by *Peter Gille*. *Furetiere* therefore was led into a palpable er-ror, when he affirm'd after *Dr. Mentel* and *Father Jacob a Carmelite*, that the firſt printed books known in *Europe* were *Durandus de Ritibus Ec-clefiæ* printed *anno* 1461, a bible printed *anno* 1462, *St. Auſtin de Civi-tate Dei*, and *Tully's Offices* ; feeing here are no lefs than four printed books before the oldeſt of them ; befides this book *de Ritibus Ecclefiæ* was not written by *William Durand*, but by *John Stephen Durant*, who was firſt prefident of the parliament of *Tholoufe*, and is therefore a dif-ferent book from the *Durand's Rationale* we are now fpeaking of, and of a much later date.

THE *fourth* is the fecond edition of the *Latin Bible* printed *anno* 1462. in *folio* with the following infcription at the end [1]. " This pre-

---

[1] Prefens hoc opus finitum ac completum & ad eufebiam Dei induſtria in civitate *Moguntina* per *Johannem Fuſt* civem & *Petrum Shoeffer de Gernfheim* clericum Diœcefis ejufdem eſt.

confummatum anno incarnationis Dominicæ MCCCCLX I in vigiliâ Affumptionis gloriofæ virginis *Mariæ*.

,, ſent work was finiſh'd and perfected for the ſervice of God in the city
,, of *Mentz* by *John Fuſt* citizen, and *Peter Schoeffer de Gernſheim* clerk
,, of the ſame dioceſs, it was compleated in the year of our Lord's in-
,, carnation MCCCCLXII on the eve of the aſſumption of the glorious
,, virgin *Mary*. " I have ſeen one in the library of *Dr. Mead*, and another at the late Mr. *Wooodman*'s bookſeller, in Vellum, and *Chevillier* ſaw
two more at *Paris* in two volumes. Of this bible *Walchius* [1] relates a
ſtory, which ought to be mention'd here, as far as reſpects the common
opinion. *Fauſt* went to *Paris* with ſome copies of it finely illuminated,
where he ſold one of them for 750 crowns, and another for 500 ; till
at length he reduc'd his price to 50 and 40 crowns. The great quantity which he ſold, and the exact likeneſs of every copy, made it ſuſ-
picious that they were done by a more eaſy and expeditious way than that
of writing ; whereupon the buyers thinking themſelves impos'd upon,
began a proſecution which oblig'd him to fly the country, and return to
Mentz. Thus far *Walchius*, who ſays nothing of *Fauſt*'s being accus'd
of magick, as ſome others affirm. What relates to the perſon of *Fauſt*
will be beſt conſider'd in the next chapter. As to the *bible* itſelf, 'tis
my opinion, that the reaſon why the generality of authors have thought
this ſecond edition to have been that which he ſold for MS. is, that they
ſcarce knew of any other book printed before it [2] : but for my own
part I cannot ſuppoſe that *Fauſt* would offer a book to ſale for a written
one, which had ſuch an inſcription, as muſt infallibly diſcover the cheat.
'Tis urg'd, that he might print a certain number of them without this,
and after the diſcovery, reprint the laſt ſheet with this colophon at the

[1] *Walchius decas fabularum generis humani printed at Strasburgh* 1609 *in* 4to. *pag.* 181

[2] *Mr. Le Gallois* in his treatiſe of the fineſt libraries pag. 160. tells us that there was no-thing printed before this bible of 1462, which *Fauſt* brought to *Paris*. [*quoiqui, en ſoit il eſt certain qu' on ne voit rien d'imprimé avant cette Bible que* Fauſt *apporta luy meme a Paris*] *Father de St. Raomuld* affirms likewiſe in his *Theſaur Chronolog.* pag. 324. that we have nothing printed before the year 1462 : and the great *Naude*, who in his addition to the hiſtory of *Lewis* XI. ſays that he had ſeen about 1000 old books in 20 or 30 of the moſt celebrated li-braries in and about the city of *Paris*, and hath writ a treatiſe *ex profeſſo* upon this ſubject, in the afore-mention'd book, chap 7. pag. 268. expreſſes himſelf thus ; " but we have no book printed before 1462 ; and pag. 69 he ſays that we muſt needs ſuppoſe them (the firſt printers) to have made an infinite number of proofs and maculatures, before they could juſtify, and get all their implements fitted together ; after which they began at length to compoſe, not *Tully*'s *Offices*. &c. but the great bible in *folio*, which was finiſh'd anno 1462, Vide *Chevillier* pag. 17.

end:

end: but this is improbable upon two accounts; firſt, he had already
printed three books with inſcriptions, *viz.* the *Pſalter*, the *Rationale*, and
the *Catholicon*; all which import particularly *that they were not done with
pen and ink or any writing tool, but by a fine new invented art of caſting
Letters, and printing with them.* Now ſince ſome of theſe muſt of neceſſity have been known in *France* long before this year; it was impoſſible
to have deceiv'd them by any but the firſt impreſſion, unleſs we did ſuppoſe that he kept the three former unſold and unſeen; which would be
moſt abſurd to imagine. But ſecondly 'tis plain that his deſign in ſelling them for MSS. was to reimburſe himſelf for the vaſt charges which
he had been at in deviſing this invention, preparing all the neceſſary
materials, making eſſays, *&c.* Such expences muſt have reduc'd him a-
bove twelve years before this to the neceſſity of a recruit, ſeeing he had
perfected the new invention, and began to print with it on or ſoon after
the year 1450. as has been fully prov'd; nor can we in any probability
ſuppoſe that he ſhould work on for twelve whole years ſucceſſively and
print three editions, two of which were very large, without vending
them; eſpecially ſince he is reported by moſt authors to have enrich'd
himſelf exceedingly by this time, and conſequently wanted no ſuch ſtrategem? If I could have obtain'd with all my endeavours any certain information of the year in which he went to *Paris*, it would have deter-
mined the diſpute. However, if I may be allow'd a conjecture, ſince
we find by the unanimous conſent of writers that the art was perfected
in the year 1450, and no books printed in his name till *anno* 1457 as yet
known: *Fauſt* might moſt probably ſpend theſe ſeven years in Printing,
illuminating and ſelling his firſt *Bible*; after which, his new art being
diſcover'd, he thought it in vain to keep it ſecret longer; and therefore
in his next book gave the world an account of his method, as we find
in the *Pſalmorum Codex* and thoſe that follow'd it. What confirms my
conjecture is, that *Guttenburgh*, who was proſecuted by *Fauſt* for the moiety
of the money expended, and gave a deed bearing date 1455 for the payment, purſuant to the judge's determination, inſtead of complying with
it, eſcap'd to *Strasburgh*, and left his partner in the lurch, this we may
reaſonably ſuppoſe, reduc'd *Fauſt* to ſuch ſtreights, as oblig'd him to go
to *Paris* with what books he had, in order to ſell them to the beſt advantage.

vantage. Theſe reaſons induce me to think that it was the *firſt*, and not the *ſecond bible*, which *Fauſt* ſold at ſuch extraordinary rates: The reader is at his liberty to judge as he pleaſes in this matter.

THE *fifth* is the *Tully's Offices* printed at *Mentz ann*. 1465; tho' ſome editions have a later date by one, and others by two years, all of which are printed at *Mentz*, with the ſame inſcription in every reſpect, as we ſhall ſhew immediately. The Right Honourable the Earl of *Oxford* ſhew'd me this book; 'tis a ſmall 4*to*, and very beautifully printed, and well preſerv'd. Sir *Thomas Bodley* had this in his library, which he preſented to the univerſity of *Oxford*, where it is ſtill kept. Dr. *James* publiſh'd a catalogue of all Sir *Thomas's* books intitled *Catalogus Bibliothecæ Bodleianæ* in 4*to anno* 1605, in the 197 page of which book we find this *Tully's Offices* with the following inſcription, *Ejuſdem liber de Officiis*, &c. *an*. 1465. About 70 years after this, Dr. *Thomas Hyde* publiſh'd his catalogue of all the books in the univerſity library, printed at *Oxford* in *fol. ann*. 1674, in which he gives the date of the book *pag*. 162; which is the ſame with the former, and confirm'd by *Antony Wood's* hiſtory of that univerſity, printed likewiſe *ann*. 1674, *pag*. 228 [1]. Mr. *Beughen* mentions the ſame date in his liſt of the firſt editions [2], and tells us, that it was reprinted at *Mentz* two years after, *viz. ann*. 1467, and at *Rome* 1468. Father l'*Abbé* [3] ſpeaks of one which he ſaw in the *French* king's library dated 1466, and *Chevillier* ſaw another in the library of the *Mazarin-college*, with theſe words in red letters [4] *This preſent noble work* Tully's Offices *was done by* John Fuſt *citizen of* Mentz *not with pen and ink*, &c. *but by a new art*, &c. *by the hands of my boy* Peter de Gernſheim *ann*. MCCCCLXVI *on the fourth of* February. Several eminent writers, as I have already hinted, have eſteem'd this the firſt printed book; among whom is *Peter Ramus* or *de la Ramee*, Royal profeſſor of Mathematicks in the univerſity of *Paris*, who had this edition in his library, and affirm'd it to be the firſt work

---

[1] Immo anno Domini 1465 ut fert aliud exemplar in *Bodleiana* [bibliotheca.]

[2] *Moguntia* in 4*to* ann. 1465, quæ poſtmodum ſunt recuſa ibidem, *an*. 1467 in 4*to*, & *Roma* 1468, *&c. Incunab. Typograph*. 46.

[3] *Nov. Biblioth. MSS. lib. ſeptim. pag*. 353.

[4] Præſens *M. Tulli* clariſſimum opus *Joan. Fuſt Moguntinus* civis, non atramento, plumali canna neque ærea, ſed arte quadam perpulchra, manu *Petri de Gernſheim*, pueri mei feliciter effeci. Finitum *an*. MCCCCLXVI, quarta die menſis februarii. *Chevil*. p. 18.

produc'd

produc'd by the art of Printing [1] in this he has been follow'd by our country-man *Anth. Wood* in the book before quoted ; by *Paſquier* in his *Recherches de la France*, lib. 4. ch. 4 ; and by ſeveral others. 'Tis very probable that the edition of 1465 and 1466 may be the ſame, the laſt ſheet only reprinted ; which may be eaſily known by comparing them together ; and it were to be wiſh'd, that ſome of the Curioſo's of *Oxford* would take that trouble, ſince they are both there, as appears from *Ant. Wood*'s liſt.

AFTER the finiſhing of this book, *Fauſt* is ſuppos'd to have died, or loſt his ſight (as ſome report,) or at leaſt to have grown ſo rich, that he left the buſineſs wholly to his ſon-in law *Peter Schoeffer*, who then inſtruced his ſon *John* in that art. We find no more books printed in *Fauſt*'s name, all the reſt being in *Peter Schoeffer*'s, ſome of whoſe inſcriptions are given in the *fourth* chapter.

I have dwelt ſomewhat longer upon theſe noble relicks of our firſt printers, becauſe I am ſenſible of the great value, which the curious and learned have for them.

I come now to thoſe of other, but fictitious dates, which it will not be improper to ſay ſomething of, in order to prevent the reader from being deceiv'd or puzzled by them.

AMONG all the apocryphal editions that are to be met within any library, excluſive of thoſe which are ſuppos'd to have been printed with wooden blocks, and diſcours'd of already in a diſtinct chapter, that which bears the oldeſt date is the Book of Sermons *de Sanctis* by *Leonard de Utino.* *John Godfrey Olearius, Lutheran* miniſter of St. *Mary*'s church at *Hall* in *Saxony*, ſays it is ſtill preſerv'd in the library of that church, and dated 1446, tho' there be no mention of the place where it was printed: the reader will find his account of it quoted in the margin [2], in his book de *Scriptoribus Eccleſiaſticis*, publiſh'd under the title of *Abacus Patrologi-*

---

[1] Cum primum *Typographiæ* exemplum *Moguntiæ* editum ſit anno 1466 — ut conſtat ex *Ciceronis Officiis*, quæ primum omnium librorum typis æneis impreſſa ſunt : Exemplar *Officiorum* iſtorum habeo in membrana impreſſorum. *P. Ramus Schol. Mathem. lib.* 2.

[2] *Leonardus de Utino*, ordin. *prædic.* ――――

Ejus *ſermonum de Sanctis* liber ſub ipſa *Typographica* artis incunabula *anno* 1446 impreſſus, abſque tamen loci mentione, habetur in bibliotheca templi *Mariani* noſtri *Hall.* Confer. Dn. parentis *Halygraph.* Appendice T. t. t. 1. B. Sermones ejuſdem Quadrageſimales & Dominicales ann. 1479 prodierunt. *Abac. patrolog.* p. 291.

M

cus

cus in *8vo* at *Jena* 1673, in which he quotes the teftimony of his father *Godfrey Olearius,* who wrote the hiftory of *Hall,* printed at *Leipfick* in 4to. *ann.* 1667.   *Chevillier* obferves very juftly, that *Olearius* hath mention'd neither the fize nor printer of this ancient book ; and that all who have fince fpoken of it, rely upon his teftimony : he thinks therefore that it ought to have been more nicely enquired into, fince if the date be true, it entirely overturns the receiv'd opinion that this art was not perfected 'till the year 1450: the reafons of his fufpecting it is, becaufe *Utinus* liv'd in *Italy ann.* 1445, according to *Poffevinus,* and can hardly be fuppos'd to have had fuch credit in *Germany,* as that his fermons fhould be printed after a new method fcarce known to above *five* or *fix* perfons: he is therefore of opinion, that the book is a manufcript, or that *Olearius* has guefs'd at the date, or which is moft likely, that this is the date of the compiling, not of the printing of it.

M**r.** *Mattaire* has taken the pains to folve the greateft part of thefe doubts, and given the following account of it [1] ; ,, That a very curious ,, and learned gentleman of his acquaintance met with a copy of it at ,, *Aix la Chapelle* in a monaftery of regular monks, out of which he tran- ,, fcrib'd the following colophon printed at the end of it, in *Englifh* thus ;

Thus end the golden fermons upon the Saints throughout the whole   *year, compil'd by Mafter* Leonard de   Utino, *doctor of divinity, of the order of the fryars*

[1] Jam dabo tibi, lector, quod in votis ha- buit *Chevillierus*; unde editio tantæ vetuftatis fpecie venerabilis teftimonio novo certior fiat & notior. Vir quidam literarum peritus——

dum Aquisgrani peregrinabatur ibi in *Regulari- um* cœnobio vidit librum fupra memoratum, ir *fol.* ex quo defcripfit hæc, quæ in libri ipfius fine adjiciuntur.

Expliciunt fermões aurei de Sanctis per totum annum, quos compilavit mgr. *Leonardus de Utino* facre Theologie doctor, ordinis fra‑rum predicator, ad inftanciam & complacentiam magnifice civitatis *Utine jis* ac nobilium vi- rorum ejufdem MCCCCXLVI in vigilia beatiffimi patris noftri Dominici ofefforis, ad laudeʒ & glꞌaʒ Dei omnipotentis & totius curie triu...phantis.

Libri ipfius character impolitus & rudis ; abbre- viaturifque frequenti us adeo refertus, ut ejus lectio nequaquam fit, quam illorum *Moʒuntia*

annis 1459 & 1460 excuforum facilior. *An- nal. Typogr.* p. 25.

Preachers

Preachers, at the inſtance and intreaty of
the magnificent city of Utino, *and the noble*
citizens thereof MCCCCXLVI, *on the eve of our bleſſed*
father Dominick confeſſor, to the praiſe and glory
of almighty God, and of the whole triumphant court.

Mr. *Mattaire* adds, that the characters of it are very rude and ill ſhap'd and ſo full of abbreviations, that they are as difficult to read, as thoſe printed at *Mentz ann.* 1459 and 1460.

THIS makes it abundantly plain, that tho' the book carries the abovemention'd date, yet it bears teſtimony that the compiling and not the printing of it, is there intended; ſo that not only the difficulty diſappears, but *Chevillier's* conjecture is manifeſtly ſupported: And Mr. *Mattaire* ſeems entirely of this opinion, and beſides inſtances in a book or two which he hath, whoſe dates as he aſſures us, were thoſe of their being compil'd; tho' the obſcurity of their inſcription, might poſſibly lead an unwary reader to take it for that of its impreſſion: and indeed it is an unreaſonable ſuppoſition, that Printing could have been brought to ſuch a degree of perfection at that time, againſt the general teſtimony of writers: beſides neither the abbreviations, nor the rudeneſs of the character, can be a ſufficient index of their antiquity, ſeeing, as he obſerves, they continued in uſe among ſome eminent Printers even beyond the year 1500. In the next place I ſhall mention ſome editions, whoſe dates are certainly prov'd to be wrong. The firſt is the *Regula Paſtoris* of Pope *Gregory*; a copy of which is in the *French* king's library, with this inſcription ſuppos'd to be written at the end; *Tentamentum Fauſti,* an eſſay of *John Fauſt ann.* 1459: now it is plain from what has been ſaid before that *Fauſt* was ſo far from making any eſſays at that time, that he had already printed ſeveral perfect editions, Mr. *Mattaire* gives us this account of it *p.* 22. that he met with a book in 4to in the king's library at *Paris,* without the name of either place or Printer, only with this title, *Liber Regulæ paſtoralis* Gregorii *papæ ad* Johannem *epiſcopum* Ravenenſem: at the beginning of which *Gabriel Naudé* had written two verſes to the reader with his own hand, intimating that book to have been certainly printed by *Fauſt* at *Mentz,* becauſe the mark of the paper which is the head and horns of

an heifer, is an infallible criterium of *Fauſt's* books. And an advertiſement in which he confirms his aſſertion, from the rudeneſs of the types,
the want of diphthongs, and ſome other circumſtances that favour the
infancy of the art ; and concludes, that *Fauſt* would not put his name,
&c. to it, 'till his frequent eſſays had embolden'd him to make himſelf
publick, as he did afterwards in the *Durand's Rationale* of 1459, *Catholicon,* &c.

Mr. *Mattaire* doth indeed prove plainly enough, that the rudeneſs of
the types, and want of dates, names, &c. continued ſome conſiderable
time after the diſcovery of the art, and conſequently that that could be
no certain mark of its being one of *Fauſt's* firſt eſſays : however as nothing certain can be affirm'd concerning this book, we ſhall dwell no longer upon it. I have ſeen *Æneas Sylvius's* letters printed by *Koelhoff* of
Lubeck, which is certainly antedated, for this reaſon, ſeveral dates in the
letters being ten years older than the date of the book itſelf. There is
another of his books in *fol.* in the library of the *Sorbon,* with a falſe date at
the end of theſe words, *Flores de diverſis ſermonibus & epiſtolis* B. Bernardi
per me Joan. Koelhoff *de Lubeck colonienſem civem impreſſi an.* MCCCC,
feliciter finiunt: for 'tis plain the art was not ſo much as thought of at that
time, nor perfected 'till 50 years after : but what demonſtrates the falſeneſs
of the date is, that this *John Koelhoff* was ſcarce born then, ſince he printed
the works of *N. Gerſon* in 4 *vol.* in *fol.* at *Cologn ann.* 1483, which are of the
ſame make and character as the *Flores* abovemention'd, as *Chevillier* p. 10
and 11 obſerves, who therefore thinks that the following numbers LXXXII
were omitted at the end of MCCCC. The ſame author mentions two or three
editions more of the ſame nature, the laſt of which is the *Manipulus Cu-
ratorum* of *Guy Mout Rocher* with the following uncommon date at the
end [1] *Printed at* Paris *in the year one thouſand* CCCC *and twenty three,
amen:* 'tis plain that the art was not brought to *Paris* 'till the year 1470,
as ſhall be ſhown in its place; ſo that the laſt C muſt have been taken
up by the balls, or loſt ſome other way. Upon the whole it may be
eſteem'd a general rule that all dates before the year 1450 are falſe;
and this is corroborated with the ſuffrage of all learned writers upon this

---

[1] Completus *Pariſiis* anno Domini milleſimo CCCC viceſimo tertio, amen. *Chevil.* p. 11.

ſubject.

ſubjeԀ.   In the mean time as it is not reaſonable to imagine, that *Fauſt*
and *Schoeffer* could be altogether idle from the year 1452, in which they
are ſuppos'd to have finiſh'd their firſt *Bible,* to 1457, in which they publiſh'd the *Pſalter,* (unleſs we can ſuppoſe that *Fauſt's* law-ſuit with *Guttenbergh,* and his journey and ſtay in *France,* could take him up *five* whole
years, and that his ingenious ſon did not venture upon any work by himſelf;) if time and induſtry ſhould, as we may reaſonably hope it may,
diſcover any more of thoſe old and valuable monuments of the infancy
of the art ; provided ſuch impreſſions bear either a certain date or mark
of their being done at *Mentz,* and by our *Protodædali* before the diſperſion of their ſervants, or even after that time ; I doubt not but the learned will allow them a proper rank in the liſts, which ſhall be publiſh'd
hereafter.

C H A P. X.

Remarkable Occurrences between the year 1450, *and the Divulgation of the* Art.

THO' I propos'd to avoid all unneceſſary repetitions, yet this chapter being deſign'd as a ſhort recapitulation of the hiſtory of the
firſt *twelve* years, the thread of which has been unavoidably interrupted
by controverſy; and to introduce ſome material occurrences, which could
not properly be inſerted in any other chapter, or ſuch as may have eſcap'd
the readers memory ; I find the impoſſibility of joyning theſe notable
events together, without interſperſing them with moſt of thoſe already
touched upon : and this has render'd an apology before hand highly neceſſary.

I begin with the year 1450, in which 'tis agreed by moſt authors, that
the art was perfeԀed in theory and praԀice, the inventors having prepar'd
their tools and materials, and made a great number of eſſays ; thinking
they might with ſafety attempt ſome conſiderable volume : Their next
care was to carry on the buſineſs without danger of being diſcover'd: to
this end they admitted as few ſervants as poſſible into any part of the ſe-

cret,

cret, and such only upon whose fidelity they might depend, engaging them to the greatest secrecy by an oath. This being done they allotted to them their several provinces; but conceal'd every branch of Letter-founding and composing. If my authority be required, since all our accounts relating to these beginnings are so obscure and imperfect; I answer, that this may reasonably be infer'd from a remarkable passage out of the learned *Hen. Pantaleon*, a physician of *Basil*, part of which I have already quoted in a former chapter, as far as it related to *Fauft* and *Schoeffer*'s being the authors of this art; the remainder of it is as follows [1]: ,, This art was at the first kept very secret and communicated to ,, but very few; for they (*Fauft* and *Schoeffer*) tyed up the types in bags, ,, which they brought into the work-room, and took away when they ,, went out, 'till at length in process of time the business increasing caus'd ,, the Art to be divulg'd. ,, All the authors quoted by us agree with *Pantaleon* about their keeping the Art with all imaginable secrecy, but scarce any have inform'd us of this circumstance, of their carrying their types with them to and out of the work-room; which would have been a vain precaution, had they intrufted any but themselves in the compositor's part. However it is evident that the whole secret did not consist therein; the cutting the Punches, sinking them into the Matrices, making the Moulds and casting the Letters, might be still a secret to any one that had been intrufted so far as to go through all the branches of the business of Printing; and he must have been a person of a surprizing genius who could have found out the mystery of Letter-founding by barely seeing the letters, therefore the keeping that part to themselves was making it a greater secret than all the oaths they could bind them with.

T H E next remarkable occurrence is that of their admitting *John Guttenbergh* a wealthy goldsmith into partnership with them, as it is related by the last nam'd author, by *Salmuth*, and others quoted in the *third* chapter. This gentleman finding his neighbour *Fauft* engag'd in a new and advantagious invention, which he wanted money to carry on, and attra-

---

[1] Erat enim ars illa primo abscondita & pauculis manifeftata; litteras enim in facculis clausis secum in Officinas ferebant, ac dum abeunt, auferebant; donec temporis fucceffu ars aucta atque plurimum illuftrata fuit. *Do illuftribus Germann.* part. 2. pag. 397.

&ed by a profpect of gain, offer'd his purfe and affiftance upon good terms to *Fauft*; who gladly accepted the propofal. But *Guttenbergh* purfuing his own private rather than the common intereft, and having attain'd fome infight into the art, began to object that *Fauft* had converted fome of the money to his own ufes, and refus'd the payment of his dividend of the charges; 'till *Fauft* had obtain'd a decree, which oblig'd him to pay his moiety of what the plaintiff fhould fwear had been expended upon the common fund: this he evaded by giving a bond payable fome time after, and efcaping to *Strasburgh* his native city, before it was due. But he firft took care to learn as much of the art, as he could, to furnifh himfelf with Printing-tools, and to draw off fome of *Fauft's* fervants with him. At *Strasburgh* he communicated to *John Mentel* or *Mentelin* the fecret, and his defign of fetting up a Printing-houfe there: however neither he nor his workmen were fo throughly inftructed in the bufinefs, but they were oblig'd to demur a confiderable time before they could perfect every thing for the work, and to make many tryals in order to attain the right method; which is evident from this, that there is no book extant with *Mentel's* name 'till the year 1473, and not at all with *Guttenbergh's*; for it is fcarce probable, that if they had printed any confiderable volumes before that time, they fhould all have perifh'd without being fo much as taken notice of by any author, and efpecially by their learned townfman *Wimpheling:* whilft there remain fo many of *Fauft's* in the writings and in the hands of the learned and curious. During this time *Fauft* finding himfelf impos'd upon by *Guttenbergh*, and difappointed of the money expected, and wanting either will or power to fue him in that city where he fled, form'd a ftrategem to raife himfelf a frefh fupply, which fucceeded according to his wifh; for he went to *Paris* with fome of his fineft vellum *bibles*; one of which was fold to the king for 750 crowns, and is ftill to be feen in the royal library at *Paris*, a mafter-piece in that kind: another was bought by the Archbifhop of *Paris* for 300 crowns: but as people were unwilling to give fo exorbitant a price, he offer'd fome of the laft for 50 crowns and lefs, in hopes to have difpos'd of them all before he was difcover'd. It is not indeed to be fuppos'd, that they were all equal in the ornamental part; yet the beauty of the work,

the

the elegancy of the flower-pieces, initial letters, &c. the variety of the fineft colours intermix'd with gold and filver, with which they were exquifitely variegated, made the purchafers fond of fhewing them to their acquaintance; as every one thought the whole world could not produce fuch another. 'Tis reported that the Archbifhop thinking his *bible* worth his majefty's feeing, carried it to him; who view'd it with furprize, and in return fhew'd his own: upon a ftricter examination and comparing 'em together, they found that the ornaments were not exactly the fame; but as to the other part fuppos'd to be written, they obferv'd fuch a conformity in the number of pages, lines, words, and even the letters, as foon convinc'd them that they were done by fome other method than tranfcribing: befides two fuch *bibles* were the work of a man's life-time to tranfcribe; and upon enquiry he was found to have fold a much greater number. Hereupon orders was given to apprehend *Fauftus*, and profecute him as a **Conjurer**: I fhould have been apt to think this charge too abfurd to gain belief, except among the vulgar; and that it was only conniv'd at, in hopes it would terrify him to a difcovery of his art, were it not for a paffage which I have met with in Mr. *Maichel's* hiftory of the *Paris* libraries, wherein he mentions a ftrange problem publifh'd by Father *Bouhours*, a learned Jefuit — *Whether it be poffible that a* German *fhould be a wit?* Mr. *Maichel* juftly takes the part of his country-men, and proves them much wifer for the invention of Printing, than thofe ftupid *Paris* doctors, who rather believ'd it an effect of **Magick**, than of human wit or invention. *De la Caille* relates that he fled to *Mentz*, and fufpecting his fafety there, departed to *Strasburgh*, where he taught *John Mentel* or *Mentelin* his Art: but there is not the leaft probability for this affertion, fince he could not be fafer at one place than at another; and with refpect to *Mentel*, it is much more probable that he learn'd the invention from *Guttenbergh*, than from *Fauft* who perhaps was never at *Strasburgh*, unlefs he pafs'd thro' it in his journey to and from *France*.

HOWEVER, the parliament of *Paris* thought fit to make an arreft in favour of him, and to difcharge him from all further profecution, in confideration of his noble invention; and as I am credibly inform'd, a falary was paid by that crown to *Fauft's* defcendants for many years after, as a reward for his fufferings and merit: this was the end and fuccefs of that

expedition,

expedition, and prov'd at length very advantagious to him ; and made some amends for the melancholy hours of his confinement, and the terrors of an approaching death.

FAUST discharg'd thus with honour and a large supply of money, return'd to *Mentz*, where being inform'd that his quondam partner *Guttenbergh* was endeavouring, with the assistance of *Mentel*, to set up a printing-house at *Strasburgh*, and to challenge to himself the whole glory of the invention ; he began to consider, that it was not only in vain, but even dangerous to conceal himself and his art any longer from the world ; and 'tis probable, resolv'd at last to make both as publick as possibly he could in all the editions, which came from his press, 'till at least, *ann.* 1466 or 1467, in which he is suppos'd to have reprinted the last leaf of *Tully's Offices*, the last book known to be printed by him. During the interval between 1457, and the taking of *Mentz ann.* 1462, *Faust* meeting with prodigious encouragement, was oblig'd to increase the number of his workmen, and open more of the art to them, than he had done 'till then. Some of these having attain'd a sufficient insight into the mystery, were induc'd to go somewhere else, and set up for themselves ; to which they were encourag'd, both by the example of those who went away with *Guttenbergh*, and probably by invitations from other places, which were desirous of having the Art brought to them. *Pantaleon* tells us, that some of those who signaliz'd themselves the first in *Italy*, were of that number ; and indeed if we consider how soon they began to print in that kingdom, especially *Rome, Venice, &c.* and make a just allowance for preparing the great apparatus of a Printing-house, with their first essays, before they came to work off those volumes, which are of the oldest date, some of them pretty large ; we cannot but think that they left *Mentz* long before it was taken. *Faust* however had a sufficient number of servants left to finish his last editions, which are mention'd before ; after this we hear no more of him 'till the year 1471, wherein *Peter Schoeffer* and one *Henlif* a bookseller gave a book to a monastery, in order to obtain the prayers of it for *Faust's* soul : by which it was apparent he was dead before that time, or perhaps before 1470, because *Schoeffer* in that year printed St. *Jerom's Epistles* in his own name, without any mention of his master *Faust*.

N

HERE

HERE therefore I am oblig'd to conclude the hiftory of that *illuftrious man*, tho' I fhould have been vaftly more fatisfy'd in communicating other particulars of his life and death, could I have found 'em in the writers of thofe times.   But *Germany* is not the only ungrateful country that has neglected fuch as have beft deferv'd of her ; for the following books will furnifh us with inflances of this in other parts of the world.   I fhall only obferve, that as it is the property of falfe defert to be folicitous for panegyricks and monumental records, whilft true and intrinfick merit is filent, and equally contemns both ; fo whilft the *Dutch* beftow the higheft encomiums upon a *fuppofitious and imaginary inventor :* the *Germans* have been fo regardlefs of a *true* and *real* one, as to leave it entirely to his own works to tranfmit his praifes to pofterity.   If *Fauft* had died before the facking of *Mentz*, we might have had grounds to fuppofe, that fome monument had been erected to his memory by his fellow-citizens, and deftroy'd by the conqueror ; but as he furviv'd thofe times at leaft *fix* or *feven* years, and carry'd on and improv'd the Art during that interval, 'tis impoffible to entertain fo favourable an opinion of the *Moguntines*.   However his books and the art which he left us, will more effectually and univerfally proclaim and perpetuate his name and memory, than any monumental infcriptions, *&c.* and endear both to the learned and curious, as long as the Art or the world itfelf fhall endure.

THERE is one occurrence worthy to be mention'd, which I omitted in this chapter, not fo much out of forgetfulnefs or neglect, fince it is an inflance of *Fauft's* gratitude and generofity, as becaufe it is not eafy to fix the time of it, nor fo likely to have happen'd within the compafs of thefe *ten* years, as of fome of the former,*viz.* betw een 1440 and 1450. That is, his giving his only daughter in marriage to his fervant *Peter Schoeffer*, admitting him into partnerfhip, and procuring him the freedom of the city of *Mentz*, as a reward for his fervices, and the improvements which he made to the Art ; fuch as the invention of punches, matrices, metal-types ; and, as fome report, Printer's ink : if thefe difcoveries are owing to him, *Fauft* made him as ample amends as he could poffibly.   I wifh *Schoeffer* had been fo grateful to his generous mafter, as to have tranfmitted to us a fuller account of his life and character, than what we enjoy ; or if he perform'd this, that time had not depriv'd us

of

of fo valuable a monument; the want of which obliges me, much againſt my will, to bring this chapter and hiſtory to a concluſion, and reſt fatisfy'd with what we have.

C H A P. XI.

The Conclusion with an Account of the antient Method of Printing.

I AM now come to the cloſe of the firſt book of this hiſtory, which I have endeavour'd to inrich with collections from dead and living authors, and every thing valuable that I could procure upon this ſubject, from many of the moſt curious libraries. The next book will open a large and pleaſant ſcene. In the mean time I cannot conclude this better, than by giving a ſhort ſummary of the whole, and digeſting it into diſtinct periods, that the reader may, as it were at one view, ſee the whole progreſs of the Art, and fix it more eaſily in his memory; and by cloſing it with an account of the old way of printing us'd during the time of *Fauſt,* his ſon-in-law, &c.

1. THIS Art was devis'd a conſiderable time before any thing done that way appear'd.

2. 'TIS not improbable that the firſt hints of engraving upon woodenblocks might come from the *Chineſes,* who practis'd it above 300 years before it was thought of in *Europe.*

3. THE attempts to imitate it began about the year 1440, and not before.

4. THE new and more perfect method of Printing with fuſile-types did not ſucceed it 'till 10 years after, *viz.* 1450.

5. THIS

5. This new invention was difcover'd by *John Fauft* in the city of *Mentz*; in the perfecting of which *Peter Schoeffer* affifted him very much, and was amply rewarded by his mafter.

John Guttenbergh had no other fhare or merit in this difcovery, than by promoting it with fupplies of money from time to time, and that not from a principle of a publick fpirit, but for his own intereft, which made him drop both the Art and Artift when he found it lefs gainful than he expected.

6. This invention was kept with all imaginable fecrecy by thefe three parties, 'till *Guttenbergh*, upon a difference between them, took fome of their fervants with him to *Strasburgh*, where he began to practife it, and to teach it to *John Mentel:* The perfon in whofe favour the *Strasburgh* pretenfions were afterwards ftarted.

7. This contention not happening 'till the year 1455, they had already printed the *latin bible,* and perhaps privately difpos'd of fome number of the copies, feeing their difpute was about ftating their accounts, and balancing the charges and profits of the bufinefs.

8. Whether their firft feparate types were of wood, or lead, or any other metal; they ventur'd to print their firft effays but on one fide of the page, 'till they had found out a better ink than the common fort which they then us'd.

9. It is probable from this circumftance, that their firft improvement upon common ink, to prevent its fpreading, was only by charging it with a proportionable quantity of fome watery gum ; fuch as gum arabick, maftick, &c. which tho' it remedied that defect, would not fuffer the paper to be printed but upon one fide: but either *Schoeffer* or his mafter having found out the way of making it with oyl, they then printed on both fides.

10. They did not begin to put their names and infcriptions at the end of their books, as we can yet find, 'till the year 1457: this they continued to do 'till *Fauft* either dyed or left off the bufinefs.

11. Gutten-

11. GUTTENBERGH's name was never joyn'd with theirs, nor put to of the books which he printed after he abandon'd *Fauſt*.

12. SOME others of *Fauſt*'s ſervants forſook him before the taking of *Mentz*, and ſettled ſome at *Cologn*, others in *Italy*.

13. THE greateſt diſperſion of them was, when that noble city was taken and plunder'd by Archbiſhop *Adolph*, *ann.* 1462; ſo that the Art became univerſally known throughout *Europe*.

THERE remains now only to give the reader an idea of the firſt way of Printing, and of what is moſt peculiar to it; which, tho' a ſubject well known by the curious, may not be unacceptable to ſeveral perſons, to whoſe hands this work may chance to fall.

1. WITH reſpect to their forms, they were generally either large or ſmall *folio's*, or at leaſt *quarto's:* the leſſer ſizes were not in uſe.

2. THE leaves were without running-title, direction-word, number of pages, or diviſions into paragraphs.

3. THE character itſelf was a rude old *Gothic* mix'd with *Secretary*, caſt on purpoſe to imitate the hand-writing of thoſe times; the words were printed ſo cloſe to one another, that it was difficult and tedious even to thoſe who were us'd to MSS. and to this method; and often lead the in-attentive reader into miſtakes.

4. THEIR orthography was various and often arbitrary; and as for the diphthongs æ and œ, they were not at all careful about them.

5. THEY had very frequent abbreviations, which in time grew ſo nu-merous and difficult to be underſtood, that there was a neceſſity of writing a book to teach the manner of reading them.

6. THEIR periods were diſtinguiſh'd by no other points than the double and ſingle one, *i. e.* the *colon* and *full ſtop*; juſt after the ſame manner

ner as the reading *pfalms*, in our *Common prayer-books* are pointed; all other punctuations being of much later invention.

7. THEY us'd no great letters to begin a sentence or proper name of men or places.

8. THEY left blanks for the places of titles, initial letters, and other ornaments, in order to have them fupply'd by the illuminators, whofe ingenious art, tho' in vogue before and at that time, yet did not long furvive the mafterly improvements made by the printers in this branch of their Art. Thofe ornaments were exquifitely fine, and curioufly variegated with the moft beautiful colours, and even with gold and filver; the margins likewife were frequently charged with variety of figures of faints, birds, beafts, monfters, flowers &c. which had fometimes relation to the contents of the page, tho' moftly none at all: thefe embellifhments were very coftly; but for thofe that could not afford a round price, there were others done after a more ordinary manner and at much cheaper rates.

9. THE names of the printer, place, &c. were either wholly neglected or put at the end of the book, not without fome pious ejaculation or doxology.

10. THE date was likewife omitted or involv'd in fome crampt circumftantial period, or elfe printed either at full length, or by numerical letters, and fometimes partly one and partly the other, thus; *one thoufand* CCCC and *fixty*, &c. but all of them at the end of the book.

11. THERE was no variety of characters, no intermixture of *Roman* and *Italick*; which were of later invention; but their pages were continued in a *Gothick* letter of the fame fize throughout.

12. THEIR *Rubricks* which were very frequent and added no fmall beauty to the pages, were fometimes done by the fame hands as the initial letters.

13. WHEN-

13. WHENEVER they met with any *Greek*, they either left a blank for it, to be afterwards fill'd up by writing if the paſſage was long; or if ſhort, confiſting only of three or four words, they got it cut on wood, tho' after ſuch a rude and ill-ſhap'd manner, that it required ſome pauſe to be read.

14. THE quotations of the places out of which they were taken, were very often neglected both in Manuſcripts and printed books, which caus'd the curious no ſmall trouble to find them out.

15. THEY had ſeldom dedicatory or prefatory epiſtles; and when they began afterwards to retail them in their impreſſions, they generally plac'd 'em at the end of the work; a piece of juſtice as much neglected, as wanting in our age.

16. THEY collected no *table* of *contents*, no *index* nor *ſummary*, (which are indubitably a great help to the reader,) nor any *errata's* at the end; for what faults were in their editions were rather owing to the manuſcripts which they printed after, than to the careleſneſs of the Printer.

17. THEY printed but few copies at once, for 200 or 300 were then eſteem'd a large impreſſion; tho' upon the encouragements receiv'd from the learned, they increas'd their numbers in proportion.

18. LASTLY, If I may be allow'd this article, they were not ſolicitous to obtain *privileges* and *patents* for the ſole printing of any particular volume, tho' towards the later end of *Fauſt's* time ſeveral of his ſervants ſet up Printing-houſes, and were ambitious to excel their maſter: How ſoon after thoſe privileges began, appears from that granted by the Emperor to *John Schoeffer*, *Fauſt's* grandſon *ann.* 1519, for the ſole printing *T. Livius*, and to prohibit any other to reprint thoſe books which had come from his preſs: and as this had been granted upon the account of his being the grandſon of the firſt inventor of the Art; ſo ſeveral Popes and Princes gave like patents to their firſt Printers as a mark of their favour.

I ſhall

I shall here mention something concerning their way of Book-binding, an account of which we find in *Scaliger*[1], who tells us, that his grandmother had a printed Psalter, the cover of which was two inches thick ; in the inside was a kind of cupboard, wherein was a small silver crucifix, and behind it the name of *Berenica Codronia de la Scala*. This book seems to have been printed with wood, but probably bound like the rest.

As to the prices of their books, I cannot find any thing particular except what I have before quoted out of *Campanus's* dedication to the Pope ; from which it may be infer'd, that in his time at *Rome* they were sold for about one fifth part of what the MSS. had done. To this I shall add an instance of the gift bequeath'd by *P. Schoeffer*, and *Conrad Henlif* of the same profession, to a library of monks, which will enable us to guess at the great rate they still were sold for. *La Caille* relates it out of the annals of the abby of St. *Victor* at *Paris*, and it is as follows[2] ; ,, The ,, anniversary (office for the souls) of the honourable *Peter Schoeffer*, ,, *Conr. Henlif* and *John Faust* citizens and Printers in the city of *Mentz*, ,, as also for the souls of their wives, parents, children, friends and bene- ,, factors ; which said *P. Schoeffer* and *C. Henlif* have given us the book ,, of St. *Jerom's Epistles* printed upon vellum (*in two vol. fol. ann.* 1470,) ,, excepting nevertheless the sum of twelve golden crowns, which the ,, aforesaid Printers receiv'd from our Lord *John Abbot* of this church ,, *Oct.* 29, 1471.

HENCE 'tis plain that the *twelve crowns* (which in those days were more than equivalent to as many *pounds* now) were but part of the price or value of the said book ; and that the other part, whatever proportion it bore to this, was remitted to them in consideration of this anniversary office, to which there us'd to be no price fix'd, tho' the least for it was generally *five* or *six crowns.*

I conclude this chapter with an observation of Monf. *de la Monoye* concerning the phrase of *Libri editi*, which I hope the curious will be pleas'd with : he tells us, that this phrase was us'd before the invention of Prin-

---

[1] *Scaligeriana, Hag. edit. in 8vo.* p. 173.

[2] Anniversarium honorabilium virorum *Petri Schoeffer & Conradi Herlif*, ac *Joan. Fust*, civium de *Moguntia*, impressorum, necnon uxorum, filiorum, parentum, amicorum & benefactorum ; qui *Petrus & Conradus* dederunt nobis *Epistolas beati Hieronymi* impressas in Pergameno, excepta tamen summa duodecim scutorum auri quam præfati impressores receperunt per manus Domini *Joannis* Abbatis hujus ecclesiæ, 3 kalend. Novemb. *ann.* 1471. *De la Caille*, pag. 14.

ting.

ting, and fignified only books publifh'd and difpers'd abroad in fome confiderable number, in oppofition to thofe that were writ fair to be fet up in libraries, which were call'd *Libri fcripti.* This obfervation he proves from a paffage out of *Philelphus,* who fpeaking of his ten books of *latin odes,* expreffes himfelf as follows; *Carminum libri editi quinque, verfuum quinque millibus ; nam alteri quinque qui tantundem verfus compleEtentur, partim fcripti funt non editi, partim ne fcripti quidem,* i. e. *five books of the latin odes are already publifh'd, containing* 5000 *verfes* ; *the other five, which will contain the fame number, are partly written not publifh'd, and partly ftill unwritten:* he obferves further, that the firft *five* books of odes were not fent to the prefs 'till the year 1497, when they were printed in *4to.* at *Brefcia :* befides the fame *Philelphus* tells his reader in one of his epiftles written *ann.* 1453, that he defign'd to publifh all the ten books in that year, *Libros decem hoc anno edere inftitui,* which could not be underftood of Printing, feeing tho' the art was perfected about this time, yet it was ftill kept fecret 'till *four* years after, when *Fauft* put his firft colophon to the Pfalter. Whether this obfervation be as certain as it is curious, I fhall leave to the judgment of my readers.

C H A P. XI.

An Account of the first printed Bibles *before the year* 1501.

AS thofe authors who have wrote any thing fully upon the fubject of Printing, have given their readers an account of the firft Bibles, that have been printed, from the difcovery of the Art to the year 1500 or even beyond: I thought our *Englifh* readers would not be difpleas'd to have a fhort abftract given them of thofe antient and valuable monuments of the art; and I can't but think it will be more acceptable to have them all in one view, than difpers'd, as they would be, were I to give them under their refpective Printers, who liv'd at a vaft diftance of time and place from one another; efpecially confidering that fome famous cities, and even univerfities, as that of *Louvain,* have not printed fo much as one fingle Bible in all the interval between the year

1450 and 1500, and even beyond; whereas others, for instance, that of *Nurembergh* has produc'd at least 13 in that time : I shall place them according to the years in which they were printed, and add such farther particulars concerning them, as I have been able to meet with in those authors, who have given us an account of them ; and such as my own observations have enabled me to collect from those noble libraries I have formerly mention'd.

B Y this the reader will be sufficiently appris'd, that I intend to speak only of those which bear any certain date ; but as for those, which are either printed without date, or with a disputed one, I shall just say so much of them, as will let him see how little they are to be rely'd on, and what reasons I have to pass them by : I have, I think, already ventur'd to give the reader a rule how to judge of such works, *viz.* if their dates are before the year 1450, they must be suppos'd to have been wrong printed, either designedly, or by mistake : the reader will find proofs sufficient of the former in our next book, and the later is too well known to require any : however in this later respect I shall give him an instance or two of it, because it will be a kind of a key to rectify any other that may hereafter fall in his way.

W E meet with an account of a *German* Bible, still kept in the library of the city of *Ausburgh*, affirm'd by *Hottinger*, who saw it there, to have been printed with fusile types *ann.* 1448, but with this caveat however, *ni fallor, if I am not mistaken,* as writing at some distance of time and place : other authors have given it that of 1449, but as either of them preceded the time of the invention, *Malinkrot* tells us, that *Martin Zeiler* thought it 'twas only a manuscript version made *ann.* 1449: but Mr. *Beughen* doth not scruple to tell us in the preliminary discourse to his *Incunabula Typographiæ*, that they only misplac'd the two last figures of the date, and printed 1449 instead of 1494. *Chevillier* mentions two more out of *Lipenius*, whose dates are demonstrably false, the one is a Bible printed at *Paris ann.* 1443, and the other at *Lyons ann.* 1446 : whereas it is certain, that Printing was not brought to *Paris* 'till *twenty seven* years after the date of the first, *viz. ann.* 1470, nor to *Lyons* 'till *six* or *seven* years after that: the same may be said of another printed at *Basil*, and affirm'd, by two booksellers of *Geneva* in the catalogue of their books, to bear date

1459,

1459, fince 'tis plain that that city did not receive the Art 'till about 1475: if the reader therefore will take this rule with him, to examine the time in which the Art was brought to any place, which he will find in the following Book, he will eafily rectify any wrong date that may come in his way, and as for thofe, which do not mention the place or Printer's name, he may fafely rank them amongft the apocryphal ones, and them which have no date at all, but as the former have been taken notice of by all our annalifts, I fhall be obliged fo far as I am able to afcertain their refpective dates, as we go along.

1. Before I come to fpeak of thofe, which bear a certain and indifputable date, I muft not omit the *firft* printed by *Fauft* and *Schoeffer* about 1450 or foon after, and mention'd by *Trithemius*, the *Colognian Chronicle*, and fome other authors, as the firft confiderable work printed with fufile types by thofe two *Protodædali*. I have already given the reafons of its being printed without date or colophon, which would have betrayed the difcovery of their new Art, and prevented *Fauft*'s felling it for MS: but this however ought by no means to hinder us from giving it the firft rank, feeing the fact is fo undeniably attefted. It is pity they have been long ago, either deftroy'd, or buried in fome private libraries, where the moft diligent fearches have not as yet been able to find them out: perhaps its being printed fo like MS, may be one reafon why they are ftill lookt upon as fuch by the owners, if any fuch there be; for which reafon I am ftill willing to hope, that time may difcover and bring fome of them to light, and that what has been faid in this hiftory, and by authors of a much higher character, will fpur up fome curious perfons to make a more diligent fearch after fo valuable a monument; 'till when, no farther account can be expected of it than what we have already given.

2. The next is that, which I have ventur'd, after other authors, to call the fecond impreffion of the Bible, printed at *Mentz* by the fame worthy inventors *ann.* 1462, and which is confequently the moft antient we know extant in any library; we have already given fome account of it in a former chapter *p.* 31, and of the colophon printed at the end of it, which we need not therefore repeat here: as there are feveral copies of it here in *London* where I have feen them, and elfewhere in *England*, we need not

go to any foreign authors for an account of it: it is printed in *fol.* as indeed all their other works were.   For tho' I have follow'd *Peter Lambeck*'s
notion of the Pſalters being printed in 4*to*, becauſe its ſize may be very
much like that of a *quarto*, yet if I may here venture to give my judgment
of a book I have not ſeen, I think I have ſufficient grounds to believe
that the firſt Printers had their paper made of all ſizes ; and that the
five books printed on Blocks of Wood, already mention'd to be in the Earl
of *Pembroke*'s library, would appear to any one like *quarto's*, were it not
that the ſignatures ſhew the contrary.

THE next impreſſion we meet with, is one which Mr. *Mattaire* gives
us upon the authority of a learned friend of his, who deſires to have his
name conceal'd, and the want of whoſe date is ſupply'd by a colophon of
three *latin* verſes importing, that it was printed in the *third* year of *Lewis*
XI. reign, *i. e. ann.* 1464 by the three *German* partners, who brought
the Art to *Paris*, tho' there be no mention made of the place where it was
printed, vid. *Annal. Typogr.* p. 41, and 60.   I am perſuaded that Mr. *Mattaire*'s friend was miſtaken in the firſt verſe, and I ſhould not have given
it a rank here, nor even mention'd it, were it not to prevent the reader's
being puzzled with this account of it under the year 1464 ; or his ſuppo
ſing me guilty of an omiſſion : but as *Chevillier* gives us the ſame colophon printed at the end of the firſt *Paris* Bible by the ſame three partners, with this variation however from the former ; that in the firſt verſe,
inſtead of *Semi luſtrum*, it has *tribus luſtris*, that is inſtead of the *third*, it
imports the *thirteenth* year of that king's reign : we may eaſily ſuppoſe,
that it was the firſt *Paris* Bible of 1475, and that this unknown gentleman
might poſſibly be miſtaken : however the book being in *Queen's-college*
library, in *Cambridge* it may be eaſily conſulted.

3. The next impreſſion therefore to that of *Mentz* 1462, is that of *Auſburgh*, [in latin *Auguſta Vindelicorum*] printed by *John Bemler ann.* 1466 in
latin *fol.*   It is mention'd by *Martin Cruſius, Melchior Adamus,* and after
them by *Malinkrot* ; *Chevillier* ſeems indeed to think their teſtimony in
ſufficient to aſcertain ſo old a date, but I cannot ſee any reaſon for it,
ſeeing it is four years more recent than the taking of the city of *Mentz*,
and the diſperſion of *Fauſt's* ſervants ; beſides the city of *Ausburgh* was ſo
near *Mentz*, and ſo conſiderable withal, that it is no way improbable,
but

but some one of them might go and settle there even sooner than the year 1466.

4. The *latin* Bible *fol.* printed at *Reutlingen* [*Reutlingæ*] a small town in *Germany* in the dutchy of *Wirtembergh ann.* 1469, mention'd by *Hallevor-dius,* Father *le Long, De la Caille, Chevillier* and others ; but more parti-cularly by *John Saubert* in his catalogue of the *Norican* or *Nurembergh* li-brary, where he saw it : the Printer of it was *John de Averbach,* we have nothing else extant of him at least with his name.

5. The *latin* Bible *fol.* printed about 1471 *Mar.* 15. at *Rome* by *Conrard Sweynheym* and *Arnold Pannariz* [or *Panaratz* as I have seen it printed in one of their books] who were the first Printers that settled in that city : it has a preface, and at the end four *latin* distichs in praise of those two *Germans,* and a small work or history of *Aristeas,* and is translated by *Matthias Palmerius:* the Printers tell Pope *Sextus* IV, in the lists which they gave him of their works, that they had printed 575 copies of it : concer-ning this Bible *Spondæus* gives us the following account, *we have,* says he, *the Bible printed at* Rome *in two very large volumes* [*ingentibus volumi-nibus*] *ann.* 1471 *in the house of the* Maximis *by two* Germans *named* Con-rard Sweynheym *and* Arnold Pannartz.

6. The *Italian* Bible translated by *Nicholaus Malherbis* (in Italian *Ma-lermi*) a *Venetian* abbot of the order of the *Calmaldules,* printed at *Venice ann.* 1471 *Calend. Aug.* in *fol.* by *Vindelin de Spire,* who with his brother *John,* was the first who brought the Art of Printing unto that city. *Che-villier* tells us, he has seen it in the library of the *Mazarine-college* at *Paris* in two volumes, and that tho' the *imprimatur* doth not mention the Prin-ter, yet it is easy to guess at him by the *Italian* verses, which *Squazafica* has put to that edition.

7. Mr. *Mattaire* mentions another *fol. Italian* Bible printed in the same year 1571, of *Malhermi's* translation, without Printer or places name. Fa-ther *le Long* is the author he has taken it from.

8. The *latin* Bible reprinted at *Mentz* by *Peter Schoeffer ann.* 1472, on the eve of St. *Matthias* the apostle *fol.* the learned *Walton* (editor of our *English* edition of the *Polyglot)* thought this the first impression of the Bible, and seem'd doubtful of what some authors had affirm'd, that they had seen some more antient editions than that ; how much he was mistaken

the

the reader may judge by the foregoing ones: this Bible has a colophon at the end, not unlike thoſe us'd by his maſter and himſelf, in the former edition and ſome other of their works.

9. Mr. *Mattaire* (after Father *le Long,*) mentions a *latin* impreſſion *ann.* 1473 without Printer or places name.   *Annal. Typogr.* p. 100.

10. The *latin* Bible *fol.* printed at *Paris* by *Ulric Gering, Martin Crantz,* and *Michael Friburger*, the firſt who ſet up a preſs in that city.   This Bible, which *Chevillier* has ſeen in the library of the *Celeſtin* monks, and has given us the colophon of; importing its being printed in the 13th year of *Lewis* XI. reign, *i. e. ann.* 1475, is the ſame which we ſuppoſe Mr. *Mattaire's* friend did inform him to have been printed in the 3d year of that monarch, *i. e. ann.* 1464: we need not therefore repeat here, what we ſaid juſt before under that head; Mr. *Mattaire* however places this under the year 1476.

11. The *latin* Bible printed at *Nuremberg* in the ſame year 1475 in *fol.* by *Anthony Koburger* or *Coburger* firſt Printer of that city ; in which library *J. Saubert* tells us, they have a copy ſtill extant, we have another in the publick library at *Oxford*.

12. Another *latin* Bible without Printer or places name, printed alſo *ann.* 1475. *fol. Mattaire* p. 110.

13. The Bible in *Italian* printed by *James de Rubeis,* alias *des Rouges,* at *Pignerol* in *Piedmont, ann.* 1475, *fol.* idem.

14. ———— in *latin quarto,* printed at *Placentia* by *John de Ferratis Cremoneſe ann.* 1475.

15. ———— in *low dutch, fol.* at *Cologn ann.* 1475, without Printer's name, *idem.*

16. ———— in *latin* printed in *fol. ann.* 1476 at *Venice,* by *Nicholas Jenſon* in *Gothick* character, a copy of which is ſtill to be ſeen in the library of the *Celeſtin* monks at *Paris.*

17. ———— printed at *Venice* by *Francis Hailbrun* and *Nicholas de Frankford* partners, *ann.* 1476 *fol. Chevillier* ſeems doubtful, whether this and the laſt are not the ſame edition under different partners names; but Mr. *Mattaire* and father *Orlandi* give them as two different editions.

18. The

18. The Bible in *latin* with canons and concordances *fol.* printed at *Nu-rembergh* by *Anthony Koburger ann.* 1476. *Orlandi* is the firſt author that has mention'd it: but doth not tell us where he ſaw it or how he came by the knowledge of it.

19. ———— *ead.* printed at *Naples, ann.* 1476, *fol.* by *Matthias Moravus de Olomuntz* ; the colophon of which has ſome lines in commendation of the Printer.

20. ———— *ead.* printed at *Nurembergh* by *Anthony Koburger ann.* 1477, *fol.* it has the arguments and references like that printed by the ſame Printer *ann.* 1476.

21. ———— *ead. fol.* printed by *Bernard Richel* citizen of *Baſil, ann.* 1477, without places name.

22. ———— in *Italian* by *Malhermi fol.* printed at *Venice* by *Anthony de Bononia, ann.* 1477.

23. ———— *ead.* printed at *Venice* by *Gabriel de Piero,* a native of *Treviſo, ann.* 1477, *fol.*

24. ———— in *high dutch, fol.* by *Anthony Sorgius* at *Ausburgh,* 1477.

25. ———— *ead.* 1477, without Printers name.

26. ———— in *low dutch, fol.* at *Delph* 1477.

27. ———— *ead.* in *quarto,* 1477.

28. ———— in *latin* with *Gothick* character, *fol.* at *Venice* by *Leonard Wild* for *Francis de Hailbrun* and *Nicholas de Franckford,* 1478.

29. ———— *ead.* in *Gothick, fol.* by *Theodoric de Reynsberg* and *Reynald de Novimagio, fol.* 1478.

30. ———— *ead.* with the arguments and references of *Menardus Monachus, fol.* printed at *Nurembergh* by *Anthony Coburger,* 1478.

31. ———— *ead.* in Gothic *fol.* at *Venice* by *Nic. Jenſon,* 1479.

32. ———— *ead.* with arguments and concordance *fol.* by *Anthony Coburger* at *Nurembergh,* 1479.

33. ———— *ead. fol.* at *Lyons* by *Perrin de Lathomi de Lotharingis,* 1479.

34. ———— *ead. fol.* without Printer's name at *Cologn* 1479.

35. ———— in *low dutch, fol.* at *Goude* in *Holland* by *Gerard Leeu,* 1479.

36. Bi-

36. The Bible in *latin* with the apoſtils of *Nic. de Lyra, fol.* by *John de Cologn* and *John Manthen,* 1480; the place is not mention'd, but theſe two printed at *Venice* from 1471 to 1481, if not beyond. *Orland.*

37. ———— *ead. quarto* at *Venice* for *Octavian Scot,* 1480. by *Francis Halibrun.*

38. ———— in *High Dutch* at *Ausburgh,* 2 vol. *fol.* by *Ant. Sergius* citizen of it, 1480.

39. ———— in *Latin fol.* by *Anthony Coburger,* at *Nuremberg* 1480.

40. ———— *ead.* with ſummaries and references *fol.* by *John Zeiner* of *Reutlingen* at Ulms, 1480.

41. ———— *ead.* with apoſtils of *N. de Lyra* 7 vol. *fol. Cologn,* 1480 without printers name.

42. ———— *ead.* with *Gothic* character, by *Leonard Wild* of *Ratisbon, fol.* at *Venice* 1481.

43. ———— *ead.* with poſtills of *N. de Lyra* by *John de Cologn, Nic. Jenſon,* and partners *fol.* 1481; no place nam'd, but they printed at *Venice.*

44. ———— *ead.* in *fol.* by *Conrard Lentorius* at *Nurembergh,* 1481.

45. ———— in *Italian,* by *Malermi fol.* printed at *Venice* for *Octavian Scot,* 1481.

46. ———— in *latin quarto* at *Venice* by *Francis Renner de Hailbrun,* 1482.

47. ———— *ead.* by *Reynhard* of *Strasburg,* and *Nichol. Philipi de Gernſheym fol.* at *Strasburg* [Argentoratum] 1482.

48. ———— by *Ant. Coburger* at *Nuremberg,* 1483.

49. ———— in *quarto* by *Francis Renner de Hailbrun* at *Venice,* 1483.

50. ———— in *fol.* by *John,* ſirnam'd the Great, *Herbort, German* at *Venice,* 1483.

51. ———— in *high dutch* by *Ant. Coburger* at *Nuremberg,* 1483.

52. ———— *ead.* in *fol.* at *Ausburg* 1483 without printers name.

53. ———— in *latin fol.* by *John Zainer de Reutlingen. Ausburg* 1484.

54. ———— *ead.* by *Ant. Coburger fol.* at *Nuremberg,* 1484.

55. ———— *ead.* in *quarto* by *John,* ſirnam'd the Great, *Herbort* of *Selgenſtat* at *Venice,* 1484.

57. — Bi-

56. The Bible in *Latin fol.* at *Nuremberg* without Printer's name 1484.

57. ———— in *Italian fol.* at *Venice* by *Andrea de Pattaſichis de Catharo*, 1484.

58. ———— in *high Dutch* at *Lubeck* by *Stephen Arnold*, 1484.

59. ———— *ead.* at *Stratzburg* no printers name, 1485.

60. ———— in *Latin* at *Antwerp fol.* by *Nicholas Keſter*, 1487.

61. ———— *ead.* in *quarto Venice* 1487, without Printer's name.

62. ———— *ead.* in *fol. Baſil*, 1487, *id.*

63. ———— *ead.* in *fol.* with *Lyra's* apoſtils, 5 vol. *fol.* no Printer's name but known to be printed by *Ant. Coburger, Nuremberg*, 1487.

64. ———— in *French fol.* by *Antony Verard, Paris*, 1487.

65. ———— in *high Dutch fol. Auſburg* 1487. no Printer's name.

66. ———— in *Hebrew* with points, *fol.* by *Abraham Ben Rabb. Hhajim* at *Soncino*, 1488.

67. ———— in *Latin, fol.* at *Venice* for *Octavian Scot*, 1489.

68. ———— *ead.* in *Gothic* character, *fol.* revis'd by *Stephen Pariſetti* and printed by *James Malieti*, no place's name, 1490.

69. ———— in *high Dutch*, 4to, *Auſburgh*, 1490, no Printer's name.

70. ———— *ead.* 4to, at *Nurembergh*, 1490; no Printer's name, but ſuppos'd to be printed by *A. Coburger.*

71. ———— in *Latin, fol.* at *Venice* by *Simon de Gara*, 1491.

72. ———— *ead.* at *Baſil*, 4to, 1491 ; no Printer's name.

73. ———— *ead.* at *Venice*, 4to, 1491, *id.*

74. ———— *ead.* at *Baſil* by *John Froben*, 8vo, in a ſmall letter, 1491.

75. ———— *ead.* with *Lyra's* apoſtils, 4 *vol. fol. Stratzburg*, 1492.

76. ———— *ead.* cum gloſſa ordinaria *vol. 6. fol. Nurembergh* by *Anthony Coburger*, 1493.

77. ———— in *high Dutch* by *Stephen Arndes, fol.* at *Lubeck*, 1493.

78. ———— *ead. Gothic* character, 4to, at *Venice*, by *Fr. Renner de Hailbrun*, 1494.

79. ———— in *Italian, folio*, by *John Roſſo*, 1494 ; *Venice.*

80. ———— in *Latin* 4to, at *Venice* by *Simon Bevilaqua* citizen of *Pavia*, 1494.

81. ———— in *Hebrew*, 8vo, by *Gerſon Ben Moſes* of *Soncino* at *Brixia*, 1494

P

82. The

82. The Bible in *Hebrew*, 4*to* and 8*vo*, at *Pisauro*, 1494 ; without Printer's name.

83. ———— in *Latin* by *Matthew Hus German, fol.* 1494 ; no place's name, but we find him printing at *Lyons* three years before this.

84. ———— in *high Dutch* 4to, at *Ausburg*, 1494 ; no Printer's name.

85. ———— in *Latin* with *Ord. Gloss.* and *Lyra*'s apostils, *fol.* by *Paganino de Paganinis*, 1495.

86. ———— *ead. Gothic* character, by *John Froben de Hamelburgh*, 8vo *Basil* 1495.

87. ———— *ead.* 4to, by *Jacob* and *Angelus Brittans* at *Brescia*, 1496.

88. ———— *ead.* with *Ord. Gloss.* and *de Lyra*'s apostils, 6 *vol. fol.* at *Nuremberg*, 1496 ; by *Ant. Coburger.*

89. ———— *ead.* corrected by *Angelus de Monte Ulmi* 8vo, printed by *Jerom de Paganinis* at *Venice*, 1497.

90. ———— *ead.* in *Gothic* character with summaries, &c. by *Franc. Fradin* and *John Pivard* 4to, 1497 ; no place's name.

91. ———— *ead. fol.* at *Cologn* 1497 ; without Printer's name.

92. ———— *ead.* at *Strasburgh*, ditto.

93. ———— *ead.* with *Lyra*'s apostils 6 *vol. fol. Basil* 1498 ; no Printer's name.

94. ———— *ead.* by *Simon Bevilaqua* 4to, *Venice* 1498.

95. ———— *ead.* 4to, by *John Pivard* 1500 ; no places name.

96. ———— *ead.* by *Simon Vostre, fol. Paris* 1500.

97. ———— *ead. fol.* at *Nuremberg* 1500 ; no Printer's name.

98. ———— *ead.* by *John Froben, Basil* 1500.

99. ———— *ead.* 8vo, *Lyons* 1500.

I have purposedly omitted some less considerable ones, which are either without Printer or places name, or both ; because such were only the wretched performances of a few, who made it their business to reprint the editions of some of the most famous Printers of *Europe*, whether of the Bible, or of any other considerable work ; and to vend them under-hand for the right ones : this was an abuse which began very early to be complain'd of ; for no sooner had a *Froben, Badius, Aldus* or any other

great

great Printer publifh'd a work, which had coft him infinite pains to correct, as well as great fums of money to purchafe the beft manufcripts,
but they pyrated them in fuch a fhameful and incorrect manner, that
they could afford to fell them for lefs than half the price. And as there
wanted not fordid perfons to encourage this vile practice, and to prefer
thofe maim'd performances to the more correct ones, if they could but
fave money by them; it often prov'd that the fale of a valuable edition
was hinder'd, to the great lofs and difcouragement of the Printer, whilft
the bad ones went off with eafe : this occafion'd them to complain of
the abufe, in their prefaces to their works, and to appeal to the learned
againft fuch practices ; fome of whom (in particular *Erafmus*) did not fail
to write very fharply againft thofe enemies to learning, who were at length
come up to fuch a degree of impudence, as to counterfeit the names,
marks and rebus's of the famous Printers, of which we fhall have occafion
to give an account hereafter. In the mean time, all their complaints and
efforts proving ineffectual towards the fuppreffing fuch pyracies ; they
were forc'd to have recourfe to the higher powers, and to employ the
affiftance of their learned patrons, to obtain them patents and privileges
for the fole printing of thofe works, upon which they had beftow'd fo
much pains and coft: but this more properly belongs to the next book
to which I am now haftening.

P 2   B O O K

BOOK II.

The Hiſtory of the Diſperſion, Progreſs and Improvements of PRINTING, from 1462 to 1520.

The INTRODUCTION.

ITHERTO we have ſeen the *Art of Printing* kept with the utmoſt ſecrecy by its inventors, and confin'd to the city of *Mentz*, till the fatal year of its being taken plunder'd and depriv'd of all its former rights and franchiſes, as we have hinted already : which occaſion'd the diſperſion of the greateſt part of *Fauſt's* ſervants whom we muſt ſuppoſe by that time to have been very numerous : theſe ſeeing the deplorable condition to which that noble city was reduc'd, and the difficulty of carrying on the buſineſs any longer with that freedom and encouragement they had till then enjoy'd ; and being perhaps inclin'd enough of themſelves to leave their maſters, to go ſettle in ſome of the moſt famous cities of *Europe*, where they were ſure to gain, not only wealth and honour, but the friendſhip of the learned, immediately diſperſed themſelves and ſettled, ſome in the neighbouring cities of *Cologn* and *Auſburgh*, others went to *Rome, Venice, Paris, &c.*

where

where they foon met with all the encouragement they could wifh: this happen'd, as we have hinted in the former book in the year 1462. So that *Fauft* and *Schoeffer*, had happily conceal'd the art from the reft of the world, at leaft the fpace of *twelve* years from the time of its being perfected: we muft, however, except one of his fervants *viz. Nic. Jenfon*, who if the date of his firft book be true and genuine, muft have given his mafter the flip before that fatal period, fince we find this book finifh-ed at *Venice an.* 1461 with great advantage and improvement; we fhall have occafion to enquire further into this man and his work, in the fequel of this book : however, if we except this one fingle work, we don't find any footfteps of the infant art, being carry'd out of its nurfe's arms du-ing thofe twelve years.

BUT now we muft confider it in a different view, difperfing it felf over divers nations, patroniz'd by Popes and Kings, and efteem'd a di-vine blefling to mankind. It feems now to have left the city of *Mentz*, where it yet fhines there brighter than ever ; and at the fame inftant dif-covers it felf at *Rome, Venice, Oxford* and *Paris* ; and in a fpace fhorter than can be imagin'd, becomes confpicuous over all *Europe*.

As there is fo great a number and variety of events and remarkable occurrences, which happen'd in feveral cities of *Europe*, at the fame time, or immediately after one another, with refpect to the firft printers who fettled there, the improvements made by them, and the encouragement they receiv'd; it will be abfolutely impoffible to difpofe them in fuch an order, as may give the reader at once a full view of them all, with-out interrupting the feries, either with refpect to time or place. Thus, for inftance, while we fhew the tranfactions at *Rome*, during the *two* cr three firft years, *Venice, Paris, Oxford, Cologn, Milan, &c.* will open new fcenes to our view, attracting our eyes towards them, and oblige us to break the thread of one to begin with that of another ; which continual diverfions would rather confound than inftruct the reader, and render the hiftory confus'd and tedious. Our beft annalifts and hiftorians being fenfible of this, have follow'd a better method. Father *Orlandi* in par-ticular, the lateft that has wrote upon this fubject, hath taken that of *De la Caille* ; who proceeds with every city by it felf, from the time it is fuppos'd to have receiv'd the art, to the end of the century, according to their faireft claim to priority in point of time ; and then goes on with

the

the next in order. This method I have chofe, and given under the head of each city the names, character and merit, of each printer that has wrought there, from the time of its receiving the art to the end of the year 1500; and pointed out the excellencies of thofe who have been eminent in this art, either by the beauty of their types, the elegance and correctnefs of their works, the number of their editions, or any improvements which they made. By this means, I hope the reader will clearly fee the early progrefs of printing in every place; if not at one view, yet at leaft in fuch an order as more eafily to form an idea, not only of the printers and cities wherein they refided, but likewife of the moft confiderable patrons for wealth, learning, &c. of that time, to whofe character and merit, I have not failed to do juftice throughout this whole work.

I propos'd at firft to have clos'd this hiftory with the fifteenth century; but when I came to confider that the moft eminent printers, to whom we owe many important improvements of this art, fuch as *Aldus* at *Venice*, *Amerbach* and *Froben* at *Bafil*, *Badius* at *Lyons* and *Paris*, with many others, did not begin to appear upon this ftage, till almoft the clofe of it: and that their merit was not difcover'd till the beginning of the next; I thought it an unpardonable injuftice to them and my readers, to curtail their hiftory by too fcrupuloufly adhering to my propos'd epocha; and therefore have chofen to continue this hiftory *twenty* years longer, *i. e.* to 1520; and fometimes made an excurfion beyond that time, when ever any of thofe excellent mafters have outliv'd it. This has afforded me another agreeable opportunity, *viz.* of mentioning fome others who did not enter the province of printing till after the fifteenth century.

ANOTHER motive which induc'd me to continue this hiftory 20 years longer, was, that I found all the improvements that had been made to the art, were made by that time *i. e.* by the year 1520 at leaft; the foundation of them was fo far lay'd before that year, that whatever has been done fince, either with relation to the beauty of letter, elegancy of impreffion, variety of types, printing in different languages, efpecially in the eaftern ones, in different columns, correctnefs and the like, all thefe and many more, had already been carry'd on to fuch a perfection before this time, that it admitted but of fmall improvements to be made to it afterwards. I have therefore thought it a much better period to clofe

this

this hiſtory with, than that of 1500 where *Orlandi* concludes his ; this has
given me an opportunity of mentioning not only the improvements them‑
ſelves, but likewiſe thoſe glorious printers to whom we owe them. How‑
ever, as it would ſwell this book too much to inſert the names of all the
printers, that appear'd within thoſe 20 years, they being too numerous,
and a great many of them, deſerving rather to be remember'd with
ſhame than honour : I have reſolv'd to ſpeak only of thoſe who ſignaliz'd
themſelves, either for ſome improvements they made to the art, the
beauty and correctneſs of their editions, or any other merit they have
been conſpicuous for : it is for that reaſon I have choſen to ſpeak of them
in a chapter by it ſelf, after I have clos'd the 15th century, to which I
ſhall alſo add in another chapter, an account of the abuſes which crept
into the art from its promulgation to 1520, that there may be nothing
wanting to make this hiſtory as compleat and inſtructing as poſſible.

I t will be neceſſary to acquaint the reader that tho' we have follow'd
the method of the beſt annaliſts, in ſettling the priority of every city, ac‑
cording to the date of the oldeſt extant work, that was printed there,
which is certainly the ſureſt way and leaſt liable to miſtakes ; yet it is more
than probable that they might receive the art much ſooner : ſeeing ſome
time muſt reaſonably be allow'd for ſetting up a printing-houſe, and
furniſhing it with the neceſſary apparatus, which in the infancy of the
art was more difficult to procure, for want of proper workmen acquaint‑
ed with all the branches of ſuch a tedious work, for which leſs than a
year or two could ſcarce ſuffice : and becauſe we are not abſolutely ſure
that thoſe editions, which we give for their firſt, were really ſo : Mr.
Mattaire, who has taken ſuch pains to ſearch the beſt libraries of *London,*
Oxford, Paris, &c. for thoſe old monuments, that he thought he had exhau‑
ſted that ſubject, has nevertheleſs poſt dated the claim and rank of ſeveral
cities by ſome years ; if *Orlandi* may be credited, who afterwards rectify'd
them by the diſcovery of ſome older editions ; and who can tell what
time may produce, that may wholly invert our preſent order : thus for
inſtance ſome of the hiſtorians quoted in the laſt book, tell us that *Stras‑*
burgh, Cologn, Francford, &c. receiv'd the art before any others ; yet as
we have none of their works extant, but ſuch as were printed ſome years
                                                            after,

after, we have been oblig'd to give them a lower rank, and place them
after *Rome, Paris, Venice,* &c.   The reader may eafily remember that
Guttenbergh left *Mentz,* and fettled at *Strasburgh* fome years before the taking of the former, *i. e.* before *ann.* 1462; and that he taught *John Mentel* the Art in the latter: yet we meet with no edition done there of older
date than 1471, *viz.* the *Decretum Gratiani* printed by *Henry Egeftein.*
Tho' *Cologn* receiv'd fome of *Fauft's* fugitive fervants foon after his rup-
ture with *Guttenbergh,* yet the oldeft edition there, as yet known, is the
works of Pope *Leo* I, printed 1470.   What became of thofe impreffions
before that time, is fcarce worth our enquiring, fince the beft of thofe
which have been fince publifh'd, are far inferior to thofe done in *Italy,*
France, &c. in beauty of character, elegancy of compofition, correctnefs
and choice of MSS to print after; while themfelves proved indolent
enough to neglect thofe improvements even after they had been made in
other countries.

However 'tis probable they might have fufficient bufinefs in printing
fmall books of devotion, lives of faints, and legends; which, according
to the taft of thofe times, and of that nation in particular, were eagerly
bought up and thumb'd over, 'till fcarce a leaf was left; while the men
of learning and politenefs were more curious in laying up fuch only as
were a credit not only to the author and Printer, but to the Art it felf.
But however that be, I hope what I have faid will fufficiently convince
the reader, how cautious we fhould be in fixing the epocha's, and confequently the rank and claims of every city, in this refpect; fince we know
not but the next diligent fearcher may find matter enough to give this order a new turn.

I have fhown in the clofe of the laft book to what a degree of perfection the Art of Printing was advanc'd even before the year 1467, and given
there fome account of that noble edition of *Nich. Jenfon,* which is fuppos'd to be done *ann.* 1461, with the encomium which Mr. *Mattaire,* to
whom we are beholden for the firft account of it, about *eight* years ago, gives
to that mafter-piece of the Art, fince which I faw it at the Earl of *Pembroke's.*   What feems ftrange in that Printer, is, that from the time of this
date 1461 to 1471, not one of his impreffions is to be met with; fo that
neither their beauty, nor the efteem which they merited among the curious,

ous, have been able to preferve them, unlefs they are ftill latent in fome libraries, 'till fome accident brings them to light, as happen'd to the *Decor Puellarum*. 'Tis unreafonable to fuppofe that a man, who could, in fo fhort a time improve the Art, to a degree equal to the beft Printers of the next age, and publifh'd fo many excellent volumes from 1470 to 1480, fhould have continued idle for *nine* or *ten* years.

For this reafon many learned perfons are of opinion that the date of the book is wrong printed, and that one of the X's was either carelefsly or wilfully omitted, or taken up by the balls: but Mr. *Mattaire* will by no means allow this fuppofition, and gives his reafons againft it. But tho' I am partly of his opinion, yet there are two reafons that induce me to differ from father *Orlandi*, in allowing the preference to *Venice* before thefe laft mention'd cities: the firft is that this impreffion of the *Decor Puellarum*, doth not mention the place where it was done, and therefore might as well have been printed in any other place as at *Venice*; our annalifts give no other reafon for its being done there rather than any where elfe, but that *Jenfon* is found, ten years after the date of it, flourifhing in that city for the fpace of another ten years; but how to fill the chafm of the firft ten is what they are at a great lofs, as we fhall fee by and by. My fecond reafon is that had this book been really printed at *Venice, ann.* 1461, it would have been abfurd for the two *Spires*, who did not fettle there till about *ann.* 1468, to have taken upon them in their firft colophons the title of the firft perfons who taught the city of *Venice* the art of printing, or if they had, I doubt not but *Jenfon* would have taken care to have confuted fuch an affumption in fome of his own works, which he never did: allowing therefore the date of this work to be genuine, yet it would be too prefumptive to build the claim of that city upon a book, which for ought appears was not printed there.

I have ventur'd to fay fo much concerning this impreffion, in this introduction, becaufe of its being dated one year before the time our fecond book begins; fo that it could not fo properly be brought into the book itfelf, without antedating of it by that one year for the fake of one impreffion. Before Mr *Mattaire* gave us an account of it in his *Annal. Typogr.* moft authors gave the city of *Rome* the preference, to that of *Venice* by at leaft 4 or 5 years; and with refpect to the latter the two

Spires

Spires were allow'd to have been the firſt Printers there, according to the verſes that are at the end of their firſt works: this impreſſion therefore, doth at moſt prove *Jenſon* to have began to print ſome where, before thoſe two brothers were ſettled at *Venice*. What diſcoveries may be made hereafter, which may perhaps invert the preſent order, is what I am not concern'd about at preſent : my buſineſs is to ſettle it now according to the beſt light I have been able to get. I hope the reader will excuſe me, if the reſpect which I bear to thoſe noble cities, who gave the firſt encouragement to this infant Art, hath made me ſomewhat prolix, and what he may perhaps call over curious in ſettling this point of precedency ; for ſince it may be ſo eaſily ſettled and adjuſted from authentic records, it would have been an unpardonable omiſſion in me to have neglected it ; ſeeing every one of thoſe cities do ſtill value themſelves upon their rank, and have taken all poſſible pains to find out all the old monuments that would both ſupport and advance their reſpective claims.

I know that ſome annaliſts, in order to fill up the chaſm of *nine* years, have ſuppos'd that *Jenſon* went from *Venice* to *Paris*, where he taught the Art of Printing, and ſet up ſome preſſes, and inſtructed ſeveral, who became eminent Printers. But this is improbable on many accounts ; 1. Becauſe there are none of his works done at *Paris* ; 2. Becauſe his character is much finer than any us'd in *France* by the firſt Printers there ; 3. Becauſe he would have met with ſuch encouragement there, eſpecially conſidering it was his native country, that there had been no occaſion to return to *Venice* ; *laſtly*, becauſe, if he had taught ſo many ſkilful workmen in the Art, of which himſelf was then by far the greateſt maſter, it would have been unneceſſary to ſend for the three partners out of *Germany*, who did not however come to that city 'till about the year 1469, that is, *ſix* or *ſeven* years after his ſuppos'd coming thither. To this we may add, that upon this ſuppoſition the Art muſt have been brought to *Paris*, ſeveral years ſooner than the moſt authentick records, and the beſt writers allow, which ſeems as improbable ; as it is difficult to aſſign a place where *Jenſon* printed this work. From all which, allowing the date of the *Decor Puellarum*, as no place is mention'd where it

was

was printed, we are oblig'd for the reafons before mention'd to give the preference to *Rome*.

C H A P. I.

The City of *Mentz*, Monaftery of *Subiaco*, and the City of *Ausburgh*.

§. 1. Fauſt *and* Schoeffer *continue to print at* Mentz, *after the* Diſperſion *of moſt of their Servants, and the taking of that City.*

IF thoſe cities which gave the earlieſt invitations and encouragements to the Art of Printing, do ſo juſtly merit to be recorded in their re-ſpective ranks, that of *Mentz* certainly deſerves to be placed at the head of them, upon two accounts ; 1. becauſe it was the mother and inventreſs of it ; and 2. becauſe it ſtill continued to promote and cheriſh it, after it had been reduc'd to a foreign yoke. In the firſt book we conſider'd her in the former view, whilſt ſhe was the only one in the world, that engroſs'd both the Art and Artiſts to herſelf : but the conqueror's ſword was the occaſion of its being diſpers'd through the moſt eminent cities of *Europe* : 'till this time the beſt of *Fauſt's* ſervants being tyed by an oath of ſecrecy, and perhaps by ſome more powerful engagement, had not dar'd to for-ſake their maſter ; and if ſome few had ventur'd to break through their en-gagements, yet were they ſtill ſo imperfectly acquainted with the Art, that they never perform'd any work that could abide the teſt of time, if we except *N. Jenſon's* : but now as the city was depriv'd of its freedom and pri-vileges, it aboliſh'd the difference between maſter and ſervant, citizen and foreigner ; they began to look upon themſelves as free from all former ties, and at liberty to accept of the invitations which they receiv'd from *England, Italy, France,* &c. ſo that in the ſpace of very few years, there was ſcarce a metropolis or conſiderable city, where there was not one or more Printing-houſes ſet up : ſeveral monaſteries likewiſe began to entertain thoſe fugitives very early, as we ſhall ſhow anon ; and wherever any of thoſe workmen chanc'd to ſettle themſelves, they did not fail of meeting

with

with all the affiftance and encouragement, which the moft eminent men either for power or learning could give them.   However as they cannot be fuppos'd to have been all men of equal capacity and induftry, fo we need not wonder if they did not fignalize themfelves every where alike; but whilft one fort of them did in a fhort fpace improve the Art to a very confiderable degree, others of a more fluggifh nature, contented them-felves with going on in their old way, and fome of them even from bad to worfe.

W E need not doubt but that *Fauft* and *Schoeffer*, during this fad inter-val, were as much courted by other nations to leave *Mentz*, and betake themfelves to a place of greater tranquillity, and in a more flourifhing ftate: but their love to their native city, which had favour'd them fo much in its profperity, prevail'd upon them to continue there, and to car-ry on their bufinefs, as before.   This is apparent from the lift of their works, given in the firft book; and the edition of the great *Bible* which they printed in this very year, with that of *Tully's Offices three* years af-ter, gives ground to fuppofe, that the merit of this invention procur'd them fome particular regard and privilege from Archbifhop *Adolph*, as foon as it became known to him; which might induce them to go on with the bufinefs, as they had done formerly: however if they printed nothing between the year 1462 and 1465, (as we don't as yet find that they did) we may reafonably fuppofe, that the confufion in which the city then was, might obftruct it for that time, fince we don't find fuch a length of time between any of their other works: the truth is, we have very few or no particulars concerning them, except what we have given in the firft book, wherein I endeavour'd as well as I could to trace *Fauft*'s hiftory to the end of his life.   All that we can add concerning *Peter Schoeffer*, is, that he continued printing feveral confiderable volumes 'till the year 1479, which he then fubfcrib'd with his own name, and to fome of which (towards the latter end of his life) he added his coat of arms, which might in all probability have been given to him either by the Archbi-fhop or fome crown'd head: accordingly we find thefe words added to his colophons, *Suis configuando fcutis*, that they were mark'd with his own arms. He left a fon *John Schoeffer*, who became likewife an ex-cellent Printer at *Mentz*; but he muft in all likelihood have been very young

young when his father dy'd, feeing we find nothing printed by him 'till *ann.* 1503, when he acquainted his readers in the colophons to his firſt impreſſions, that he was the ſon of *Peter Schoeffer* and grandſon to *J. Fauſt, &c.* the firſt inventors of the Art ; and that himſelf was an excellent maſter of it, and an eminent citizen *(primarius civis)* of the metropolis of *Mentz,* but as this is beyond my propos'd epocha, I ſhall ſay no more of him.

I don't find any other Printer in the city of *Mentz,* during *Peter Schoeffer's* life : about 1480, we meet with one ſingle work of no great conſequence done there by one *Erhard Rewick,* and between the year 1470 and 1500, there are about *fifteen* impreſſions printed there without any Printer's name ; and therefore are ſuppos'd to have been done by ſome of *Fauſt's* ſervants, who dared not put their names to them, whilſt *Schoeffer* and his ſon liv'd.

Tho' I do not deſign to ſwell the following book with a liſt of the works done in every city, it having been done by the indefatigable Mr. *Mattaire* and father *Orlandi,* but only to give my readers an account of the moſt eminent Printers, that have ſignaliz'd themſelves in any of them, with the names and dates of the leſs conſiderable ones ; yet I hope the reader will forgive me, if my reſpect for *P. Schoeffer,* whoſe works are ſo much valued by the curious, as well for their antiquity, as for their elegance, correctneſs, and thoſe ornaments, which he ſtill caus'd the illuminators to beſtow on them to the laſt, induces me to ſubjoin a liſt of them ; they are as follows, with their colophons.

1. The edition of *Tho. Aquinas's Secunda ſecundæ,* printed in *fol. ann.* 1467, with an inſcription at the end to this purpoſe [1] ; ,, This noble ,, work intitled *Secunda ſecundæ* was finiſh'd in the famous city of *Mentz* ,, in *Germany* (which nation the divine goodneſs hath vouchſaf'd to ſig- ,, nalize with ſuperior gifts to all other nations of the earth,) by a new ,, invented Art of Printing, *&c.* without the help of any writing inſtru- ,, ment, *&c.* for the ſervice of God, by *Peter Schoiffer de Gernſheim,*

[1] Hoc opus præclarum *Secunda ſecundæ* alma in Urbe *Moguntina* inclitæ nationis *Germanicæ,* quam Dei clementia alti ingenii lumine donoque gratuito cæteris terrarum nationibus præferre illuſtrareque dignatus eſt, artificioſa quadam adinventione imprimendi ſeu characterizandi abſque ulla calami exaratione ſic effigiatum, & ad euſebiam Dei induſtria eſt conſummatum per *Petrum Schoiffer de Gernſheim.* Anno Domini MCCCCLXVII. Die ſexto menſis *Martii.*

,, *ann. Dom.* 1467, on the *fixth* day of *March.* ,,   In this he hath alter'd one letter of his firname, *viz.* the firft *e* into an *i*, in the next he chang'd the *i* into a *y*, according to Mr. *Mattaire*'s lift ; who likewife juftly cenfures his *latin fyntax* in writing *Dei clementia dignatus eft* ; tho' this hinders not his being a correct Printer, as well as tolerable good clerk for thofe times.

2. THE next is the *Inftitutiones Juris Imper. Juftinian. cum Gloffa*, in *fol.* ann. 1468.   The colophon is much to the fame purpofe with the former, in which he is very liberal of his incenfe to *Mentz* and the whole *German* nation.   It is fuperfluous to give a tranflation of it ; but the original may be feen in the margin[1] ; tho' *Schoeffer's* infcriptions in the following impreffions are fomewhat fhorter, yet we fhall likewife take the liberty of abridging them to avoid repetition.

3. ST *Jerom*'s *Epiftles* with an introduction in *2 vol. fol.* printed upon vellum *ann.* 1470. In this he ftyles himfelf that famous perfon *Peter Schoiffer*[2], the colophon of it has been given in another place ; and this is the book, part of the price of which, as we faid before, was remitted by him to the monks of St *Victor*, in order to procure their prayers for *Fauft* and himfelf.   Cardinal *Briffonet*, abbot of St *Germain* in the fields near *Paris*, gave another copy of it to the library of that monaftery ; and a *third* was prefented by *Arthur de Montauban* archbifhop of *Bourdeaux* to the library of the *Celeftins* at *Paris*, of which order he had been formerly.   Thefe are all ftill extant in the libraries abovemention'd.

4. VALERII MAXIMI *dictorum factorumque memorabilium libri* X. in *fol. ann.* 1471, in the noble city of *Mentz* upon the *Rhine* by *Peter Schoeffer de Gernfheim*, mafter of the Art of Printing[3].

---

[1] Præfens Inftitutionum præclarum opus alma in urbe *Moguntina* inclitæ nationis *Germanicæ* ; quam Dei clementia tam alti ingenii lumine donoque gratuito cæteris orbis nationibus præferre illuftrareque dignatus eft ; non atramento omni, non plumali canna neque ærea, fed artificiofa quadam ad inventione imprimendi feu characterizandi fic effigiatum, & ad eufebiam Dei induftrie eft confummatum per *Petrum Schoyffer de Gernfheim*, anno Dominicæ Incarnationis M CCCC LX VIII. 24 die Menfis *Maii*.

[2] Epiftolare beati *Ieronymi* cum introducto-rio per *virum famatum in hac Arte Petrum Schoiffer*, &c.   At the end of the introduction are thefe two verfes addrefs'd to the Saint ;

Nunc memoris memor efto tui, Ieronyme, *fancte,*
Ne pereat, Chrifto veniam pro crimine dante.

At the end of the book are the fix verfes quoted before at *pag.* 33, which begin thus ;
    Jam decet ut noftris concordent, &c.
[3] In nobili urbe *Moguntina Rheni* ——— per *Petrum Schoeffer de Gernfheim* artis imprefforiæ magiftrum, viii *Cal. Jul.*

5. THI

5. The *Latin bible* reprinted *ann.* 1472 by *Peter Schoeffer* with the same colophon as the former *Bible* of 1462.   It was finish'd on the eve of St. *Matthew* the apostle.

6. The *Corpus Canonicum* without the Printer's name, *ann.* 1472, *fol.* The *Catholicon* reprinted *ann.* 1472 with the same colophon as the former; and finish'd on St. *Matthew's* eve.   These three last being finish'd about the same time, show that *Schoeffer* had already more than one press at work.

7. St. *Austin's* book *De civitate Dei* in *fol.* with the commentaries of *Thomas de Valois* and *Nicholas Thevet,* printed *ann.* 1473, at the end whereof are the following words in *latin,* [1] *viz.* , This most excellent work of
,, *the city of God* written by *Aurelius Augustine,* the bright star of the or-
,, thodox city, with the commentaries of two learned professors of divi-
,, nity, distinguish'd with rubricks and a *table* of *contents,* was with great
,, labour finish'd in the famous city of *Mentz* in *Germany,* not with a
,, writing instrument, but by an artificial disposition of the figures of let-
,, ters, to the glory of the undivided trinity, and by the aid of the city
,, of God, by *Peter Schoiffer de Gernsheim,* on the *fifth* day of *September,*
,, 1473.

8. Henrici Harp or *Harpian. Ord. Min. Fr. Speculum aureum de-em præceptorum Dei,* by *Peter Schoiffer,* &c. in *fol.*   The colophon is almost the same with that of the *Secunda* of *Tho. Aquinas.*   It was finish'd on the *fourth* of the ides of *September ann.* 1474.

9. S. Bernardi *Clarevallensis Abbatis sermones,* fol. *ann.* 1475 [2]. Here *Schoeffer* began to put his mark, rebus, or coat of arms to his impressions.

10. Justiniani *Institutiones cum notis Accursii,* fol. *ann.* 1476, *Schoeffer* dedicated this work to Pope *Sixtus* IV, to the Emperor *Frederic,* and to the Archbishop of *Mentz* [3].

---

[1] Igitur *Aurelii Augustini,* civitatis orthodoxæ fidei is præfulgidi, *de civitate Dei* opus præclarissimum, binis sacræ paginæ professoribus eximiis id commentantibus, rubricis tabulaque discretum, celsa in urbe *Moguntina* partim *Alemania,* non calami per phrasim, characterum autem apicibus artificiose elementaum, ad laudem *Trinitatis individua, civitatis Dei præsidio,* operose est consummatum per *Petrum Schoiffer de Gernsheim* die V mensis *September* CIↃCCCCLXXIII.

[2] In nobili urbe *Moguntina Petrus Schoyffer de Gernsheim* suis consignando scutis consummavit, die xiv *April.* MCCCCLXXV.

[3] Sanctiss. in *Chrsto* P. ac Dom. D. *Sixto* Pap. IV invictissimo Dom. D. *Frederico* Roman. Imperat. semper *Augusto* generoso Dom. *Diethero de Isemburg* electo & confirmato *Mo-*

11. De-

11. DECISIONES *Rotæ Romanæ*, in *fol. ann.* 1477. The original o
the colophon may be seen in the margin [1].

12. JOHAN. *de Turre-cremata ord. prædic. Card.* expofition of the *pfalms*
in *fol.* by *Peter Schoiffer* at *Mentz*, 1478.

13. PAUL. *de S. Maria* Bifhop of *Burgos*'s *Scrutinium fcripturarum, fol*
ann. 1478. This work is infcrib'd to the fame Archbifhop of *Mentz* [2].

14. THE book of *Decretals* in *fol.* at *Mentz* by *P. Schoiffer*, 1479.

THIS is the laft book that is known to have been printed by him, who
is therefore fuppos'd to have dy'd about this time.

WE have now done with the city of *Mentz*; whofe fame in this ref
pect feems to have been intirely confin'd to *Fauft*'s family, and that no
further than to his grandfon *John Schoeffer*; feeing nothing confiderable
was ever printed there by any other perfon, except the travels of *Bernar*
Bredembach Dean of *Mentz*, into the *Holy-land ann.* 1486, by one *Erhar*
Rewick a native of *Utrecht*, whom we have juft mention'd. 'Tis now
time to come to thofe places, which fhow'd the earlieft fpecimens of this
Art; and to give the beft account we have of them.

§. 2. *The* MONASTERY *of* SUBIACO.

THE next place, that we know of, which fignaliz'd it felf in the Art
of Printing, is the monaftery of *Subiaco*, in *latin Monafterium Subla-*
cenfe, in the territories of *Campania*, in the kingdom of *Naples*, and fubject to the Pope; the monks of which are of the *Benedictin* order, and
very rich, having the lordfhip of no lefs than fourteen caftles. Here the
Art was introduc'd fo foon, that in the year 1465, there was publifh'd
an edition of *Lactantius*'s *Inftitutions* in *fol.* fo correct and elegant, and
in fuch a beautiful *Roman* character, that nothing feems wanting but the

---

guntino in nobili urbe *Moguntia Rheni* imprefforiæ artis inventrice elimatriceque prima, præfens Inftitutionum opus præclarum *Pet. Schoef-*
fer de Gernfhiem fuis confignan o fcutis, omni-
potente favente Deo, confummavit. 10 kal.
Jun. MCCCCLXXVI.

[1] Gravi labore, maximifque impenfis, *Ro-*
manam poft impreffionem, opus iterum e-
mendatum antiquarum novarumque decifionum
fuis cum additionibus Dominorum de *Rota*, in

civitate *Moguntia* artis imprefforiæ inventrice &
elimatrice prima, *Petrus Schoiffer de Gernfheim*
fuis confignando fcutis a te magiftra feliciter
finivit, prid. Non. *Jan.* MCCCCLXXVII.

[2] R in Chrifto *Pat.* D D. *Diethero* Archi-
præfule *Moguntino*, in nobili civitate *Moguntia*,
domicilio *Minervæ* firmiffimo, *Petrus Schoeffer*
de Gernfheim arte magiftra fuis confignando fcutis feliciter finivit, ad VIt Idus *Januarias.*
MCCCCLXXVIII.

name

name of the Printer.   What is ftill more furprizing is, that *Lactantius's*
quotations from the *Greek* authors are printed in a very neat *Greek* letter,
and extremely like that which the firft Printers of *Rome, Conrard Sweyn-*
heym and *Arnold Pannartz,* became noted for.   This induc'd father *Or-*
landi to think it was one of the firft effays, which thofe two *Germans* made
in that convent,   before they went to *Rome* ;   but this can by no means
be allow'd, becaufe tho' the character be like theirs, yet it appears by the
eight firft impreffions, which they printed at *Rome* ;   that they had no *Greek*
alphabet 'till *four* or *five* years after the date of this impreffion, as we fhall
fee in the next chapter : the following colophon is at the end of it.

> *In the year of our Lord* MCCCCLXV, *and the fecond year*
> *of the pontificate of Pope* Paul II. *in the* XIII *indiction,*
> *and on the laft day but one of the month of* October, *in the*
> *venerable monaftery of* Subiaco.

T H I S fcarce and curious edition is mention'd by *Montfaucon* in his *Di-*
arium Italicum p. 255, *& feq.* who hath given it an earlier date, *viz.* 1461 ;
but the miftake arifes from the laft figure's being imperfectly printed.
We know nothing of any other impreffion, which came from that Monaftery's prefs.

§. 3. *The* CITY *of* AUSBURGH.

T H E next is the city of *Ausburgh* [in *latin Augufta,*] one of the moft
opulent of the imperial cities in *Germany* ; in which the learned *John Bem-*
ler fet up a Printing-prefs,   about the year 1466.   The only two books,
that are known to be printed by him, are the *Latin Bible* in *fol.* with
this infcription —— *Per* Joh. Bemler, *Auguftæ Vindelic. ann.* 1466 ; and his
tranflation of Joh. Nach's *fumma præcipuorum capitum fidei chriftianæ,* out
of *Latin* into *high Dutch,* printed *ann.* 1472.   Whether he printed any
books during that fix years interval,   or was employed wholly in tranflating this laft work,   is difficult to determine, as well as whether he publifh'd any thing after 1472,   However there were *five* other eminent perfons in that city,   who,   tho' they did not begin fo foon as he,   yet prin-
R   ted

ted divers learned works ; moſt of them, being either citizens or natives of *Auſburgh*, might in all probability learn the Art from him.

As we have little or nothing particular concerning them except their impreſſions, we ſhall content our ſelves with giving their names, chara-ćter, and the time in which they printed, as far as we can diſcover it by their known works.

After the above nam'd *John Bemler* came.

2. John Shusler citizen of *Auſburgh*, a very good Printer, but whoſe works reach only from *ann.* 1471 to 1472.

3. Gonter Zainer *de Reutlingen*, who printed from *ann.* 1471 to 1484, we have but *eight* of his impreſſions.

4. Ant. Sorgius citizen of *Auſburgh* from 1477 to 1487, we have but *four* of his editions.

5. Erhard Raldolt of *Auſburgh*, who after having printed ſome works at *Venice*, with his partner *Bernard Pićtor*, 'till the year 1485 or be-yond, return'd to his own native city, and there ſet up a preſs about or before the year 1488, and continu'd printing 'till 1490, if not beyond: however he was a very diligent Printer for thoſe times, ſeeing he prin-ted in that ſhort ſpace *ſeven* books in *latin*.

6. The *laſt* we find in this city, is *John Schenſperger*, who printed a chronical work in *Latin*, with cutts *fol. ann.* 1497 ; but whether any be-ſides that, is not as yet known.

We find likewiſe two or three *Dutch* books printed here without Prin-ter's name, and of no great conſequence.

C H A P. II.

1. *The firſt* Printers *at* Rome; *their Patrons and Correćtors* ; *Books printed by them*, &c. *their Pe-tition to the* Pope.   2. *The City of* Tours, 1467. 3. *The Town of* Reutlingen, 1469.

SOON after *Auſburgh* had receiv'd the Art of Printing, it was brought to *Rome* by two Germans, *Conrard Sweynheim* and *Arnold Pannarts* ; who ſet up a printing-houſe there *anno* 1466, the ſecond year of the pontificate of *Paul* II. under the patronage of *John Andreas* Bishop of *Aleria*, who was the Popes library-keeper, justly fam'd for his learning and generosity. These printers affisted with that prelates purse, did immediately prepare an elegant, round, *Roman* character, and a sufficient quantity of the finest paper; they invented likewise such variety of spaces, as kept a beautiful distance between the words, and made their impreffions appear with the greatest neatness and exactness. Their margins were broad, and not only added a grace to the pages, but rendered them likewise convenient for the writing of notes, &c. and their ink was so excellent, that it still looks as fresh as if newly printed. In short, they were persons who valu'd their credit, and the honour of pleasing their patron more than riches; and spar'd neither cost nor labour, in order to make their impreffions as beautiful and correct, as poffible; which any one that has seen them, will own with pleasure.

I doubt not but the great acquaintance amongst the learned, which their noble patron's friendship procur'd them, might be a great means of their improving the art to such a degree; seeing such persons were best able to difcover the faults and inconveniences of the first printed books, which these *Germans* might more easily rectify when they became acquainted with them. These two partners settled themselves in the house of *Peter* and *Francis de Maximis*, brothers and Roman knights; where the Bishop of *Aleria* not only furnish'd them with the most valuable manufcripts, out of the *Vatican* and other libraries, but also prepar'd them himself, corrected their proofs, and prefix'd prefaces and dedications to their works, in order to recommend them the more to the learned world. This laborious tafk was follow'd by him with such application, that he fcarce allow'd himself time to sleep. What a value this great Bishop had both for the art and these two great masters of it, appears from his dedication to Pope *Paul* II. prefix'd to the edition of St. *Jerom's Epiftles*, which I shall now give the *Englifh* reader a translation of. ,, It was, says he, in your days, that among many other divine ,, favours this bleffing was beftow'd on the Chriftian world, that every ,, poor fcholar can purchafe for himfelf a library for a fmall fum,—— ,, that thofe volumes, which heretofore could fcarce be bought for an ,, hundred crowns, may now be procur'd for lefs than twenty, very well

,, printed

,, printed, and free from thofe faults with which manufcripts us'd to
,, abound. —— for fuch is the art of our printers and letter-makers,
,, that no antient or modern difcovery is comparable to it. Surely the
,, *German* nation deferves our higheft efteem, for the invention of the moft
,, ufeful arts. The wifh of the noble and divine Cardinal *Cufa*, is now ——
,, in your time accomplifh'd, who earneftly defir'd that this facred art,
,, which then feem'd rifing in *Germany*, might be brought to *Rome*.
,, Your Pontificate, (glorious in every refpect,) will be as immortal as
,, learning it felf. In which this art was brought and laid at your Holi-
,, nefs's feet. ——It is my chief aim in this epiftle to let pofterity know,
,, that the art of printing and type-making was brought to *Rome* under
,, *Paul* II. This blefling was certainly confer'd on us by our heavenly
,, Shepherd, that a book is now purchas'd for lefs than a binding for-
,, merly. Receive then, great, generous and glorious Pontif, the firft
,, volume of St. *Jerom*, gracioufly, —— and take the excellent mafters of
,, this art, *Conrard Sweynheym* and *Arnold Pannarts*, *Germans*, under
,, your protection, *&c.*

T HUS were thefe two printers carefs'd and encourag'd by moft of the
men of letters and fortune at *Rome*, and even by the Pope himfelf, who
frequently vifited their Printing-houfe, and examin'd with admiration
every branch of this new art ; which feem'd defign'd to recover learn
ing, and reflore that city to its antient luftre. This excited them to
approve themfelves worthy of all that efteem, which was fhew'd them, by
publifhing a vaft number of elegant impreffions, fome of which were fo
large that they could not be done without great labor and charges, as
will be evident from the lift of their works, which they prefented to the
Pope, of which we fhall give an account in its proper place.

W H A T their firft impreffion was, whether *Cicero*'s *Familiar Epiftles*
or St. *Auftin*'s book *de Civitate Dei*, is what authors can by no means agree
about ; that the former was printed at *Rome ann.* 1467, with a latin epi
gram, at the end of which their names are at full length ; and on the fol
lowing year, a new edition of St. *Auftin*'s book [1] is plain beyond contra

---

[1] Anno igitur codem 1468, opus *Auguftini*
de Civitate Dei eruditiffimum ; *Epiftolis Hiero-*
nymi difertiffimas, cum luminibus orationis tum
viribus argumentorum inftructas vulgaverunt.

—— Anno fuperiore *Tullianos* dederant *Epi*
tolas, hoc dant *Hieronymianas,* &c. *Annal. Typo*
graph. p. 44.

diction

diction : the difpute therefore feems to be about an edition of it, older by a year ; in which the Printer, without either naming himfelf, or the place in which it was done, contents himfelf with this colophon in *latin*, MCCCCLXVII, *in the third year of Pope* Paul II, *&c.* from which laft words, and the likenefs of the character with the *Lactantius* printed at *Subiaco*, and their firft impreffions at *Rome* ; they venture to affirm it to have been printed by them, without deciding whether at *Rome* or any where elfe. *Orlandi*, the laft writer upon the fubject, fpeaks of it as follows, *p.* 67 [1]. ,, It is certain that the firft work, that came out of their prefs has ,, been univerfally believ'd by authors to be St. *Auftin*'s book *de civitate* ,, *Dei* ; and tho' it mentions neither the name of the place or of the ,, Printer, yet being printed in a round Roman character, and in the ,, *third* year of *Paul* II. *ann.* 1467, as may be feen at the end of the faid ,, book ; ,, it cannot but have been done by them ; but I think I have two material objections againft it : the *firft* is, that if they had printed it at *Rome*, they would not have omitted it in their lift to the Pope ; and if at *Subiaco* or any where elfe, I cannot fee how they could print the *Cicero* at *Rome* in the fame year. *Secondly*, tho' the likenefs of the character feems to carry fome proof, and inclin'd him to believe the edition of *Subiaco* to have been alfo done by them ; yet it is evident by what we hinted in the introduction, that they were fo far from being furnifh'd with a *Greek* alphabet, that their firft works have all the *greek* done upon wood in a very inelegant manner ; and that whenever the quotation was above *three* or *four* words, they left a blank fpace to be fill'd afterwards with the pen ; whereas this of *Lactantius* has all the *greek* quotations printed in a beautiful caft letter : and therefore tho' we may allow this edition and that difputed one of St. *Auftin*'s, to have been done by the fame hand, yet it is plain it could not be done by thofe two *Germans*. If we can believe them, they'll tell us, that they began their firft tryal with a lefs confide_ rable work, *viz. Donatus*'s *grammar*, of which they printed only 300 cc_ pies : this is plain, both by their putting it at the head of their lift, and

[1] Egli e ancora certiffimo che il primo Libre, il quale ufci dalle ftampe di *Roma*, e fempre ftato creduto dagli autori il Sant. *Agoftino de civitate Dei*, il quale fe bene non addita il luogo, ove ftampato, ne il nome degl' Impreffori, tutta volta e di carettere tondo *Romano*, ftampato nel anno terzo di papa *Paolo* II, e nel milleſimo 467, come fi legge in detto libro. *Orland. origin. della Stamp.* pag. 67.

by their prefacing it with the words — *unde imprimendi initium sumpsimus*, after which they went on with [1] *Cicero's Epistles*, and the rest of their works without mentioning any edition of St. *Austin's* before the year 1468 : the epigram which we mention'd before, to be at the end of both these editions is as follows,

> *Hoc* Conradus *opus* Sweynheim *ordine miro*
> Arnoldusque *simul* Pannartz *una æde colendi*
> *Gente Theotonica* Romæ *expediere sodales*
> *In domo* Petri de Maximis.

I have already hinted their method of managing the *Greek* quotations, which they follow'd in the first volumes they printed, that is 'till the middle of the year 1469 : perhaps were they forc'd to it for want of workmen to cut the *Greek* alphabet; but at length, notwithstanding the neglect of that tongue might have excus'd them from the labour and expence of procuring setts of punches and matrices for Printing in that language, and the difficulty of finding workmen fit for such a task, they surmounted every obstacle of this nature, and form'd a compleat *Greek* alphabet, which they us'd in the edition of *Aulus Gellius*. Concerning this edition the Bishop of *Aleria* speaks thus; ,, However, this prov'd a very ardu-
,, ous task at first ; —— for a great part of the *Latin* was corrupted thro'
,, the negligence of the transcribers ; and a much greater part of the
,, *Greek* deprav'd, maim'd, and mutilated. Even that, which remain'd
,, entire, was scarce understood by *Latin* scholars, by reason of their ig-
,, norance in *Greek*. Some attempts have been made by persons skill'd
,, in both tongues, to restore this jewell to its former lustre ; but they,
,, either discourag'd by the difficulty, or diverted by other affairs, de-
,, sisted from the undertaking. ,, Thus writes that learned prelate, who
by the assistance of *Theodore Gaza*, a man of great abilities and universal
learning, perform'd this admirable work, rectify'd the *Latin* text, and
render'd the *Greek* intelligible. This edition was printed *ann.* 1469 in a
fine character, with the arguments to each book done in red by the illu-

[1] Concerning these two editions the letter on which they were printed, gave names to two sizes of *Printing-letter*; *viz.* from *Cicero's* Epistles, that siz'd Letter has been call'd *Cicero* ever since in *Italy, France,* and *Germany,* and answers to our *Pica*; *Holland* alone calls it *Mediaan :* the other is from St. *Austin's* book, which is call'd *Augustin* in several parts of *Europe,* but with us *English* ; but this I shall treat of more largely in the second volume.

minators.

minators. The quotations, which are long and more frequent, than in any other author, are printed in a fair *Greek* character, confidering this kind of printing was but in its infancy ; and what is extremely remarkable, they were fo correctly printed, that, as we are affur'd by Mr. *Mattaire*, in two whole pages, which contain'd feventy fix lines of a confiderable length, there were but *fourteen* faults of impreffion. The place, mention'd by that author, may be feen in *pag.* 46 of his *Annales Typogr.* where he has fet down thofe places, which were wrong printed, in order to convince the world, by the fmallnefs of their number, of the accuracy and diligence of thofe two Printers.

He tells us likewife that their *Greek* character was fomewhat large, round and even, without accents, ligatures, abbreviations, or any thing that might perplex the reader, except only that fometimes two or more words were join'd together without any fpace between them ; and that the periods had either no full ftop, or one in the wrong place ; fo that a perfon, not us'd to MSS. was doubtful where the fenfe ended. To this edition was prefix'd a dedicatory Epiftle of the Bifhop of *Aleria* to the Pope, wherein he acknowledges the kindnefs of his Holinefs and the Cardinal of *Oftia*, in fupplying him with money in his greateft exigencies ; and promifes to proceed with the utmoft induftry in furnifhing the learned world with new productions from the prefs. At the end of the book is a copy of verfes, fuppos'd to be written by the fame prelate, in praife of that edition, which are elegant for thofe times, the reader may find them at length in Mr. *Mattaire's Annals* p. 47. I fhall only give a *latin* octaftich, which was printed at the end of feveral of their impreffions, in commendation of the printers ; wherein the poet apologizes for the harfhnefs of their *German* names, offenfive without doubt to an *Italian* ear. They are inferted particularly in the firft edition of St. *Jerom's Epiftles*, and the great work of *Nich. de Lyra* entitled *Gloffa ordinaria in univerfam Bibliam*, 5 vol. *fol.* and in feveral others. The reader will find them in the margin [1]. Thus they continued printing without inter-

---

[1] Afpicis illuftres, lector, quicunque libellos, Si cupis artificum nomina noffe, lege. Afpera ridebis cognomina Teutona forfan : Mitiget ars Mufis infcia verba virum,

Conradus Sweynheim, Arnoldus, Pannartzque magiftri. *Roma* imprefferunt talia multa fimul, *Petrus* cum fratre *Francifco Maximus*, ambo Huic operi aptatam contribuere domum.

miffion.

miffion for feven years, whilft their patron procur'd 'em all poffible affiftance, and overlook'd their impreffions.   This is manifeft from the editions of *Tully*, *St. Jerom*, *Livy*, *Lucan*, the works of St. *Leo*, *Ovid*, *Nicholas de Lyra*, and efpecially of *Pliny*, with many more; in which the
Bifhop acquaints the world with the pains, taken by himfelf and his conftant affiftant *Theod. Gaza*, in correcting the originals, and prefiding
over the editions [1].   For this reafon Dr. *Mentel*, mention'd in our firft
book, affirms him to have been corrector of *Sweynheim's* prefs, and
Campanus Bifhop of *Teramo*, who was *Ulric Han's* patron, to have perform'd the fame office in his [2].   This is likewife afferted by *Naudé* in his
fupplement to the hiftory of *Lewis* XI [3], and divers other writers.   But
it is queftionable whether thofe excellent perfons can properly be call'd
correctors, or rather do not deferve the title of authors or editors.

H o w e v e r, there is an eminent paffage in this Epiftle of the Bifhop's
before *Pliny's* works, which as it demonftrates his care and diligence in
his province, ought not to be omitted.   ,, It was, fays he [4], the earneft
,, requeft of *Ireneus* Bp. of *Lyons*; and of *Juftin*, who of a philofopher
,, became a martyr, and likewife of St. *Jerom* and *Eufebius* of *Cefarea*, to
,, the lateft pofterity, that thofe, who were to tranfcribe their works,
,, would diligently compare the copies of them, and carefully correct
,, them: the fame requeft I make now, both with refpect to other books,
,, and in particular to *Pliny*, left that work, which coft fo much labour
,, and ftudy, (for he fpent above nine whole years in it) fhould again
,, fink into its former errors and inextricable darknefs. ,,

[1] — Juvit mirifice vir fummæ eruditionis ac
fapientiæ *Theodorus* meus *Gaza*, atque ita quidem, ut abfque illo nec, pene dixerim, mundus
hoc munus fuerit impleturus.   *Epift. Dedic.
ad Pap* Paul. II. prefix'd to *Pliny*.

[2] *Joannes Andreas* præful *Alerienfis*, qui in
ipforum libraria taberna ἐπανορθωτης effe non
dedignatus eft; ut nec *Campanus* in *Uldaric.
Mentel. de vera Typograph. origin.* p. 11.

[3] *Rome* fut une des premieres ou la preffe
roula par le moyen d'un *Uldaricus Gallus*, qui
dona fujet a l'eveque *Jo. Campanus*, lequel fe
rendit correcteur de fon imprimere de compo-

fer cette epigramme a fa louange, que raporte
Faernus. *Addit.* ad Hift. *Lud.* XI, p. 297.

[4] *Irenæus Lugdunenfis* epifcopus; item *Ju-
ftinus* ex philofopho martyr; item cum divo
Hieronymo Eufebius Cæfarienfis feram pofteritatem
adjurarunt, ut eorum defcripturi opera confer-
rent diligenter exemplaria, folerti ftudio emen-
darent: idem ego tum in cæteris libris, tum
maxime in *Plinio* ut fiat, vehementer obfecro,
obteftor, atque adjuro, ne ad priora menda &
tenebras inextricabiles tanti fudoris opus rela-
batur.

H i t h e r t o

HITHERTO we have feen the flourifhing ftate of this prefs, which in the fpace of fix or feven years at moft, *viz.* from *ann.* 1467 to 1472, oblig'd the world with no lefs than twelve thoufand four hundred and feventy five volumes, in eight and twenty editions, fome of them very large, and all beautiful and correct; fo that if their vaft labours and coft had met with fuitable fuccefs, they muft have rais'd a prodigious eftate. But, whatever be the caufe, 'tis certain that the greateft part of this library remain'd ftill in their hands for want of buyers; which reduc'd them to the moft neceffitous circumftances.   Father *Orlandi* endeavours to account for this ill-fuccefs, by fuppofing that their impreffions, being in Roman character, were diflik'd in thofe days, becaufe the learned had been fo accuftom'd to the old Gothick, as not to approve of this new, tho' preferable one.   This conjecture feems the more probable upon two accounts; 1. Becaufe feveral eminent printers were oblig'd to comply with the taft of the age, and ufe the old character, refembling that of MSS. 2. Moft of the firft Printers of *Paris, Venice, Rome,* &c. who began with the Roman, were forc'd by degrees to refume the old Gothick, which continu'd till almoft the middle of the next century, and prov'd the ruin of many valuable impreffions in divers parts of *Europe.* However that be, our two *Germans* under thefe preffing exigencies had recourfe to their great patron, who immediately drew up a petition in their names and behalf to Pope *Xyftus* IV, fubjoin'd to the fifth volume of *Nich. de Lyra's Gloff.* and prefented on the 20th of *March* 1472.   In this he reprefents their great merit and mifery in the moft pathetick terms imaginable; gives a catalogue of all the volumes printed by them, the greateft part of which was ftill unfold; prays his Holinefs to confider their deplorable cafe; and declares their readinefs to deliver up the unfold books either to him, or to whomfoever he fhould command, for their prefent fubfiftance.   The Bifhop, to fhew that he was fenfibly touch'd with their misfortune, prefaceth the petition in his own name, and requefts the Pope to hear the juft complaint of his worthy and induftrious Printers; and afterwards expofes their circumftances in their own words.   As this curious piece has never yet, that I know of, been tranflated into *Englifh*; I prefume the reader will be pleas'd to fee it, with the promis'd lift of their works, both which they printed with the

S   works

works *N. de Lyra*; *Chevillier* tells us he faw it at the beginning of *Tome* 5, of that great work. It is as follows,

„ ¹ Jo. Andr. to Xystus IV.

—„ Your Holinefs's humble petitioners *Conrard Sweynheim* and *Arnold*
„ *Pannartz*, our printers and the firft artificers, who practis'd this moft

¹ Jo. And. *ad* Xyst. IV.

—— Ut digneris mifericorditer occurrere, fervuli tuæ fanctitatis *Conradus Sweynheim* & *Arnoldus Pannartz*, impreffores noftri ac utiliffimæ hujus fictoriæ artis primi in *Italia* opifices implorant. —— Vox imprefforum fub tanto chartarum fafce laborantium, &, nifi tua liberalitas opituletur, deficientium ifta eft. —— Nos de *Germanis* primi, tanti commodi artem in *Romanam* curiam tuam multo fudore & impenfa deceffori tui tempeftate deveximus. Nos opifices librarios cæteros, ut idem auderent, noftro exemplo incitavimus —— Indicem fi perlegeris imprefforum a nobis operum, miraberis —— vel chartas huic librorum copiæ potuiffe vel lineamenta fufficere—— Impreffi funt noftro ftudio libri, qui in fubjectis fuo ordine tibi recenfebuntur.

1. Donatus pro puerulis, ut inde principium dicendi fumamus, unde imprimendi initium fumpfimus, —— *without date.* —— CCC.
2. Lactantii Firm. Inftitutionum divinarum lib. vii. —— *Anno* 1468　DCCXXV.
3. M. Tull. Cicer. Epiftolæ familiares —— 1467　DL.
4. M. T. Cicer. Epiftolæ ad Atticum —— 1470　CCLXXV.
5. Roderic epifcop. Zamorenfis Speculum vitæ humanæ —— 1468　CCC.
6. D. Auguft. de civitate Dei —— 1468　DCCCXXV.
7. D. Hieronymi epiftolæ, vol. II —— 1468　MC.
8. M. T. Cicero de oratore cum cæteris, —— *without date* —— DL.
9. M. T. Cicer. pars libelli de philofophia —— 1471　DL.
10. L. Apuleius Platonicus cum Alcinoo —— 1469　CCLXXV.
11. Auli Gellii noctium Atticarum lib. —— 1469　CCLXXV.
12. C. Cæfaris Commentaria —— 1469　CCLXXV.
13. Divi Platonis defenfio, —— *without date* —— CCC.
14. P. Virgil. Maron opera omnia, —— *without date* —— DL.
15. T. Livius Patavinus cum Epitome decadum, ——*without date*—— CCLXXV.
16. Strabonis Geographia, —— *without date* —— CCLXXV.
17. M. Annæus Lucanus —— 1466　CCLXXV.
18. C. Plinii Veronenf. Natur. hiftor —— 1470　CCC.
19. C. Suetonius Tranquillus de xii Cæfar. —— 1470　CCLXXV.
20. Div. Leonis Pap. fermones —— 1470　CCLXXV.
21. M. Fab Quintilian. Inftitution. Oratoriar. —— 1470　CCLXXV.
22. D. Thom. Aquin. Continuum catenæ aureæ, —— *without date* —— DL.
23. D. Cypriani Epiftolæ —— 1471　CCLXXV.
24. Biblia cum Opufculo Arifteæ —— 1471　DL.
25. Silius Italicus cum Calphurnio & Hefiodo —— 1471　CCLXXV.
26. M. T. Orationes cum invectivis in Verrem, *&c.* —— 1471　CCLXXV.
27. P. Ovid. Nafon. opera omnia, 2 vol. —— 1471　DL.
28. Nichol. de Lyra, Gloffa in tot. Bibl. 5 vol. —— 1471 -- 1472　MC.

„ ufeful

,, ufeful invention in *Italy*, implore your affiftance. ———— This is the
,, voice of thofe printers, who labour under fuch a load of printed vo-
,, lumes, that they muft fink under it, unlefs timely reliev'd by you.
,, ———— We were the firft of the *Germans*, who introduc'd this excellent
,, art, with vaft labour and coft, into your territories, in the time of
,, your predeceffor; and encourag'd, by our example, other printers to
,, do the fame. If you perufe the catalogue of the works printed by
,, us, you will admire how and where we could procure a fufficient
,, quantity of paper, or even rags, for fuch a number of volumes. ————
,, The books, done by us, are fubjoin'd in the following order. ,,

The lift of thofe books confifting entirely of *Latin*, I have put them
with the original of the petition in the margin, and have added the date of
the year wherein each was printed, as far as it could be procur'd, ther
being none in the catalogue. The order of time is not obferv'd, bi
only the number of copies of each. We may likewife infer what book
were then moft efteem'd, not upon the account of their authors, but o
their ufefulnefs, by the proportionate number printed of them. The
petition thus proceeds.

,, The total of thefe volumes amounts to twelve thoufand four hun-
,, dred feventy five, a prodigious heap, and intolerable to us, your Holi-
,, nefs's printers, by reafon of thofe unfold. ——— We are no longer able
,, to bear the great expence of houfe-keeping for want of buyers; of
,, which there cannot be a more flagrant proof, than that our houfe,
,, otherwife fpatious enough, is full of *Quire-books*, but void of every
,, neceffary of life:——— we are ready, if your goodnefs fhall judge it

Horum omnium voluminum fumma — effi-
cit codices duodecies mille quadringentos feptu-
aginta quinque; acervum quidem ingentem, &
nobis imprefforibus tuis, qua parte reftat, in-
tolerabilem —— ingens fumptus ad victum ne-
ceffarius, ceffantib s emptoribus ferri amplius a
nobis nequit; & ementes non effe nullum eft
gravius teftimonium, quam quod domus noftra
fatis magna plena eft quinternionum, inanis rerum neceffariarum -- parati fumus pro clementiæ
tuæ arbitrio de noftra merce *i. e.* de impreffis
quinternionibus noftris tibi tot tradere, quot
volueris, & quibus volueris. ——— Tua incredi-
bilis manfuetudo fubveniat nobis de aliquo offi-
cio, unde poffimus nos & noftros alere. Impenfa eft facta in folius *Nicolai de Lyra* a nobis
voluminibus tanta, ut amplius nihil nobis fu-
perfit ad vivendum. Si venderemus opera
noftra, non folum a pietate tua nihil peteremus,
fed ultro in præfentium temporum articulo, in
quo te plurimum egere non nefcimus, ipfi noftra offerremus; faciemufque quotiens tuo ad-
jumento fortuna nobifcum uf effe videbitur
fronte fereniore Interea, Pater Sancte, adju-
vent nos miferationes tuæ, quia pauperes facti
fumus nimis —— xx facti CCCCLXXII,
Pontificatus tui Clementiffimi anno primo.

,, meet,

„ meet, to deliver up as much of our wares, *i. e.* printed fheets, as you
„ pleafe, to your felf, or to whom you fhall order. -- We therefore be-
„ feech your great Clemency to beftow fome place upon us, whereby
„ we may be enabled to maintain our felves and families.   The im-
„ preffion of *Nicol. de Lyra*'s works hath prov'd fo chargeable, that we
„ have nothing left to live upon.   Could we fell our books, we fhould
„ be fo far from defiring any thing at your hands, that on the contrary
„ we fhould willingly contribute of our own to you, whofe exigencies
„ at this juncture we are well acquainted with ; and this fhall readily be
„ perform'd, whenever fortune, by your affiftance, fhall fmile upon us.
„ In the mean time, let your Holinefs pity and help us, whofe neceffity
„ is fo exceeding great. ---- *March* xx, *ann.* MCCCCLXXII, and in the
„ firft year of your moft gracious pontificate. „

Thus were thefe indigent perfons oblig'd to expofe their mifery to
the world; with what fuccefs, I cannot learn : tho' it is evident from
their printing a confiderable time after, as fhall be fhewn, that fome
method muft have been taken to extricate them from thofe wretched circumftances. *Sweynheim* indeed publifh'd nothing after the year 1473,
and for that reafon is fuppos'd by fome to have dy'd about that time ;
yet his partner *Pannartz* continu'd printing till *ann.* 1476, in a fmaller
character than what was us'd by him in company with the former.   It
will not perhaps be amifs to remark that the word *quinternio* in the petition, tranflated by us *Quire-books*, fignifies a quire of five fheets fo impos'd, that they are put into one another by the book-binder, and the
firft fheet contains the *firft* and *laft* of the 10 leaves, the *fecond* the 2d and
9th, *&c.* this method oblig'd 'em to compofe *twenty* whole pages of matter, before they work'd it off at prefs ; and requir'd a prodigious quantity of letter to every Font.   All the editions of thefe two partners as yet
known, from their firft fettlement at *Rome*, *ann.* 1467 to 1473 in which
Sweynheim is thought to have dy'd, are 40 in number, all folio's and in
latin; fome of them pretty confiderable, fuch were their Bible of 1471
mention'd in the former book in two large volumes, and *Nicol. de Lyra* in
five larger ones; the works of Pope *Leo* firnam'd the Great, *&c.*   As for
thofe which *Pannartz* printed afterwards by himfelf, we have not been able
to difcover above fix, all *latin* folio's, but none fo confiderable as the three
laft

laft named: he began to ufe the *Regiftrum Chartarum* (which is the fignatures plac'd at the end of the book thus, A B C D, &c. and fo on for as
many fheets as the book contains) in his edition of *Herodotus* tranflated by
Laurent. Valla, and printed *ann.* 1475; his latter works are done in a very
elegant charaƈter; the laft of which is the *Quæftiones de Veritate* of *Thom.
Aquinas.* It muft be obferv'd that many of thefe editions are printed without date, and fometimes without their names, but moft of them have
one or the other of the Epigrams mention'd before *viz. Hoc Conradus opus*
&c. or *Afpicis illuftres,* &c. but oftener the latter.

THESE are all the particulars I could meet with concerning thefe two
Printers. The next in rank is,

ULDRIC HAN ann. MCCCCLXVIII.

ULDRIC HAN is commonly call'd in *Latin, Gallus,* in *Italian Gallo,* and
in *French Coq,* which fignifies a *Cock*; for every writer upon this fubjeƈt,
has thought fit to tranflate his name into that language in which he wrote.
This Printer came and fet up a Printing-prefs at *Rome* within a very
fhort fpace after *Sweynheim* and *Pannartz.* He was a perfon fo accomplifh'd in his art, that feveral nations have claim'd him, and in particular the *Germans* and *French.* Thefe latter grounded their pretences upon the following authority. *Anthony Campanus* bifhop of *Terumo,* the
moft diftinguifh'd poet and orator of his time, perform'd the fame office
to him, which the bifhop of *Aleria* did to the two *Germans, viz.* of preparing and correƈting his copies, revifing his editions, and writing epiftles and commendatory verfes upon them. He obferving that *Han* had
latiniz'd his name, and fubfcrib'd one or two of his impreffions *Uldaricus
Gallus,* particularly the edition of the univerfal hiftory of *Rodoricus San-
ius* a *Spaniard,* whom Pope *Paul* II made governour of the caftle of St
Angelo and bifhop of *Palentino,* took occafion to miftake his name will-
ully, (for he could not poffibly be ignorant of his being a *German,*) and
o reprefent him as a *Frenchman,* not fo much out of refpeƈt to that na-
ion above the *Germans,* as for the fake of a pun in his epigram, which
ou will find in the margin [1]. The witticifm confifts chiefly in this,

---

[1] Anfer *Tarpei* cuftos Jovis, unde quod alis   *Uldricus Gallus*: ne quem pofcantur in ufum,
   Conftreperes, *Gallus* decidit; ultor adeft   Edocuit pennis nil opus effe tuis.

that the *Gauls* or *French* being difcover'd by the noife of the geefe one night in their attempt to furprize the *Roman* Capitol, a countryman of theirs had found out a way to be reveng'd of them, by teaching the world an art of writing without the help of their quills. Thefe verfes are annex'd to an edition of *T. Livy* by *U. Han* without date, and quoted by feveral authors.

MICH. FERNUS in his life of that Bifhop tells us, that he learn'd this epigram of a *Turk*, whom he met with in a journey to the Pope's territories; and who gave him account of his converfion to the chriftian religion, and his early love of eloquence, which induc'd him to leave *Turky* and come to *Rome*, to fee the famous *Paul* II. and *Campanus*, whofe works he had carefully collected; and amongft other things recited this epigram. However, 'tis evident that he was a *German* by his adding the name of his country to that of *Gallus* in feveral of his editions. Thus, in that of *Cicero de Oratore, ann.* 1468. he calls himfelf *Ulricum Gallum de Wienâ*; in St *Auftin de civitate Dei ann.* 1474, *Ulricum Gallum Almanum*; in fome others *Ulricum Gallum de Bienna* & *de Ingolftat*. *Wimpheling* undertook to prove him a *German* againft *Fernus*, who in his life of *Campanus* chang'd *Gallus* into *Gallicus* to make him an abfolute *Frenchman*, and afcrib'd this miftake to his having tranflated his name into *latin*; which, as *Hermolaus Barbarus* afferts, ought never to be done. But in this he did no more than what was frequent among the *Germans* and others, who to foften the harfhnefs of their firnames, either alter'd or latiniz'd them; fo *Fuft* chang'd his into *Fauftus*, *Schoeffer* into *Opilio*, *Leichtenftein* into *Levi lapis*, *des Rouges* into *de Rubeis*, and the learned *Stephens* into *Stephanus*; which cuftom ftill prevails in foreign parts: and the famous Monf. *le Clerc* of *Amfterdam*, ftiles himfelf *Joan. Clericus* in all his *latin* works. To return to *Ulric Han*.

THE time of his firft coming to *Rome* is not eafily determin'd. Some affirm that he was fettled there before *Sweynheim* and *Pannartz*, as *Wimpheling*, *Monf. Naude*, and Dr. *Mentel*; but this feems improbable upon two accounts. 1. Becaufe we have no edition of his fo ancient as thofe of the two laft nam'd; 2. Becaufe the Bp. of *Aleria*, who was the editor of all the firft impreffions of thefe, determines in their favour; and his teftimony is of much greater weight in this cafe, than that of

thofe

thofe writers. He attributes *the honour to* Sweynheim, *&c. of having founded the firſt Printing-houfe at* Rome, *and brought the Art from* Germany, *in the preceding Popes reign, and by their example encourag'd others to do the like* ; as he fpeaks in the petition to *Xyſtus* IV, above quoted. Now *Xyſtus's* predeceſſor was *Paul* II, who was advanc'd to that dignity in *Auguſt* 1464; and in his days they came to *Rome.* If *Campanus*, the patron of *Ulric*, had known of his fettling there before them, he would certainly have contradicted the Bp. of *Aleria*, and maintain'd the priority to the man, who, under his protection, prov'd fo indefatigable in his bufinefs, that himfelf was engag'd night and day in revifing his works [1]. The merit of this Printer appears from his fine impreſſions, and the choice that his patron made of him to publifh thofe works, which he had procur'd and corrected with the utmoſt application, as well as from the praifes, which he gives him in his prefatory epiſtles and verfes. We find by the liſt of his books, that he frequently neglected the date of the impreſſion and his own name. The former defect is fupplied, as far as poſſible, from fome material circumſtances, either in the epiſtles affix'd to them, or elfewhere in the book ; and the latter by a diligent comparing of one edition with another ; for there is fome peculiar difference between the characters of the firſt Printers, by which a nice obferver may judge of the author.

Thus Mr. *Mattaire* remarks that the types of *Con. Sweynheim* and *Arn. Pannartz*, were eafily known by their having a long *ſ* at the end of words, the *i* without a point, and no diphthongs : thofe of *Nic. Jenfon* were much more round and neat, with the diphthongs, æ and œ ; whereas *Jo. Spires* made ufe of ę for æ, and *Ulric Han* ufes a fingle *e* inſtead of a diphthong.

About 1473, *Han* took *Simon Nicolai de Luca* into partnerſhip with him till the end of the year 1474, after which he printed by himſelf till 1476. There was alfo a brother of his, call'd *Lupus Han*, whofe name ſtands alone in fome of thofe impreſſions, which are neverthelefs allow'd to be *Ulric's*

---

[1] Cum Ulricus quidam *Gellicus*, qui formas in urbem literarias nuper intuliſſet, illum interquiefcere aſſiduis emendationibus non permitteret, remque literariam ex magnis difficultatibus inopiaque ad ingentem ubertatem gloriofiſſimo illo & divino opificio evocaret, *&c. Fern. in Vita Campani.*

by reafon of the likenefs of the character &c. and added to the lift of his works by the two lateft annalifts, Mr. *Maittaire* and Father *Orlandi.* He affected to put at the end of fome of his editions, the colophon of *John Fauft* and *Peter Schoeffer*. *Non atramento, plumali calamo*, &c. *i. e.* that it was not done with pen, ink, or any other writing inftrument, &c.

ANN. 1473 he began to print a regifter in two columns at the end of his *Virgil*: all his other editions, as yet known, are 21 in number, the firft of which is *Cicero de Oratore* in 3 books *ann.* 1468, the laft *Tit.* *Livy* in *Italian* 1476: this laft is in three volumes *fol.* the 2d of which has an error in its date, where they have printed 1460 inftead of 1476. This work has not indeed his name, but thofe who have feen it make no doubt but it was printed by him.

THE two *Germans* had reafon to tell the Pope in their petition, that their example had encourag'd many more Printers to come and fettle at *Rome*, feeing we find no lefs than *thirteen*, who practis'd the fame Art there between 1470 and 1490, befides the brother of *Uldric Han*, and his partner *Simon de Luca*; and *eight* or *nine* of whom were actually fettled there within a few years after the two former; but as we have nothing left particularly concerning them, except their names and their works, we fhall juft mention them as they came in courfe of time.

4. GEORGE LAVER *de Herbipoli* 1470 alias *Wortsburg*, he wrought in the Monaftery of St. *Eufebius* at *Rome*, as we find by an epigram of eight verfes in *latin* rhyme written, as is fuppos'd, by his corrector *Celeftine Pulverinus*; and printed at the end of his edition of *Tractatus de Inftituti-one fimplicium Confefforum, ann.* 1472; he had a partner fome fpace of the time, *viz. Leonard Pelugi*; we have but *five* editions of his; the *firft* is that of St. *Chryfoftom*'s homilies, tranflated into *latin* by *Fr. Aretine, fol. ann.* 1470; the *laft* is *Durandi Speculum, ann.* 1479; he had another corrector nam'd *Pomponius*.

5. ADAM ROT 1471, he us'd likewife *Fauft*'s colophon, and in the firft of the two editions we have of him, ftyles himfelf *Clericus Metenf. Diocef.* his laft edition is dated 1474.

6. JOHN

6. John Philip *de Lignamine* 1472, he was a native of *Meſſina* and a *Sicilian* knight, and intimate with Pope *Sixtus* IV, to whom he inſcrib'd a book of his writing, *De unoquoque Cibo & Potu utili homini & nocivo, & eorum primis qualitalibus.* *Malinkrot* mentions him *pag.* 84 upon the authority of *Simler,* which laſt affirms him to have printed the following works at *Rome, viz. Quintilian, Suetonius,* the works of St. *Leo, Laĉlantius,* St. *Ambroſe,* *Tully's Offices, Laur. Valla's Elegantiæ,* and *Horatii opuſcula:* but we find none of theſe editions in the liſt of his works, but only four leſs conſiderable ones, the *three* firſt in *Italian,* and the laſt, *Euſebius's* hiſtory tranſlated into *Latin* by *Rufinus,* and printed *ann.* 1476.

7. Stephen Planck of *Padua* 1472, we have *eight* editions of his, the laſt of which is dated 1497.

8. George Sachel *de Reichenbalt,* 1474; his laſt edition of *three* is dated 1477.

9. John Reynard *de Eningen,* 1475; we have but one edition of his printed at *Rome, ann.* 1475, 14 years after which, we find him printing at *Strasburgh.*

10. John *de Nicolao Haneymar de Openheim,* ⎫
11. John Schusener *de Bopardia,*   ⎬ 1475,
⎭

we have but two editions of theirs, both dated 1475.

12. John Tibull *de Amidanis Cremoneſe,* 1475; the two editions we have of his bear the ſame date.

13. Eucharius Silber of Wirtzburgh, 1475.

This *Silber,* alias *Franck,* a *German* and native of *Wirtzburgh,* ſignaliz'd himſelf at *Rome* by the fineneſs of his letter, which were of the *Venetian* ſort. He ſet up his Printing-houſe in *Campo di Fiore;* and not only tranſlated his name *Silber* [*Silver*] into *latin,* but likewiſe into *greek;* ſo that ſome of his editions are ſubſcrib'd *Achirion* and *Argyrion,* others *Argenteus,* added to that of *Franck.* The works we have of his are *twenty one* in number, from *ann.* 1475 to 1500: however he continued printing there many years after, but either the greateſt part of theſe laſt have been loſt, or elſe he printed but little, ſince we meet only with two editions of his from 1500 to 1509, in Mr. *Mattaire's* annals.

T   His

His correctors were *Michael Fern* firnam'd *Archipoeta, Bartholomew Salicetus,* and *Ludovicus Regii*; the firſt of whom collected with prodigious induſtry all biſhop *Campanus*'s works, which he caus'd to be printed in two different places within *ſix* months of each other, *viz.* at *Venice* and *Rome*, in the order in which he had digeſted them. Theſe impreſſions were printed ſo incorrectly, that he was oblig'd to inſert an *Errata* in *Silber*'s edition ; wherein he expreſſes a vaſt deal of indignation, that a work, in which he had labour'd ſo much, ſhould yet be publiſh'd ſo full of faults ; and gives it the following title, *Vis ex ſtulto demens, idemque ex demente inſanus fieri? Libros* Romæ *primus imprime, Corruptorum recognitio.* After this he proceeds to the *Errata,* with an acknowledgement of his own errors, and endeavours to clear the Printers of others. He ſhows the care which he had taken to render the edition correct ; but that his efforts were fruſtrated by the careleſſneſs of the Printers, who, being tir'd with a days labour, correct their proofs imperfectly, and frequently neglect or omit the author's corrections.

In the ſequel of this hiſtory we ſhall have occaſion to mention ſome *Errata's* of a much greater length than the foregoing, which *Fern* complains ſo loudly of, tho' this contain'd four large pages in *fol.* The two laſt Printers in this city before 1500 are :

14. Simon *de Nicolo* of *Luca* 1478, who had been ſometime partner to the fam'd *Uldric Han,* and of whom we have but one edition. And,

15. Peter *de Turre,* ann. 1490, in which year he printed *Ptolemy*'s *Coſmography* in a large *folio* with maps and cutts, and in a beautiful character, [*Orland.* p. 79.] which is all that we have of his. We find about twenty more editions without Printer's names ; however the reader will eaſily ſee by this liſt of Printers, and the ſcarcity of their works, that the Art began to dwindle very much before the cloſe of the century ; and if he conſults Mr. *Mattaire* upon the next, he will find it ſtill much thinner of both ; but whether for want of encouragement, or what other cauſe, is not my buſineſs to enquire.

§. 2. *The*

§. 2. *The City of* Tours, 1467.

TOURS is an Archiepifcopal city of *France*; in which we meet with but one book printed. This, 'tho done in an old *Gothick* character, (which was not as yet us'd in any place but *Mentz*) is fo elegant, that it may be efteem'd a mafter-piece of that kind. 'Tis to be regretted, that the Printer of fuch an excellent work fhould be unknown. The impreffion was done in the Archbifhop's palace; but if the reader upon that account, fhall expect it to be a piece of devotion, he will be vaftly miftaken; for it is not unufual with ecclefiafticks of the moft elevated ftations in that church, to have a greater relifh for gallantry than religion. The book is the loves of *Camillus* and *Emilia*; to which is fubjoin'd another upon the fame fubject, tranflated from *Boccacio* by *Aretin*, and is infcrib'd as follows.

FRANCISCI FLORII *Florentini* de Amore *Camilli* & *Æmiliæ* liber, *expletus eft* Turonis, *editus in domo* Guillelmi Archiepifcopi Turonenfis, *anno millefimo quadringentefimo fexagefimo feptimo, pridie calendas Januarii,* 4to. De duobus Amantibus Libellus in latinum, ex *Boccacio*, transfiguratus per *Leonardum Aretinum*. This book is join'd to the former, and printed in the fame character and form.

THE following book was printed in the fame city a long time after, *viz.* La vie & miracles de monfeigneur St. *Martin* tranflatee de Latin en Francois: *imprimee par Mathieu Lateron, fol. 7me de May, Tours. 1496.*

N. B. *Tho' we defign to treat in a diftinct book of the introduction and progrefs of Printing in* England; *yet it is not amifs to remark here, that* Oxford *comes next in courfe to the city of* Tours, *according to our premis'd criterion of the oldeft editions; for the moft ancient impreffion printed in that univerfity, is St.* Jerome's *expofition of the apoftles creed* 4to, *bearing date* ann. 1468, a copy of which is now in the Earl of *Pembroke's* library.

§. 3. *The Town of* Reutlingen, 1469.

THIS town of *Reutlingen*, and the city of *Venice* are next; the former of which being nearer to *Mentz*, may fo far be allow'd the firſt rank: It is a fmall town in the dutchy of *Wirtembergh*, in which *John de Averbach* fet up a Printing-houfe *ann.* 1466, and publifh'd the two following editions;

 1. Biblia Latina, *fol.* per *Johannem de Averbach*, 1469.

 2. Alvari Pelagii Hifpani ordin. min. fumma de planctu ecclefiæ Chriftianæ, *Reutlingæ.* 1474.

This is a very fcarce book, and has not the Printer's name, but is neverthelefs fuppos'd to have been printed by *Averbach*: It is in *fol.* and the next edition of it was printed at *Ulm* ann. 1473. This *John Averbach* muſt not be confounded with the learned *J. Amerbach* of *Bafil*, of whom we fhall fpeak in its proper place.

C H A P.   III.

The City of Venice, 1469; *the Names, Character, &c. of the Printers who flouriſh'd in this City from* ann. 1469, *to* Aldus Manutius's *Time,* 1494

AS the city of *Venice* has excelled all others, not only in the number of workmen and editions, but likewife in the goodnefs and excellency of them, I fhall be forc'd to divide it into two chapters; in the firſt of which I fhall fpeak of thofe Printers who flouriſh'd from its firſt fettlement there by *John* and *Vindelin de Spira*, to the time of the great *Aldus Manutius*, whofe merit alone will very well deferve to be fpoken of in a chapter by it felf, tho' there were no others to bear him company in it.

With refpect to thofe firſt Printers, 'twill be fuperfluous to repeat here what I have faid, in the introduction of this book, concerning

Nich.

Nich. Jenson, and the reasons for suspending my judgment concerning his edition of 1461, and allowing the priority to the foregoing cities before that of *Venice*.　　There will be further occasion of speaking of that Printer, when we shall come to thoseother works of his, printed between the years 1470 and 1480.　　In the mean time I beg leave to remind the reader of the remark upon this head, which we just hinted in the introduction, *viz.* that the verses at the end of the first impression by *John* and *Windelin* of *Spire ann.* 1469, evidently prove them to have been the first who brought the Art to that city.　　The reader will find them in the margin [1].　　Mr. *Mattaire* who hath a particular regard for his countryman *Jenson*, and first discover'd to the world the edition in dispute, very justly intimates, that there was such an emulation among the first Printers, that they made no scruple of claiming the priority from each other, right or wrong; either by false dates, as we hinted before, or by pompous verses annex'd to their works; from which he infers a probability that these two brothers might do so: whereas *Jenson*, in his opinion was too modest, to have been guilty of such a piece of arrogance. For my part I can't see any necessity of accusing either side of such a fault, seeing they never charg'd each other with it; besides *Jenson* in all probability printed his book somewhere else, and therefore might indeed be too modest when he came to *Venice*, to challenge the priority from them as to that place in particular.　　However, as to the point of modesty, I own I am at a loss to what side to give it, seeing all the first impressions, both of *Jenson* and of the two brothers, are back'd with epigrams equally magnificent, and I don't see where there would have been the least immodesty in either to have ascertain'd a just claim, against an unjust assuming rival.　　Let me add, that (if there was any wilfull mistake on either side, which I think there was not) it is more probable *Jenson* should have committed it, than the two brothers; because he might easily, if there was occasion, excuse it by making his date pass for an error of impression; whereas the two *Germans* publish'd themselves, in words at length and

[1] Primus in Adriaca formis impressit aenis
　　Urbe libros *Spirâ* genitus de stirpe *Johannes.*
　　In reliquis sit quanta, vides, spes, lector, habenda,
　　Quam labor hic primus calami superaverit artem.
　　　　　　MCCCCLXVIIII.

in

in the plaineſt terms, the firſt Printers at *Venice*, and ſo left no room for evaſion.   I ſhall therefore begin with them, who were not inferior to *Jenſon* himſelf.

John and Vindeline of Spire, 1469.

They were natives of *Germany*, but whether of the city of *Spire*, whoſe name they bear, or whether that was only their ſirname, I cannot determine; for tho' ſome of the epigrams annex'd to their books ſeem to imply the former, yet it is difficult to affirm certainly that it was not a poetical licence, which, in this caſe, might have been more excuſable than that of *Campanus* upon *Ulric Han*, mention'd in the preceding chapter.   However, 'tis plain that many of the *German* Printers had no other ſirnames than thoſe of the places wherein they were born.

These two brothers ſoon ſurpaſs'd all their predeceſſors in the beauty and neatneſs of their characters, and the elegance of their impreſſions, which to this time render them admir'd and eſteem'd by the curious, above all other ancient editions.   *Venice* by this gain'd ſo much reputation for the fineneſs of her types, that ſome eminent Printers at *Rome* and elſewhere either furniſh'd themſelves with ſetts of them, or endeavour'd to imitate them, acquainting their readers in their next impreſſions, that they were printed *characteribus Venetianis*, with *Venetian* types.   *Chevillier* indeed thinks this to have been an impoſition upon the world; nor can it be denied but that ſome of them pretended this, in order to recommend their own wretched performances.   But this demonſtrates the ſuperior merit of that city, and the laudable emulation of her Printers, not only to excell thoſe of other places, but even one another.   And indeed theſe two brothers with *John de Cologn* and *N. Jenſon*, ſeem to have brought the Art to its utmoſt perfection, becauſe none of the moſt famous Printers which ſucceeded till our time, ſuch as *Vaſcoſan*, the *Stephens*'s, &c. have ſurpaſs'd them in this reſpect; as well as becauſe this, like other arts, ſeem'd obnoxious to a certain fatality and decline, when carried to a particular height, as it happen'd in the ſpace of *ſix* or *ſeven* years after their firſt ſettlement at *Venice*.   What I mean is, that they ſhould ſo unaccountably ſuffer themſelves to be carry'd away by the degenerate

taſte

tafte of that age, and change their beautiful Roman character, for the old, obfolete and difagreeable Gothick, which they began to print with about the year 1477.

THE *Spires* had the two following learned men for their correctors, viz. *Chriftopher Berardus* of *Pifauro*, and *George Alexandrinus* ; *John*, the elder brother, is reported to be the firft who put the direction-word at the end of the page, and that upon good grounds, fince no book, to our knowledge, before his *Tacitus*, hath it ; the fingular ufe of which is too obvious to want explanation. He liv'd no longer than to the year 1470, and was fucceeded in the whole bufinefs by *Windelin*, who manag'd it with great applaufe by himfelf 'till 1472, in which year he took *John de Cologn* into partnerfhip with him. We find but one book, viz. *Plautus*, printed by them joyntly ; fo that it is probable each of them return'd foon after to his feparate prefs. This *Windelin* was fo highly efteem'd as a Printer even by his own countrymen, (a thing very uncommon !) that he was twice invited into *Germany* by fome eminent counfellors at law of that nation, to print there the following confiderable volumes, viz. 1. *Bartholi commentarium juridicum*, which he perform'd *ann.* 1471, without the name of the place, adding only two verfes inferted in the margin [1] ; and 2. The commentaries upon the five books of *Decretals* of *Nic. Tudefchi* of *Sicily*, firnam'd *Abbas Panormitanus*, *ann.* 1474 [2] ; he printed likewife in *Germany*, about the fame time, the firft edition of the *Tractatus Tractatuum* five *Oceanus Juris* 15 vol. *fol.* But as he had engag'd himfelf, prefently after his brother's death, not to leave *Venice*, (as appears by the verfes at the end of St. *Auftin de civitate Dei*, *ann.* 1470 [3] begun, but not finifh'd by his brother,) he return'd thither, and continued printing with prodigious honour till the year 1477, wherein he began to fall in with the Gothick character beforemention'd. In this he was followed by all the reft, and even by the celebrated *Nic. Jenfon*, tho' this laft ftill preferv'd the beauty and neatnefs of his forms, which the others very much

---

[1] Hos *Windelinus* clara virtute magifter
　　Tranfcripfit; celeri formula preffa pede.
　Maittaire Annal. Typogr. p. 94, fub not. (*b*)
[2] *Vide Orlandi* pag. 19.
[3] Qui docuit *Venetos* exfcribi poffe *Johannes*
　　Menfe fere trino centena volumina *Plini*,
　　Et totidem magni *Ciceronis Spira* libellos ;

Cœperat *Aureli*, fubita fed morte peremptus
Non potuit cœptum *Veretis* finire volumen.
Vindelinus adeft ejufdem frater, & arte
Non minor; *Adriacaque* morabitur urbe.

degene-

degenerated from. About this time *Windelin* probably dy'd, becaufe we meet with no impreffion of his that bears a date later than 1477. Such was the efteem the learned had of this excellent Printer, that of *twenty eight* impreffions we have extant of his, above *twenty* of them have a *latin* epigram at the end in praife of him ; fome of which are of a confiderable length, and moft of them by different hands. The firft edition is that of *Cicero*'s *Epiftolæ familiares, ann.* 1469 ; the laft we know of with a date, is *Dante*'s *Poems, ann.* 1477 ; fome of his editions are without date.

3. NICHOLAS JENSON, JANSON or GENSON, 1470.

NICH. JENSON is allow'd by the generality of writers to have been a Frenchman ; and as he was one of the firft of that nation, who was eminent in this Art, all his countrymen have been more than ordinarily lavifh of their praifes on him ; fo that whoever reads fome of their encomiums, would be apt to think him the only Printer of merit in that age, and that there had never been any edition worth their confideration, 'till it came out of his prefs ; and this they did, even before they fo much as dreamt of that early mafter-piece of his, the *Decor Puellarum:* we need not therefore wonder at Mr. *Mattaire*, if we find him fo highly pleas'd at the difcovery of this fingular work ; for it muft be own'd, that unlefs we will difpute the date of it, the higheft encomiums muft fall fhort of his merit ; fince it will plainly follow, that he was not only the earlieft by fome years, who improv'd the Art, but likewife who brought it to its greateft perfection, with refpect to the finenefs of his Roman characters, and elegancy of compofition. Whereas were the fuppofition of thofe, who think it antedated by *ten* years, to be allow'd, it will be manifeft that there had already been feveral eminent Printers at *Rome, Venice,* and elfewhere before him, who introduc'd that noble and elegant character; and that tho' his fhould be allow'd to be fomewhat finer than thofe of his predeceffors, yet would his merit be inferior to theirs, and his improvement upon them be but fmall in comparifon of that, which they made upon the old *Moguntine* types. However that be, I acknowledge with the greateft freedom and fincerity, that he was an excellent mafter of the Art, and his impreffions as beautiful, and, for the laft *ten* years fpace,

wherein

wherein he follow'd the bufinefs, as numerous as any of his contempo
raries. *Polydore Vergil* highly commends him for having fo wonderfully
improv'd the Art of Printing, and *Sabellicus* owns, that he and his partner
John de Cologn, excell'd all the Printers of their time, in the richnefs and
elegancy of their impreffions [1]. The learned *Omnibonus Leonicenus*, who
prepar'd copies for him, and corrected fome of his editions, hath, in an
epiftle to the bifhop of *Belluno*, left us an excellent character of him,
prefix'd to his *Quintilian anno* 1471 [2]. wherein he extols his types, and
mentions him as a fecond *Dædalus*, and as one to whom the greateft
fhare of this invention was due.

THE learned therefore are very juftly furpriz'd, that fo excellent a
mafter and fo great an ornament to the Art of Printing fhould be the
firft who brought the Gothic character to *Venice*, in which he printed
his bibles, divinity, and law-books. This method was follow'd by all
his brethren, both in that city, and in feveral others of *Europe*; tho' it
muft be own'd that he far furpafs'd the reft even in that refpect, and
fhow'd a more exact tafte and judgment; for his Gothic types had all
the beauty and elegancy, which they were capable of, and may be ftill
read with pleafure and admiration.

I don't find that he had any other corrector befides *Omnibon. Leonice-*
nus above-mention'd, if we except *Francifcus Colutia Verzinenfis*, who in
his dedication prefix'd to the work of *Palladius de Agricultura*, of which
he was the editor, tells *Jenfon* to whom he dedicates it, that it was at his
defire that he had undertaken to correct that work. By this it feems
as if *Jenfon* was the firft printer who had any of his impreffions dedicated to himfelf. Moft of his works, like thofe of the two *German* brothers, have a *latin* epigram at the end in praife of him; but, what is remarkable, not one of them fpeaks of him as the firft *Venetian* Printer,

---

[1] Sed omnium maxime opibus & eleganti
literarum forma multum cæteros antecelluerunt
Nicholaus Jenfo & *Johannes Colonienfis* : *Sabel-*
lic. Enead. 10. l 6.
[2] Accedebant juftæ preces magiftri Nicolai
Jenfon Gallici, alterius, ut vere dicam, Dædali,
qui librariæ artis mirabilis inventor, non ut
fcribantur calamo libri, fed veluti gemma im-
primantur, ac prope figillo, primus omnium
ingeniofe monftravit : ut huic viro, qui de re
literaria tam bene meruit, nemo fit qui non
favere debeat. Idcirco non difficulter impe-
travit, ut non folum hoc opus, verum etiam
utramque Ciceronis artem corrigerem.

which

which circumstance alone would be sufficient to justify us for postponing him to them. We meet with four of his editions printed in one year, *viz.* 1470, which shews him to have been a very diligent work-man. And in the space of ten years, we have thirty-nine of them, still extant ; exclusive of the *Decor Puellarum,* besides those which may have been lost, or are still undiscover'd. The first edition printed by him in *Gothic* character, is St *Austin*'s book *de Civitate Dei, anno* 1475. the two last of his works are dated 1481.

4. CHRISTOPHER WALDARFER OF RATISBON, 1470.

CONCERNING this Printer we know little, except that we have four of his editions still extant corrected by *Ludovicus Carbo* or *Carbone :* the *third* of which *viz. Servius Comment.* on *Virgil* fol. *anno* 1471, has an epigram of *four latin* distichs in his praise, by which we may guess that he printed a great many more works than these *four*, especially *Classicks.* The last of them, *viz. Pliny's Epistles,* hath neither the name of the Printer nor place ; but by a dedication prefix'd to it by the said *Carbo* to *Borso* duke of *Modena,* one may conclude it to have been done by *Waldarfer.* He remov'd from *Venice* soon after, and set up a Printing-house at *Milan,* where we shall find him, when we come to that place.

5, 6. JOHN *de* COLOGN, *&* JOHN MANTHEN *de* GERETZEN. 1471.

THESE two *Germans* came and settled at *Venice,* soon after the two *Spires,* and were equal to any of their contemporaries, in the beauty of their Roman types, the fineness of their paper, and elegance and correctness of their works. But they likewise gave into the Gothic way of printing ; and it is observable that *Venice* and *Lyons* have produc'd more of those impressions, than almost all *Italy* and *France* together. Whether these Printers were more modest than their brethren, is uncertain ; but, however, in the list of their editions, we meet with none of those pompous epigrams and panegyricks upon themselves, so frequently us'd at that time. They took *Nic. Jenson* into partnership with them, towards the later part of their printing. *John de Cologn* is affirm'd by

fome

fome to have invented the *Regiſtrum Chartarum* about *anno* 1475 ; but it is obvious to the reader, from the catalogue of *Uldric Han*'s works at *Rome*, that the latter us'd it at leaſt two years before him.

THERE is one thing remarkable in one of their colophons, at the end of their editions of *Valerius Maximus, fol. anno* 1474; and which, for that reaſon, I have ſubjoyn'd in the margin [1] : that they were rather book-ſellers than Printers : becauſe they acquaint the readers in it, that they had given this work to be printed by men hir'd for that purpoſe. We ſhall meet with many more in the ſequel of this hiſtory, who follow'd their example.

HOWEVER it muſt be own'd, that all the works that came out of their preſs, or were printed for them, are an honour to them : the laſt liſt of their editions according to father *Orlandi* amounts to 28, from *ann.* 1471 to 1481.

AS we know little or nothing concerning the following ones, beſides their names and their works; we ſhall juſt mention them in their rank, according to the date of the works we have of them.

7. ANTONY BOLOGNESE, or *Antonio de Bartolomeo, de Bolonia,* 1472. we have *five* editions of his from 1472, to 1486.

8. LEONARD ACHATES of *Baſil,* 1472. 1 edition.

9. GABRIEL *de Pietro* of *Treviſo,* 1473. 6 edit. to 1478.

10. FRANCIS *de Hailbrun* and
11. NICOL. *de Francford* } 1473. 3 edit. to 1475.

12. BARTOLOMEW CREMONESE, 1473. 3 edit. to 1475.

13. JAMES *des Rouges* 1474.

THIS was his true name, he being a *Frenchman*, tho' in his *latin* editions he writes himſelf *Jacobus Rubeus* or *de Rubeis* ; and in his *Italian* ones *di Roſſi* and *Roſſi* : He was juſtly eſteem'd one of the beſt Printers in his time. 'Tis affirm'd by ſome that he aſſiſted *Nic. Jenſon* in improving his Roman characters ; but this is improbable, becauſe it doth not appear, that he came to *Venice* 'till two or three years, at leaſt, after the other had publiſh'd ſome of his fine editions. However, the beauty of his letter, and the fineneſs of his impreſſions are incomparable ; particularly the two

---

[1] Venetiis impreſſoribus expoſitus fuit per *Joh.de Cologn.Agrippin.* ac *Joh. Manthen de Gher-* *retſteim,* MCCCCLXXIV, qui una fideliter viventes, eoſdem impreſſores ad hoc duxerunt.

hiſtories

hiftories of *Florence* in *Italian,* one written by *Leonard de Arezo,* and the other by *Poggius,* are accounted mafter-pieces in that kind.   At length he left *Venice,* and fettled at *Pignerol* in *Piedmont,* where he printed an *Italian Bible,* the fatyrs of *Juvenal,* and fome other work, which we fhall fpeak of in its proper place.   There is one thing more to enhance his merit, which is, that he comply'd not with the degenerate tafte of thofe times, in introducing the Gothic characters into his Printing-houfe ; his impreffions from *anno* 1474 to 1476, are ten in number.

14. CHRISTOPHER ARNOLD : we have but two editions of his from 1474 to 1478.

15. ANDREAS JACOBI of *Cathara* ; 5 editions from 1476 to 1482.

16. MARC. *de Conti* and
17. GERARD ALEXANDER } 1 edit. 1476.

18. BERNARD PICTOR and
19. ERHARD RALDOLT of *Ausburg,* } 5 edit. from 1476 to 1477.

20. GERARD *de Flandria,* 1 edit. 1477.

21. JAMES LUNESE *de Fivizano,* 2 edit. 1477.

22. PHILIP PETRI or *de Petro, Venetian,* 13 edit. from 1477 to 1482

23. GUERIN *the young,* 1 edit. 1477.

24. ANDREAS *de Patafichis* and
25. BONINO *de Boninis* } 8 edit. from 1478 to 1488.

26. MARTIN SARACEN, 3 edit. from 1478 to 1488.

27. LEONARD WILD *de Ratisbon,* 3 edit. from 1478 to 1481.

28. FRANC. RENNER *de Hailbrun,* 5 edit. from 1478 to 1494.

29. THEODORIC *de Reynsberg* and
30. REYNALD *de Novimagio* } 2 edit. 1478,

31. GEORGE WALCH *German,* 1 edit. 1479.

32. NICHOLAS GERARDENGO, 2 edit. from 1479 to 1480.

REYNALD *de Novimagio* by himfelf, 7 edit. from 1479 to 1494.

ERHARD RALDOLT by himfelf, 13 edit. from 1480 to 1485, after this he went to his own city *Ausburgh,* and fet up his prefs there, as we have faid under that head.

33. PETER PIASII
34. BARTHOL. BLAVII } 11 edit. from 1480 to 1495.
35. ANDREA TORRESANI *de Azola*

36. JOHN

36. John Lucilius Santriter and }
37. Francis Theodore   } 3 edit. 1480 to 1489.

38. Octavian Scot was a nobleman of the city of *Mons*, who set up some presses at *Venice* at his own charge, and printed a great number of curious editions, all which are marked with O. S. M. his chief corrector was *Maurice de Hibernia*, or of *Ireland*, a Francifcan monk, who was afterwards made bishop of *Triamo:* all the editions we have of *Octavian Scot* are 39, from *ann.* 1480 to 1498.

The chief workmen he employ'd to print for him are the three following,

39. Christopher Pensi,

40. Bennet Locatellus,

41. Bartholomew Zani.

The laft of thefe did likewife print for himfelf, and we have 15 editions of his printed with his own name, from 1487 to 1500.

42. John *de Forlivio* and   } thefe two printed 26 edit. from 1481 to
43. Gregory *de Gregoriis* }   1500.

44. Lucas *de Dominico, Venetian*, 5. edit. from 1481 to 1482.

45. Baptista *de Tortis*, 18 edit. from 1481 to 1498.

46. Thomas of *Alexandria* and partners, 6 edit. from 1481 to 1486.

47. Antony *dalla Strada Cremonefe*, 10 edit. from 1481 to 1488.

48. Mathew Capcasa of *Parma*, 10 edit. from 1481 to 1495.

49. Antony Pap and   }
50. Bernardin Moreni *de Lecho* } 1 edit. 1482.

51. Peter Loslein *German*, he was both partner and corrector to *Bernard Pictor* and *Erhard Raldolt* at *Venice*, we have two editions printed with his name both 1483.

52. Bernardin Benatio, or *de Benateis*, 12 edit. from 1483 to 1498.

53. Peter Maufer a Frenchman and } 1 edit. 1483.
54. Nichol. de *Contengo* of *Ferrara* }

Maufer was a very good Printer, but mov'd often from place to place; he began firft to work at *Padua*, then went to *Verona*, and afterwards came to *Venice:* where we find but one fingle edition done by him.

55. Herman Litchenstein in *latin Levilapis*; this was another unfettled workman, he wrought at *Vincenza*, *Trevifo*, and now at *Venice*; where we have 5 edit. of his, from 1483 to 1494.

56. A n-

56. ANDREA BONETTI *de Pavia*, 3 edit. from 1484 to 1486.

57. PEREGRIN PASQUALI and   ⎫ 12 edit. from 1484

58. DIONIS BERTOCH, or *de Bertochis* of *Bolonia* ⎭   to 1494.

59. PAGANINUS *de Paganinis*, 7 edit. from 1485 to 1498.

60. BERNARD STAGNINO *de Trino*, 5 edit. from 1485 to 1498.

61. ANTONY RACTIBOVIUS, 1 edit. 1485.

62. ALEXANDER CRETENSIS, he was a native of *Crete*, the only work we have of him, is a *Greek Pfalter* 4to *ann.* 1486, with a *latin* colophon, in which he ftyles himfelf, *Filius fapientiffimi & celeberrimi Domini Georgii* Prefbyteri.

63. WILLIAM *de Trino* firnam'd *Anima mia*, 5 edit. from 1486 to 1491.

64. BERNARD RIZZI *de Novara*, 10 edit. from 1486 to 1492, it is to be obferv'd, that his five firft, *i. e.* from 1486 to 1489, are fubfcrib'd only *Bernard de Novara*, and the five laft *Bern. Rizzi de Novara*, which has made fome authors queftion whether they were not two different Printers : his corrector was *Dominic Canali*.

65. LEONICUS CRETENSIS, of him we have only *Homer*'s *Batrachomuomachia*, or battle of the frogs and mice in *greek*, *cum græcis fcholiis* 4to, *ann.* 1486.

66. PETER CREMONESE firnam'd *Veronefe*, 2 edit. from 1486 to 1490.

67. JOHN ROUGES *alias Rubeus*, *Roffi*, 9 edit. from 1486 to 1499.

68. JOHN HAMMAN *de Landoja* ⎫

69. JOHN EMERICH *de Udenhem* ⎭ 4 edit. from 1487 to 1500.

70. HANIBAL *de Parma*, 1 edit. 1487.

71. THEODOR. RAGAZONI *alias de Ragazonibus*, 6 edit. from 1488 to 1500.

72. BERNARDINE *de Choris Cremonefe*, 9 edit. from 1488 to 1492.

73. GEORGE ARRIVABENUS of *Mantua*, 4 edit. from 1488 to 1492.

74. CHRISTOPHER *de Penfis de Mandello*, 11 edit. from 1489 to 1500.

75. BERNARDINE *de Renatis*, 1 edit. 1490.

76. JAMES PAGANINI of *Brefcia*, 1 edit. 1490.

77. PHILIP PINCIUS *de Caneto*, this was a very diligent as well as excellent Printer : he continu'd printing 'till after the year 1510 with great applaufe :

applaufe : his corrector was the learned *Bennet Brugnoli*, a man very well verfed in the *greek* and *latin* tongues ; his works from 1490 to 1500 are 24 in number.

78. THOMAS *de Blancis* of *Alexandria*, 1 edit. 1491.

79. SIMON *de Gara*, only a *latin* bible, 1491.

80. LAZARUS *de Siviliano*, 2 edit. from 1491 to 1492.

81. MANFRED. *de Montferrat*, 2 edit. from 1491 to 1492.

82. MAXIMUS *de Butricis* of *Pavia*, 1 edit. 1491.

83. FRANCIS GERARDENGO of *Pavia*, 1 edit. 1492.

84. JOHN *de Cereto de Tridino* firnam'd *Tacuino*, 23 edit. from 1492 to 1500.

85. BARTHOL. VENETUS *de Ragazzonibus*, 1 edit. 1492.

86. SIMON BEVILAQUA citizen of *Pavia*, 21 edit. from 1492 to 1500 ; he wrought alfo at *Pavia*, as we fhall fee when we come to that city.

87. JOHN PETER *de Querengis*, 5 edit. from 1492 to 1498.

88. DAMIAN *de Milan*, 2 edit. from 1493 to 1494.

89. MARTIN *de Rovado de Lazaronibus*, 1 edit. 1493.

90. JEROM *de Paganinis*, 2 edit. 1493 to 1497.

91. JOHN RAGAZZO and ⎫
92. JOHN MARIA   ⎬ 1 edit. 1494.

93. PERRIN LATHOMI, 1 edit. 1494, befides a Bible he printed at *Lyons*, 1479.

94. BERNARDINE VITATIS of *Venice*, 14 edit. from 1494 to 1500.

C H A P. IV.

Aldus Pius Manutius Romanus *a* Venetian *Printer, and the Inventor of Italick Letters* ; *his Life, Character and* Greek *Editions, with an Account of the other Printers at* Venice, *till the Year* 1500.

ALDUS MANUTIUS, the moft eminent Printer of the fifteenth century, was born *anno* 1445, when Printing was yet in its infancy ; who as he grew up, became fuch an admirer of this new Art, that

that tho' his education, learning and genius might have juftly excited him to greater employments, yet he chofe to devote his whole time and ftudy to the cultivating and improving all the branches of it. This defign he perform'd with fuch indefatigable application and vaft charges, that his whole ambition feem'd to be confin'd to this province and the advancement of learning [1]. After he had receiv'd the rudiments of Grammar, under *Gafpar* of *Verona*, he apply'd himfelf to the *Greek* and *Latin* tongues under the great *Baptifta Guarini* of *Verona* ; and in a fhort time made fuch a progrefs in thefe languages, as not only to furpafs his fellow ftudents, but even to rival his mafter himfelf. Thus he continued furnifhing his mind with every part of literature, in order to fit himfelf for that bufinefs, of which he was afterwards to become the ornament. The war breaking out in *Italy*, and the city of *Ferrara* being befieged, he removed from thence to *Mirandula*, where he became acquainted with the great *Picus* of that name, a prince of the brighteft genius that age had produc'd, and one of the greateft lovers of learning, and of learned men, who not only receiv'd him with open arms, but procur'd him the acquaintance of many learned men, by whofe converfation and correfpondence, *Aldus* receiv'd no fmall advantage toward the acquiring that great knowledge of the *Greek* and *Latin* Tongues, which he became afterwards fo famous for. In the 45th year of his age, *anno* 1490, he began to prepare the neceffary *apparatus* of a Printinghoufe, wherein he fpent *four* years, and confequently did not begin Printing till about *anno* 1494. During this interval he obferv'd with regret to what degree the abbreviations, us'd by all the former Printers every where, were multiply'd ; fo that they became unintelligible, without fome key to direct the reader, an inftance of which is given in the margin [2]. Upon this, he confider'd a method to remedy this inconve-

---

[1] Omnem enim vitam decrevimus ad hominum utilitatem confumere——nam etfi quietam ac tranquillam agere vitam poffumus, negotiofam tamen eligimus & plenam laboribus. *Ald. præfat. ad Lafcar. Creten.*

[2] This curious example of the abbreviations, us'd in thofe times, is extracted from *Okam's* logick, folio verfo, leaf 121, as follows;

Sĩ hic ẽ fãls̃m q̃'d ãd fimplr̃ ã e p̃ducibile a deo g̃ ã i̊&ꝯlr̃hic a ñ e̊ g̃ a ñ e̊ p̃ducibile a deo

&c. which words printed at full length, will run thus; *Sicut hic eft fallacia fecundum quid ad fimpliciter, A eft producibile a deo. Ergo A eft, & fimiliter hic. A non eft, ergo non eft producibile a deo.* Vide Chevil p. 110.

Thefe abbreviations were grown in time fo numerous and univerfal, that books were oblig'd to be publifh'd to teach the method of reading and underftanding them.

nience,

nience, and fet them quite afide in his editions. But becaufe the printing the words at length would enlarge the volumes a fourth part, (for
there was fcarce one word in five that was not abridg'd) and encreafe the
price ; he refolv'd likewife to remedy that. To which end he invented
the *Italick* character, call'd from him *Aldine*, or *Curfivus* and *Cancella-
rius*, from its refemblance to hand-writing ; which by its figure and
clofenefs, gain'd as much upon the round Roman, as the abbreviations
did, and reduc'd the volume to near an exact bulk, thereby rendering them
abfolutely ufelefs. This is the main, tho' not the fole advantage, which
he propos'd by this new character ; for the world has fince found its
extraordinary ufefulnefs in many other refpects ; which being obvious to
every perfon, I fhall not particularife here, but mention only the agree-
ablenefs of a mixture of Roman and Italick. However, it muft be own'd,
that *Aldus* made too great ufe of the latter, in printing whole volumes in
that character, which is known to tire the eyes much more than the Roman. Upon this account feveral eminent Printers afterwards rejected it
in their quotations, when they were of any confiderable length, and
fubftituted Double comma's or Guillemets at one end of the lines, to diftinguifh the citations from the body of the book : which Guillemets
were fo call'd from their Inventor, a *French* Printer of that name.

To return to *Aldus* ; as foon as he had perfected this new character,
which muft neceffarily coft him prodigious fumms of money, he obtain'd
a privilege from three feveral Popes, for the fole ufe of them during the
fpace of *fifteen* years ; and thefe pontifs give him great encomiums upon
the account of this invention. The firft of thefe was granted him by
Alexander VI, and is dated *Sept.* 17 1502, with the following preface [1].
,, For as much as our beloved fon *Aldus Manucius Romanus* hath, for the
,, common benefit of the learned, invented a new fett of characters, and
,, been at vaft pains and charges in correcting and printing of books, ——
,, and is afraid left fome thro' envy or emulation fhould get patterns

---

[1] Quoniam dilectus filius nofter *Aldus Manucius Romanus* ad communem doctorum utilitatem, novis excogitatis characterum formis, affi-
duam operam libris emendandis imprimendifque
impendit, magnofque in ea re labores fumptuf-
que facit, vereturque ne infurgente invidia æmu-
lationeque excitata, aliqui, fumpto de ejus characteribus exemplo, ad eandem formam libros
imprimant, deque alterius invento novum fibi
lucrum quærant ; ideo nobis fecit humiliter fup-
plicari, &c.

X

,, of

,, of his chara&ers and print with them, thereby reaping the benefit o
,, another man's invention; he hath therefore humbly befought us, &c. ,,

He obtain'd the like privilege from Pope *Julius* II, within four month
after the firft, *viz.* *Jan.* 27 1503, which begins thus ; ,, For as mucl
,, as thou—— haft been at the pains to print with fuch diligence and ele
,, gancy, within thefe few years, and for the common benefit of all the
,, learned, many *greek* and *latin* volumes, corre&ted and revis'd with the
,, utmoft care and diligence, in thofe new chara&ers, which are vulgar-
,, ly known by the name of *Curfivi* and *Cancellarii*, and are fo beauti-
,, ful as to feem written by hand, &c.

His fucceffor *Leo* X, likewife granted him a brief to the fame purpofe
within ten months after, exprefly prohibiting any perfon to print in on
imitate that chara&er during the fpace of *fifteen* years[2].

'Tis apparent from the tenour of thefe briefs, that this Italick chara&er
was not the only particular, wherein *Aldus* fignaliz'd himfelf; for the
number and corre&nefs of his editions, with the beauty of his chara&ers,
gain'd him the efteem and admiration of the learned; nor need I tell the
reader how highly all his works have been valued ever fince, as well as
thofe of his fon *Paulus Manucius*, of his fon-in-law *Andreas Azolanus*, and
his grandfon *Aldus*; which are of equal merit with his own, and of equal
value. His ambition of being efteem'd not only a man of letters, (as he
really was,) but alfo the moft corre& Printer of the age, was fuch, that
he fpar'd no coft in procuring the beft MSS, nor labour in revifing them;
and his care was fo great, left any errors fhould efcape him either in the
MS. or proofs, that, as we are affur'd by *Angel. Roccha*, keeper of the
Vatican library, he would not allow himfelf to print above two fheets
in a week[2]. But this muft be underftood only of fuch works, as re-

---

[1] Cum tu——Græcorum & Latinorum au-
&orum volumina fumma cura & diligentia ca-
ftigata, a paucis annis, ad communem omnium
litteratorum utilitatem, chara&eribus, quos vul-
gus *Curfivos* feu *ancellarios* appellas, imprimi
tam diligenter & pulchre curaveris, ut calamo
confcripta effe videantur, &c.

[2] Ne per fpatium quindecim annorum iis
chara&eribus, quos ipfe invenit vel edidit pri-

mus, imprimere —— neve chara&eres, quos
Curfivos feu *Cancellarios* appellant, imitari præ-
fumant, &c.

[3] Audivi ab iis qui cum eo verfati funt ——
duo ad fummum folia fingula quaque hebdomada
imprimi folere; cum hodie totidem fere in fingulo quoque prælo quotidie cudantur. *Ang.*
Roc. de bibliotheca Vaticana, pag. 112.

quir'd

quir'd a more than ordinary diligence and application ; otherwife it were difficult to reconcile this with what *Aldus* fays in his preface to *Euripides ann.* 1503 [1], that he publifh'd fome good author every month, of which he printed above a *thoufand* copies ; or with what *Erafmus* fays of him in his proverbs [2] ; that he was erecting a library, whofe limits would be thofe of the world it felf. However that be, his accuracy and diligence is unqueftionably attefted by all the learned ; and he tells Pope *Leo* X, in his petition beforemention'd, that the height of his ambition was to prefent the world with authors, corrected with the utmoft exactnefs ; and that nothing was more mortifying to him, than to fee any faults in his impreffions, *every one of which he would gladly, if poffible, have redeem'd at the price of a crown of gold* [3]. What affiftance he had from the learned in correcting his books may be gather'd from his preface to the *Greek* edition of *Ariftotle's Logick*, where he affures us, *that he had fome of the ableft criticks with him, to affift in the correction* ; and in the preface to the *phyficks* of that philofopher, he boafts, *that his impreffions were more perfect and correct than the very originals from which they were printed* [4].

But it muft be own'd that the learned are far from granting him this laft piece of merit, which he challenges ; and fome of them have objected, that he either printed them not according to the beft manufcripts, or corrected them by his own conjectures, or follow'd fometimes too fcrupuloufly thofe which were faulty and imperfect. Upon this account *Erafmus*, tho' a great friend of his, complains that *Michael Bentius*, who printed his proverbs, *had follow'd the corrupt editions of* Aldus *in the quotations from* Homer *and* Cicero [5]. The fame author tells *John Betzemius*, in a letter fent with a catalogue of his works, *that fome of* Plutarch's *books were printed by* Aldus *after fome very corrupt manufcript* [6]. Yet he excu-

---

[1] Quandoquidem mille & amplius boni alicuus auctoris volumina fingulo quoque menfe mittimus.

[2] *Aldus* bibliothecam molitur, cujus non alia cpta funt quam ipfius orbis. *Erafm. Chil.* 2. *Jent.* 1. *Prov.* 1.

[3] Sic doleo, ut, fi poffem, mutarem fingula errata nummo aureo.

[4] Dicere queo, quicquid meo labore formis excuditur, ipfis exemplaribus longe correctius

ac magis perfectum exire ex ædibus noftris.

[5] Nam *Michael Bentius* contulit quædam loca a me citata ex Græco *Homero* ab *Aldo* excufo, item ex *Cicerone Aldino*, cum *Aldina* fint depravatiffima. *Vita Erafmi, Lugdun. Batav. in* 16º, pag. 173.

[6] Hoc unum erat incommodi, quod *Aldus* hoc opus excudit fecundum exemplar multis locis depravatum. *Tom.* 1. *oper. Erafm.*

fes

fes him in another letter [1], and lays the blame upon fome *Pedagogue, whom* Aldus *intrufted with the care of fome of the editions of ancient authors.* If this be fact, 'tis very much to be regretted, that fo great a Printer, to whom the republick of learning is in all other refpects fo much oblig'd, fhould be overfeen in a matter of fuch importance. And this, in all probability, is the reafon why he thus exprefles his diffatisfaction at his own editions, in the petition to the Pope beforemention'd ; [2] *that he was fo far from regarding the flatteries of fome perfons, that he had not as yet publifh'd one book, with which he could be fatisfied* [2].

B e s i d e s this, he carries his complaints ftill further, and inveighs loudly againft two forts of men, who alone are capable of depriving the learned world of the benefit of printing, unlefs fome fpeedy ftop be put to their wretched performances : the firft are thofe, who, notwithftanding their notorious ignorance and incapacity, prefume to print any kind of books : the *fecond* are the half learned editors, who not only venture upon publifhing ancient authors, but likewife write notes and commentaries with their own corrections upon them. Thus was this great man concern'd to fee the corruptions already crept into the Art, thro' the avarice of fome, and ignorance of others ; whilft himfelf found by fad experience, that all his care, as well as learning, was fcarce fufficient for fuch a tafk. As no Printer ever furpafs'd him in the latter, fo none ever equall'd him in the former ; for fo indefatigable was he in that laborious province, that he fcarce allow'd himfelf time to eat, fleep, or attend his domeftick affairs ; and, which is ftill more, was fo regardlefs of his health, as to neglect thofe pleafures and recreations fo neceffary and conducive to the prefervation of it. The learned *Zuinger*, in his *Theatrum vitæ humanæ* p. 3713 of the *Bafil* edition 1604, tells us, that his mind was entirely engaged in the care of his Printing-houfe ; that, as foon as he had order'd his other neceffary affairs, he fhut himfelf up in his ftudy, where he employ'd himfelf in revifing his *greek* and *latin* manufcripts, reading the letters which he receiv'd from the learned out of all parts of the world, and writing

---

[1] Officina Veneta dedit nobis *Feftum Pompeium* egregie depravatum ; non infimulo *Aldum* ; folet ille tales operas alicui Pædagogo committere. Pag. 148, fupradict. edit. *Lugdun. Batav.*
[2] Sed ego non credulus illis ; nullum enim adhuc dedi librum, in quo mihi ipfi fatisfecerim.

anfwers

anfwers to them.   To prevent interruption by impertinent vifits, he caus'd the following infcription to be plac'd over his clofet door [1]; *Who-ever you are,* Aldus *earneftly intreats you to difpatch your bufinefs, as foon as poffible, and then depart ; unlefs you come hither, like another* Hercules, *to lend him fome friendly affiftance ; for here will be work fufficient to employ you, and as many as enter this place.*   Thefe words were afterwards borrow'd by the learned *Oporinus,* (who from a profeffor of the *greek* tongue in the univerfity of *Bafil,* became one of the moft eminent Printers, either of that city, or even of *Europe* ;) and were fet over his ftudy door for the fame intent.

ALDUS is affirm'd by many authors to have been the firft who printed whole volumes in *greek,* particularly the learned *Henry Stephens,* afferts, both in the *Complaint of the Art of Printing* written by him, and in his epitaph upon *Aldus,* that he was the firft Printer in that language [2] ; and *Gefner* tells *Paul Manutius Aldus*'s fon, in the 11th book of his Pandects, that if he is not miftaken, there were no *greek* books printed before thofe of his father, or at leaft, not with equal beauty and correctnefs with his [3]. Tho' this is not ftrictly true, as we fhall immediately fhew, yet as he was the greateft Printer in *greek,* and inventor of a beautiful character, thefe and feveral other authors might eafily attribute to him the firft rank in this province.   The firft *greek* book was publifh'd by him, *anno* 1494, as appears by the lifts, which the annalifts give us of his works, and from what *Aldus* himfelf fays, in his preface to *Stephanus de urbibus, anno* 1502 [4], that he begun his firft *greek* impreffions in the year wherein the war in *Italy* commenc'd, *viz. anno* 1494, at the time of the expedition of *Charles* VIII king of *France* to feize upon the kingdom of *Naples.*   Some writers, from a miftaken paffage in his preface to *Ariftotle, anno* 1495, wherein he tells his patron Prince *Carpi,* that he prefents him with the prince of phi-lofophers, *Plato* excepted, now firft printed and very correct, have thought

---

[1] Quifquis es, rogat te *Aldus* etiam atque eti-am, ut fiquid eft quod a fe velis, perpaucis agas, deinde actutum abees, nifi tanquam Hercules veneris fuppofiturus humeros; femper enim erit quod & tu agas, & quotquot huc attulerint pe-des.

[2] Qui graphicis primus tradidit illa typis.

[3] Exemplaria Græca ante patrem tuum aut nulla, ni fallor, aut pauca, nec ea induftria typis publicata funt.

[4] Eodem anno, quo vexari bello cœpit *Italia,* difficillimam hanc ego imprimendorum libro-rum provinciam accepi.

it

it to have been his firft *greek* impreffion ; whereas he publifh'd at leaſt *three* the year before. However 'tis plain he had printed no book in any language before *anno* 1494.

IT appears from what has been faid in a former chapter concerning the *Lactantius* printed in the monaftery of *Subiaco, anno* 1465, the *Gellius* at *Rome* 1469, and others, that feveral confiderable fragments were printed in *greek* with no fmall elegancy and correctnefs. But befides thefe there were feveral editions in that language printed in divers cities of *Italy* fome years before ; the principal of which we fhall mention.

THE *firft*, as yet known, is the *greek* grammar of *Conftantine Lafcari* 4to, revis'd by *Demetrius Cretenfis*, and printed by *Dionyfius Palavifinu* at *Milan, anno* 1476, afterwards reprinted at *Venice* by *Leonard* of *Bafil, anno* 1488.

THE next is the *greek* pfalter printed at *Venice, anno* 1486 by *Alexander* of *Crete* 4to, and *Homer*'s *Batrachomuomachia*, or battle between the frogs and mice 4to, at *Venice* by *Leonic* of *Crete* in the fame year. But as thefe may be efteem'd only preludes or effays in that language, we fhall come to a more confiderable edition, *viz.* that of *Homer*'s works in *greek*, which B. *Neril* caus'd to be printed at *Florence* in a large *folio, anno* 1488 by *Demetrius* of *Milan*, a native of *Crete*. This excellent work I have feen in the curious library of the learned Dr. *Mead*, and I dare affirm that whoever examines the whitenefs and ftrength of the paper, the finenefs of the character, the elegant difpofition of the matter, the exact diftance between the lines, the large margin, and in fhort, the whole performance with its various ornaments, will eafily own it a mafter-piece in that kind. There was likewife a fine edition of *Ifocrates* printed at *Milan* in *fol.* by *Henry German* and *Sebaftian ex Pontremulo, anno* 1493, a year before any of *Aldus*'s impreffions appear'd.

HOWEVER, tho' he was not the firft *greek* Printer, yet no perfon ever fignaliz'd himfelf more in that province than he, nor equall'd him in beauty, correctnefs and number of editions. Concerning the beauty of his *greek* characters, of which he is faid to be the inventor, Mr. *Mattaire* tells us *pag.* 237, *Annal. Typogr.* that thofe, in which he printed the *Pfalter, Æfop, Ariftotle, Ariftophanes,* &c. were fomewhat larger, rounder, more beautiful and elegant, adorn'd with frequent ligatures, which added no fmall

beauty

beauty to his *greek* editions, *&c.* Nor is this is the only particular, for which the learned world is so much oblig'd to him; since his designs reach'd still farther, and were answer'd to his great satisfaction before his death, which happen'd *anno* 1515. He observ'd, with no small regret, how much and how long the *Greek* tongue had been neglected; in order therefore to revive that noble language, and accustom the learned by degrees to read nothing but the originals, he resolv'd to publish most of his books in *Greek* only. This succeeded so well, that the oldest men began to acquaint themselves with it, and as many youths engaged in the study of that tongue, as of the *Latin*; which gave him such sensible pleasure, that he mentions it in several of his prefaces, and particularly in that prefix'd to *Aristotle's Logic*, wherein he thus expresses himself[1]: ,, In our ,, days we may see many old gentlemen, who follow *Cato's* example in ,, learning the *Greek* tongue. For with respect to the youth, they equally ,, apply themselves to that, as to the *Latin*. Upon which account *Greek* ,, books, of which there is now a prodigious scarcity, are come into very ,, great request, *&c.*,, In his preface to *Stephanus de urbibus* he observes with pleasure[2], ,, That *Italy* was not the only nation wherein the *Greek* ,, tongue was in vogue; but that in *Germany, France, Hungary, Britain,* ,, *Spain,* and almost every place, where the *Latin* was known, not only ,, the young, but even the old study'd *Greek* with the utmost eagerness ,, and application.

ALL his impressions were not of that nature; for in some of them, printed before and afterwards, as *Musæus, Greek grammar, Proclus's Sphæra,* the works of *Philostratus, Eusebius contra Hieroclem,* &c. he first gave the whole *Greek* text, and then the *Latin* translation.

SOON after this, he invented a method, entirely new, of printing these *Greek* editions with their translations, which I do not find practis'd by any Printer since.

---

[1] Nostris vero temporibus multos licet videre *Catones,* hoc est, senes in senectute Græce discere. Nam adolescentulorum ac juvenum Græcis incumbentium jam tantus fere est numerus, quantus eorum qui Latinis. Propterea Græci libri vehementer ab omnibus inquiruntur, quorum quia mira paucitas est, *&c.*

[2] Nam non in *Italia* solum, sed etiam in *Germania, Gallia, Pannonia, Britannia, Hispania,* & ubique fere, ubi Romana lingua legitur, non modo ab adolescentibus, juvenibusque, sed a senibus quoque summa aviditate studetur literis Græcis.

THEY

THEY were impos'd after such a manner, that the purchaser might have them bound either with the *Greek* and *Latin* feparate, or with a leaf of the one, and a leaf of the other alternately ; for inftance, the *firft* leaf was *Greek*, then follow'd the *firft* in *Latin*, then the *fecond Greek* leaf, and the *fecond Latin*, and fo on to the end ; but with this precaution, that the *Greek* of the *firft* leaf was only printed upon the *fecond* page of it, and the *Latin* verfion oppofite to it ; the *Latin* upon the *fecond* page of the *Latin* leaf was the verfion of the *Greek* upon the *firft* page of the *third* leaf, and all the *Greek* upon the *fecond* page of this leaf, fell exactly over againft the *Latin* of it in the *firft* page of the *fourth* or *fecond Latin* leaf.   This order being obferv'd throughout, every other leaf being *Greek*, and the reft *Latin*, it was eafy either to bind it in two volumes, the one *Greek*, and the other *Latin* ; or into one, with the original firft, and verfion afterwards, oppofite to each other.

BUT, as we remark'd before, this excellent method was never obferv'd, not even by thofe, who reprinted fuch of *Aldus*'s editions, as had been done after this way ; *viz. Efop*'s and *Gabriel*'s fables, *Lafcaris*'s grammar, *&c.* for they printed the *Greek* in one page, and the *Latin* upon the other ; which is vaftly more inconvenient than his method ; the manner of printing both languages in two columns not being invented 'till after the year 1550, *Vide Chevil.* pag. 238.   I conceive there is no neceffity of giving a more particular defcription of *Aldus*'s *Greek* types, becaufe his works are fo univerfally known to the curious ; but whoever defires to know further concerning them, and their fuperior excellence to thofe us'd before, may confult Mr. *Mattaire*'s *Annals*, pag. 237.

ALDUS has been likewife fuppos'd the firft, or, at leaft, one of the firft, who printed in *Hebrew*.   But this is certainly a miftake ; for, tho' he had a font of *Hebrew*, yet he made but little ufe of it ; and 'tis evident, that the jews of *Soncino* in the duchy of *Milan* began to print books in that language about *twelve* or *fourteen* years before *Aldus* appear'd, as fhall be fhewn in its proper place.   *Chevillier* p. 267 tells us, that he faw nothing of his in this tongue, but the *Hebrew* alphabet, which is ftill preferv'd in the *Sorbon* library.   We find however, that he wrote and printed an introduction to the *Hebrew* tongue ; as appears from a book printed by him, *ann.* 1501, intitled, *Aldi Manutii Grammaticæ Latinæ*
linguæ

linguæ rudimenta; *de literis Græcis & Diphthongis*, &c. *ut & introductio ad Hebræam linguam*, 4to.   Indeed *Justin Decadius* a *Grecian* and inhabitant of *Venice*, who caus'd the *Greek* psalter to be printed by *Aldus* in 4to, flatters those of his own nation, to whom he dedicates it, with a promise which that Printer made him, of printing an edition of the bible in *Hebrew*, *Greek* and *Latin*; but it is not known, that he ever perform'd it, at least, with relation to the *Hebrew*.

BEFORE we close the character of this great man, it will be proper to acquaint the reader with the reason of his assuming the name *Pius* after the year 1503; because even this is another testimony of his merit.   He receiv'd it from his patron prince *Albertus Pius de Carpi*, whose tutor he had formerly been, and who, on account of his singular desert, adopted him into his family, and contributed large sums towards defraying the charges of procuring and correcting manuscripts, preparing three fonts, of *Italick*, *Greek* and *Hebrew*, characters, entertaining so many learned correctors, and such a number of workmen, beside the other charges common to every Printing-house.   His chief correctors were *Peter Alcyonius*, *Demetrius Chalcondylas*, *Marcus Musurus*, and *Alexander Bondinus*.

THE mark of his Printing-house, which shall be given, with the rest of the marks or rebus's of the Printers of the 15th century, at the end of this book, was a dolphin twin'd about an anchor, and nibling at it; signifying his close and indefatigable application to business, which he went through with deliberation and judgment.   *Chevillier* tells us, that he took it from the emperor *Titus*; and that *Peter Bembus*, who was afterwards made a cardinal, presented him with a silver medal, which had that emperor's head on one side, and on the reverse, a dolphin twisting himself round an anchor.   This was likewise, according to some authors, the device of *Augustus* the emperor [1], the anchor being design'd to signify rest, as lightning or the dolphin were to denote swiftness.   These *Titus* afterwards express'd by the dolphin, signifying swiftness, and an anchor, design'd to stop the course of a ship, denoting slowness.   *Aldus* himself seems to hint at this signification, when he tells prince *Carpi*, in his epistle dedicatory prefix'd to *Proclus*'s *Sphere*, anno 1499 [2], that he could testify

---

[1] Σπευδε Βραδεως *festina lente*.

[2] Sum ipse mihi optimus testis me semper habere comites, ut oportere aiunt, delphinum & anchoram; nam & dedimus multa cunctando, & damus assidue.

Y   for

for himfelf with the greateft fincerity, that he had always thofe two companions with him, which they fay are fo neceffary, *viz.* the dolphin and anchor, and publifh'd many things with deliberation, and yet without intermiffion.   His fon *Paul*, who was Printer to the *Vatican*, his fon-in-law *A. de Azola*, and his grandfon *Aldus* us'd the fame mark.

Some vile Printers of *Florence*, finding the impoffibility of equalling *Aldus*'s editions, refolv'd to counterfeit them as well as his rebus, and carry'd on the cheat for fome time, 'till it was difcover'd by means of a miftake committed by the engraver, who revers'd the dolphin, fo that his head was on the left fide of the anchor, whereas in *Aldus*'s mark it was on the right.   Whether his fon-in-law *Andreas de Azola* firft perceiv'd this difference, I will not affirm ; but he firft gave publick notice of it, to prevent the world's being any longer impos'd upon.   This paffage in the preface to his *Livy* in 8vo *anno* 1518, is given at full length in the margin [1].   I am fenfible that in this fketch of the hiftory of that Printer, I have exceeded in many cafes my propos'd limits ; yet, I hope, the worth and character of the perfon will fufficiently excufe me for not keeping too fcrupuloufly to our epocha.

The works, which we have of him, from 1494 to 1500, are in number twenty four ; fourteen of which are *Greek*, and the reft *Latin*, or *Latin* and *Greek*.

The reader may eafily perceive, how fhort this lift comes of the number, which we might have reafonably expected from fo induftrious a Printer, within the fpace of fix or feven years ; efpecially confidering, that as himfelf affures us, he publifh'd an author every month, which amounts to almoft four times our number.   Whether the reft are perifh'd, or are ftill latent in fome libraries, I fhall not determine, but am willing to hope the latter, and that time will by degrees bring them to light.

However he ftill continued printing many years after the clofe of the century, and took his father-in-law *Andreas de Azola* [in *Latin Azola-*

---

[1] Extremum eft ut admoneamus, *Florenti-* *nos* quofdam impreffores, cum viderint diligentiam noftram in caftigando & imprimendo non poffe affequi, ad artes confugiffe folitas, hoc eft grammaticis inftitutionibus *Alai* in fua officina formatis, notam delphini anchoræ involuti no- ftram appofuiffe; fed ita egerunt, ut quivis me- diocriter verfatus in libris impreffionis noftræ animadvertat illos imprudenter feciffe.   Nam roftrum delphini in partem finiftram vergit, cum tamen noftrum in dexteram totum demittatur.

nus]

nus] in partnerſhip with him. As to the time of his death, or any particulars of it, I have not been able to diſcover any thing certain ; I ſhall
therefore conclude his hiſtory with a remark or two concerning an edition of his, which I hope will not be diſagreeable to the reader : it is
that of *Poliphili hypnerotomachia*, written by *Franciſcus Columna*, to prove
that all the world is but a dream; wherein he relates many things worth
learning : it has been ſuppos'd to be printed at *Treviſo*, *anno* 1467, becauſe
at the end are the following words ; *Tarviſii cum decoriſſimis Poliæ amore
lorulis diſtineretur miſellus Poliphilus*, MCCCCLXVII *kalendis Maii*, *i. e.*
when the unfortunate *Poliphilus* was in love with the charming *Polia*, 1467.

THIS they thought to have been the year, when the book was printed ;
whereas *Mattaire* and *Orlandi* obſerve, that the words plainly demonſtrate
it to be the year, in which *Colonna* finiſh'd it. Beſides, it is evident from
the character, the regiſters, direction-words, comma's, interrogatory
points, and other particularities, as well from the laſt leaf, which contains
the errata, and concludes thus, *Venetiis menſe Decembri* MID *in ædibus
Aldi Manutii accuratiſſimé*, that this edition came out from *Aldus*'s preſs.
However, *Orlandi* tells us, that this leaf was deſignedly torn off, becauſe
there is no date of the year, in which it was printed ; but Mr. *Mattaire*
gives us an account of theſe errata *pag.* 255, which bore this title, *Gli er-
rori del libro fatti ſtampando, liquali corrige coſi* : then follows the errata
containing fifty nine full lines, a greater number than *Aldus* ever put at
the end of his works. After the errata are the *Latin* words abovemention'd, *Venetiis*, &c. 'Tis plain from this, that 1467 was the year, in which
the author finiſh'd it at *Treviſo*, and the date of the edition, 1499. With
reſpect to the author's name, *Orlandi* deduceth it from the initial letters
of each chapter, which being joyn'd together form theſe words, *Poliam
frater Franciſcus Columna peramavit. Orland.* pag. 57, 58.

THE remainder of the *Venetian* Printers to *ann.* 1500 are as follows.

96. ANTONY MORETUS of *Breſcia* and ⎫
97. JEROM *de Alexandria*   ⎬ 1 edit. 1495.
                                        ⎭
98. ANTONY ZANCHI or *de Zanchis*, 1 edit. 1497.
99. OTINUS *della Luna* of *Pavia*, 3 edit. from 1497 to 1499.
100. JOHN ALVYSIUS *de Vareſio Milaneſe*, 1 edit. 1498.

101 BARTHOL. JUSTINOPOLITANUS, ⎫

102. GABRIEL *de Brifighella*,   ⎬

103. JOHN BISSOLI,   ⎬

104. BENEDICT MANGI of *Carpi*, ⎭

WE have but two editions of thefe four partners, *viz. Phalaris Epiftles* 4to 1498, and *Æfop*'s life and fables 4to 1500, both in *Greek:* the former of thefe editions has a privilege from the fenate of *Venice*, for their fole printing of it during the fpace of ten years ; and an epiftle of *Bartholomew Juftinopolitan* to *Contarenus* a fenator of *Venice*, wherein he complains of the great abufes, which were crept into the Art of Printing ; and the difadvantages thence arifing to the common wealth of learning, thro' the ignorance and negligence of Printers, which encreas'd every day among them : he feems therefore rather to have been an editor than a Printer, and to have hir'd the other three to print in partnerfhip with him.

105. ANTONY *de Guzzago* of *Brefcia*, 1 edit. 1498.

106. SEBASTIAN MANILIUS a Roman and partners, 1 edit. 1499.

107. JOHN BAPT. SESSA of *Milan*, 2 edit. 1499.

108. ZACHARIAH CALIERGI of *Crete*; he was a very eminent Printer of *Greek:* we have two editions of his, both of 1499, *viz. Simplicius Comment.* upon *Ariftotle*'s *Cathegorics fol.* and *Etymologicum magnum, fol.* in *Greek*, the laft of thefe printed at the defire of a *Conftantinopolitan* lady : he remov'd to *Rome*, and printed there till *ann.* 1523 if not beyond ; and the *Lexicon Varini* was printed by him in that year.

109. LUCANTONIUS *de Giunta* or *Zunta* of *Florence*, 1500.

ALL the Printers of this name [*de Giunta* or *Zunta*] have been perfons of the moft diftinguifh'd merit for their performances at *Rome*, *Florence*, *Lyons* and *Venice* ; their common rebus or mark was the *flower-de-luce*, and fometimes the *eagle*. The firft of that name is this *Lucantonius Giunta*, a man of noble extract, who employ'd *John de Spira* to print for him at *Venice*.

WHETHER this *Spira* was a fon or grandfon of one of the two brothers, who firft brought the Art to this city, is uncertain. However, the *Giunta*'s fignaliz'd themfelves in that Art, 'till the middle of the fixteenth century. The following edition is the only one, we know of, printed by him before the clofe of this century, *viz. Regulæ fancti* Benedicti,

dicti, *fancti* Bafilii, *fanct.* Auguftini & Francifci; *collectæ atque ordinatæ per* D. J. Franc. Brixianum *monachum congregationis* S. Juftinæ *ordinis* S. Benedicti *de obfervantia,* 4to, *cura & impenfis nobilis viri* Luc. Antonii *de* Giunta Florentini, *arte & folerti ingenio magiftri* Johannis *de* Spira, *idibus April.* Venetiis. Some of the impreffions of *Matthew Capcafa* at *Venice,* 1482, are faid in the colophon to be printed at the defire of *Lucant. Zunta.*

109, NICHOLAS BLASTI, one *Greek* edition dated 1500.

110. ALBERTINE VERCELLENSIS, 1 edit. dated 1500.

THESE are all the Printers hitherto known to have wrought at *Venice,* from the time of its receiving the Art, to the year 1500, but there were many more, who, as was hinted before, made a trade of reprinting fome of the beft editions in a flovenly incorrect manner, and to underfell the good ones; for which reafon, they did not dare to fet their names to them. Father *Orlandi* gives us a lift of 90 of them done at *Venice* during that interval, the greateft part of which, I am apt to fufpect, are of that forry kind.

C H A P. V.

Of the three firft Printers at Paris, *and their Succeffors; the Encouragement which they met with; fome Account of the Books printed by them; with other Particulars. A fecond Printing-houfe fet up in the* Louvre *by King* Lewis XI. *The reft of the* Paris *Printers.*

WHOEVER defires a compleat account of the firft fettlement, progrefs and improvement of the Art of Printing, in the city and univerfity of *Paris,* the metropolis of *France,* will find that fubject copioufly treated of by *De la Caille* in his *Origine de l'imprimerie* printed *anno* 1689, and more particularly by *Chevillier* in his *Origine de l'Imprimerie* printed at *Paris, anno* 1694.

THESE

THESE two authors have chiefly confin'd their hiſtory to that kingdom; and, as they had all poſſible opportunities of ſearching the records and
libraries of that univerſity, have been enabled to acquaint the world with
a vaſt many particularities relating as well to the Art, as to the moſt eminent Printers there. But ſince an induction of them would ſwell this work
to too great a bulk, I ſhall ſelect the moſt curious and material parts,
and refer the reader for the reſt to the authors before mention'd. Sufficient reaſons, I hope, are already given, againſt the opinion of thoſe,
who, contrary to all the moſt inconteſtable records, aſſert that *Nich. Jenſon* firſt brought printing to *Paris*. This particular is further confirm'd
by the two laſt mention'd *French* hiſtorians, whoſe account of that matter
is as follows.

SOME time before the year 1470, *William Fichet* and *John Heynlin de
Lapide* or *Lapidanus,* two famous doctors of the univerſity of *Paris,* and
of the college of *Sorbon,* obſerving the progreſs of printing in ſeveral
cities of *Europe,* began to uſe their utmoſt efforts in order to introduce
it not only into that city, but even into their college, where they might
give it all neceſſary help and encouragement. They were both perſons
of great reputation for their learning and publick ſpirit. The former
was a *Savoyard* by birth, and a great reſtorer of the long neglected art
of rhetorick, and all polite literature. The latter was a *German,* and
had been rector of the univerſity, and prior of the college of *Sorbon,* to
which laſt dignity, he was choſen again about this time. As there were
then but few, if any, except *Germans,* eminent in printing, *Lapidanus* undertook to bring ſome of the moſt ſkilfull thither. This could not but
ſeem eaſily attainable by him, who had ſuch a numerous acquaintance
amongſt the learned in *Germany,* and is ſuppos'd, upon good grounds, to
have been of the ſame dioceſs, if not the ſame city with *Uldric Gering,* a
native of *Conſtance.* The latter being influenc'd by the kind invitations
of a perſon of ſuch eſteem, who promis'd him the college of *Sorbon* for
his abode, and his aſſiſtance in procuring and preparing manuſcripts,
and reviſing his editions; and allur'd by the hopes of conſiderable gain in
ſo rich a city, wherein the Art was yet unpractis'd, brought two other
countrymen with him, *viz. Martin Crantz* and *Michael Friburger* or *de
Columbaria* or *Colmar* in *Alſace,* to *Paris*; where he ſet up preſſes in the
hall

hall of *Sorbon*, and in the year 1470 publifh'd the firft book, that ever was printed in any city of *France*, except that of *Tours* mention'd in a former chapter. Father *Orlandi* tells us, that *Lewis* XI gave *Fitchet* and *Lapidanus* orders to fend for fome of the beft Printers to *Paris*, at his own charge; and that by this means the three *German* partners were induc'd to fettle there. *Chevillier* takes no notice of this, but attributes the honour wholly to the *Sorbonifts*. However, it is certain that this king was a great encourager of learning; as appears by the magnificent library which he form'd at his palace in *Paris*; whither he brought not only all the books, which his predeceffors, and in particular *Charles* V firnam'd the wife, and *Charles* VI had collected and fet up at *Fountainbleau*, but likewife all that he could purchafe at any rate, together with a great number of editions printed at *Mentz* by *Fauft* and *Schoeffer*; and what manuſcripts he could not purchafe, he order'd to be curioufly tranfcrib'd, and to be fet up there. A remarkable inftance of this, mention'd by the *French* writers, is as follows.

THE king underftanding that the college of phyficians at *Paris* had in their library the works of *Rhafis* a phyfician, tranflated out of *Arabick* into *Latin*, fent to borrow it, in order to have it tranfcrib'd; but the college reprefenting it as againft their conftitutions to lend any of their books without a fufficient pledge; his majefty was contented to obtain the ufe of it, by depofiting a large quantity of his own plate. Whether therefore the king or the two doctors brought the firft Printers to *Paris*, 'tis beyond doubt, that he gave them fufficient encouragement, and acceſs to the library at the *Louvre*, with liberty to print from any of thofe volumes, in the choice of which, it is probable, they were directed by their two patrons.

As the Art was then in its infancy at *Paris*, their firft editions were in a large round Roman character but greatly inferior in beauty to that of their contemporaries in *Italy*; their paper was fmooth and ftrong, tho' lefs white; their impreffions were maim'd and imperfect, with letters and words half printed, and finifh'd with a pencil; the infcription and title of fome epiftles, and the large initial letters of books and chapters were done with the hand, for which a blank was left in the page; they had no capitals, nor regular fpaces, but were full of abbreviations; in fhort,
there

there was nothing to recommend them except the newnefs, and the beauty of the ink. They us'd few rubricks, and thofe only upon vellum; fome of their books begin at the *folio verfo*, or even page; and all of them are without titles, number of pages, fignatures or direction-words; they us'd no fignatures 'till the year 1476, and then plac'd them not at the bottom, but at the top of the pages; they added neither date, nor names of Printer and place; all which are only to be gathered from the prefaces, or epigrams at the end, or fome other circumftances, as will appear from the lift of their works, efpecially of thofe printed in the three firft years 1470, 1471, and 1472. It is certainly very furprifing, that neither *Gering* nor his two learned patrons, who muft infallibly have feen fome of the *Italian* editions, efpecially thofe of *Rome* and *Venice*, which had all thefe neceffary ornaments, fhould not make them fenfible of their deficiencies in all thofe refpects. However, fo few were the elegant Printers in thofe days, that the learned men of *Paris*, who efteem'd the Art of more confequence than thefe embellifhments, fail'd not to acknowledge their obligation to the *Sorbon* doctors, for the fervices they had done to the univerfity in fettling the Printers there, upon whom they were equally liberal of their encomiums. Enough of thefe may be feen in *Chevillier* pag. 41, *& feq.* I fhall only cite in the margin an epigram printed at the end of *Gafpar Pergamenfis*'s epiftles, which was their firft impreffion, and had prefix'd to it a letter of thanks to thofe great men, upon their bringing the Art to that city.

THE epigram[1] is addrefs'd to the city of *Paris*, and fufficiently fhews not only that this edition was the firft fruits of the Art both in that city and kingdom, againft thofe who afcribe that honour to *Jenfon*; but likewife that the *Parifians* congratulated themfelves for their fuccefs in introducing it thither, fince it gave the univerfity an abfolute authority over

Ut fol lumen, fic doctrinam fundis in orbem,
　Mufarum nutrix regia, *Parifius.*
Hinc prope divinam tu, quam *Germania* novit,
　Artem fcribendi, fufcipe promerita.
Primos ecce libros, quos hæc iuduftria finxit
　Francorum in terris, ædibus atque tuis.
Michael Uldaricus Martinufque magiftri
　Hos imprefferunt, ac facient alios.

all

all Printers and bookfellers, in the *feven* following particulars, mention'd by *Chevillier* pag. 327, *viz.*

1. THAT all the Printers and bookfellers of *Paris*, after the firft fettlement of printing there, have ftill continued in their former ftate, that is, been efteem'd as agents and fervants to that univerfity.

2. THAT they are oblig'd to take the oaths to the rector of it.

3. THAT they are not allow'd to follow that bufinefs 'till the univerfity has judg'd them qualify'd for it.

4. THAT the univerfity exercifes their jurifdiction over them by fummoning them to appear, &c. by fining, punifhing and depofing them for any mifdemeanor.

5. THAT the edicts and ordinances of the king impower that body to vifit and fearch all Printing-houfes, ware-houfes for books, and bookfellers fhops, &c.

6. THAT the univerfity fet a price upon their books, which was affix'd to their catalogues, and plac'd in fome confpicuous part of their fhops, left any perfon might be impos'd on by them. This part of their province they exerted, long before the Art of Printing was difcover'd, over all tranfcribers, illuminators, bookfellers, &c.

7. LASTLY, that the bookfellers, &c. fhould fell no books of religion, &c. 'till they had been examin'd and approv'd by the univerfity, or, at leaft, by the faculty of doctors of divinity.

WE fhall fhew in the third book of this hiftory, that the univerfity of *Oxford* had the fame authority over the Printers and bookfellers of that city.

To return to our three Printers, they continued printing but three years at the houfe of the *Sorbon*; after which one of their patrons, *Fichet* being invited to *Rome* by Pope *Sixtus* IV, and the other intending foon after to return to *Germany*, they remov'd to St. *James's-ftreet*, at the fign

Z   of

of the *Golden Sun*. Upon this they immediately rejected all their old punches, matrices and letters, and furnish'd themselves with some entirely new, and printed several considerable volumes 'till the year 1477; at which time *Crantz* and *Friburger* either return'd into *Germany*, or, at least, left off printing, for there is no edition with their names after that year; but *Gering* printed in his own name many years longer, as shall be shewn in its place   In the mean time, it will be proper to give the reader an account of this new set of characters, which they made use of in their new house.

'Tis to be observ'd, that they were of three or four sorts, all different from each other, and from those us'd at the house of the *Sorbon*, and cast in new matrices.   One sort is vastly inferior to their former, and resembles the hand-writing of that time, but such as was done (*stannea manu*, as *Aldus* expresses it) with a heavy hand.

It is not, however, altogether Gothic, but rather like that which *Schoeffer* us'd at *Mentz*.   Another sort was not unlike this in shape, but of a much larger face.   The *third* was a Roman much more round and fine than the two former; but the *fourth* sort, not us'd by *Gering* 'till after the year 1478, that is, after his partners had left him, is a very beautiful, large Roman, which (if we may believe *Chevillier*, who saw and compar'd them) is in no case inferior to that of the *Spira*'s, *Jenson*, or any other of the famous *Venetian* and *French* Printers, either before or since.   Thus *Gering* attain'd to a degree of perfection equal with any of his brethren; but was at last oblig'd to comply with the custom, and print several books in Gothic, such as *Virgil* and some others, besides those for the use of churches.   The editions printed at this house, and in these new characters, are still defective with respect to their dates or Printers names, some wanting the one, some the other, and some both, as appears by the list of his works given us by the foremention'd author, *anno* 1480. *Gering* took into partnership with him for some time, *William Maynyal*; and in the year 1483 remov'd from St. *James's-street*, and took a lease, during life, of a house belonging to the college of *Sorbon*, where he set up his old sign of the *Golden-sun*.   As he was now become very rich, and had contracted an intimate friendship with the *Sorbon* collegians, he made them some considerable donatives both in books and

and money; upon which account they chofe him fellow of that college, and affign'd him chambers and commons in it: and as he was not engag'd in matrimony, he took the more pleafure in converfing with them, communicating his defigns, and ufing their advice about the books which he was to print, and their affiftance in correcting them; in return for which he prefented them with copies of all his editions.   It was no fmall advantage to that college (which was call'd at firft by the founder *Robert Sorbon, Societas pauperum magiftrorum Parifiis in theologica facultate ftudentium*) to have fo generous a friend and benefactor admitted into it; who requited them for this honour with vaft legacies, left by him in his will to this college, and that of *Montague* in the fame city.   For by his fuccefs in printing 'till *anno* 1510, in which he died, he had amafs'd a prodigious quantity of wealth, all which he bequeath'd to thofe two colleges.   What he endow'd the *Sorbon* in particular with, was fufficient to maintain *eight* fellows, to be added to thofe on the old foundation, and two lectures every day, one in the morning for the Old, and another in the afternoon for the New Teftament; befides feveral other donatives to thofe of the houfe whom he had a particular efteem for.

Now confidering, that he was the firft Printer of that city and kingdom; that he was invited thither by the college of *Sorbon*; that he had been fo great a mafter of his art, and fo liberal to that poor fociety in his life-time, and after his death; the reader may perhaps expect to hear of fome monument erected by them to his memory: but 'tis plain from what *Chevillier*, a fellow of that college, tells us, that they did not fo much as fet a grave-ftone over him, to let the world know where that great man was bury'd; fo that our laft mention'd author, after a vaft deal of pains, could not gain the leaft certainty about it.   However, to do them juftice, they order'd an anniverfary-mafs to be faid on the 23d of *Auguft*, on which he dy'd.   Who his correctors were, is difficult to determine; but it is probable he made ufe of any of the collegians, whom he pleas'd.   He had fome other partners befides *Maynyal* beforemention'd, and inftructed feveral Printers, who fignaliz'd themfelves both during his life and after he dy'd.   There were likewife divers other Printing-houfes fet up at *Paris* foon after his, of which we fhall fpeak, when we have given fome further account of his works; *Chevillier* in his lift of

them

them divides them into three claffes, *viz.* thofe which he printed with his two partners in the college from 1470 to 1473; next thofe printed at the *Golden Sun* in St. *James's-ftreet* 'till *anno* 1483; and *laftly*, thofe which he printed from that time 'till his death, either by himfelf or with his other partners. Of the firft clafs there are *eleven* editions ftill extant all printed in the fame charaƈter, fome of the firft of which have epiftles affix'd and infcrib'd by *Fichet* above-nam'd, to feveral princes and prelates, and are dated 1470 and 1471; one of which, to cardinal *Beffarion*, has the following, *Ædibus Sorbonæ fcriptum, impreffumque uno anno & feptuagefimo quadringentefimo fupra millefimum:* thofe of the *fecond* clafs are 23 in number: and fixteen of the *third* clafs, exclufive of thofe, which he printed after the year 1500: all which the reader will find either in *Chevillier* or Mr. *Mattaire*. *Gering's* laft work is dated 1508, which fhews that he left off printing two years before he dyed: for his death did not happen 'till *anno* 1510, *Aug.* 23. The next Printing-houfe, to that of the three *Germans* laft fpoken of, was fet up by,

4. Peter Cæsaris and 5. John Stol, 1473.

These two Printers were likewife natives of *Germany*, but had already ftudied fometime in the univerfity of *Paris*, where the former had attain'd to the degree of mafter of arts: thefe two became acquainted with their countryman *Gering*, and inform'd him of their defign of fetting up a Printing-houfe, begging his affiftance and inftruƈtions therein, which he readily granted: and thus was the fecond Prefs fet up at *Paris* by thefe two learned perfons, who became foon after, no lefs famous, for their induftry and application, than they had been for their learning. They pitch'd upon one of the houfes, belonging to the college of *Sorbon*, to print in, which *Chevillier* tells us, was in St. *James's-ftreet* at the fign of the *Soldier* and *Swan:* their charaƈter was fhort of the beauty of *Uldric Gering*, tho' far from being of the Gothic kind; this may be one reafon why a great many of their works are loft: they were likewife guilty of negleƈting to affix either their names or dates to their works: fo that the former is only to be gather'd from the likenefs of the charaƈter to their

other

other works, that are printed in their names, and the latter is either fupply'd by fome circumftance, or wholly guefs'd at.

Their firft work is fuppos'd to be the *Speculum Zamoræ*, which tho' printed without date, yet is known to have come out *anno* 1473 by the epigram at the end: one of their fineft impreffions is that of *Ocham's* decalogue, which *Naudeus* thought to have been done by *Gering*, but *Chevillier* who has compar'd them with other of their works, affures them to have been printed by them: we have but ten editions of theirs from 1473 to 1500: but they continu'd printing beyond that time efpecially *Cæfaris*. The next *Paris* Printer was,

6. Peter Caron, of whom we have but one edition dated 1474.

7. Pasquier Bon-homme 1475, he printed the chronicle of *France*, and that of St *Dennis* in three volumes *fol. a fcarce book*, and the only one we have left of him, it is dated 1475.

8. Anthony Verard, 1480.

He was one of the moft confiderable Printers and bookfellers of his time, and very eminent for the curiofity and number of his editions. The greateft part of his books confift in romances and the like, printed in a Gothic character, but fo elegant as to pleafe the eye extremely. Many of them are printed upon fine vellum ; *La Caille* tells us, that there are above an hundred volumes of his romances printed curioufly on vellum, embellifh'd with exquifite miniatures or fmall cutts, painted in water colours, in imitation of the manufcripts which he printed after, all which are to be feen in the French king's library. However, tho' he engag'd moft in romantick pieces, yet he likewife publifh'd feveral learned volumes, all in *French*, with equal care and beauty, in the fame Gothic letter.

He kept his Printing-houfe and fhop upon the bridge of *Nôtre Dame* at the fign of St. *John* the *Evangelift*. Sometimes he fubfcribes his books only with the firft letters of his name, A. V. His mark is enclos'd with four *French* verfes in a pious ftrain : the reader will find them in the margin [1]. Whatever is become of the great number of his editions, fome of

---

[1] Pour provoquer ta grand mifericorde　　　*Antoine Verard* humblement te recorde
A tout pecheur faire Grace & Pardon　　　Tout ce qu'il a, il fsent de toy pardon.

which

which were printed by the *French* king *Charles* VIII's order, I can find no more in *Orlandi's* lift than 32, from 1480 to 1500.

THE reſt of the *Paris* Printers are as follows,

9. NICHOLAS *de Philippis* and

10. MARK REYNHARD *de Strasburgh,* }

WHERE they printed in partnerſhip before they came to *Paris:* we have but one edition of theirs dated 1482.

11. ANTONY CAYLLAUT and ⎫ we have 4 edit. of theirs from 1483

12. LEWIS MARTINEAU,   ⎭   to 1492.

13. GUIDO MERCANT, 10 edit. from 1483 to 1499.

14. GEORGE MITTLH or *Mittelh,* 2 edit. from 1484 to 1489.

15. DENNIS JANNOT, 1 edit. 1484.

16. ROBINET MACE, 1 edit. 1486.

17. JOHN BONHOME, who was alſo a bookſeller, 3 edit. from 1486 to 1489.

18. PETER LEVET, 5 edit. from 1487 to 1497.

19. JOHN CARCHAGNI, 1 edit. 1489.

20. PETER ROUGE the king's Printer, 3 edit. from 1487 to 1488.

21. JOHN DUPRE, 1 edit. 1488 : he went to *Lyons* ſoon after.

22. PHILIP PIGOUCHET, 3 edit. from 1489 to 1500.

23. WOLFGANG HOPYL *German* and ⎫ 4 edit. from 1489 to 1498.

24. JOHN HIGMAN,   ⎭

THE former of theſe became afterwards partner of the great *Henry Ste-phens.*

25. MICHAELLE NOIR, 1 edit. 1489.

26. DURANT GERLIER, 1 edit. 1489.

27. JAMES MAILET, 1 edit. 1491.

28. GEORGE WOLF of *Baden* and partners, 7 edit. from 1491 to 1499.

HIS partners, who printed afterwards by themſelves ſhall be mention'd in their place.

29. WILLIAM CARON,

30. JOHN BELIN with *John Dupre* abovemention'd, } 1 edit. 1492.

31. GILLET COUSTEAU and ⎫ 2 edit. from 1492 to 1494.

32. JOHN MENARD,   ⎭

33. JOHN

33. J OHN L AMBERT and } 2 edit. 1493 to 1494.
34. C LAUDE J AMMAR,

35. J OHN P HILIPPI *de Cruczennach*, German, one of *George Wolph's* partners : we have 3 edit. of his from 1494 to 1495.

36. P ETER P OUILLAC,
37. S TEPHEN J ANNOT and } 4 edit. from 1495 to 1498.
38. J OHN T REPEREL,

39. J OHN B OUYER and } 1 edit. 1496.
40. W ILLIAM B OUCHER,

41. A NDR. B OCARD one of the beſt Printers of his time: *De la Caille* affirms him to have printed a great number of books, both for himſelf and other bookſellers : and among others, the *Figuræ Biblicæ* of *Anth. de Rampengol:* his mark was the arms of *France*, and thoſe of the univerſity, and of the city of *Paris* with four *French* verſes, which you will find in the margin [1] : we have however but 4 edit. of his, 3 dated 1497, and the laſt 1498.

42. A NTONY N IDEL or *de Nydel* a citizen of *Paris*, and maſter of arts : we have but one impreſſion of his dated 1497.

43. J OHN P OITEVIN,
    J OHN H IGMAN, } we have but 1 edit. of each of theſe dated
44. J OHN R ICHARD, } 1498.

45. J O. P ETIT, *Pariſian*, 1498.

J OHN P ETIT was a native of *Paris*, and rather a bookſeller than a Printer : he is juſtly eſteem'd one of the moſt eminent and induſtrious ones of his time. He kept the greateſt number of the beſt workmen of any of his contemporaries, with no leſs than fifteen preſſes continually at work at his own charges, whilſt himſelf was engag'd in the buſineſs of his ſhop, at the *ſilver Lyon,* and procuring the moſt ſkilfull correctors to reviſe his works. He gain'd a prodigious reputation by the beauty and correctneſs of his impreſſions, which, tho' printed in a Gothic character, are much eſteem'd by the curious. He began to print *anno* 1498, tho' ſome copies

Honneur au Roy, & a la Court,   Dont nôtre bien procede & ſourt
Salut a l'Univerſite,   Dieu gard' de *Paris* la cite.

of

of editions by feveral former Printers have likewife his name, as Mr. *Mattaire* informs us, yet all have not ; he continued printing 'till *anno* 1532, and many of his impreffions are as fcarce as they are curious.   The learned *Henry Stephens*, father of fo many great Printers of that name, was fo well fatisfy'd of his merit, that he was glad to have him for his partner with *Wolfgang Hopyl* mention'd above, who was a Printer of much older date: *Petit* became fo famous, both for the beauty and correctnefs, as well as the number of his editions, that he was afterwards fworn Printer and bookfeller to the univerfity of *Paris*, and chofen fyndic or mafter of that company ; among thofe Printers which he employ'd, was the famous *Jodocus Badius*, who printed feveral confiderable editions for him.   In the title page of his books, he us'd the words *Petit a Petit* [*by little and little*] alluding to his own name, which he alfo us'd for his motto.   The books which we find printed in his name from 1498 to 1500, are only three, the firft of which is much valued by ftudents in law, *viz.*

MODUS *legendi abbreviaturus in utroque jure*, 8vo, per *Jo. Petit, Parifiis*, 1498. For as we hinted before, abbreviations were become fo frequent and intricate in moft fciences, but efpecially that of the law, that fuch a help as this was become abfolutely neceffary.

46. JOHN DRYART,
47. SIMON COLIN,   } we have but one impreffion of each of
48. GODFREY MARNEF, } thefe dated 1498.
49. MICHEL TOLOSA, 1 edit. 1499.
50. ALEXANDER ALIATE, }
51. THIELMAN KERVER, } 1 edit. of each 1500.

WE find alfo in *Orlandi*'s lift about 44 editions without Printers names.

BEFORE I difmifs this chapter, I cannot omit obferving, that *Paris* hath been a noble patronefs of the Art of Printing. 'Tis true, *Venice* is juftly fam'd upon this account ; yet it ought to be remember'd, that moft of her celebrated Printers were of the *French* nation, and fignaliz'd themfelves as much in this Art, as any other nation ; and that *Paris* excell'd all other cities of that kingdom in this refpect.   The encouragements which their kings, and the learned of that and other countries, have given the Art, and the care of the univerfity over the Printers, have

contri-

contributed extremely to the great improvements made therein.   Befides
this, the *French* have fhewn an extraordinary genius and fkill in the cutting of their punches for all languages; they have been very curious
about their paper, and more particularly in adorning their editions with
cutts, head and tail pieces, initial letters, rubricks and other embellifhments of that nature.   This I mention not fo much with refpect to the
15th century, as to the following.   No city has produc'd a greater number of the fineft bibles than *Paris*.   Their large, royal and polyglot bibles
are juftly efteem'd mafter-pieces of that kind; their editions of general
and provincial councils, of canon and civil-law, the works of the fathers,
chronological and hiftorical books, and, in fhort, in every art and fcience,
are very numerous, rich, and valuable; and many of them contain feven,
eight, and ten large volumes, and fome twenty, thirty, and even thirty
feven, as the acts of the council printed by the famous *Anthony Vitré* at
the *Louvre*.   The women likewife were very eminent in this province;
and particulaily, *Charlotte Guillard*, the widow of *Berthold Rembolt*, *Ulric
Gering*'s partner, who for the fpace of 50 years kept feveral preffes, and
printed a great number of large and correct editions both in *Latin* and
Greek, her beft editions were publifh'd after fhe became a widow the fecond time, *viz.* the bible, the fathers; in particular, the works of St.
Gregory in two volumes were printed fo accurately, that the *errata* contain'd but three faults.   Her fame at laft increas'd fo, that the learned
Lewis Lippoman, bifhop of *Verona*, made choice of her to print his *Catena SS. patrum in Genefim*, which he finifh'd in *Portugal*.   This edition fhe
perform'd fo much to his fatisfaction, that when he affifted at the council
of *Trent*, he came on purpofe to *Paris* to return her thanks, and prevail'd
upon her to print likewife his fecond volume, *viz. Catena in Exodum*,
which fhe perform'd with equal beauty and correctnefs.   Thefe with many other particulars relating to that admirable woman, may be feen in
Chevil. p. 48, *& feq.*

A s *Paris* has always abounded in excellent Printers, and furnifh'd moft
other cities of *Europe* with fome of them; fo, on the other hand, it muft
be own'd, that it has produc'd feveral equally bad, who have publifh'd
many wretched editions; and 'tis probable they might have ftill increas'd,
had not the univerfity check'd their growth.   For as it has fuch power

over

over all Printers and bookfellers, as to refufe admitting thofe into the bufinefs, who are not fufficiently qualify'd, and to turn them out of it, or fufpend or fine them for any mifdemeanors, as was hinted before; it can more eafily reftrain them, than where fuch checks are wanting. However thofe, whofe merit recommends them, enjoy all the encouragement they can reafonably defire, both from their princes and the univerfity. They are endow'd with privileges, exemptions, and immunities beyond any other city; and have had frequent opportunities of raifing themfelves to great dignities, of acquiring large eftates, and in fhort, every thing fuitable to their merit.

C H A P. V.

The Settlement and Progrefs of Printing *in the Cities of* Cologn, Milan 1470, Strasburgh, Bolognia *and* Trevifo 1471, *the Names, Dates, and other Particulars of their* Printers.

Article I. COLOGN. 1470.

T H E city of *Cologn*, (which is one of the moft opulent Hans-towns in the empire, and an archiepifcopal fee, pleafantly fituated upon the *Rhine*,) by its nearnefs to *Mentz*, muft neceffarily have receiv d the Art of Printing very early. We have taken notice, in the firft book of this hiftory, that fome of *Fauft's* fervants left him even before the taking of that city, and fettled at *Cologn*; and the author of the Chronicle of that name mentions it as the firft city, which receiv'd the art after *Mentz*. 'Tis unqueftionable that if her firft impreffions had been preferv'd, we muft have given it the precedency to almoft all the cities hitherto mention'd; but whether the firft printers of it neglected to add their own, and the cities name at the end of their editions, (a fault too common in thofe days) or whether their works were too inconfiderable to be preferv'd; it is certain that there is no book, as yet known, printed there with an authentick date, before this year 1470; which is

the

the reason why, according to our propos'd method, we can allow it no higher rank. We have indeed, in the introduction to this second book, taken notice of one of the most eminent printers in this city, *viz. John Koelhoff*, who antedated some of his impressions; but, I hope, the reader is fully satisfy'd from the reasons which we have given there, that he began not to work so early, since one of his dates is even much older than either himself or the Art of Printing. *Cologn* did not abound with great Printers during the first 30 years, *viz.* till 1500; tho' in process of time it became very famous in that art, as well by those who liv'd in it, as those that dispers'd themselves into many cities of *Europe*. It is call'd *Colonia Agrippina* in *Latin* from the empress *Agrippina, Nero*'s mother: the following are all the Printers we know of 'till the end of the 15th century.

1. CONRARD WINTERS *de Hombergh*, a citizen of *Cologn*, of whom we have but one edition dated 1470.

2. PETER *de Olpe*, 2 edit. both 1471.

3. ARNOLD TERBORN or *Terburn*, 2 edit. from 1473 to 1477.

4. JOHN KOELHOFF *de Lubeck*, 9 edit. from 1474 to 1494: besides the two following ones, which tho' printed with his name, have a date manifestly false.

1. FLORES *de diversis sermonibus & epistolis* B. Bernardi *per me* Joan. Koelhoff *de* Lubeck Coloniensem *civem impressi anno* MCCCC, *feliciter finiunt.* The reader may see by the time in which he printed, that either the last C must have been taken up by the balls, or omitted by the compositor; and that it was done *anno* 1500, or that some other figures are wanting to the date: but it appears to me to be done by design rather than mistake.

2. SILVII *Senensis Epistolæ*, at the end; *Pii secundi pontificis maximi, cui ante summum episcopatum primum quidem imperiali secretario, mox episcopo, deinde etiam cardinali Senensi,* Enee Silvii *nomen erat, familiares epistole date ad amicos in quadruplici vise ejus statu finiunt, per me* Joannem Koelhoff de Lubeck *coloniæ incolam, anno incarnationis* MCCLCLVIII.

We have already obferv'd, that there are fome letters in this book, which are of a later date by feveral years than that of the book ; fo that it muft neceffarily be falfe.

5. Henry Quentel an excellent Printer, tho' omitted by the laft annalift father *Orlandi*, continued printing long after the year 1500, and had a fon *Peter Quentel* and a grandfon *John Quentel*, who likewife diftinguifh'd themfelves for the goodnefs and correctnefs of their editions ; we have but 4 edit. of his from 1480 to 1500.

6. John Guldenschayff, 4 edit. from 1484 to 1487.

Mr. *Mattaire* mentions likewife fome bibles, and a few other books printed here without Printers names.

Article II.   M I L A N, 1470.

Milan [in *latin Mediolanum*] is one of the four chief cities of *Italy*, fituate near the rivers *Adda* and *Tefino*, and faid to have been built by the *Trojans* after their expulfion by *Bellover* king of the *Gauls*. This city, after a variety of chances and wars, was almoft ruined by *Frederic Barbaroffa* ; but now flourifhes under the emperor of *Germany*. It received the Art of Printing very early, and had many excellent artificers from the beginning, whofe works are equally valuable with thofe of any other cities. We cannot pofitively affirm any thing concerning the time, in which this Art was brought hither, nor who were the men that fet it up. The firft both in time as well as excellency was.

1. Anthony Zarot, 1470.

He was a native of the city of *Parma*, tho' of *Cretenfian* parents, as appears by fome of his colophons, and gain'd a great reputation for 30 years, in which he continued printing, by his elegant and correct impreffions in a beautiful Roman character, which are fufficiently known among the learned. He was oblig'd indeed to comply with the cuftom in printing fome editions in old Gothic ; yet even thefe have all the elegancy and beauty they can admit of. He is efteem'd the inventor of fignatures, or alphabetical letters at the bottom of every fheet, which

at

at firſt he plac'd under the laſt line of the page, where they ought to be : But afterwards he put them, upon what account is hard to gueſs, at the end of the laſt line, ſo as to make them ſerve, as it were, for the laſt word in the page. This appears by his edition of *John Simoneta de geſtis Franciſci Sfortiæ ducis Mediol.* anno 1486. This whim of his was not follow'd by any Printer, nor by himſelf long ; for he ſoon return'd to the firſt method. His main province was printing of claſſicks, which he executed with extraordinary diligence and accuracy. He is ſaid to be the firſt that printed miſſals or maſs-books for the uſe of the clergy, who were hitherto us'd to MS ones. That which he printed *anno* 1478, had the four *Latin* verſes in red letters, which you will find in the margin [1]. His chief corrector was the famous *Peter Juſtin Philelphus*, a perſon of learning and great application, eſpecially in correcting the faulty editions which *Zarot* was oblig'd to procure from *Rome* or other places. His next corrector was the learned *P. Steph. Dulcinio*, prebend of *Scala*, who tells the marquiſs of *Palavicino*, to whom he dedicates the ſecond edition of *Manilius*, anno 1499. that he had corrected that author in above three hundred places, and clear'd it from the barbariſms, and other faults of the tranſcribers, as far as it was poſſible to be done in a very corrupt copy. *Zarot* continued printing till the year 1500, from which time we hear no more of him.

We have twenty ſix of his impreſſions ſtill extant, many of which have either an epigram or a colophon in his commendation. Some are without Printer or places name, and even without date; the laſt of which muſt be gueſs'd at, the former are eaſily known by the particular beauty of his character, and becauſe he printed no where but at *Milan*.

2. Philip *de Lavagna Milaneſe*, 13 editions, from 1474 to 1480. The laſt of which, *viz. Euſebii Chronicon* in *Latin*, is without date, and has a *Latin* epigram of ſix lines written in his commendation by *Boninus Mambritius*.

3. Christopher Valdarfer *de Ratisbon*, an excellent artiſt, who printed at *Venice* from 1470 to 1471, then came to *Milan*, where

[1] Anroni patria Parmenſis gente Zarote,
Primus Miſſales imprimit arte Libros.
Nemo repertorem nimium ſe jactet ; in Arte,
Addere plus tantum quam peperiſſe valet.

he

he wrought till *anno* 1477, if not beyond. He made ufe of the fame
corrector here which he had at *Venice*, *viz.* *Ludovicus Carbo* or *Carbone*,
a native of *Ferrara* ; we have but four impreffions of his done at *Milan*
from 1474 to 1477.

4. Dominic *de Vefpolate*,　⎫
5. Dionys Paravicino, 　⎬　4 edit. from 1476 to 1478.

The former alfo took another partner, *viz.*

6. James Marlian, of thefe we have 2 edit. 1477, 1478.

7. Ludovic and ⎫
8. Albert　　 ⎬ *Piedmontefe.* Of thefe two Brothers we have only

one edition, *viz. Dante's* comedies with comments : The text is printed
in an elegant Roman, and the comments in a fine Gothic character, with
the colophon which you'll find in the margin [1].

9. Leonard Pachel,　　　⎫
10. UldricScinzenzeter, ⎬ 1479.

Thefe two partners were Germans by birth, and printed fometimes together and fometimes feparately, till after the clofe of the 15th century.
The former of them printed a great many of the claffcks, and is reported to have printed a very confiderable number of law books, many of
which are not yet come to light. Their corrector was *Benedict. Rhetho-
ricus.* The number of their impreffions hitherto difcover'd from 1479 to
1500, amounts to 36.

11. Simon Magnagus, 1 edit. 1480.

12. Benignus and 　⎫
13. John Antony　 ⎬ *Bonafo* brothers, 2 edit. 1482, 1488.

14. James *de S. Nazaro,* 2 edit. 1489, 1494.

15. Philip *de Montegaliis,* 1 edit. 1490.

16. Peter Antony *de Caftillione,* 1 edit. 1493.

17. Henry German, and 　⎫
18. Sebastian *de Pontremoli,* ⎬ 1 edit. 1493.

---

[1] Edente Martino paulo Nidobeato Nova-
rienfi DIVA. BO. MA cum dulci nato JO.
GZ. Ducibus feliciff. Liguriæ valida pace reg-
nantibus, operi egregio manum fupremam LUD.
& ALB. FR. Pedemontani amico Jove impo-
fuerunt. Mediolani urbe illuftri. Anno Gra-
tiæ M. CCCC. LXXVI I. V. .D. F MP. N.
N. CUM. GU. T. FA. CU.

19. Wil-

19. WILLIAM SIGNER of *Rouen*, 2 edit 1496, 1498.

20. JOHN BAPT. ALVISIANUS, 1 edit. 1497.

21. ALEXANDER MINUTIANUS, 1 edit. of all *Cicero's* works in 4 volumes fol. the two firſt *anno* 1498, the other two 1499.

22. DEMETRIUS CHALCONDYLLA and partners, 1 edit. 1499.

23. AMBROSE CAPONAGUS, 1 edit. 1499.

24. JOHN ANGEL. SCINZENZELER and

25. BARTHOL MINIATOR, } 2 edit. both 1500.

26. PETER MARTYR MONTLEGATIUS, 1 edit. 1500.

There are alſo many editions printed at *Milan*, from 1471 to 1500 without Printer's names.   Fath. *Orlandi* tells us, that he has on purpoſe omitted many works done at *Milan*, becauſe his learned friend Dr. *Joſeph Antonio* keeper of the *Ambroſian* library in that city, was then (*ann* 1722) compiling a hiſtory which would ſhortly appear under the following title, *Hiſtoria Literaria Mediolanenſis ab an.* 1470 *ad* 1500. *qua occaſione de Origine & progreſſu Typographiæ, Libris editis intra illud tempus, ac Viris Illuſtribus, eo ſeculo in eadem Urbe florentibus.*   By this we may eaſily gueſs, that we have as yet but an imperfect hiſtory of that city.   We may ſay the ſame of almoſt all the reſt, except thoſe that have met with ſome learned perſons who have taken the pains of ſearching the libraries, in order to give a more perfect and full one of them, ſuch as that of *Paris, Nurembergh, &c.*

Article III. STRASBURGH.

STRASBURGH, in *Latin Argentina* and *Argentoratum*, is an epiſcopal See, and the metropolis of *Alſatia* upon the borders of *France*, celebrated for the number of learned men, which it has produc'd ; and the beauty and magnificence of its churches, towers, buildings, *&c.* according to the poet's deſcription [1].

IT was the native place of *John Guttenbergh*, to which, after his diſagreement with *Fauſt*, he brought the Art of Printing together with ſome of his artificers ; ſo that it may be juſtly eſteem'd, at leaſt, one of the

[1] Imprimiſque altas propius fert inclyta turres
Argentina Domus doctorum clara virorum.

firſt

firſt cities, that practis'd it after *Mentz*, tho' all the monuments of it are ſo far loſt to us, that we know not any books with a certain date, printed there before the year 1471.

WE have ſeen, in the firſt part of this hiſtory, how much this city hath been celebrated by ſome authors, upon the account of *John Guttenbergh*, whom they ſuppos'd to have been the inventor of this Art, or at leaſt to have laid the firſt foundation of it here, tho' he was oblig'd to retire to *Mentz* in order to perfect it. But as this, I conceive, has been ſufficiently confuted already, it is unneceſſary to repeat it here. I have likewiſe given the reader an account of another controverſy in favour of *Strasburgh* and *John Mentel* ſtarted about two hundred years after the diſcovery of this Art, by Dr. *Mentel* of the univerſity of *Paris*, who aſſerted that his anceſtor was the Inventor of Printing ; which diſcovery he was robb'd of by a treacherous ſervant, whom he ſuſpects to be our famous *John Fauſt*. I hope, I have fully expoſed the vanity of this author's pretences, and his unfaithfulneſs in quoting teſtimonies in behalf of *Mentel*; againſt whom, were there no other evidence, it would be ſufficient to allege, that there is not one book printed in his name before the year 1473, and that without any mention of the city of *Strasburgh*.

ALL that is proper to add at preſent is, that our author, to elude, if poſſible, the force of this objection, affirm'd that this book, which *John Mentel* finiſh'd *anno* 1473, was no leſs than twenty years a printing, and contain'd ten large volumes in *fol.* ſo that it muſt have been begun about 1453, *i.e.* four years before *Fauſt* had printed any work in his name, but this is a groundleſs conjecture.

THIS book is the *Speculum Morale* of *Vincentius Belvacenſis*, a very voluminous work ; but that it ſhould have taken up 20 years in printing is only ſaid without any authority or teſtimony for it; however we may allow it to have taken up ſome conſiderable time, without leſſening the validity of what has been heretofore affirm'd after ſeveral eminent authors, *viz.* that *John Fauſt,* at his return from *Paris,* where he had been ſelling his printed bibles for manuſcripts, ſtay'd ſome time at *Strasburgh,* where he taught *Mentel* his Art. The only difficulty againſt it is, that if this laſt had been let into the ſecret ſo ſoon, there would be ſome earlier and a greater number of his productions to be ſeen. The former is
eaſily

eafily anfwer'd by the fad experience we have, of too many of the old monuments of the Art being either loft, or not yet difcover'd; and the latter, *De la Caille* endeavours to account for, who peremptorily afferts this *Mentel* to be the fame with *John Mentelen* or *Manthen de Geretzfheim*, who went and fettled at *Venice*, and affociated himfelf with the famous *John de Cologne*, one of the moft eminent and firft Printers of that city about the year 1474, with whom he printed feveral valuable editions, mention'd in the chapter of *Venice*.

IF this affertion be well grounded, 'tis fuperfluous to feek for any of his works at *Strasburgh*, except the *Speculum* beforemention'd, if even that was printed there. But as *la Caille* has not mention'd his authority, I fhall not dare to affert the truth of this too pofitively. We muft not omit taking notice, that this *John Manthen* continued printing at *Venice*, with his partner aforefaid, 'till the year 1480, as the reader may fee by what has been faid of him there; whereas *John Mentel* is affirm'd by the Dr. from the authority of *Gafpar Benegerus* to have dy'd at *Strasburgh* two years before, *viz.* 1478, in honour of whom the great bell of that city was or-der'd to be rung the funday following [1], which is never done but upon the death of a prince or fome very great man. I fhall not take upon me to decide the controverfy, but only fay, that if the *Speculum* aforefaid, be *Mentel's* firft edition at *Strasburgh*, it will follow, that he was outftript, at leaft by two years there, by the famous *Henry Eggelftein*, of whom we have only two volumes, both printed *anno* 1471; the laft of which is per-haps one of the largeft that ever was printed, the paper of it being of an extraordinary fize, exceeding even that which is commonly call'd *Charta magna*. It hath likewife another remarkable particular, which is, that the beginning and end of it are printed in red, and is therefore the firft edition done after that manner.

THE Printers therefore of *Strasburgh* from 1471 to 1500 are as fol-lows,

1. HENRY EGGELSTEIN abovemention'd, 2 edit. dated 1471.
2. JOHN MENTEL, 1 edit. *viz. Vincentii Speculum morale* in ten large

---

[1] Obiit dominus *Johannes Mentel* fabatho poft conceptionem virginis *Maria*, anno MCCCC LXX IIX; et factus eft ei pulfus cum campana magna Dominica fequenti. Pa-ræn. &c. *pag* 93.

B b

volumes, *fol.* and suppos'd to be printed at *Strasburgh*, tho' no mention is made of the place where it was done ; it is dated 1473.

3. MARTIN FLACH or *Flachen* citizen of *Basil*, 7 edit. from 1475 to 1500.

4. LEORIUS USNER citizen of *Strasburgh*, 2 edit. from 1476 to 1477.

5. MARC REYNHARD of *Strasburgh* and

6. NICOL. *de Philippis* of *Gernsheym*, } 2 edit. from 1480 to 1482.

7. JOHN PRUS, 1 edit. 1487.

8. GEORGE REYNHARD or *de Grunynger*, 3 edit. from 1489 to 1498 : he had likewise printed at *Rome*, as we have seen under that head *anno* 1475.

ORLANDI has likewise given us a list of 84 edit. printed at *Strasburgh* without Printers names.

Article IV. BOLOGNA, 1471.

BOLOGNA or *Bolonia*, in *Latin Bononia*, an ancient and famous city of *Italy*, at the foot of the *Alps*, upon the river *Rhine*, in the territories of the pope, was formerly call'd *Felsina*, from *Felsinus* king of the *Thuscans*, which signifies a shield. This name she preserv'd above nine hundred years, and always was eminent for the number of learned men and brave warriers which she produc'd. This city afterwards was call'd *Bojona* from *Buoi* king of the *Gauls*, and in process of time *Bononia* and *Bolonia*. It is at this day a celebrated university, endow'd with extraordinary privileges from emperors, popes, &c. and such a concourse of students resort thither, that it is recorded of one of their doctors and professors, the learned *Azzo*, that he was oblig'd to read his lectures in some publick market places, to above ten thousand students. For these and other reasons, not necessary to be given here, it has been styl'd *Archigymnasium mundi*, and the mother and founder of universities[1]. 'Tis no wonder therefore that the Art of Printing receiv'd such early encouragement from it, and that it had so many famous workmen, eminent for the beauty and correctness of their impressions.

Bononia docet Mater studiorum,
Petrus ubique Pater, Legumque Mater.

I

IT is likewife obfervable that it had not the Art brought to it by foreigners, as other famous cities, *Rome, Venice, Paris,* &c. but was oblig'd for it to one of her own citizens, *viz.*

1. BALTHAZAR AZZOGUIDI, *anno* 1471.

A perfon well born and of good education, who fet up his Prefs in that city, and continued printing, at leaft, till the year 1480, after which we hear no more of him. His editions are all in a neat Roman character, and printed with great accuracy, the firft of which, *viz. Ovid's Metamorphofes* anno 1471, has the colophon which you'll find in the margin [1]. By which it is plain that he was the firft who practis'd the Art of Printing, of which he improperly calls himfelf the inventor in his own city of *Bolonia.* We have 12 editions of him from 1471 to 1480.

2. HUGO RUGERIUS and
3. DONINUS BERTOCH } of *Regio,* 6 edit. from 1474 to 1495.

4. DOMINIC *de Lapis,* 3 edit. 1476 to 1477.

5. JOHN SCRIBER of *Ausburgh,* call'd alfo
JOHN *de Annunciata de Augufta,* } 2 edit. both 1478.

6. HENRY *de Colonia,* 5 edit. from 1479 to 1486.

7. JOHN *de Noerdlingen* and
8. HENRY *de Harlem,* } 8 edit. from 1480 to 1488.

THE laft of thefe did likewife affociate himfelf firft with

9. MATH. CRESCENTINUS, and afterwards with

10. JOHN WALBECK; fo that 3 of the 8 editions above-nam'd were printed, one with the former, and two with the laft.

11. BALTHASSAR *de Hyruberia,* 2 edit. both 1481.

12. DOMINIC *de Silveftro de Cini,* 1 edit. 1482.

13. PLATO *de* BENEDICTIS; or DEI BENEDETTI of *Bologna,* 1483.

This Printer hath never been excell'd by any perfon in the beauty and elegance of his Roman character; and as his editions are extremely fine

---

[1] Baltheffar Azzoguidi civis Bononienfis ho-　artis imprefforiæ Inventor, ad Utilitatem Hu-
neftiffimo loco natus, primus in fua Civitate　mani generis impreffit, A. M CCCC LXX .

and

and correct, fo he hath taken care to tell the world of it in almoft every colophon at the end of his books, by adding fome pompous title to his name, fuch as *impreffor folertiffimus, artis hujus exactor probatiffimus, quam pulcherrimis Characteribus,* &c. He is thought to have either learn'd the Art at *Venice*, or furnifh'd himfelf with his Fonts from thence. The firft is moft probable, becaufe we find an edition of *Dion. Chryfoftom's Oratio de regno*, 4to. fuppos'd to have been printed by him at *Venice anno* 1483. But *F. Orlandi* thinks this fuppofition ill-grounded, and therefore hath mention'd neither him, nor that edition under the article of *Venice*, but has put it at the head of thofe printed by him at *Bologna*, where having found a book, printed *anno* 1481, intitled *Baptiftæ Mantuani Carmelitani parthenices*, he reprinted it with his own name and colophon. All his impreffions as yet known, the two foremention'd ones included, amount to fixteen, the laft of them, *viz. Vegetius* and others *de Re Militari* is dated 1495.

14. BENEDICT HECTOR, 1478.

He was a very good Printer and Bookfeller, who employ'd many Printers of this city, and kept likewife fome preffes of his own a-going, as appears by thofe impreffions we have of him ; all which are fo correct and beautiful, that he is juftly rank'd among the beft workmen of his time, and *Ugerius de Pontremulo* has honour'd fome of his impreffions with epigrams in praife of him. We have four and twenty of them ftill extant from 1488 to 1499.

15. BACILIERUS ⎞ ⎛ *Bacilieris,* ⎞
    BASSALERUS ⎬ or *de* ⎨ *Baffaleris,* ⎬ 1489.
    BAZALERUS ⎠ ⎝ *Bazaleris,* ⎠

WE have but three editions of this Printer from 1489 to 1493, in each of which he fpells his name differently. He was an excellent Printer, and a rival of the famous *Plato de Benedictis*, whom he endeavour'd to furpafs in beauty of letter, finefs and accuracy of his impreffions, which tho' they do not excel, yet are not at all inferior to thofe of his corrival, and he doth not fail accordingly to give himfelf fome of thefe pompous epithets which we have feen of the other ; and it is obferv'd that fome of *Plato's* impreffions were no fooner come out of the prefs, but *Bacilierus* went immediately to work upon them, and publifh'd another
other

other edition in a ſmall time after.   Such an emulation could not chuſe but have proved an honour and ſervice to the Art had it liv'd till now.

16. JOHN JAMES FONTANESE, 2 edit. both dated 1492.

17. HECTOR FAELLI *Bologneſe*, 2 edit. from 1492, to 1500.

18. HERCULES NANI, 2 edit. from 1493, to 1494.

19. JUSTINIAN *de Ruberia*, 2 edit. from 1495, to 1499.

JOHN ANTONY *Platonides Benedictorum Bologneſe*, 1 edit. 1499. With a ſmall number printed at *Bologne* without the Printers names.

Article V. *The City of* TREVISO.

TREVISO, in *Latin Tarviſium*, a noble and ancient city of *Italy*, and the capital of the province of that name, by reaſon of its vicinity to *Venice*, under whoſe dominion it is, had the Art of Printing ſoon introduc'd.   *Gerard de Liſa*, a *Flemming* by birth, and an excellent Printer, was the firſt that ſet it up here.   We can only ſay in general both of him and this city, that the few editions we have left of theirs are very elegant and in a neat character.

1.   GERARD *de* LIZA *or* LISIS, *or* GERARD *de* FLANDRIA, 1471.

WE have but four editions of him ; the two firſt are dated 1471, the third 1476, and the laſt 1492, which makes me hope that more of them will ſtill come to light, theſe being eſteem'd very curious, not only for their elegancy, but likewiſe for their correctneſs.

2.   HERMAN LICHTHENSTEIN *or* LEVILAPIS *of* COLOGN, 1477.

THIS Printer we have ſpoken of under the chapter of *Venice* ; and we ſhall again mention him under the city of *Vincenza*, where he printed for ſome time.   At *Treviſo* we have only two editions printed by him, both dated 1477.   He died *anno* 1494, whilſt he was printing that voluminous work of *Vincentius*, entituled, *Speculum Morale.*

3. BERNARD *de Colonia*, 2 edit. 1477, 1478.

4. MI

4. MICHEL MANZOLI or MANZOLINI, 7 edit. from 1477 to 1480.

5. BARTHOLOMEW *de Conſoloneriis*, 4 edit. from 1478 to 1483.

6. BERNARDIU CELERIUS *de Luere*, 2 edit. 1480, 1483. after which he went to *Venice*, where he aſſociated himſelf with *Bernardin de Novaria* as has been mention'd under that Head.

7. JOHN VERCELLIUS, or *Vercellenſis*, 6 edit. from 1480 to 1494. after which he went to *Venice*, where you will find him under that head, from *anno* 1486 to 1499. In this laſt place he calls himſelf *John Rubeus Vercellenſis*.

8. PAUL *de Ferrara* and ⎫
9. DIONYS BERTOCH, ⎬ 2 edit 1481, 1482.

DIONYS BERTOCH and ⎫
10. PEREGRINE PASQUALI, ⎬ 2 edit. 1482, 1485.

THERE is ſcarce one Printer to be met with in hiſtory, who chang'd oftner his place of abode, his partners, and even his name, than *Denni Bertoch*; who ſometimes calls himſelf *Bertoch Doninus*, and ſometimes *Dionys*, ſometimes *de Bononia*, and at other times *de Regio*. His firſt works, *viz.* for 1482 to 1490, were printed at *Treviſo*; immediately after which we find him at *Venice*, where he ſtay'd till 1492; thence he remov'd to *Regio*, and aſſociated himſelf with *Marc Antony de Baccilieris*; and laſtly he ſettled at *Modena* about the year 1499. We find but two of their impreſſions under this head, dated 1482 and 1485.

BUT tho' we have rank'd them under the article of *Treviſo*, yet they bear no name of any place, and may indeed be ſuppos'd done by them at *Venice*, where they printed about this time; however I have choſen to follow *F. Orlandi*, who thinks it more probable that they were done at *Treviſo*.

THERE is an edition printed by *Peregrine Paſquali* at *Scandian* near the city of *Reggio*, but with a date impoſſible to be underſtood o gueſs'd at;

IT is as follows,

DILIGENTIS *ac ingenioſi calchographi Peregrini Paſquali exaɛliſſim tum operâ, tum curâ hæc Candidi ex Apiano hiſtorico & ſophiſta traduɛlio Scandiani Camillo comite, impreſſa eſt.* Anno a natali Chriſti, 1ſ M CCCC LCXV.

Appen

Appendix to the foregoing chapter ; Printing *fet up at* Ratisbon, Amberg, *and* Colle, 1471.

THESE three cities, tho' diftant from each other, we have join'd together at the end of this chapter, for the fake of the editions printed at each of them in the fame year 1471, which were too few to deferve a diftinct article ; fince we meet with no impreffions at either of them, except the four following ; *viz.*

1. AT *Ratisbon* an imperial city in *Germany* upon the *Danube*; *Servii comment. in Virgilium*, fol. without the Printer's name.   1471. *Orl.*

2. AT *Amberg* in the *Palatinate*, now fubject to the elector of *Bavaria* ; *Marc. Tull. Cicer. Orationes omnes*, fol. without the Printer's name. 1471. *Orl.*

3. AT *Colle* a citadel fituate upon a hill in *Tufcany*, and fubject to the duke of that name ;

(1.) OPPIANI *Cilix, qui claruit fub imper. Caracallâ, halieuticon five de naturâ & venatione pifcium libri quinque*, 4to. per. Gallum Bonum. 1471. *Orl.*

(2.) JACOBI *de Voragine legenda aurea.* ibid. without the Printer's name, *Orl.* 1471.

CHAP.   VII.

Printing brought into the Cities of Naples, Florence, *and* Ferrara, *anno* 1471, *and to* Nurembergh, Verona, Parma, Mantua, Derventer *and* Padua, *anno* 1472 ; *a Lift of the Printers, and their Works, with other particulars, till* 1500.

Article. I. *The City of* NAPLES.

NAPLES, in *Latin Neapolis* and *Parthenope*, is the metropolis of the kingdom of that name, in *Italy*. It was formerly govern'd by kings of its own, but afterwards became fubject to the crown of *Spain*, and is

now

now under the emperor of *Germany*. This city has been the residence of men of the most distinguish'd wit and learning, in ancient and modern ages ; as *Virgil*, who is said to have writ his Georgicks here ; *Livy, Horace, Claudian, Petrarck, Bocatellus Panormitanus, Laurentius Valla*, the great restorer of latinity and eloquence ; *Perillus*, an elegant *Italian* poet ; and many others of conspicuous merit. The great number of learned men in this city, particularly, when printing became known and spread itself over *Europe*, was a sufficient inducement for some of the best Printers to settle there. But none encourag'd the Art and artists more, than *Ferdinand* III. king of *Naples*, whom we had occasion to mention before, upon the account of the free access, which the learned had to his person, and their epistolary correspondence with him, and who liv'd at the time of the infancy of the Art. As his learning was equal to the esteem he had for the learned, I doubt not but it was he who procur'd the famous *Sixtus Russinger* a learned and pious priest, who was a native of *Strasburgh*, to settle in his capital. This seems more than probable, not only because he was the first who set up a press at *Naples*, but from the great marks of esteem which that prince shew'd him ; insomuch, that having discover'd his intention to return to his own country, he try'd all possible means to divert him from it, and even offer'd him a noble bishoprick, or any other preferment, if that could have fix'd him in his dominions. But this venerable old man, whether out of modesty, or rather a desire of spending the small remainder of his days in his native city, refus'd the king's offer, and return'd home loaden with the presents of that generous monarch. *Riessinger* was not only a Printer, but a clergyman, and famous for his great learning ; yet as he continued but a short time at *Naples*, we have few editions of his. *Orlandi* gives him a contemporary and fellow citizen, *viz. Peter* of *Strasburgh*, who settled there about the same year ; but as I do not find that he printed any thing in company with *Riessinger*, or that any of his impressions are left, I shall say no more of him.

We have but four impressions of *Sixtus Russinger*, or *Riessinger*, two dated *anno* 1471 and 1472, the other two without date. They are all curious and correct, and two of them have *Latin* epigrams at the end

in

in his commendation. We don't find that he carried on the bufinefs after he came again to his native place.

2. BARTHOLD RING of *Strasburgh*, 1 edit. 1475.

3. MATTHIAS MORAVUS *de Olumuntz*, 7 edit. from 1475 to 1499.

THE firft of whofe impreffions, *viz. Seneca's* works is remarkable for its wrong date MLXXV for MCCCCLXXV. We find likewife an impreffion of his done at *Genoa* in company with *Michael de Monacho, viz. Supplementum Summæ quæ pifanella vocatur,* fol. Januæ 10. Cal. *Julii millefimo quadringentefimo* LII. quarto, *inftead of* LXX. quarto: his corrector was *Junianus Majus* a *Neapolitan,* and a profeffor of grammar and rhetorick, who publifh'd the following edition, *Juftiniani Maii Parthenopei liber de prifcorum proprietate verborum,* fol. with this colophon, *Impreffere Matthias Moravus impreffor folertiffimus & venerabilis Monachus Blafius Theologus* 1475, which book has been much efteem'd and reprinted in many places.

4. ARNOLD *de Bruxella* or *Bruffels,* 5 edit. from 1475 to 1477.

5. JOHN ADAM *de Polonia,* 1 edit. 1478.

6. CONRARD GULDEMUND, 1 edit. 1478.

7. FRANCIS *de Dino* of *Florence,* 2 edit. 1480 to 1487. He went afterwards to *Florence,* where we fhall find him under that head.

8. AYOLF *de Canthono* citizen of *Milan,* 1 edit. 1492.

THIS piece which is known but by few, is intitled, *L' Aquita,* and was compos'd in *Latin* by *Leonard Aretino,* and by him tranflated into *Italian.* It confifts of four books, the firft treats of the origin of the world, and the off-fpring of *Jupiter.* The fecond of the departure of *Æneas* from *Troy,* and of the kings of *Italy.* The third of the actions and fayings of *Julius Cæfar.* And the fourth of the defcendants of *Julius Cæfar.*

THERE are many others done here without Printer's name.

Article II.   *The City of* FLORENCE.

FLORENCE, the metropolis and feat of the dukes of *Tufcany,* and a noble univerfity, was not oblig'd to foreigners for this Art, fince it was brought within her gates by one of her own citizens *Bernard Cennini.*

We

We do not find that he went to any other city in order to learn it, but being a confiderable gold-fmith, and having two fons, *viz. Dominic* and *Peter,* who were very ingenious artificers, and the latter a perfon of letters, they fet themfelves about cutting of punches, finking of matrices, and, in fhort, got the whole apparatus of a Printing-houfe made within their houfe ; infomuch that they were in a capacity of printing before the year 1471. The firft book and only one we have left, which is the reafon why he has been unknown to all our annalifts till *F. Orlandi,* was *Virgil's* works with *Servius's* commentaries, which they began to print on the 7th of *November* 1471, and finifh'd *October* the 5th 1472. The preface and colophon of this not only giving an account of their ingenuity and diligence, but containing likewife fomething remarkable, I fhall refer the original to the margin, and infert it here in *Englifh.* The book is printed in the father and his fon *Dominic's* name, and *Peter* the other fon was the revifer and corrector of it.

1. Bernard, and 2. Dominic Cennini *Citizens of Florence,* 1471.

Virgilii *opera omnia cum comm. Servii, & in fine Æneid. ejufdem Servii de Natura fyllabarum libellus ad Aquilinum,* fol. Florentiæ. *Orl.* 1471.

[1] In principio poft præfationem ad lectorem;
Florentiæ VII idus Novembres
MCCCCLXXI.
Bernardus Cenninus auritex omnium judicio præftantiffimus, & *Dominicus* ejus F. egregiæ indolis adolefcens, expreffis ante calibe characteribus, ac deinde fufis literis volumen hoc primum imprefferunt. *Petrus Cenninus Bernardi* ejufdem filius quantâ potuit curâ & diligentiâ emendavit, ut cernis.
Florentinis ingeniis nil ardui eft.
Finis.

Bernardus Cenninus auritex omnium judicio præftantiffimus, & *Dominicus* ejus F. optimæ indolis adolefcens imprefferunt. *Petrus* ejufd.

Bernardi F. emendavit ; cum antiquiffimis autem multis exemplaribus contulit, imprimifque illi curæ fuit, ne quid alienum Servio afcriberetur ; neu quid recideretur, aut deeffet, quod Honorati effe pervetufta exemplaria demonftrarent. Quoniam vero plerofque juvat manupropriâ fuoque more Græca interponere, eaque in antiquis codicibus perpauca funt, & accentus quidem difficillimi imprimendo notari poffunt, relinquendum ad id fpatia duxit. Sed cum apud homines perfectum nihil fit, fatis videri cuique debebit, fi hi libri (quod vehementer optamus) præ aliis emendati reperientur.
Abfolutum opus nonis Octobris MCCCC LXXII Florentiæ. Orl. p. 130, 131.

After

After the preface (which was at the end of the book) are the following words:

" At *Florence* VII Ides *Novemb.* 1471.

" Bernard Cenninus a moſt excellent gold-ſmith, in the opi-
" nion of all men, and *Dominic* his ſon, a youth of an extraordinary
" genius, having firſt made their ſteel punches, and afterwards caſt their
" letters from them, printed this their firſt work. *Peter Cenninus* ano-
" ther ſon of the ſaid *Bernard* hath us'd his utmoſt care in correcting
" it, as you ſee it.

Nothing is too hard for a Florentine genius.

Finis.

And after,

The colophon runs thus:

" Bernard Cinninus a moſt excellent goldſmith, *&c. as in the*
" *laſt,* and *Dominic* his ſon, a youth, *&c.* printed (this book); *Peter*
" the ſon of the ſame *Bernard* corrected it, having firſt compar'd it
" with the moſt ancient manuſcripts. It was his firſt care that nothing
" ſhould paſs under the name of *Servius,* but what was truly his, or
" any thing, that was plain from the moſt ancient copies to be his, might
" be maim'd or wanting. But becauſe many perſons chooſe to write
" the *Greek* quotations with their own hands, and there are but few to
" be met with in the old copies, and their accents cannot be printed
" but with great difficulty, he thought proper to leave blank ſpaces
" for them. But as man can produce nothing abſolutely perfect, it
" will be ſufficient for us, if theſe books be found (as we heartily wiſh)
" more correct than any other.

The work was finiſh'd on the Nones of *October* 1427 at *Florence.*

3. Fr. Dominic *de Piſtoria* and ⎰
4. Fr. Peter *de Piſa*   ⎰ *Monks,* 1477.

There are ſome *Florence* editions with this inſcription, *Apud ſanc-*
tum Jacobum de Ripoli, which have given *F. Orlandi* no ſmall trouble to
diſcover the Printers, who liv'd near that place; at length he found that
it was a cloiſter of *Dominican* fryers, who liv'd in a little convent upon
the plain of *Ripoli,* without St. *Nicholas*'s gate at *Florence,* near which
place he found four editions, the firſt of which is printed with the above-

C c 2

mention'd

mention'd *Monk*'s name as follows, *Improntata in Firenze al Monaſterio di ſanto Jacopo di Ripoli del'Ordine del Fratri Predicatori per Mano di dua religioſi Frate Dominico da Piſtoja e Frate Piero da Piſa* Firenze 1477. The other three mention only the name of the place, *Impreſſ. apud ſanctum Jacobum de Ripoli.* The ſecond and third are dated 1478, the laſt is without date.

5. Nicolas Allemanus, or *Nicolas de Lorenzo Dallamagna,* and *Della Magna,* 5 edit. from 1477 to 1485.

6. Nicolas *de Breſtaw,* 2 edit. 1478.

7. Antonius Bartholomæi *Miſcomini,* 12 edit. from 1481 to 1494.

8. Franc. *de Dino* of *Florence,* 2 edit. 1487, 1490.

This Printer work'd at *Naples* about the year 1480 as we have ſeen before ; after which he remov'd to *Florence,* and printed the above-mention'd editions, the firſt of which wants the place's name, but is reaſonably ſuppos'd to have been printed there rather than at *Naples,* becauſe its character is different from that us'd at the latter.

9. Antonius Francisci *Venetian,* 1 edit. 1487.

10. Demetrius Calcondilla Milanese, *a native of Crete,* 1488.

He was a perſon of admirable skill in the *Greek* and *Latin* tongues, and at firſt a corrector of the preſs ; but afterwards he turn'd Printer, firſt at *Florence,* and then at *Milan, anno* 1499, where we have mention'd him under that article. The only book known to have been printed by him at *Florence,* is a beautiful edition of *Homer* in *fol.* of which I have ſeen two copies. It is printed in a fine *Greek* character with a large margin and diſtance between the lines ; and conſidering that it was the firſt volume printed in *Greek,* is a very curious and valuable piece, and bears the following title.

Homeri *opera omnia cum textu Græco, Labore & Induſtriâ Demetrii Mediolanenſis Cretenſis. Sumptibus Bernardi Neriſii & Nerii Tenaidis Florentinorum, fol. idib. Jan. Florentiæ,* 1488.

11. Francis Bona Corsi, 9 edit. from 1490 to 1499.

12. Bartholomew P. *Florentine,* 2 edit. 1492 1493.

13. Lau-

13. L a u r e n c e F r a n c i s c i *de* A l o p a, *Venetian,* 1494,

T h i s was a very ingenious and famous Printer both in the *Greek* and *Latin* tongues. *Jo. Andreas Lafcaris,* a noble *Grecian,* and one of the moſt diſtinguiſh'd criticks and poets of that time, deſigning to revive, as much as poſſible, the ſtudy of thoſe languages, eſpecially of the *Greek,* choſe this *Laurence* for his Printer, and correƈted his copies. 'Tis remarkable that his editions in the *Greek* are all printed in fine capi_ tals throughout, the uſe of which was till then unknown, if we except four or five to be met with in ſome old impreſſions and manuſcripts. Mr. *Mattaire* hath given us a ſhort ſpecimen of the firſt of theſe curious editions, with the preface of *Lafcaris,* in *Latin* capitals likewiſe, inter_ ſpers'd with *Greek* words; the figures and letters of which, as well as the number of words in each line, and of the lines in each page, anſwer ex_ aƈtly to thoſe of that edition.   He hath added ſome remarks upon them, which the curious reader may find in his *Annales Typograph.* from p. 267 to 285.   We have five editions of his, all in *Greek,* the firſt and ſecond are dated 1494 and 1496, the reſt are without date.

14. L a u r e n c e M o r g i a n i,   ⎱ 4 edit. from 1495 to 1497.
15. J o h n of *Mentz,*   ⎰

16. S o c i e t a s C o l u b r i [*or the fraternity of the Snake*] 1 edit. 1497.

17. P h i l i p J u n t a or *de Junta,* 2 edit. 1497 and 1500 both *Greek.*

18. G e r a r d *de Harlem,* 1 edit. 1498.

19. L e o n a r d *de Arigis de Ceſoriaco,* 1 edit. 1499, beſides many others which have no Printers names.

Article III. *The City of* FERRARA, 1471.

F e r r a r a is an ancient city built in the time of *Theodoſius* II, ſur_ rounded afterwards with a ſtrong wall by the Exarch of *Ravenna:* it was made an univerſity by the Emperor *Ferdinand* II, and has always been famous for men of learning and valour and for ingenious artificers. *An.* 1598 it paſt from the dominion of the Marqueſſes of *Eſte* to that of the

Popes

Popes of *Rome*, under which it has continu'd ever fince: hither the Art of Printing was brought by one of its own citizens, *viz.*

1 ANDREAS GALLUS, 1471.

IT appears by the colophon to his firft impreffion, which you will find in the margin ¹ that he was either a *Frenchman* or of *French* extraction, tho' a citizen of *Ferrara*, which laft might be beftow'd on him upon the account of his being the firft perfon who fet up his prefs there; the like encouragement having been given by many other cities to their firft Printers: but whether he brought it thither from fome other place, or devis'd it at home as *Cennini* did at *Florence*, is neither eafy, nor very material, to guefs: he was a good Printer and his editions are ftill efteem'd by the curious.

WE have but twelve of them extant from *ann.* 1471 to 1493.

THE reft of the Printers of *Ferrara* are as follows,

2. CARNERIUS AUGUSTINUS whofe father *Bernard Auguftinus* was a bookfeller of the fame city. We have four editions of his from 1474 to 1475 one of which, *viz. Boccacio* in *Italian* is the firft poem printed in that language, it has neither date nor name of Printer or place, but the character fhews it to be *Auguftines*.

3. SEVERUS of *Ferrara*, 1 edit. 1476.

4. SEVERINUS bookfeller of *Ferrara*, but whether this and the former be the fame, or father and fon, is uncertain: we have but one edition of his, *viz. Alberti Trotti de vero & perfecto Clerico* 4to 1476, in which he writes himfelf *per Severinum Bibliopolam Ferrarienfem.* This edition *Orlandi* tells us was afterwards reprinted at *Lyons, ann.* 1535, with a *Latin* preface, importing that it was about feventy years fince *Severinus* bookfeller had publifh'd it at *Ferrara*, by which it would appear that he had printed it *ann.* 1465, even before either that city or even *Rome* had receiv'd the Art: our author therefore gueffes the miftake to be in the word *feptuagefimus annus*, which he thinks was printed inftead of *fexagefimus*, which laft brings it almoft to the very time.

---

¹ Impreffi *Andreas* hoc opus cui *Francia* nomen
Trdaidit, at civis *Ferrarione's* ego, &c.

5 THE

5. T H E fifth and laſt Printer was *Laurence Roſſi* or *Rubeus*, of whom we have 6 editions from 1492 to 1497.

T HERE are a few more without Printers names, the laſt of which is the hiſtory of Pope *Joan* in *Italian* 1497.

Article I. *The City of* N U R E M B E R G H, 1472.

NUREMBERGH or *Norimbergh*, in *Latin Norimberga*, is a free city in *Germany* upon the confines of *Swabia*, *Franconia*, and *Bavaria*, ſituate upon the river *Pegnitz*. It was formerly a democratical commonwealth, but upon ſome domeſtick ſedition, it reduc'd itſelf to an ariſtocracy, in the reign of the emperor *Charles* IV, under the government of twenty four ſenators choſen out of ſo many of their ancienteſt families; which form of government hath been continued ever ſince. The city is very rich, large and populous, ſurrounded with a double wall above eight miles in circuit, and 180 lofty towers. It was always celebrated for producing the beſt artificers in every kind of handicraft, and particularly for a beautiful metal of their own making, call'd *Nurembergh* copper; the compoſition of which was kept with all imaginable ſecrecy within their walls, every workman being firſt ſworn to it; ſo that the metal was almoſt equally dear with ſilver; till about the latter end of the laſt century, one of their own citizens came over and ſold the ſecret here in *England*, which has made it more common, and conſequently leſſen'd the price of it. This metal I purpoſely chuſe to mention becauſe it was reckon'd very excellent for making of matrices, being far more ductile than the common copper, and not ſo apt to break the punches.

I T will be no eaſy matter to fix the time when the Art of Printing was brought to this city. *John Andreas Endters* a Printer of *Nuremberg*, who publiſh'd a piece on Printing, in *High Dutch*, anno 1722, and in it has given us an account of its progreſs in that city, acquaints us that he had met with ſome MS. annals, which affirm, that the Art was no ſooner found out at *Mentz*, but it was immediately communicated to *Nuremberg*, which did therefore receive it about the year 1444 according to one, or 1440 according to another. 'Tis true, our author is ſo far from being ſatisfy'd with their account, that he has even taken the pains to confute them from more authentic teſtimonies; however, tho'

I do

I do not defign to enter into a detail of that difpute, yet I could not forbear mentioning thus much, becaufe it ferves to confirm a former obfervation, *viz.* that not only the Printers, but likewife the *Cities* themfelves have taken no fmall pains to antedate their refpective claims to this Art.

I have already taken notice in the firft part of this hiftory, *pag.* 22. that the difcovery of the Art of Printing had been attributed by *Purbach*, and *Peter Ramus* to that learned mathematician and aftronomer *John de Monte regio*, or *Regio-Montanus*, and mention'd *Manilius*'s aftronomy printed by him without date or places name. Our *German* author acquaints us upon the authority of *Gaffendi*, one of the *French* royal mathematicians, ,, that *Regiomontanus* came to *Nuremberg* about *anno* 1471, ,, with a defign to fet up a Printing-houfe there, in order to print his ,, own works and thofe of other learned men, with greater accuracy ,, and fpeed, and to improve the Art of Printing in feveral of its branch- ,, es ; but that he met with fo many obftacles to his defign, that he ,, faw himfelf forc'd to make ufe of foreign Printing-houfes, fuch as ,, they were, till one *Bernard Walter* offer'd to bear the charges of erect- ,, ing a Printing-houfe for him (as he likewife did towards many other ,, curious inventions of his) and enabled him to print *Purbac*'s new ,, theory, *Manilius*'s aftronomy, and his own *Ephemerides* for the ufe of ,, the publick.

Our author obferves further, that as this account of *Gaffendi*'s doth quite overturn *Peter Ramus*'s fuppofition of *Regiomontanus* being the inventor of the art, fo it likewife fhews him to have contributed much towards the improvement of it. It likewife proves that there were fome Preffes in this city before he came thither, but who they were that fet them up, and what works they printed before that time, is what he has not been able to find out, becaufe they have no dates or Printer's names.

The oldeft book he could find with a date, is the *Commeftorium Vitiorum* of *Francis de Retza* a *Dominican Fryar*; at the end of which are the words which you'll find in the margin[1] with this odd date $\tilde{n}$ LXX°.

---

[1] Hic Codex egregius Comeftorii vitiorum facre Theologie Profefforis eximii *Francifci* de *Retza* Ordinis predicatorum finit feliciter. *Nu- remberge anno* $\tilde{n}c$ LXX$_0$. Patronarum formarumque Concordia & proportione impreffus.

which

which our author feems to take for 1470. This book was afterwards reprinted by *Ant. Koburger anno* 1476, and afterwards *anno* 1496, under the following title, *Summa quæ deſtruĉtorium vitiorum nominatur,* without Printer's name.

The author mentions another book of the fame date, *viz. Gerſon,* chancellour of *Paris, Commentarium ſuper ſapientis hebrei cantica,* &c. but as neither of theſe have the Printer's name, we ſhall ſeek fomewhere elſe for the firſt Printer of *Nuremberg.* According therefore to our pro-pos'd method of the oldeſt edition known, that rank will fall upon.

I. Antony Koburger.

A perſon eminent for learning, and the number, elegancy and cor-rectneſs of his editions, which gain'd him the title of the prince of Printers among the learned of his time. At firſt indeed his character, tho' of the *Venetian* ſort, was fomewhat imperfect, and inferior to that of many of his cotemporaries ; but he afterwards procur'd a new ſett, which hath been juſtly eſteem'd ever ſince as fine as any that have been us'd ei-ther before or after him. He was no leſs ſolicitous in correcting his works ; ſo that tho' he was alone ſufficient for that task, yet he took the learned *Frederic Piſtorius* for his affiftant. He ſpar'd no coſt nor pains in procuring the beſt manuſcripts, and always deſir'd the judgment of the learned before he ventur'd to print them. The great *Jodocus Badius* hath made this ſhort but juſt panegyric upon him, in a letter written to him *anno* 1499, and printed at the beginning of the works of *Angelus Politianus anno* 1519 [1]; That he was a great friend and lover of the learned, and indefatigable in printing the beſt copies faithfully, neatly and correctly. Mr. *Mattaire* hath given us an extract of this letter in his *Annales Typogr.* p. 79. by which the reader may ſee what eſteem this great man was in, not only among the learned, but likewiſe among the beſt Printers of his time ; and it may be ſaid of him, that he printed more works than any of them, particularly bibles, of which the reader

---

[1] Litteratos omnes & colis & foves, pervi-gilemque curam ad bonos codices vere terſe & fine mendis imprimendos adhibes.

will

will find no lefs than 12 editions ftill extant, one of which is in 5, another in 6 volumes in folio, and a third with fine wooden cuts.

He was no lefs diligent in printing other works, and we are told by *John And. Endters*, " That he kept daily twenty four preffes at work, " and employ'd no lefs than an hundred journeymen whom he main- " tain'd without doors; they had a fet hour to come to work, and to " leave off, and he admitted none fingle into his houfe but oblig'd them " to wait at his door till they were altogether, and then they were ad- " mitted in, and enter'd upon their refpective works.

" He was likewife a confiderable Bookfeller, and kept a fpacious " printing-houfe at *Lyons* in *France*, where he had fundry law-books " printed for him; befides this, he had his factors and agents in the " moft confiderable cities in *Chriftendom*, and kept fixteen open fhops " befide ware-houfes, and in all of them a confiderable ftock of the beft " books then extant, fo that he never was at a lofs for any good edi- " tions to fupply his cuftomers with.

Thus he continued printing both at *Nuremberg* and at *Lyons* with great fuccefs and applaufe, till the year 1501 if not beyond; however we don't find any edition of his of a more recent date, which makes me believe that he left off printing about that time. In 1513. *James Sachon* one of his workmen at *Lyons*, printed *Caftellanus*'s *Latin* bible for him with this colophon, *Lugduni per Jacobum Sachon expenfis Antonii Koburger*. The fame is likewife dated from *Nurembergh*, but is fuppos'd to be the fame edition with that of *Lyons*; he dy'd in this year after having been for fome time a member of the chief council of *Nuremberg*; all the editions that we have of him, his bibles inclufive, from 1472 to 1500, amounts to but thirty feven, a number too inconfiderable for the many preffes and workmen that he kept, which gives me room to hope that time will difcover a great many more.

2. Mr. *Mattaire* p. 79 tells us of one *Adam* of *Amberg* [the metropolis of the *Bavarian* palatinate] who flourifh'd *ann.* 1472, but doth not tell us where he wrought. Our German author fays that he had met with a fmall treatife in 4to. of a fheet and half, with his name, and the city of *Nurembergh* at the end; fo that he moft probably refided there, but tho' this work be without date, yet his edition of *Cicero's Orationes* print-

ed

ed *ann.* 1472, tho' without places name, may be so far presum'd to be
done here, as to allow him the next place after *Koburger*,

THE rest of the Printers of this city are as follows,

3. FREDERIC CREUSNER, 5 edit. from 1473 to 1479.

4. JOHN SENSENSCHMID of *Eger*, ⎫
5. HENRY KOLER of *Mentz*, and ⎬ 1473.
6. ANDREW FRISNER *de Wunsiedel*. ⎭

KOLER was a native of *Mentz*, and in all likelyhood one of *Faust's*
servants who left that city soon after it was taken, and took sanctuary
at *Nuremberg*.

THE last of these *viz. Frisner* after having been corrector and assistant
to *John Sensenschmid* till 1478, set up a Printing-house himself, which appears from many of his books which bear his name, as Printer and editor. He had study'd for some time in the university of *Leipsick*, with a relation of his, *Erasmus Frisner*, a Dominican Fryar, who tho' but twenty
seven years of age had compos'd several books, the printing of which he
committed to his kinsman *Andrew*, who printed them some time after at
Nurembergh where he dwelt, as appears by several of his books from
1473 till 1478, after this having taken his degree of master of arts he
remov'd again to *Leipsick*, where he was soon after chosen professor of divinity, and attain'd even to the honour of *Rector Magnificus* of that university, to which place he got all his Printing-tools convey'd: he went from
thence to *Rome*, where pope *Julius* II. made him *Papæ & sedis apostolicæ
primarius ordinarius*. By his last will which he made at *Rome ann.* 1504,
he left a noble legacy for the erection of a college at *Wonsiedel*, for the
education and maintenance of young students of the family of the *Frisner's* which they enjoy to this day, he left them also his *Historia Lombardica* which he had printed whilst at *Leipsick*. He likewise bequeath'd
all his printing materials to the convent of the dominicans of *Leipsick*,
and expresses himself thus, *Item, I leave my iron chest, presses, instruments
and other utensils and materials for printing, together with twenty florens
rhenish to pray for my soul and for buying the monks a better dinner than
they us'd to have in the Prior's refectory———the day when they perform my
obsequies.*

D d 2

WHAT

WHAT ufe the monks made of the Printing-prefs, &c. I can no where find: we have but four editions printed by the aforefaid three partners from 1473 to 1487.

7. CONRARD LENTORIUS. We have but one *Latin* Bible with the apoftills of *Nich. de Lyra* fol. 1482.

8. GEORGE STUCHS or *Flucks de Sultzbach*, we have but one miffal of his, adorn'd with rubricks 1484.

9. GASPAR HOCHFEDER, our German author calls him *Hochfelder*. 2 edit. 1491 and 1494.

WITH about 60 more without Printers names.

MR. ENDTERS mentions fome other Printers before 1500, but as he gives us no account of their works, we fhall fay no more of them.

BEFORE I eave the city of *Nuremberg* I cannot but take notice that it is alfo famous for being the native place, and conftant refidence of the great Painter, Engraver, Mathematician and Printer *Albert Durer*.

MARK ANTONIO, *Raphael's* learned engraver, gives him this cha-racter, fpeaking of his fkill in engraving and of his other excellent ta-lents; „ That if fo excellent, fo exact, and fo univerfal a genius had „ been cultivated in *Tufcany*, inftead of *Germany*, and had form'd his „ ftudy according to the excellent pieces which he might have feen at „ *Rome*, as the reft of our celebrated painters have done, he would have „ prov'd the beft in that refpect that *Italy* ever produc'd, as he really „ was the greateft and moft accomplifh'd genius that *Germany* could „ ever boaft of.

THIS great man was born *ann.* 1471. His father obferving the ear-ly marks of his genius to all the liberal fciences, fpar'd no coft to have it improv'd by all poffible means (travelling excepted) and by the beft mafters in *Germany*. But tho' his other talents have been highly cele-brated by the learned, yet I never met with any who took notice of his having been a printer, (no not even his countryman and fellow-citizen, author of a Piece on the Subject of Printing &c. in *Nuremberg*, mention-ed in the beginning of this article) tho' feveral of his works are preferv'd in divers libraries both publick and private. I have feen fome of them

very

very beautiful, nor do I doubt but that his genius for painting and engraving, led him to the other two branches of cutting upon wood and Printing, that he might be able to perform the whole work himfelf, without the danger of having any part of it fpoil'd by unfkilful hands, and the better to print the defcriptions of his cuts, *&c.* in a more elegant manner than cou'd poffibly be done in wood. His improvement in the art of engraving or cutting upon wood, was carried by him to its utmoft perfection, as all perfons muft own who have feen any of his works.

The part of fhadowing which is call'd crofs-hatching, and which has been loft for many years, and conducted (if not wholly invented) by him with fuch extraordinary beauty and truth, join'd to the uncommon luftre of his ink, has furpafs'd all the wood-cutters ever fince. His reafon for preferring this method of cutting on wood to that of copper plates ; were ; 1. The rouling-prefs, which is wholly us'd in the later, was not then fo perfect as fince ; 2. His moft confiderable works (of which he was the author, for he fcarce printed any other) being chiefly geometry, perfpective, fortification and architecture as well as hiftory, wooden cutts were much the more eligible method upon feveral accounts, efpecially when cut by fuch a mafterly hand as his. The only difficulty was to make it fubfervient to his hiftory-pieces ; but that he eafily furmounted by the ftrength of his genius ; and thofe who have feen any of his performances even in this kind, will readily own that nothing of that nature ever equall'd them. His ufual mark was the initial letters of his name AD joyn'd together thus ▨ but his moft effectual way to prevent counterfeits was by giving his works a degree of beauty never yet attain'd to.

WITH refpect to his Printing, I have already hinted, that he feldom meddled with any works but his own, as I can find ; but as I have met with none done before the year 1500, tho' he probably entred into that province before that time ; I fhall not trouble the reader with a lift of them, but content my felf with fubjoining an account of a few of the moft confiderable, which I have feen : They are efteem'd by the learned mafter-pieces of the kind, and preferv'd as monuments of the author's merit, being as follow ;

1. THE

1. The hiftory of the *Apocalypfe*, confifting of a fine fet of draughts upon that fubject, all cut upon wood with his own hand, and with the utmoft beauty and truth.

2. The hiftory of the *four gofpels*, done after the fame manner, and with the fame beauty. Both thefe fets are printed with the common prefs, with explanations and hiftorical accounts of the defigns placed either under them, or on the other fide, or upon a diftinct leaf. They are both in *fol.*

3. His book of proportions, which he did not live to finifh, but was printed by his widow after his death, is likewife efteem'd another mafter-piece in that kind. I fhall only add, that the fingular beauty of his ink, the excellency of the Prefs work, and in a word, the exactnefs of his performances do juftly rank him amongft the greateft genius's of the age. I hope therefore the reader will excufe this digreffion in favour of a perfon to whom the world owes the great improvements made in the art of cutting upon wood, which has been fo ferviceable to the Printers in the ornamental part of their works.

Article V. The City of VERONA.

Verona, an ancient city in *Lombardy*, famous for fome noble relicks of the old *Roman* architecture, fuch as amphitheatres, triumphal arches, *&c.* which ftill retain fome part of their former magnificence, is like-wife remarkable for having been the native place of feveral eminent per-fons, in particular, of *Cornelius Nepos, Emilius Maurus, Pliny, Vitru-vius, Guarini,* and others. It receiv'd the Art of Printing very foon, yet made but fmall advantage of it. We find very few Printers in it, and we have but a fmall number of their works left. The firft of them was;

1. John *de* Verona.

Who was a native of *Verona*, and fon to *Nicolas* a doctor of phyfic, and the firft who fet up a Printing-prefs in that city, as appears by the
colophon

colophon of the only book extant of his, *viz. Valturius de re militari liber.* fol. *per Jo. Veronenf. Veronæ* [1]. anno 1472.

2. FELIX ANTIQUARIUS & ⎱ we have but 1 edit. of theirs, dated
3. INNOCENT ZILETI. ⎰ 1476.

4. PETER MAUFER, 1480.

PETER MAUFER, was a Frenchman and an excellent Printer. The firſt place where he ſet up his preſs was the city of *Padua*, about 1474, as we ſhall ſhew in its proper place. Thence he came to *Verona* in 1479, and after a ſhort ſtay there, went to *Venice* in 1483, and aſſociated himſelf with *Nicol. Contengo*, as mention'd in the chapter of that city. We have only the following book printed by him here.

JOSEPHI *opera Latinè, Ludovico Contrada interprete,* fol *per Petrum Maufer Gallicum,* oct. cal. Jan. pont. max. Sixto 4. Venetorum duce Joanne Mocenigo, *in inclytâ civitate Veronæ* 1480.

5. BONINO *de* BONINI *de* RAGUSIO, 1482.

WHO printed at firſt in the city of *Venice,* with *Andreas de Paltaſichis anno* 1478 ; whence he remov'd to *Verona,* and at laſt to *Breſcia,* where he continued printing much longer ; we have but three of his editions done at *Verona,* 1482 and 1483.

6. PAUL FRIDENPERGER of *Paſſaw* in *Germany,* 1 edit. 1486. with a ſmall number without Printer's names.

Article 6. *The City of* PARMA, 1472.

PARMA is another ancient city in *Lombardy,* call'd by the Romans *Gallia Ciſalpina,* ſituate in a very pleaſant large plain, and ſo well furniſh'd with paſture ground, that it is recorded by *Martial* for the great number of cattel it bred, *Tondet & innumeros Gallica Parma greges.* It

[1] Joannes ex Verona oriundus Nicolai Cyrurgiæ Medici filius, Artis impreſſoriæ Magiſter hunc de Re Militari librum Literis & figuratis ſignis in ſua Patria primus impreſſit, MCCCCLXXIII.

was

was once under the pope's government, and given by *Paul* III. to his nephews, with the title of dukes of *Parma*, under whom it has continu'd ever since. Tho' this city receiv'd the Art of Printing so early as the year 1472, yet it had but very few artificers, and a small number of editions printed there. It may indeed be reasonably suppos'd that these being so much inferior to those of *Venice*, *Rome*, *Paris*, &c. have been mostly destroy'd; and the same may be said of many other cities. However *Parma* deserves to be remember'd, if not for the number and excellency of her Printers, yet for having given birth to some of the greatest of that time, who were (perhaps for want of sufficient encouragement here) oblig'd to settle in other parts of *Italy*. Among these were the famous *Antony Zarot*, who printed at *Milan* a great many fine and correct volumes, as we have shewn under that article, *Fausto*, *Vincenzo*, and *Pellegrino del Bonardi*, and *Bartholomew de Parma* in *Bolognia*, and *Matthew Capcasa* in *Venice*, *Mich. Manzoli* in *Treviso*, with many more whose name and place of birth, &c. the reader will find in the article of each of those cities. The first book, we meet with printed here, is the works of the famous lawyer *Baldus*; but hath no Printer's name, tho' it is dated at *Parma ann.* 1471. However 'tis probable it was printed by *Stephen Corali*, a native of *Lyons*, who is the first in our list, and printed (or rather might reprint) the same work the year following.

1. STEPHEN CORALI, 5 edit. from 1473 to 1476.
2. AUGUSTINE GENOENSIS (or of *Genoa*) 1 edit. 1477.
3. ANDREA PORTILIA, 4 edit. from 1479 to 1481.
4. ANGELO UGOLETTI *de Parma*, 4 edit. from 1493 to 1499.

AND near twenty more without Printers names.

Article VII.   MANTUA.

MANTUA one of the most ancient cities of *Lombardy*, situate in the middle of an island, form'd by the river *Mincio*, had its name and origin from *Manto* daughter of *Tiresias* a Theban augur, she bore a son call'd *Ocnus*, who built a city near the river *Po*, and from his mother's name call'd it *Mantoa* or *Mantua*. After a great variety of changes, it is now subject to the house of *Austria*. It has given birth to many learned men

both

both ancient and modern, and particularly to the immortal *Virgil*. This city cannot boaſt of any great merit with reſpect to the Art of Printing, except that it was brought thither *ann.* 1472 by ſome *Germans,* who came to ſettle there; but, as it is probable, for want of encouragement, were oblig'd to remove. We find but four of theſe Printers at the moſt, and at a conſiderable diſtance of time from each other. Of the two firſt we know but one edition; and two of each of the reſt, as will appear from the following liſt.

    1. GEORGE, and 2. PAUL, *Germans,* 1 edit. 1472.

    3. PAUL JOHN *de Burſchbach,* of the dioceſs of *Mentz,* who was perhaps the ſame with *Paul German* the latter of the two foregoing, who takes now the name of his native town inſtead of that of his nation, 2 edit. 1479, 1481.

    4. VINCENT BERTOCH of *Reggio,* 2 edit. 1493, 1498: and ſome others which have no Printers names.

Article VIII. *The City of* DERVENTER, 1472.

DERVENTER [in *Latin Daventria*] in *lower Germany,* near the river *Iſſel* upon the confines of *lower Gelderland,* near the city of *Utrecht* began to practiſe the Art of Printing *ann.* 1472. The 1ſt impreſſion done here, *viz. Prudentius Aurelius Poeta Hiſpanus his poems,* 4to. has no Printer's name, but is dated *Daventriæ* 1472.

    2. RICHARD PAFRADIUS, 1 edit. 1481.

    3. JAMES *de Breda,* 4 edit. from 1490 to 1497, with about twenty more without Printers names.

Article IX. *The City of* PADUA, 1472.

PADUA or*Padova,* in *Latin Patavia* or *Patavium,* (ſo call'd by *Antenor* the firſt founder of it, in compliment to his companions, who were *Paphlagonians,* and for whoſe ſakes he call'd it by the name of their metropolis) is a rich, ancient and noble city upon the river *Brento,* and now under the government of the *Venetian* republick, famous for its hot baths and mineral waters, and reſorted to from all parts of *Europe.* It is one of the laſt cities we know of that receiv'd this Art in the year 1472. in which tho' it was not very eminent either for the number of Printers or impreſſions, yet it publiſh'd ſeveral curious editions, which had not as yet appear'd in any of the foregoing cities. The two firſt Printers were ;

1. BARTHOLOMEW *de Val de Zochio* of *Padua*, &c.
2. MARTIN *de Septem Arboribus,*

OF theſe we have but three editions, 1472, 1473, 1474.

3. PETER MAUFER whom we have already mention'd under the articles of *Venice* and *Verona* : we have four editions of his printed at *Padua* from 1474 to 1479.

4. LAURENCE CANOZIUS *de Lendenaro*, 1 edit. 1474.

5. ALBERT *de Stendalia*, 1 edit. 1475.

6. JOHN HERBERT or *Herbort*, 3 edit. 1476, 1482 ; and one without date or places name.

7. ANTON. *de Carcano*, 1 edit. 1478.

8. MATTHEW *de Cerdonis de Windiſchegrets*, 5 edit. from 1482 to 1487.

9. MOSES *de Caſtello*, 1 edit. 1492.

10. JEROM *de Duranti*, 1 edit. 1493, he wrought alſo in *Pavia* with *Chriſtopher de Canibus, ann.* 1488.

11. LEWIS or *Alois de Como*, &c.
12. BARTHOLOMEW *de Troſſis,* } 1 edit. 1497.

With a few more without Printers names.

CHAP.   IX.

The Cities of 1 Louvain, 2 Ulms, 3 Utrecht, *ann.* 1473. 4 Turin, 5 Genoa, 6 Breſcia, 7 Aloſt, *ann.* 1474.

Article I.   *The City of* LOUVAIN.

LOUVAIN, in *Latin Lovanium,* is a large populous and well fenced city, the capital of all *Brabant,* and one of the moſt fre-quented univerſities in *Europe,* founded by *John* duke of *Brabant anno* 1426.

1426. It abounds with magnificent colleges and other fumptuous edifices, according to that of the poet.

Poftea Mufarum Sedem, Collegiaque ampla
———— Lovani afpicienda dedit.

It is likewife famous for the vaft number of its ftudents, efpecially in divinity ; tho' the reader will fcarce forbear wondering what fort of divines they muft have been, when we tell him that they had the Art of Printing near thirty years, *i. e.* from 1472 to 1500, and God knows how far beyond, and never printed one fingle bible in all that time, at leaft as I can find in any annalift ; whereas we have obferv'd that a *Nuremberg* Printer, namely, *Ant. Koburger* printed at leaft a dozen in that time ; the truth is, if we judge by the fmall number of workmen and of impreffions done here, we fhall be apt to think that the Art of Printing met with but fmall encouragement ; fince if we except the firft Printer, of whom we fhall fpeak prefently, I can find but two more till the year 1500, after which whoever examines the fecond volume of Mr. *Mattaire*'s *Annales Typographici,* will find them run much thinner of either.

The firft prefs was fet up here by ;

1. John *de Weftphalia* of *Paderbourn* 1473, an eminent Printer invited to *Louvain* by fome of the heads of that univerfity, where he continu'd printing till *ano.* 1495, if we except 2 editions printed in his name if not by him ; the firft in the town of *Aloft* in *Flanders* not far from that of *Louvain anno* 1474, as fhall be mention'd at the end of this chapter ; and the other, *viz. Epiftola de Simonia Vitanda,* &c. *per rev'. Magift. Engelbertum Cultificis,* &c. *Novimagii* 9 Julii 1479.

We have nineteen editions of his from 1473 to 1495 fome of which are without date, place, or Printer's name ; but eafily known to be his by the chara&er.

2. John Veldener, 2 edit. of the *Fafciculus Temporum,* 1474 and 1476.

3. Egidius Vender Heerstraten, 2 edit. 1486 to 1487. And five or fix more without Printer's name.

Article

Article II. *The City of* U L M S.

ULMS a confiderable city in *High Germany*, fituate near the *Danube*, between *Ausburg, Conftance* and *Strasburgh*, and famous for the fineft linnen and cambrick, with which it furnifhes moft parts of *Europe*, began to fet up the Art of Printing fometime before the year 1473.

1. JOHN ZEINER *de Reutlingen*, 1473.

WAS the firft who practis'd it there. He was a native of *Reutlingen* a fmall city in the duchy of *Wirtembergh*, which we have mention'd as one of the firft in *Germany* that receiv'd the art, *viz. ann.* 1469. This Printer was, in all probability, the fon or brother of *Gunter Zeiner*, who work'd at *Ausburgh* from *ann.* 1470, and is mention'd under that article *p.* 122. We have but nine editions of his from 1473 to 1484, two of which are the *Latin Bible* fol. and one, *viz. Alvarius Pelagius de planctû Ecclefiæ* 1473, 2 *vol. fol.* in large paper, is reckon'd a very curious as well as fcarce edition: he ufed to fubfcribe himfelf fometimes *Jo. Zeiner de Reutlingen* or *Reutlinga,* and fometimes *Jo. Zeiner Ulmenfis Oppidi Incolam.*

2. LEONARD HOL citizen of *Ulm*, 1 edit. 1482.

3. JOHN REGER *de Kemnat*, 5 edit. from 1486 to 1497.

Article III. *The City of* UTRECHT.

UTRECHT [in *Latin Ultra trajectum*] a city in *Flanders* upon the *Rhine*, and fubject to the emperor of *Germany*, receiv'd the Art of Printing about *ann.* 1473, if not before ; but its productions have been fo few and inconfiderable that no annalift, *De la Caille* and F. *Orlandi* excepted, has taken any notice of them; and even the latter has been able to dif-cover no more than three editions, little remarkable either for bulk or beauty, for which reafon I fuppofe they are all three without Printer's name.

Article

Article IV.   *The City of* TURIN.

TURIN [in *Latin Taurinum*] the capital of *Piedmont*, and refidence of the dukes of *Savoy* now kings of *Sardinia*, is fituate upon the river *Durio* nigh the *Po*, near the weftern *Alps.*. It is a large rich and populous city and univerfity, ftrongly fortify'd, and adorn'd with magnificent palaces, churches and edifices. It receiv'd the Art of Printing about *ann.* 1474. The firft artifts who fet up their preffes here were,

1. JOHN FABRI and } 1475.
2. JOHANNINUS *de Petro*, }

THESE two printed together at firft as appears by their firft impreffion, *viz. Breviarium Romanum fol.* per *Jo. Fabri* and *Johanninum de Petro*: but *Fabri* affociated himfelf with *Martin Huz* a Printer of the city of *Lyons*, with whom he printed fome editions, and fome by himfelf: however he continu'd ftill at *Turin*, and we have three editions more of his printed there by himfelf from 1477 to 1487, wherein he fubfcribes himfelf *Jo-Fabri Lingonenfis* ; as for his partner we have nothing of him but the breviary abovemention'd.

3. NICOLAS *de Benedictis* and } 4 edit. from 1492 to 1494.
4. JACOPIN SVIGUS }

Article V.   *The City of* GENOA, 1474.

GENOA [in *Latin Janua*] is a rich populous ancient city, the metropolis of *Liguria*, and capital of the republick of *Genoa*: it is fam'd for having given birth to *Chriftopher Columbus* the firft difcoverer of *America*, and for the greatnefs and extent of her maritime trade: we meet with two noted Printers, who came and fet up their preffes there, *ann.* 1474, *viz.*

1. MATTHIAS MORAVUS *de Olomuntz* and } 1474.
2. MICHEL MONK or *de Monacho* }

BUT whether that city chofe to drive any other trade, rather than that of books, or whether they found it already furnifhed from other places, and fo met with but fmall encouragement; or for whatever other reafon, 'tis certain they tarry'd not long there. For *Moravus* printed but one book in company with *Monk*, and the next year remov'd to *Naples*, where he continued 'till *ann.* 1490, as hath been faid in the article of that city; and we hear no further of *Monk*. The book they printed here is,

Supplementum fummæ quæ Pifanella vocatur, fol. *per* Matthiam Moravum *de* Olomuntz & Michaelem *de* Monacho *focium ejus*, x *kal. Julii Millefimo quadringentefimo* LIJ. *quarto* ; where (LIJ ftands for LXX) 1474.

It is very likely, that the ill fuccefs of thefe two Printers, frighten'd others from coming thither, for we don't meet with any that ventur'd to fettle there after them, 'till a long time after the clofe of the century.

Article VI. *The City of* BRESCIA.

BRESCIA, in *Latin Brixia*, an ancient and noble city in *Lombardy*, now under the republick of *Venice*, gave much greater encouragement to the Art of Printing, than fome of the laft nam'd cities. About the year 1474.

1. HENRY *of* COLOGN, *and* 2. STATIUS GALLICUS.

CAME and fettled here, and printed the following book, the only one yet known to be printed by them here, *viz.*

Homeri Iliades per Laurentium Vallenfem *in Latinum fermonem traduEtæ* &c. viii *kal. Decemb. per* Henr. Colonienfem & Statium Gallicum. *Brixiæ* 1474.

3. BONINUS *de* BONINIS *of* RAGUSIO, 1480.

WHOSE firft works were printed at *Verona*, *ann.* 1473, as has been faid. Thence he remov'd to *Brefcia*, where he continu'd printing 'till *ann.* 1486.

HIS correEtor was *Marcus Scaramuccinus* of *Palazzolo*: there are 10 editions of his printed at *Brefcia* from 1480 to 1486.

4. BARTHOLOM. VERSELLENSIS Printer and bookfeller, 1 edition 1482.

5. JAMES
6. ANGEL } BRITANNICUS, brothers, of the city of *Brefcia*, 1485.

THE

THE firſt of theſe was ſome time partner to *John de Forlivio* at *Venice* about the year 1483, as you'll find *pag.* 149; after which he came to his own city *Breſcia,* and printed ſometimes by himſelf, and ſometimes with his brother *Angelo:* his corrector was a Franciſcan monk nam'd *Angel de Montelmo:* we have 11 edit. of the former, from 1485 to 1498: and 2 with both their names, *ann.* 1496.

7. ARNOLD *de Arundis,* 1 edit. without date.

8. RABBI GHERSON, 1492.

RABBI GHERSON was the ſon of *R. Moſes* a jew of *Soncino,* where *Hebrew* firſt began to be printed: he ſettled firſt at *Breſcia,* where he printed the two following editions in *Hebrew,* viz.

Mechaberith Rabb. Immanuelis, per Rabbi Gherſon, Brixiæ, 1492.

Biblia Hebraicé, 8vo, *per* Gerſonem F. Moſis Soncinatem, *ibid* 1494.

CHEVILLIER tells us likewiſe *p.* 265, that he printed alſo at *Riminium* in *Romania,* a *Hebrew* edition intitled, *Col bo* without date: after this he remov'd his preſs to *Conſtantinople,* where he printed ſeveral other *Hebrew* works 'till the year 1530, in which he is ſuppos'd to have dy'd.

9. BERNARDINE MISENTI *de Pavia* came firſt from *Cremona,* where he had printed in company with *Cæſar de Parma, ann.* 1492: we have but 2 edit. of his done at *Breſcia* from 1495 to 1497.

10 FRANCIS LAURINI citizen of *Breſcia,* we have only one edition of his, *viz. Homer's Iliads* tranſlated into *Latin* by *Laur. Valla,* corrected by *Baptiſta Farſengus* a prieſt of that city, 1497: it has no place's name, but is ſuppos'd to be done at *Breſcia.*

THERE are about 20 edit. more without Printer's names.

Article VII. *The City of* ALOST.

ALOST is a ſmall town in *Flanders* upon the river *Tever* between *Bruſſels* and *Gaunt,* in which the following Printers ſet up their preſſes, *viz.*

1. JOHN *de Weſtphalia,*
2. THEODORIC MARTIN of *Aloſt.* } 1474.

THE

THE former of thefe, a native of *Paderborn*, printed in the city of *Louvain, ann.* 1473, 'till 1475, as we have fhewn in that article. We find likewife a book printed by him at *Aloft, ann.* 1474 in company with *Theodoric Martin*, a native of it, as follows ;

Liber prædicabilium, 8vo, *per* Jo. de Weftphalia Paderbonenfem *cum* Theodorico Martini, *Maii die fexto in* Alofto oppido comitatus Fland. 1474.

THEODORIC MARTIN afterwards printed by himfelf, firft at *Aloft* 'till 1490 ; then at *Antwerp, ann.* 1509, and at *Louvain, ann.* 1516. His mark us'd to be a fhield hanging upon a vine with T. M. tho' at other times, he made ufe of two anchors with his name *Theodoric Martin excudebat.* His impreffions at *Aloft* are but three in number, *viz.* two dated 1487, and the laft 1490.

CHAP. X.

The Cities of Bafil, Placentia, Pignerol, Efling, Vincenza, Lubeck *and* Valentia, *ann.* 1475; Roftock *and* Bruges, *ann.* 1476. *At* Bafil, *particulars relating to* Amerbach *and* Froben; *the Characters and Names of the other Printers, and Number of their Impreffions,'till the Year* 1500.

Article I. *The City of* BASIL, 1475.

BASIL, call'd in *Latin Bafilea*, and by *Ptolemy, Augufta Rauricorum*, is an ancient city and univerfity in *Switzerland*, water'd by the two great rivers *Rhine* and *Brife*, which being navigable, increafe very much the commerce and riches of it ; fo that in fpite of all the calamities it has fuffer'd in war, it is one of the moft opulent cities of *Germany*. The univerfity is likewife very celebrated for learned men in all fciences, and was founded *ann.* 1460, and endow'd with privileges equal to any univerfity in *Europe*, by pope *Pius* II. In this city pope *Martin* V. call'd a council, *ann.* 1431 ; foon after which it became famous for the improvements,

ments, which the Art of Printing, brought thither in or before the year 1475, receiv'd from ſome of its artificers ; who have been generally the beſt and moſt learned Printers in *Europe*, and publiſh'd the moſt elegant and correct editions of the ancient fathers, and of the *Greek* and *Latin* claſſicks. Of this number were *John Amerbach* and *John Froben*, of whom we ſhall give an account in the ſequel of this article.

The firſt book we meet with printed here, has no Printer's name ; nor is it poſſible to gueſs from the character, or any thing elſe in the edition, who 'twas done by : It is as follows ;

Roberti de Licio opus quadrageſimale, Baſileæ 1475.

1. Bernard Richel, 1477.

A citizen of *Baſil,* and an excellent Printer, was the firſt who put his name to his editions there ; we have but three of them. The firſt is his *Biblia Latina,* fol. *per* Bernardum Richel *civem* Baſiliæ 1477 ; the other two are dated 1478, 1482.

2. Michel Wenkler, 7 edit. from 1477 to 1486.

The laſt of his impreſſions, *viz. Gaſparini Pergamenſis Epiſtolæ,* 4to. F. *Orlandi* tells us in his liſt *p.* 166. that this has neither date nor Printer's name ; but Mr. *Mattaire* gives us the ſame edition under the names of *Michel Wenkler* and *Fred. Biel,* with ſome verſes at the end, as you'll find in that author, *Annal. Typogr.* p. 375, only he or his Printer has miſtaken *Parmenſis* for *Pergamenſis.*

3. Nicholas Kesler citizen of *Baſil,* 1486.

Of whom we have a *Biblia Sacra* printed at *Antwerp, ann.* 1487, and five other editions at *Baſil,* from 1486 to 1494 : his firſt edition, *viz. Textus Sententiarum, fol.* has the colophon which you will find in the margin, in imitation of *Fauſt, Schoeffer* and others [1].

His laſt work, *viz. Libri deflorationum* does not bear *Keſler's* name ; yet it being printed in the ſame character with the former, is eaſily known

[1] Anno domini milleſimo quadringenteſimo octuageſimo ſexto, octavo nonas Martii, non atramentali penna cannave, ſed quadam ingeni-oſa arte imprimendi, cunctipotenti aſpirante deo, in egregia urbe *Baſilienſi Nicolaus Keſler feliciter conſummavit.*

F f

to be his. It hath at the beginning the image of an old man with a triple face, and thefe words over it, *Sancta Trinitas.*

4. JOHN AMERBACH, 1481.

JOHN AMERBACH, one of the moft excellent and learned Printers of his time, was at firft a ftudent at *Paris*, under the famous *Jo. Lapidanu.* or *a Lapide*, who, being rector of that univerfity, invited the three *Germans* thither. *Amerbach* follow'd his ftudies 'till he attain'd to the degree of mafter of arts, foon after which he came to *Bafil*, and fet up the Art of Printing, for which he became as famous, as he had been before for his learning.

WHAT countryman he was is not eafy to determine. Some *French* annalifts challenge him for theirs, and *Orlandi* calls him a *Parifian*, tho' perhaps on no other account, than that he ftudied fo long in that univerfity. His name is unqueftionably *German*; but neither the colophons of his editions, nor his epitaph, make any mention of his country; for which reafon, we fhall not pretend to affirm any thing upon that head. His firft care at his entrance into the bufinefs of Printing was to get a font of the moft perfect round Roman, which however he made no ufe of in his books of divinity, the prevailing cuftom of thofe days being to print them in old Gothic. His next was to procure fome of the beft correctors of that age, of whom, tho' no perfon was more capable of correcting his works than himfelf, he had a greater number than any of his contemporaries. Among thefe were *Martin Dodo* a prebend, *Francis Wyler* a learned Francifcan fryar, *Conrard Pelican* an eminent divine, *Beatus Rhenanus* and others. He was fo carefull and diligent in this province, that he would not let one fheet pafs unrevis'd by himfelf. *Reuchlin* gives us this character of him in the preface to his book *De verbo mirifico*, that he was a man of an excellent genius, highly valuable for the neatnefs and correctnefs of his works, and well fkill'd in feveral arts and fciences. His former mafter *Jo. Lapidanus* affures us [1], that he never read any books bet-

---

[1] Iftud ego non favoris, fed veritatis gratia aufim dicere, quod non legerim libros hac arte effictos, quos tuis emendatiores exactiorique ftilo confummatos probaverim. Vide *Chevil.* p. 128.

to

ter or more correctly printed than his. As *Amerbach* was a man of fingular piety and zeal for religion, which appears from all his prefaces, that fcarce breathe any thing elfe; fo he rather chofe to confecrate his labours to that, than any other branch of learning. This induc'd him to print the works of all the ancient fathers, a tafk hitherto unattempted by any Printer. He began with an edition of St. *Auftin*, which he finifh'd not 'till the year 1505, in the old Gothic. But as he neither had a good manufcript to print after, nor fufficient affiftance from the learned; we can only fay that it was executed as correctly, as could be expected in thofe times. What he had moft at heart was to publifh St. *Jerom*'s works, which, as he knew was impoffible to be done without a competent fkill in the *Latin*, *Greek* and *Hebrew* tongues, the laft of which he was too old and full of bufinefs to learn, he made his three fons, youths of bright parts, divide that province among themfelves; who having ftudy'd thofe languages, were oblig'd by him, whether he liv'd or dy'd, to finifh that edition; which they faithfully perform'd. But as this tafk, wherein he was engaged, was too large for one man, he took the learned *John Froben*, whom we fhall mention hereafter, into partnerfhip, and printed feveral valuable and diftinct volumes with him. The greateft part of thefe particulars we have from *Erafmus*, in his prefaces to St. *Auftin* and St. *Jerom*, which later edition he revis'd and publifh'd *anno* 1515, with a dedication to the archbifhop of *Canterbury*. He highly extolls the piety of the *Amerbachs*, he praifes the father for having taken fuch care of his fons education; and the fons for the great progrefs they made in thofe tongues, and for their piety in having fo exactly fulfill'd their father's defire, in the impreffion of a work, which had coft them fo much money and pains; he frankly owns, that as he ftood in great need of fome affiftance for the *Hebrew* tongue, fo he was chiefly beholden to thofe three learned brothers for it [1]. *Jodocus Badius* another eminent Printer gives

---

[1]. *D. Erafm.* præfat. ad *S. Hieron.* opera. —— Quod idem fecimus in Hebraicis, verum hac fane in parte, quod minus noftro marte poteramus, aliorum fuppetiis præftititimus, præcipue fratrum *Amrbachiorum*, *Brunonis*, *Bafilii*, & *Bonifacii*, quos optimus pater *Joannes Amerbachius* velut inftaurandis bonis authoribus genitos, trium linguarum peritia curavit inftruendos. Atque hi fane paternum animum & expectationem vicerunt etiam, nihil antiquius ducentes *Hieronymi* gloria, & hac gratia nec impendio parcentes nec valetudini. *Maittaire Annal. Typogr.* vol. 1. pag. 142, 143.

their

their father the following encomium[1]; that he was a man of indefatigable induſtry, and confummate ſkill in correcting the errors of corrupt copies; and adds, that if all Printers would but follow his example, they would be in much higher reputation with the learned, than they were.

He continu'd printing 'till the year 1528, and dyed whilſt his ſecond impreſſion of St. *Auſtin* was in the preſs. It will not be amiſs to repeat here a caution, which we have elſewhere given the reader, not to confound this *John Amerbach* with *John Averbach* of *Reutlingen*, who printed there a *Latin* bible in *fol. ann.* 1469, after which we hear no more of him. *La Caille* makes them to be the ſame perſon, led undoubtedly into that error by the likeneſs of their names; whereas the diſtance of time between them, *viz.* from 1469 to 1481, the different ſpelling of their names, with other obvious circumſtances, might eaſily have ſhewn him the miſtake. Mr. *Mattaire*, in the place before quoted, hath collected a great number of extracts out of prefaces, epiſtles, and other works of the learned, in praiſe of him; and it muſt be own'd, that too much could not be ſaid in a man's commendation, who had ſpent near 50 years in the ſervice of religion with ſuch conſtant zeal and application. I ſhall refer the reader to that author for them, and only add the epitaph, which his youngeſt ſon *Boniface* caus'd to be ſet upon his tomb.

E P I T A P H I U M.

Joannes Amerbachius *hic cubat*
 Cum Barbara Ortenbergia *ſingul. pudicit. fœmina,*
 Ac Brunone Baſilioque, *filiis,*
 Præpropere quidem hinc ereptis.
 Sed ante tamen eruditione ſua trilingui
 Per laborioſiſſ. Hieronym. *operum recognitionem*
 Quibus nunc Docti ubique gentium fruuntur,
 Orbi toto commendata.
Bonifacius Amerbachius
 Parentibus & fratribus optimis,

---

[1] ――― Indefatigabili virum diligentia, & ſolertiſſima vitiorum expungendorum peritia ――― cujus viri ſi omnes ſimiles eſſemus ――― longe plures apud literatos haberemur. *Jodoc. Bas. epiſt. ad Anton. Coburger, ann.* 1499.

Se

Sed & Marthæ Fufchiæ
Uxori fuæ Chriſtianarum virtutum dotibus incomparabili,
Cum Urſula *ac* Hertexe *duabus filiolis.*
Hic quiefcenti:
Item ſibi ipſi liberis ſuis ſuperſtitibus
Fauſtinæ, Baſilio, Julianæ,
Poſteriſque in humanæ fragilitatis memoriam
F. C.

*Parentibus, fratribuſque jam olim, uxore vero in ipſo ætatis flore cum fili-
olis haud ita demum expeƈtandi cenſorii noviſſimique diei ergo collocatis.*
Anno MDXLII.

We have but nine editions of his as yet difcover'd, from 1481 to 1500 :
the firſt of them is *Vincentii Bellovacenſis opuſcula*, and the laſt *Fr. Petrar-
chæ opuſcula*, 1496.

5. JOHN FROBEN, 1491.

JOHN FROBEN was a native of *Hamelburgh* in *Fraconia*, where he
ſtudy'd 'till he became maſter of the *Latin* tongue, and afterwards went
to the univerſity of *Baſil*, where he perfeƈted himſelf in *Greek* alſo, and
betook himſelf to the buſineſs of Printing, of which he ſhow'd himſelf ſo
good a maſter, that *John Amerbach* took him as aſſiſtant and partner in
his laborious and expenſive undertaking of publiſhing the ancient fathers,
as we hinted before. He acquitted himſelf ſo well both in this province
and his own particular one, that he acquir'd as great a reputation and
eſteem among the learned, as his contemporary and partner ; to whom
Germany is oblig'd for bringing thither the neat round Roman charaƈter,
hitherto fcarcely known there, and improving it to the laſt degree of perfeƈtion. No perſon was ever more curious in the choice of the works,
which he ſent to the preſs, than he ; who had this excellent quality among
many others, that he would never print any bad books, ſuch as the ſor-
did avarice of other Printers had overſtock'd the world with ; but always
chofe the beſt authors, and beſt manuſcripts of them, ſparing neither
coſt-

coſt in purchaſing them, nor pains in correcting and fitting them for the preſs; in which, tho' he was a man of ſingular learning, yet he always preferr'd the advice and judgment of the learned of his time, to his own. Among theſe were *Mark Heyland, Eraſmus, Wolfgang Muſculus, Jo. Œcolampadius, Wolfgang, Lachner* and others, all perſons of the higheſt rank in the commonwealth of learning; for which reaſons his impreſſions have ever been, and will continue in the higheſt eſteem with all the learned. He was likewiſe particularly ambitious to have his works correct; and the abovemention'd learned men aſſiſted him very much in that province; eſpecially *Œcolampadius,* who tells us [1], that he could not ſufficiently wonder that *Eraſmus,* who alone kept three preſſes continually at work, who read and compar'd the *Greek* and *Latin* manuſcripts, and conſulted the writings of all the ancients and moderns, *&c.* could yet find time enough to correct the proofs of his works; and adds, that his example had not a little encourag'd him to take the laborious taſk of a corrector upon him. However, neither *Froben's* nor his corrector's diligence could prevent that edition, juſt now quoted in the margin, from having an errata of a page and half, tho' *Eraſmus* gave the finiſhing hand to every proof.

THIS learned author, in one of his letters to *Bilibaldus Parcheimerus,* who was then at the emperor's court, complains highly of a great injuſtice done to many good Printers in general, and to *Froben* particularly, which was, that he had no ſooner publiſh'd a good edition with great coſt and labour, but it was immediately reprinted by others, and ſold ſo much cheaper, that he could never reimburſe himſelf half his charges. This reduc'd him to the neceſſity of obtaining from the emperor, *&c.* a privilege for the ſole ſelling them for the ſpace of two or more years, according to the value of the work; there being no other effectual way of preventing ſuch an abuſe: the letter is dated from *Baſil, Jan.* 28. 1522: the

[1] O *Ecolampadius* in his epiſtle at the end of *Eraſmus's* edition of the New Teſtament in *Greek* with a new *Latin* verſion, printed by *Froben, ann.* 1516, and dedicated to Pope *Leo* X ——admirabile ſpectaculum mihi erat, imo ſpectandum miraculum, dictantem recognoſcentemque quantum tria præla exciperent, videre, ac nihilo ſecius interim Græca Latinaque exem- plaria, eaque varia & vetuſtiſſima, conſulen tem, Græcos Latinoſque interpretes conferen tem priſcos ac recentiores primæ ſimul ac in- fimæ claſſis ſcriptores perpendentem —— nimi rum *Eraſmicum* imitati exemplum, qui & ipſ hic, cæteris rebus omiſſis bonam temporis par tem in hoc collocavit negotium.

reader

reader will find it in *Vita Erafmi, Leyden* edit. 1642 in 16°, *pag.* 226, what relates to our fubject, he will find in the margin [1].

We have had occafion to mention fome cheats of even a worfe nature with refpect to the *Venetian* editions, which were counterfeited with the Printer's mark, and fold for the right ones, tho' incorrect and imperfect to the laft degree.

To return to *Froben*; he is reported to have hang'd his proofs in publick fight, with a promife of a reward for every error, that fhould be difcover'd in them by any perfon. In his fhort preface to *Celius Rhodiginus* printed *ann.* 1517, he inveighs loudly againft thofe pefts of learning, thofe Printers, who regarded not the correction of their works, but had gain only in their view; and advifes the learned againft buying fuch bad books, for the fake of their cheapnefs, affuring them that they purchas'd nothing but plague and vexation, and *that fuch wretched works could not but be dearly bought, how cheap foever they were fold; whereas he that bought a correct copy, always bought it cheap, how much foever he gave for it* [2].

Jo. Froben printed few volumes before the year 1500, and the number of thofe which are extant, is ftill fmaller. One of them was his concordance of the bible in *fol. ann..* 1495; concerning which we meet with fome particulars, not unworthy the reader's knowledge, tho' a digreffion from our fubject.

First it was fo exactly printed, that there was not one error in all the numerical figures, which in a work of that nature are at leaft one third part of the matter; and is therefore very furprizing. *Froben* added a fecond part to it, which contain'd all the indeclinable particles, that are to be met with in the bible. This work was begun at *Conftantinople* by *Jo. de Raguza*, a Parifian divine of the Dominican order, embaffador

---

[1] Plerique infidiantur Homini, propemodum conjurati ut illum perdant Ubi quid novi operis prodit, quod putent fore vendibile, mox unus atque alter fuffuratus ex ipfius officina exemplar, excudit ac venditat minimo; interim *Frobenius* immenfam pecuniam impendit in caftigatores, frequenter & in exemplaria, huic iniquitati facile fuccurretur, fi fiat imperatorium edictum, ne quis librum primum a *Frobe-nio* excufum, aut cui fit aliquid ab auctore additum, excudat intra biennium. Tempus longum non eft officina *Frobeniana* vel ob hoc favore digna eft quod nihil ex ea prodit ineptum aut feditiofum.

[2] ——— Parvo emit, quifquis librum emendatum etiam magno emit; magno emit, quifquis codicem mendofum etiam minimo emit, *Ibid.*

from

from the council of *Baden* to the emperor *Jo. Paleologus* about the year
1436; yet he did little to it himſelf, but left it to his three chaplains, one
of whom was a *Scotchman* nam'd *Walter Sonaw,* who finiſh'd it in almoſt
three years. After this it was reduc'd into an alphabetical order, by the
directions of that council, by *John de Segovia* or *Secubia,* archdeacon of
Cujedo, and doctor of divinity. What gave birth to this ſecond part of
the concordance was no leſs remarkable, *John de Raguza* beforemention'd,
coming to *Conſtantinople,* found the divines there engag'd in a very warm
diſpute concerning the proceſſion of the Holy Ghoſt, *i. e.* whether from
the Son as well as from the Father; and that the controverſy ſeem'd
chiefly to be about the particles *ex* and *per, i. e.* whether it ſhould be *ex
filio* or *per filium.* He was likewiſe inform'd, that the *Sultan* and all the
Mahometans having heard, that *Paleologus* deſign'd a journey into chri-
ſtendom, in order to reconcile this difference between the *Greek* and *Latin*
churches, had rally'd the chriſtians with no ſmall ſcorn, whom two ſuch
ſeemingly inſignificant particles had divided to ſuch a degree. This
embaſſador fail'd not to acquaint the council with it, who immediately
order'd *John de Segovia* to be ready to anſwer all the difficulties, which
the *Greeks* ſhould propoſe at their arrival at *Baſil.* In the mean time the
Huſſites and *John Huſs* of *Bohemia,* who were already at *Baſil,* and inſiſted
upon a communion in both kinds from the words of our Saviour, *Unleſs you eat,* &c. and *unleſs you drink,* &c. which their oppoſers ſaid ſignify'd no more than, unleſs you eat or drink, from which they concluded
that either the one or the other was ſufficient to fulfill the command;
theſe I ſay made it ſtill more neceſſary to have a concordance, that ſhould
explain the meaning of thoſe particles *ex* and *per, niſi* and *et,* and in how
many different ſenſes they were us'd in ſcripture. This induc'd *John de
Segovia* to write the ſecond part of the concordance relating to indeclinable words, with a prolegomenon or preface, in which he hath given
us this account of the occaſion of it. The learned *Sebaſtian Brant,* author
of the *Navis ſtultifera,* caus'd it to be printed by *Froben, ann.* 1495, and
ſomewhat above twenty years after the ſame, *Froben* reprinted it with
an elegant *Latin* dialogue between a bookſeller and the buyer, relating
to the value of good books, inſtead of a preface to that edition. The
reader may ſee it at length in *Chevillier,* p. 130.

FROBEN

FROBEN had two fons *Jerom* and *John*, who fucceeded their father, and publifh'd a great number of volumes with good reputation after his death, which happen'd *ann.* 1527. *Erafmus* tells us that what he had moft at heart was to give the world a correct edition of St. *Auftin's* works, and that he defir'd to live no longer than to fee it finifh'd[1]. However he was depriv'd of that pleafure, for *J. And-Endters* tells us tho' he kept feven preffes continually at work upon that edition, yet not above two volumes of it were printed before he died, to the great lofs and grief of all the learned world: the following epitaph, written by his friend *Erafmus*, was afterwards fet upon his tomb.

Epitaphium JOANNIS FROBENII.
per Defiderium Erafmum Rot.

Arida Joannis *tegit hic lapis offa* Frobeni,
　　Orbe vivet toto nefcia fama mori.
Moribus hanc niveis meruit ftudiifque juvandis;
　　Quæ nunc mæfta jacent orba parente fuo.
Rettulit, ornavit veterum monumenta fophorum
　　Arte, manu, curis, aere, favore, fide.
Huic vitam in cælis date, numina jufta, perennem;
　　Per nos in terris fama perennis erit.

THIS epitaph was afterwards printed, according to *la Caille*, in *Henry Stephen's Artis Typographicæ Querimonia*; *Erafmus* wrote another of four verfes in *Greek*, which the Reader may fee in *Matt. Annal. Typog.* v. 2. p. 36.

ERASMUS was not contented with writing the abovemention'd epitaphs in his late friend's praife, but he made likewife a kind of funeral oration or rather elogium upon him, in a letter to *John Emfted* a learned *Carthufian*; the reader may fee it at full length in the above-mention'd *Annals*, vol. 2. pag. 36, *& feq.*

AND indeed it was no more than he ow'd him, fince *Froben* had long before given him a pleafure, which few men befide him had ever tafted, which was to fee his own elegy before his death; the occafion of it was

---

[1] Ut inter familiares fubinde dicere folitus &t, fe non optare longius vitæ fpatium, quam quod abfolvendo fufficeret Auguftino. *Erafm. epift. ad Ammonium.* Tom. 3. oper. p.759.

as follows. Before theſe two were become intimate, *Froben* had heard that *Eraſmus* was dead, and wrote much ſuch another funeral oration upon him, which he prefix'd to an edition of that great man's proverbs, which he publiſh'd *Ann.* 1513: *Eraſmus* could not but be highly pleas'd to ſee himſelf prais'd in ſo extraordinary and ſincere a manner, being well aſſur'd that ſuch encomiums could not proceed from flattery or ſelf intereſt; for *Eraſmus* being ſuppos'd dead, *Froben* could have nothing to hope from him; and had any but a man of *Froben's* integrity and honour committed ſuch a miſtake, one might be apt to ſuſpect it had been wilfully done, in hopes of procuring ſome valuable pieces from that learned author: but whoever is acquainted with that Printer's character, will undoubtedly believe him incapable of ſuch mean arts.   I think therefore it will not be amiſs to cloſe the hiſtory of this great Printer with ſome conſpicuous parts of his character, which we have not yet touch'd upon, and which will eaſily acquit him of any ſuſpicion; which is, that he was a man of the moſt diſintereſted and generous diſpoſition. *Eraſmus* in his letter to *Emſted* abovemention'd does even tell us, that he was ſo to a fault, and that he had often reprov'd him for it, but in vain, for his natural candor was proof againſt all admonitions of that kind: neither did his munificence to men of learning and merit ſhow itſelf only in the largeneſs of his preſents to them, but in the manner of beſtowing them; never, ſays that author, did he ſeem better pleas'd than when he had, either by intreaties or by ſome cunning device, prevail'd upon them to accept of ſome favour from him. The grief he ſhew'd in his countenance at their denial was ſuch, that they found it more difficult to refuſe a favour from him, than to obtain one from another perſon; and when by chance, continues he, I have bought me ſome cloath for a gown, he has privately ſent, and paid for it unknown to me. As his houſe was open to all learned men, ſo none had a heartier welcome than *Eraſmus*, who us'd it as his home all the time he continued at *Baſil*, and it is probable that he might have continued longer there, had he not obſerv'd ſomething in his family, which he could not forbear grieving at. *Froben* was under petticoat-government, which made his affairs go ſomewhat wrong, wherefore he expreſſes himſelf thus to him in a letter dated from *Louvain*; *Fama tibi parta eſt, ea poterit tibi magno emolumento*

eſſe,

effe, fi curam de tuo adhibueris ; fed mihi non placet domi tuæ regnum iftud Muliebre, &c. But *Froben* was of too eafy and patient a temper, to give himfelf any trouble about it : we have a remarkable inftance of this in the laft year of his life, when being feiz'd with fuch a violent pain in his right heel, that fome phyficians were for cutting off his foot, he had no fooner receiv'd fome eafement in it, than he went on horfeback to *Frankfort* about fome bufinefs ; and tho' advis'd by his friends to ftir feldomer abroad, to go warmer in cloaths, and to fpare himfelf as much as poffible, he refus'd to hearken to them, and took fuch care to conceal his bad ftate of health, and the anguifh of his pain, that he went ftill about his bufinefs ; 'till being feiz'd with a fainting fit, he dropt down and broke his fkull againft the pavement ; after which he continued two days, without any fenfe or motion, and expir'd *ann.* 1528. I hope the name and character of the perfon will excufe my account of thefe particularities, efpecially fince the great *Erafmus* has thought them worth recording in a much ampler manner : he left two fons *Jerom* and *John,* who became excellent Printers, and fignaliz'd themfelves by their editions of the *Greek* and *Latin* fathers ; he had likewife fome daughters, one of whom nam'd *Juftina* he marry'd to *Nicolas l'Evefque* or *Epifcopius,* an eminent Printer of *Bafil.*

His ufual mark or rebus was a dove fitting on the top of a ftaff, with two bafilifks twin'd about it, to which he fometimes added the initial letters of both his names I O. F R O. and fometimes the fourth verfe of the 125th pfalm in *Hebrew,* the fixteenth verfe of St. *Matthew*'s 10th chapter in *Greek,* and thefe words in *Latin, Prudens Simplicitas Amorque recti,* in three diftinct lines. All the works we have extant of his from 1491 to 1500 are only four, viz. a *Latin* bible, 8vo, in a fmall character dated 1491. Another in the old *Gothic,* 8vo, 1495 ; his concordance of the bible mention'd before, *fol. anno* 1495 ; and the *Speculum decem Præceptorum* of *Henry Harp.*

I can find but one more Printer after him, *viz.*

John Bergman *de* Olpe, 1497.

Of whom we have only two editions of *Sebaftian Brant*'s *Navis ftultifera,* dated 1497 and 1498. the laft of which is adorn'd with wooden cutts.

BESIDES thefe F. *Orlandi* has given us a lift of above 60 *Bafil* editions without Printers names.

Article II. *The Cities of* Efling, Placentia *and* Pignerol.

THESE three cities being inconfiderable with refpect to their Productions in the Art of Printing, except the earlinefs of their receiving it, I have joyn'd them into one fhort article.

§. ESLING is a fmall city in the duchy of *Wirtembergh* in *Germany.* It receiv'd Printing either about or before the year 1475; tho' we can meet but with the two following editions printed there by

CONRARD FYNER, 1475. *viz.*

1. PETRI Nigri Germani *ord. præd. qui claruit anno* 1475, } 1475.
traEtatus de Judæorum perfidia, per Conradum Fyner Eflingæ }

2. EJUSDEM *traEtatus de conditionibus veri Meffiæ contra Judæos, Germanicé,* by the fame, *ibid.* Orl. } 1477.

§. PLACENTIA a noble antient city upon the river *Po* in *Italy,* in which we find only one edition printed by

JO. PETER *de Ferratis* of *Cremona,* 1475. *viz.*

BIBLIA *Latina, 4to, per* Jo. Petri *de* Ferratis Cremonenfem Placentiæ, 1475.

§. PIGNEROL [in *Latin Pignarolium*] is a well fortify'd city in *Piedmont,* at the foot of the *Alps,* under the dominion of the prefent king of *Sardinia.* Here the famous *French* Printer

JAMES *des* ROUGES or *de* RUBEIS,

Set up his Prefs, after he had printed at *Venice* from 1473 to 1477 with vaft applaufe. The firft book, which we find printed by him, is a *Latin* bible dated 1475; in which all our annalifts have follow'd father *le Long:* but it is doubtful whether he was not miftaken in the year, seeing feeing *des Rouges* was ftill printing at *Venice, anno* 1477, and that we find no more impreffions of his done at *Pignerol*, 'till *anno* 1479.

However as it is not eafy to determine whether father *le Long* was in an error, or the bible antedated, or whether this Printer kept two Preffes at the fame time, one at *Venice*, and another at *Pignerol*; I have follow'd the order of the annalifts, and ventur'd to place this edition and city under that year.

We have but four editions of his printed at *Pignerol*, that of the bible of 1475 included, two of which are dated 1479, and the laft 1480.

Article III. *The City of* VINCENTIA, 1475.

Vincentia is a large ancient city and univerfity in *Italy*, now under the republick of *Venice*, which receiv'd the Art of Printing *anno* 1475, and oblig'd the world with a gieater number of editions than many cities of *Italy*, and other parts of *Europe*, which we have feen hitherto.

1. Herman Levilapis *or* Lichtenstein, 1475.

Was one of the firft that brought it hither. He was a native of *Cologn*, and a very good, but unfettled Printer. We have already feen him at *Venice* and *Trevifo*. At *Vincentia* he printed fome editions in partnerfhip with *Nicholas Petri* of *Harlem*, alias *Peter de Harlem*.

We have twelve of them extant, in fome of which he calls himfelf *Herman Levilapis*, in others *de Levilapide* or *Lichtenftein*, in others *Herman Lichtenftein de Colonia*; one remarkable edition of his, viz.

Pauli Orofii Hifpani *biftoriarum libri* vii *ad* Aurelium Auguftinum *de maximis calamitatibus ab orbe condito ufque ad fua tempora, fol.* is without date, Printers or place's name.

This edition was corre&ed by *Æneas Vulpes*, and printed at *Vincentia* by *Herman Lichtenftein*, as appears by the epigram quoted in the margin [1];

[1] Ut ipfe titulus margine in primo docet,
  Orofio nomen mihi eft.
Librariorum quicquid erroris fuit,
  Exemit Æra mihi:
Mæque imprimendum tradidit non alteri,
  Hermanne, quam foli tibi;
Hermanne, nomen hujus artis & decus,

Tuæque laus Coloniæ
Quod fi fitum orbis, ficque ad noftra tempora
Ab orbis ipfa origine;
Quifque tumultus, bellaque & cædes velit,
Cladefque noffe : me legat.

after

after which it was reprinted in the fame place, but in a larger character, by *Leonard de Basilea* with the fame verfes, except changing the word *Herman* for that of *Leonard*, and *Colonia* for *Basilea*. It was reprinted likewife in feveral other places, only the 5, 6, 7 and 8th verfes were omitted.

2. JOHN RHENISH or *John de Reno*, five editions from 1475 to 1481.

3. JOHN *de Vienna*, 1 edit. 1476.

4. STEPHEN KOBLINGER, 1 edit. 1479.

5. HENRY, bookfeller of *Vincentia*, 3 edit. from 1480 to 1486.

6. LEONARD *de Basilea* or of *Basil*, Printer to the univerfity of *Vincentia*, 5 edit. from 1482 to 1491.

7. JAMES DUSENSIS, 1 edit. 1482.

8. HENRY *de S Urfo*, 5 edit. from 1486 to 1499.

9. SIMON BEVILAQUA [*Drink water*] citizen of *Pavia*, 2 edit. both 1489.

HE went afterwards to *Venice*, where he printed a much greater number of editions, from 1492 to 1500, as has been faid under that head.

HERE are likewife a fmall number without Printer's names.

Article IV.   *The Cities of* LUBECK *and* VALENTIA.

§. THE city of *Lubeck* is one of the Hans-towns in *Germany*, between the provinces of *Saxony* and *Alfatia* upon the *Baltick* fea. It is very eminent for its trade, port, fortifications, riches, and number of inhabitants.

HITHER the Art of Printing was brought *anno* 1475, yet appears to have met with but little encouragement from its trading inhabitants, for we find only four Printers in this city from 1471 to 1502, and they were fo far from fettling here any time, that their bad fuccefs had oblig'd them to quit the place, for we have but five editions extant of them all; their names are as follows.

1. LUCAS BRANDIS *de Schafz*, 2 edit. from 1475 to 1477.

2. STEPHEN ARNOLD, 1 edit. 1484.

3. STEPHEN ARNDES, 1 edit. 1493.

4. BARTHOL. GOTHAN, 1 edit. 1494.

I SHALL

I shall only add that the firſt work of *Lucas Brandis,* viz. *Epitoma Hiſtoriarum* has the pompous *Latin* inſcription, which you will find in the margin [1], and which has led ſome authors into an abſurd notion that the Art of Printing was found out at *Lubeck.*

§. VALENTIA, 1475.

There are ſo many cities and towns of this name in *France, Italy* and *Spain,* that it cannot poſſibly be determin'd in which of them the two following books, which are all that we find under that name, have been printed; there being nothing in the titles or any other part to aſcertain it, and even the Printer's names are wanting.

   1. Salustius, 4to. *Valentiæ,* 1475.

   2. Ximenius (Franciſcus) *de vita Chriſtiana in* vi *partes diſtinĉta,* ibid, 1484.

Article V. ROSTOCH *and* BRUGES, 1475; *and* DELPH, 1477.

   §. Rostoch is an imperial free city in *Germany,* upon the *Baltick* ſea. Here was founded an univerſity about the year 1490, fourteen years before which, we meet with the following book, the only one as yet known, printed there by ſome regular prieſts, as the colophon informs us.

   Lactantii Firmiani *de divinis inſtitutionibus,* fol. *per fratres preſbyteros & clericos congregationis Domus viridis horti ad ſanĉtum* Michaelem *in oppido* Roſtochienſi *partium inferioris* Sclaviæ, *prout facultas & induſtria tulit, emendate ſatis & accurate conſummat.* milleſimo quadringenteſimo ſeptuageſimo ſexto, quinto Idus *Aprilis:* Roſtochii, 1476.

   §. Bruges in *Flanders* had a Printer ſettled there *anno* 1476, nam'd

---

[1] ———— Imperiali in urbe *Lubecana,* arte impreſſoria, ſpeciali gratia divina, animarum ob ſalutem fidelium inventa, epitoma iſtud in partes vi. juxta mundi ætates diviſum, prius alibi non repertum, quod placuit Rudimentum Novitiorum intitulari, dei adjutorio, qui ſupernas res ac ſubterraneas feliciter, ſuaviter, tranquillieque diſpenſat, per magiſtrum *Lucam Brandis* de *Schafz* feliciter eſt excuſum atque finitum; ut pauperes ſolvere libros non valentes, unum tantum haberent hoc enchiridium loco multorum ſemper ad manum librorum.

I. Colard

1. COLARD MANSION,

OF whom we have three editions from 1476 to 1486.

ORLANDI gives us another Printer of this city, *viz. John de Rey,* who printed *Centon Epiſtolas dell' Bachiller,* 4to, 1499. Mr *Maittaire* and *la Caille* date this edition from *Burgos* in *Spain,* and they ſeem to be in the right, becauſe the book is written in *Spaniſh,* and the Printer's name ſhews him to be of that nation.

§. DELPH is a fine city in *Holland,* near the *Hague* and *Rotterdam.* We meet with ſeven editions printed there, all without any Printer's name ; the firſt of which, *viz.* the *Dutch* bible is dated *anno* 1477. The reſt are dated as follows ; two 1480, two 1487, one 1491, the laſt 1497.

CHAP. XI.

The Cities of 1. Spire, 2. Lyons, *anno* 1477. 3. Geneva, Bruſſels, Coſcence *and* Pavia, *anno* 1478. 4. Goude, Zivol, *anno* 1479 ; *and* Caen, Ceulen, Cenzano *and* Quilemburgh, *anno* 1480. 5. Lignitz, Huſſelet, Regio Mont-royal *and* Wartzburgh, *anno* 1481. 6. Piſa, Aquila, Erford *and* Langres, *anno* 1482 : *And* 7. Gaunt *and* Memining, *anno* 1483.

Article I. *The City of* SPIRE, 1477.

SPIRE is an ancient city in higher *Germany,* ſituate upon the *Rhine,* between *Mentz* and *Strasburgh.* It is now call'd in *Latin Spira,* but formerly was call'd *Novimagium* and *Nemetes.*

THO' this city doth not ſeem to have cultivated the Art of Printing within her walls, ſo much as other cities of *Germany,* yet it ought to be remembred for having given birth to ſome eminent Printers, who went

and

and fettled in other parts of *Europe,* and in particular the two famous brothers, who firft fet up their preffes at *Venice,* viz. *John* and *Windelin* of *Spire,* of whom we have given an account in the third chapter of this fecond part. Here we find the firft beginnings of the Art about the year 1477, when

1. PETER DRACH *of* SPIRE.

PRINTED the *Summa* of *Archiep. Antoninus,* which is the firft book we know of printed by him ; as he is likewife the only Printer, who put his name to any impreffions done in this city. His editions are but four in number, from 1477 to 1487 ; befides which we find about ten more printed here without the names of the Printers.

IT will not be improper to obferve here, that our lateft annalifts place the city of *Weftminfter* under this year ; the oldeft edition as yet difcover'd by them being *Socrates's Sayings* printed by *Caxton, anno* 1477 ; however the reader will find by the third book of this hiftory, that there is a more ancient one by three years, viz. *The Game of Chefs,* which is dated *anno* 1474, now in the poffeffion of my worthy friend the curious Mr *Granger* of the *Eaft-India Houfe :* and it is plain from the account of the Art's being brought into *England,* that they began to print in the abbey of *Weftminfter* much fooner than that year.

Article II. *The City of* LYONS.

LYONS, a rich and populous city in *France,* upon the rivers *Rhone* and *Arare,* is call'd in *Latin, Lugdunum,* and is allow'd to be one of the moft ancient cities in *Europe* ; fo that fome *French* writers have not fcrupled to fix the date of its foundation within 600 or 700 years after the flood, which may more eafily be believ'd than difprov'd. It has been always eminent for men of learning in all arts and fciences, which were particularly cultivated there, but more efpecially after the Art of Printing was introduc'd ; which receiv'd fuch encouragement there, that it has continu'd in a flourifhing condition ever fince. Some annalifts have afferted that it is the firft city in *France* which fet up a Printing-prefs; but if we would judge of this controverfy by the dates of the oldeft impreffions,

preffions,

preffions, we fhall find that the city of *Tours,* and next that of *Paris* had the Art feveral years before, as hath been already fhewn. However, if *Lyons* hath not the preference of *Rome, Paris, Venice,* &c. either for the antiquity or beauty of its productions; it muft be acknowledg'd that it hath gain'd it by the quantity of large impreffions, than which no city in *Europe* has furnifh'd the learned with a greater number. It is ftill a great *emporium* or market for books in all languages and fciences; and as it hath encourag'd fome of the beft artifts to fettle there, and pub-lifh beautiful and correct editions, fo it has induc'd many a wretched one to chufe it as a proper place to print and vend a much greater quan-tity of bad and counterfeit ones; but this hath happen'd in moft famous cities of *Europe.* *Lyons* hath likewife been celebrated, if not for intro-ducing, at leaft for encouraging, the *Gothick* character, and publifh'd more volumes of that fort, in proportion to thofe that were done in fine Roman, than any other city; and what is more remarkable of the Prin-ters of this city, they were vaftly more fond of that inelegant character than of the Roman, efpecially for bibles, divinity, law and phyfick books.

T H E reader will be juftly furpriz'd to hear what encomiums they gave it, and how proud they were of their performances in that kind. I have fubjoin'd in the margin three or four fcraps of their colophons, to fhew what a piece of merit the Printers of the 15th and above half of the 16th century made of their works printed in this character, not only at *Lyons,* but likewife at *Venice, Paris, Rome,* &c. [1] *John de Cologne* at *Venice* us'd to phrafe it thus, *Done in fublimely fine characters,* &c. another [2] values himfelf upon the beauty and excellence of his character; a third [3] calls it the moft elegant character; and a fourth [4] the moft polite of all charac-ters: fo that if a perfon did not fee what Types they meant, he would be apt to judge it any other than the *Gothick.* The famous *Badius,* firnam'd *Afcenfius,* who had printed in this city of *Lyons* from 1495 to 1500, is reported to have gone afterwards to *Paris,* with a defign to ftop, as

---

[1] Sublimi literarum effigie, &c.

[2] Charactere jucundiffimo M. Joan: Her-bort Alemani, cujus vis et ingenium facile fu-pereminet omnes.

[3] Opus pulchro literarum charactere poli-tiffimum, &c.

[4] Certante minio purpuræ rubedine, Superante cervas nigredine fepiâ — politioribus characterum typis, &c.

much

much as poffible, the current vogue of this old Gothick ; but in vain, for he was oblig'd to continue it himfelf till almoft the very later end of his days ; and befides it ftill remain'd in great ufe long after that, infomuch that *Atenfis* complains ¹ that Printers were extremely curious, and fpar'd no coft to give elegant impreffions of the heathen poets, orators, *&c.* whereas any batter'd old Gothick Types were thought good enough for thofe of Divinity. In the clofe of this fecond book we fhall mention fome of the Printers, to whom the world is oblig'd for the total difufe of that inelegant character. To return to *Lyons* ; the firft Printer we find there, is,

1. BARTHOLOMEW BUYER, 1477.

Of whom we have only the two following impreffions : the firft, viz. the new Teftament in French is without date, and has been fuppos'd by *de la Caille*, to have been printed about 1500. but *F. Le Long* more juftly fuppofes it, both by the rudenefs of the character, and its likenefs to that of the next edition of *Buyer*, which is dated 1477 to have been printed about this time.

2. MARTIN HUSZ and ⎱
3. JOS. FABER ⎰ two edit. from 1478, to 1485.

4. PERRINE LATHOMI, 1 edit. 1479.

He printed likewife at *Venice* with fome others, about 1494.

5. WILLIAM *le* ROY, 2 edit. from 1483, to 1488.

6. JANON CARCAIGNI, 2 edit. from 1488, to 1495.

7. MICHELET TOPIE *de Piemont* and ⎱ 2 edit. from
8. JAMES HEREMBERCLE, *alias* HEREMBERCH, *German,* ⎰ 1488. to 1490.

9. JOHN CLEIN, *German,* 1 edit. 1489.

10. MATTHIAS HUSM, *German,* 1 edit. 1489.

11. JOHN DU PRE, 2 edit. from 1489, to 1493.

He printed likewife at *Paris* and *Abbeville.*

12. PETER MARESHAL, 1 edit. 1490.

13. JOHN DE LA FONTAINE of *Lyons,* 1 edit. 1490.

14. JOHN TRECHSEL *German,* 8 edit. from 1490 to 1497.

¹ Lynceis utuntur oculis & Herculeo labore, fi quando ethnicorum aliquis aut nugax poeta, aut verbofus orator eft imprimendus ; facris quof- vis typos quamvis tritos & confufaneos adhibent. Præfat. ad Gregor.

Whofe

Whofe corrector was the famous *Jodocus Badius,* of whom we fhall fpeak hereafter ; fome of whofe learned works, comments and annotations he printed *anno* 1492 *& feq.* as *Silvæ Morales, cum interpretatione* Badii *ex* Virgil. Horat. Perf. Juvenal. Ennio, Bapt. Mantuan. Sulpit. Caton. with fome others which we fhall fpeak of anon. I muft not omit mentioning, that all *Trechfel's* works are highly valuable and correct.

15. Engolhard Schultis, *German,* 1 edit. 1491.
16. Matthias Huts, 1 edit. 1491.
17. Ant. Labillon and
18. Martin Saraceni, } 2 edit. both 1491.

19. JODOCUS BADIUS, *firnam'd* ASCENSIUS, 1495.

Badius was born in the caftle of *Afe,* in the territories of *Bruffels,* and call'd *Afcenfius* from it. He fpent his younger years in ftudy at *Bruffels, Gaunt,* and laft of all in the univerfity of *Ferrara,* under the great *Bapt. Guarini,* where he became mafter of the *Greek* and *Latin* tongues, and very famous for his learning and parts. He remov'd afterwards to the city of *Lyons,* where he publickly taught thofe two languages, and became corrector to *Jo. Trechfel's* prefs, as has been faid before. He publifh'd feveral works, fome of which were his own, as *Silvæ morales contra vitia.* fol. 1492. *Epigrammatum* lib. 1. *Navicula Stultarum mulierum* ; the Life of *Thomas a Kempis* prefix'd to his works, and fome others. Several excellent commentaries were likewife written by him upon the greateft part of the clafficks, and other *Latin* authors, as *Horace, Juvenal, Martial, Lucretius, Seneca, Saluft, Valerius Maximus, Quintilian, Aulus Gellius,* and others ; all which he printed himfelf in *folio* very elegantly and correctly, tho' fome of the firft he caus'd to be printed by *John Trechfel,* whofe daughter he afterwards married and had many children by her. To all his editions, which were not a few, he us'd to prefix an epiftle dedicatory, addrefs'd to fome perfon, eminent either for his quality, piety or learning. Among others, he dedicated the firft Volume of *Tho. Waldenfis* works to pope *Clement* VII. After he had taken the bufinefs of printing upon him ; he became fo excellent a Printer, that the learned *Rob. Gaguin,* general of the Trinitarian Order, who

who was perfectly well acquainted with his merit, wrote a letter to him, to defire him to undertake the printing of his works. This with fome other invitations of the learned, brought *Badius* to *Paris* about 1499, prefently after his father-in-law's death, where he defign'd to teach the *Greek* tongue, and where his laft endeavour, after he had furnifh'd himfelf with fine fets of Roman characters, was to explode the old Gothick both in his works, and by his example, as we hinted before. And accordingly printed the *Philobiblion* of that great encourager of learning, *Richard Bury*, lord high chancellor of *England*, bifhop of *Durham*, and founder of the *Oxford* library, towards the middle of the 14th century ; which book was fent to him by Dr. *Bureau*, bifhop of *Cifteron*, and confeffor to the *French* king, in order to be printed by him. This was the firft book known that came to the prefs after he fet it up at *Paris* ; 'tis dated 1500 ; the next year he printed the *Provinciale, feu conftitutiones Angliæ, cum Annotationibus Gullielmi Lindewode* 1501, in 2 vol. fol. in a beautiful round Roman. This book, as *de la Caille* tells us, is very fcarce, and much fought for, being very neceffary for thofe who would underftand the old *French* us'd in *William* the conqueror's time, tho' I doubt he is miftaken, the work itfelf being in *Latin*. He began to print by himfelf about the year 1495, at which time the great *Aldus Manutius* began at *Venice* ; than whom neither that age nor the next produc'd two more learned or excellent Printers.

As this later was chiefly engag'd in printing and correcting of *Greek* authors, fo *Badius* was employ'd in the *Latin* ones ; and there feem'd a kind of friendly emulation between them, each carrying away the palm in a feparate province. Upon account of this merit the editor of *Guil. de Rubione* in his dedication to the earl of *Caftille* calls *Afcenfius* a perfon skill'd in all kinds of fcience, and the prince of printers [1] ; and *Trithemius* ranks him among the *Scriptores Ecclefiaftici*, when he was but two and thirty years of age, and gives him the following panegyrick, *viz.* that he was a perfect mafter of literature, not unskilful in the holy fcriptures, a good philofopher, orator and poet, a man of a bright genius and a fluent tongue, [2] *&c. Erafmus* likewife gives him a great enco-

---

[1] Omnigenere difciplinarum eruditiffimo *Afcenfio*, imprefforiæ artis primati.

[2] Vir in fecularibus literis eruditiffimus, & divinarum fcripturarum non ignarus, philofophus, rhetor, & poeta clariffimus, ingenio excellens & difertus eloquio.

mium

mium in his dialogue intitled *Ciceronianus*; prefers his ſtile to that of *Apuleius*, and highly applaudes his admirable facility of writing. I ſhall give the *Latin* reader a ſpecimen of his poetry in the margin, which is a tetraſtich inſcrib'd to the learned *Fath. Mark Benevent*, to whom the edition of *Holkoth* upon the ſentences, printed by *J. Treſchel* anno 1497, is dedicated, and of which himſelf was the corrector; in which verſes he deſires him in a moſt elegant manner to excuſe the faults ſtill remaining in it [1]. He was no leſs skillful in reſtoring of corrupt manuſcripts, than careful in printing of them with the greateſt accuracy; ſo that ſome of his *Errata*'s have contain'd but five words. In printing the work of any living author, he always follow'd the copy exactly; and he tells us in his preface to his edition of *Angelus Politianus* [2], that he endeavour'd to imitate the laudable diligence of *Aldus Manutius*, and to print from his copies with the utmoſt exactneſs. This made not only the learned very ambitious to have their works printed by him, but the moſt eminent bookſellers of *Paris* were glad, in order to have him for their Printer, to aſſociate themſelves with him; among whom, *John Petit* ſworn bookſeller to that univerſity, and one of the moſt famous of that age, caus'd ſeveral noble editions to be printed by him as the *Calepini Dictionarium octo Linguar.* 1516. *Origen. Opera Latinè* 4 vol. fol. 1519, ſome of which beautifully printed on vellum, are ſtill to be ſeen in ſeveral libraries of that city, with many others: He had other aſſociates beſides *Petit*, viz. *Andreas Bochard, Dionys Roce, Geofrey Marneff*, and many others, all eminent men in their way. Thus he continued printing and writing with great applauſe and reputation till the year 1534, in which he died. Some authors indeed have affirm'd that he died *anno* 1526, becauſe they knew of no works printed by him after that year. *Chevillier* gives us two particulars, which fix the year of his death beyond diſpute. The firſt is the laſt book printed in his name, viz. *Alphonſus a Caſtro contra Hæreſes.* fol. 1534. and *Peter Lombard in Epiſtolas Pauli.* fol. ann. 1535. *pro hæredibus Jodoci Badii, menſe decembri*, both which editi-

---

[1] Jam portum optatum per inhoſpita ſaxa
    ſecuti
  Prendimus, ex alto proſpiciente deo.
Siqua tamen laceræ portent inculta carinæ,
  Humanè ignoſces, Marce diſerte, Vale.

[2] Curavimus —— ut quam minimum ejus ſcripta quaſi degenerent ab origine, imitantes ſanè non tacendi, imo ſemper laudandi, hominis Aldi M. R. diligentiam.

ons he faw in the *Sorbon* library. He us'd to put the following *Latin*
verfe to the firft page of his impreffions ;

Ære meret Badius laude auctorem, arte legentem.

Sometimes this,
Æra meret Badio terfa atque impreffa per ipfum.

Or thus,
Æra meret Badio, nomenque decufque parenti.

Some Impreffions have only. *Æra meret Badio.*

His mark was the draught of a printing-houfe with the words *Prælum
Afcenfianum* upon the head of the prefs, the glory and credit of which
dy'd not with him, but continued above 35 years in his own family ;
for *Badius*, whofe love to learning, and in particular to the Art of
Printing, was confpicuous thro' his whole life, prevail'd upon himfelf to
breed up his only fon *Conrard Badius* to the bufinefs of Printing, after
he had perfected him in the *Greek* and *Latin* tongues, and in feveral
other branches of literature. *Conrard* became fo famous upon all thefe
accounts, that the learned *Henry Stephens* has thought fit to tranfmit to
us an elegant *Latin* epitaph made upon him, which the reader may fee
in *de la Caille* p. 131. *Badius* had likewife a brother nam'd *John*, who
became an eminent printer, and left a confiderable number of good editions behind him ; and as if this had not been enough to have three out
of his family brought up to the Art of Printing, he marry'd his three
daughters to three of the moft eminent printers in *Paris, Robert Stephens, Michael Vafcofan,* and *John de Roigny.* The two former of thefe
are too celebrated to need a panegyrick here; and the laft took his father-in-law's mark, fucceeded him in his printing-houfe with great
reputation, and fignaliz'd himfelf by the elegancy and correctnefs of a
great number of editions, which came from his preffes ; he left a fon
nam'd *Michael,* who did not prove much inferior to his father or grand-
father.

We find two epitaphs on this great man, the one in *Henry Stephen's*
book, *De artis typographicæ querimoniâ,* anno 1569 ; which is as follows ;

Jodoci

Jodoci Badii Epitaphium.

Hic liberorum plurimorum qui parens,
Parens librorum plurimorum qui fuit,
Situs Jodocus Badius *eſt* Aſcenſius.
Plures fuerunt liberis tamen libri,
Quod jam ſeneſcens cœpit illos gignere,
Ætate florens cœpit hos quod edere.

His other epitaph is to be ſeen upon his tomb in St. *Bennet*'s church at *Paris,* where he lies buried. It is as follows ;

On this ſide is the   D. O. M.   And on this ſide his
picture of *Badius.*   B. Q. V. M. S.   wife, *Trechſel.*

Viator, artes qui bonas piaſque amas,
Siſte hic. Quieſcunt ſubter illuſtres viri
Qui litteris junxere virtutem arduam.
Jacet Jodocus *hic* Badius Aſcenſius,
Candore notus ſcriptor & ſcientiâ.
Gener Jodoci Vaſcoſanus *prope ſitus eſt,*
Doctiſſimorum tot parens voluminum,
Socer Morelli, *regis olim interpretis ;*
Muſarum alumni quæ gemunt hic conditum,
Fœduſque Federici *ademptum ſibi dolent.*
Tres cyppus unus hic tegit cum uxoribus
Lectiſſimis et liberorum liberis.
Hos Chriſtus *olim dormientes ſuſcitet,*
Ad concinendum Trinitati almæ melos.

I. X. Θ. Y. C.

Federicus Morellus Pariſ. *profeſſor & interpres regius* Federici Morelli *nobilis, genere Campani, regii quoque interpretis ;* Michael Vaſcoſani *ſcutiferi Ambiani nepos,* Jodoci Badii *illuſtris Belgæ pronepos, marmoreum hunc epitaphium patris, avi, proavi piæ memoriæ, ære ſuo poſuit ; ejuſdem, cum Deus vocans volet, tumuli compos fieri optans,* ἐν Θεῷ εὐέλπις *anno ſalutis* 1603.

Qui

Qui idem Morellus unus erat è Duumviris togatis hujus aedis sacræ
D. Benedicti παροικιας γαζοφυλακείω *præfectus.*

BADIUS liv'd at the fign of the three wolves in St. *James*'s *ftreet*, and his houfe was fo much frequented by learned men of all nations, who for converfation's fake, were forc'd to ufe the *Latin* tongue, that his daughters had obtain'd fuch knowledge of it, that no converfation pafs'd in that language but they underftood it ; the fame has been affirm'd of fome of his domefticks.   He was one of the fworn Printers of the uni- verfity of *Paris,* as appears by the infcriptions to his epiftles didicatory (¹), as well as by the order which he receiv'd from the rector of it (by virtue of his oath of obedience and fidelity to it) to print the cenfure made by that body againft *Luther*'s doctrines.

BEFORE I conclude this article of that noble Printer, it will be ne- ceffary to give the reader a caution, which he gives us in the title of his *Calepin* corrected, augmented, and printed by him in 1516, that fome vile Printers had put his name to feveral editions never publifh'd by him ; for which reafon he defires the reader to fee that his mark be to them, leaft they be deceiv'd by thofe impoftors.   It feems thefe plagiaries were more modeft than fome *Italians* and others, who fcrupled not to coun- terfeit both the name and mark of his contemporary *Aldus.*

THO' we have but one impreffion of his extant done at *Lyons,* which city he left about the clofe of the century, to which we have confin'd the lifts of impreffions; yet I hope the reader will excufe our tranf- greffing thofe limits in the account of his life and excellent character, as we have done in that of other eminent Printers, who have out-liv'd that epocha any confiderable time.   The edition fpoken of is as follows;

GULIELMI OCKAM opera, fol. *per Jodoc. Badium Afcenfium Lug-* *dun.* 1495.

AS *Badius* is the laft confiderable Printer that made his entrance into the province of printing within this century, and of all the other cities and places which have receiv'd that art before the clofe of it, a fmall number excepted ; we fhall abridge the remainder of this hiftory, and content our felves with giving our readers only their names, and

---

¹ Ex officinâ noftrâ literariâ in Academiâ parifienfi, &c.

Accuratione Afcenfii in nobiliffimo Parifio-

rum Gymnafio.

Ex Ædibus noftris in Parifiorum Academiâ, &c.

number

number of their works, that we may have the more room to open the scene of the last promis'd twenty years, *viz.* from 1500 to 1520, in the two last chapters of this II. Book.

THE rest of the Printers of the city of *Lyons* are as follow ;

20. JOHN *de Wingle* of *Picardy*, 5 edit. from 1496 to 1499.

21. CLAUDIUS GIBOLET, 1 edit. 1498.

22. NICHOLAS WOLF, 2 edit. from 1498, to 1499.

23. JOHN DYAMANTIER, 1 edit. 1500.

24. JOHN BACHELIER, 1 edit. 1500.

25. GASPARD ORT, and
26. PETER SCHENCK, } 1 edit. 1500.

27. CLAUDIUS *de Huschia*, a *Latin* bible with cuts without date, with above twenty more without Printers names.

Article III. *The Cities of* GENEVA, BRUSSELS, COS-CENCE *and* PAVIA, 1478.

I SHALL not trouble the reader with a needless description of those cities, their productions in the Art of Printing being so inconsiderable, as barely to deserve a place here, especially the three first.

§. 1. GENEVA produc'd four editions, from 1478 to 1498, without printers names.

§. 2. BRUSSELS, two edit. from 1478, to 1480, without printers names.

§. 3. COSCENSA, two editions, the first by *Octavian Salamonio de Manifredonia*, 1478, the other without the printer's name, of the same date as the former.

§. 4. PAVIA, in *Latin Papia*, a noble city and university of *Lombardy*, receiv'd the Art of Printing about the same time with the three foregoing, according to the date of her first known edition, and her productions were somewhat more considerable than theirs. Her first Printer was,

FRANCIS *de S. Petro*, of whom we have but one edition, dated 1478.

2. ANTONY *de Carcano*, 3 edit. 2 dated 1478, the last 1494.

3. ANDREAS BONETI, 1 edit. 1486.

4. CHRISTOPHER *de Canibus*, 1 edit. 1488.

5. JOHN

5. John Antony Birretti
6. Francis *de Gyrardengo* } 3 edit. all 1489.

7. Gabriel *de Craſſi*, 1 edit. 1490.

8. Bernard
9. Ambrose } *de Rovelli*, brothers, 1 edit. 1493.

10. Leonard Gerota, 1 edit. 1497.

With about 10 more without Printers names.

Article IV. GOUDE *and* ZWOL, 1479. CAEN, CEULEN, CENZANO *and* QUILEMBOURG, 1480.

§. 1. Goude in *Holland*, between *Hague* and *Utrecht*, where *Gerard de Leen*, or *de Lene*, printed from *anno* 1479 to 1480, after which he remov'd to *Antwerp*, and printed there till 1491, as ſhall be ſhewn in its place. We have but ſix editions of his printed at *Goude*, the firſt is a dutch bible, fol. 1479, the laſt is dated 1484.

§. 2. Zwol, a City in *Lower Germany*, between the rivers *Iſel* and *Vider*. We find 5 editions printed here from 1479 to 1499, all without printers names.

§. 3. Caen, in *Latin Cadomum*, an epiſcopal city and univerſity, and the capital of *Normandy*, had two ſworn bookſellers, *viz. Peter Regnault*, and *Richard Mace*; but whether many Printers, or whether they had their books from ſome other place, we find but two editions printed here, *viz. Horatii Epiſtolæ*, 1480, and *Alberti Magni Compend. Theologic. Veritat.* 1500.

§. 4. Ceulen. Our annaliſts are at a loſs where to find this place, I imagine it to be the city of *Cologn*, which the Printer might not know how to ſpell right, neither do the Germans write it much unlike it. We find but one impreſſion in *Low Dutch*, it is call'd *Spiegel der Saſſen met de Gloſſen daarop*, fol. 1480.

§. 5. Quilembourg, in *Holland*, where the ſame *Dutch* edition was printed in the ſame year, and no other as I can find.

§. 6. Genzano, *Corn. Beughen* in his *Incunab. Typogr.* mentions an edition of *Joannes Annius de futuris triumphis contra Saracenos*, fol. and dates it from *Gentiæ*, 1480; *de la Caille* mentions the ſame edition of the ſame year, and dates it from *Genzano*. Father *Orlandi* is not ſure that *Gentiæ* and *Genzano* are the ſame place, but if it is, he tells us, that it

is

is a place in the *Roman* territories, more famous for an excellent wi
in great requeft at *Rome*, than for this obfcure edition which is the on
one we have printed there. The fame author mentions alfo a fing
edition, *viz. Laurent. Gilelmi de Saona Rhetorica*, printed at *Villa S. A
bani*, 1480, but whether it be our *St. Albans* in *England*, which had t
art much fooner, or any other town of that name, beyond fea, of whi
there are a great many in almoft every province, is not eafy nor
great moment to determine.

Article VI. LIGNITZ, HASSELET, REGGIO, *ana* MONT-ROYAL, 1481.

§. 1. L I G N I T Z in *Silefia*, in which was printed the following boo
Fr. Hermani dialogus ; *Lignis*, without the Printer's name, 1481.

§. 2. A T *Haffelet*, a place unknown, was printed *Recollectorium
geftis Romanormm*, fol. *Haffeleti*, Orl. 1481.

§. 3. R E G I O, a city in *Lombardy*, belonging to the Marquifs of *Ef
rich*, ancient and populous, had the Art of Printing from

1. P R O S P E R O D O A R D, and 2. A L B E R T M A Z A L I,   1471

O F whom we have 3 edit. The two firft 1481, the laft 1487.

3 B A R T H O L O M E W B O T T O N U S, *alias Brufchi* of *Reggio*, 1 edit. 148

4. D I O N Y S B E R T O C H, who wrought firft at *Trevifo*, next at *V
nice*, then at *Modena*, fettled at laft at *Reggio*, where we find 4 edit.
his from 1496 to 1498.

5. F R A N C I S M A Z A L A, of *Reggio*, 3 edit. from 1498, to 1499.

§. 4. M O N T-R O Y A L, in *Latin Mons Regalis*, in the Kingdom
Sicily, and near the city of *Palermo*, where *Dominic de Nivaldis* and h
fons printed an edition of *Æfop's Fables* in *Latin* verfe, *fol.* 1481.

§. 5. A T *Wartsburg*, in *Latin Herbipolis*, was printed *Miffale in ufu
Ecclefia Herbipolenfis*, imprefs *Herbipoli*, fol. 1481.

This book the earl of *Pembroke* told me he faw at *Oxford*; it has a *Lat
privilege at the end, impowering Mr. *Iforius Ryfer* to print thofe *Miffal
and to adorn them with rubricks. We have already taken notice, that th
book had been fet down in the lift of Archbifhop *Laud*'s books for a M
which is the reafon it has not been mention'd by any of our annalifts.

Artic

Article VII. *The Cities of* PISA, AQUILA, ERFORD
and LANGRES, 1482.

§. 1. Pisa is an antient, rich and populous city of *Tuscany*, where
he Art of Printing got but small footing and encouragement. It is ve-
y likely that the wars which rag'd in several parts of *Italy*, from the
ime of the art's being brought to it, might be a great cause of the small
progress it made in this, as well as many other, otherwise, considerable
cities of *Italy*. We find but 4 editions printed here, the three first dated
482, 1484 and 1489, are without Printers names. The only one that
as, is *Antonii Parnormit. libri* IV. *dictorum factorum,* &c. fol. by *Gre-
ory de Gente. Pisis* 1485.

§. 2. At *Aquila*, an episcopal city in the territory of *Abruso*, distant
bout sixty miles from *Rome*, was printed an *Italian* version of *Plutarch*'s
ives, by *Adam de Rotwill*, a German, who stiles himself *Stampatore ex-
ellente. Aquilæ* 1482.

Orlandi tells us pag. 196, that Mr. *Robert Frebairn*, (now the
ing's Printer in *Scotland*, and a particular friend of mine) shew'd him
mong some of his curious annotations upon editions which he had seen,
he first part of the aforesaid lives printed at *Aquila,* ann. 1472 ; but
aid, he never could see the second part which was afterwards added to
he first. The credit of this entirely depends upon that gentleman's ob-
ervation ; but our author says, that he never saw any other part but
his which we have given, nor heard of it from any but him.

§. 3. At *Erford*, a large city in *Germany*, erected into an university
nn. 1391, and subject to the elector of *Mentz*, was printed *Lutreus de
nima. Erford* 1482.

§. 4. At *Langres*, an episcopal city in *Burgundy*, the people of which
ere call'd *Lingones* by *Lucan, Claudian,* &c. and still retain that name ;
e find the following edition, *viz.*

Jo. *de Turre-cremeta ord. præd. card. expositio super psalterium.* Impres.
er *Johan. Fabri Lingonensem,* 1482.

It hath no place's name ; only *la Caille*, and after him *Orlandi* have
ppos'd it, from the Printer's appellative, to have been printed at *Lan-
es.* However the reader may find the same Printer at *Turin,* from *anno*
1474

1474 to 1477, and at *Lyons* from 1478 to 1485. *Orlandi* dates the same edition from *Turin*, by the same Printer, where I think it more properly belongs.

Article VIII. GAUNT *and* MEMINING, 1483.

§. 1. G A U N T, in *Latin Gandavum*, is too well known by most readers to need a description. Here were printed the two following editions without the Printers names.

1. G U I L L E L M U S *Parisiensis de rhetoricâ divinâ*, 4to. *Gandavi*. *Orl*. 1483.

2. B O E T I I *de confolatione Philofophiæ*, lib. 5. *cum S. Thom. Aquin. comment.* fol. *ibid.*

§. 2. A T *Memining*, a City in *Swabia*, between *Ulms* and *Ausburgh*, we find six editions printed from *ann*. 1483 to 1494, all without Printers names.

C H A P. XII.

The reſt of the Cities and Places, which began to print before the year 1500, *with an Account of the Books printed there.*

Article I. *The Town of* S O N C I N O, 1484.

S O N C I N O is a town or caſtle in the duchy of *Milan*, between *Brefcia* and *Cremona*, and famous for being the place in which the firſt *Hebrew* books were printed. The Chriſtians had hitherto eſteem'd ſuch a deſign too expenſive and impracticable ; it being ſcarce poſſible to find artiſts in thoſe early days, who could cut punches exactly enough in that difficult and unpractis'd character. Another difficulty, which ſeem'd to them almoſt unfurmountable was, that to caſt the letters with the points and accents, would multiply the caſes to an exceſſive degree ; and to print without points, accents, &c. would have infallibly prevented the ſale of their books, becauſe few at that time, except the Jews, could
read

read witnout them ; and to caſt the points and accents by themſelves, and interline them as now, ſeem'd then perhaps wholly impracticable. We have ſeen under the article of *Aldus Manucius*, that he procur'd a font of *Hebrew* types ; but tho' the Jews had already printed at *Soncino* and elſewhere for above twelve or fifteen years, which might have given him an inſight into their method of printing in that language, yet he found it ſo difficult, that he made but little uſe of them ; and I can find nothing done by him in that kind, but an *Hebrew* alphabet, which *Chevilier* tells us is preſerv'd in the *Sorbon* library. The Jews therefore, as they were the fitteſt for ſuch a province, were the firſt who ſet about it. What encouragement they might receive from the Chriſtians in ſuch an undertaking, I cannot affirm ; yet it is probable they might in a great meaſure depend upon that ; and without leave from the Pope and the Dukes of *Milan* they dar'd not have attempted it. Soon after the Jews had propagated this art into ſeveral cities of *Italy*, ſuch as *Breſcia*, *Bologna*, *Rimini*, *Fano*, *Peſaro*, and even as far as *Conſtantinople* and *Salonica*, in all which places they inſcrib'd their editions as done by ſome of the family of *Soncino* ; the Chriſtians who now began to print in *Hebrew* in moſt cities of *Europe*, in *Italy*, at *Venice*, *Cremona*, *Mantua*, *Verona*, *Ferrara*, *Leghorn*, *Padua*, *Naples*, &c. in *England*, *London* and *Oxford* ; in *Germany*, *Baſil*, *Frankford*, *Cologn*, &c. in *France*, *Paris*, *Lyons*, &c. with ſome cities of *Spain*, *Holland*, *Poland*, &c. ſet up ſome ingenious artiſts, who engag'd in that province ; tho' it muſt be own'd that the editions of the Jews were far preferable to thoſe for beauty and orrectneſs. However there were few impreſſions of this kind printed any where, but by theſe Jews of the *Soncino* family, 'till after the year 500. Mr. *Mattaire Ann. Typog.* vol. 1. p. 152. makes a curious obſervation after father *le Long*, which is, that in all the books that he had ſeen printed in this tongue before that year, as often as the name of God occurs in the text, they made uſe of the letter *Daleth* inſtead of *He*. Thus for inſtance they printed יהוד for יהוה, and אלרים for אלהים ; for which no reaſon can be aſſign'd.

I must not omit giving the reader an account, which we meet with in *Buxtorf* the father, of a book, that he tells us was in the poſſeſſion of *Joſeph Scaliger*, of a much older date than thoſe of *Soncino*. It was an

Hebrew

Hebrew grammar intitled *Mahala Scevile Haddas,* written by *R. Moses Kimchi,* which *Buxtorf* fays had been printed in *Sicily* 152 years ago; *Habuit Josephus Scaliger impreſſum in Siciliâ ante annos* 152. (Thefe words *Buxtorf* the fon did not alter, when he reprinted his father's book at *Bafil,* anno 1640 in 8vo.) This, if it be true, will oblige us to feek much higher for the origin of *Hebrew-printing,* than the year 1484; which is the time wherein *Rabbi Gedaliah,* and after him the learned *Bartolocci* have affirm'd it to have begun; for if we fubftract 152 years from 1613 in which *Buxtorf* wrote, it will bring us to the year 1461. *Chevilier* p. 267 tells us, that he faw a third edition of this grammar, printed at *Ortona* in the kingdom of *Naples,* in the fecond year of *Charles* king of *Sicily* and *Jerufalem,* i. e. *anno* 1496, which fhews that there muft have been two editions of it before; and *Cornelius a Beughen* in his *Incunab. Typog.* p. 126 mentions an old *Hebrew* edition printed at *Bologna, anno* 1471, with this title, *R. Obadia Sephorno lux populorum. Liber Hebraicus ſic dictus, Bononiæ* 1471. But as he doth not tell us in what library he met with it, and as we have not a fufficient certainty of the truth of the dates of this and the other book mention'd by *Buxtorf;* I can fee no reafon for departing from the epoch of our lateft annalifts, to affign a new one upon uncertain grounds.

T H E firft *Jew* who oblig'd the world with *Hebrew* impreffions, was

M O S E S *the Son of* R A B B I I S R A E L N A T H A N, 1484.

A N A T I V E of *Spire* in *Germany,* whofe family multiply'd fo much, and receiv'd fuch encouragement in this undertaking, that they fpread themfelves over feveral parts of *Italy,* and printed many noble editions with vaft fuccefs and applaufe. Among thefe a fon of this *Mofes* nam'd *Rabbi Gerfon,* after he had printed feveral works at *Brefcia,* of which we have given an account, went and fet up a Prefs at *Conftantinople,* fome time before the clofe of this century, and continued printing there till *ann.* 1530. Some of his fons remov'd to *Salonica,* and other cities of the *Ottoman* empire, where they met with the fame fuccefs. But as their works, at leaft as far as we know of them, were done after the year 1500,

I fhall

I ſhall not give the reader a liſt of them, but confine myſelf to thoſe printed in *Italy* before that time. The editions at *Soncino* are as follows.

1. M I N C H A H *Happenini* 4 *to*. *Soncini*, anno mundi 5244. which anſwers to our 1484.

2. B E C H I N A L *Olam.* (Hebr.) *ibid.* 1485.

3. P R O P H E T Æ *priores.* (Hebr. abſque punctis) cum Com. *R. David Kimchi.* fol. *ibid.* 1486.

4. I K K A R I M. per *R. Joſeph Albo.* ibid. 1486.

5. B I B L I A *Hebraica cum punctis per Abraham fil. Rabb. Hhajim.* fol. *ibid.* 1488.

6. B E R A C H O T H and *Beitzah. ibid.* 1489.

7. J A D H H A S A K A H R A M B A M. 2 fol. 1490.

Article II. L E I P S I C K. 1484.

L E I P S I C K, in *Latin Lipſia,* the Capital of *Saxony,* and founded into an univerſity in 1404 by *Frederic.* 1. elector of that name, receiv'd the Art of Printing in 1484 ; and tho' it produ'd but few impreſſions before the year 1500, and yet it is become one of the moſt famous cities in *Germany* for the numbers of books printed there. The firſt Printer who ſettled there was,

1. M A R K B R A N D T,

O f whom we have only the following edition, *viz.*

A L B I C I I *Archiepiſcopi Pragenſis praxis medendi.* 4to. *per Marcum Brandt. Lipſiæ.* 1484.

1 At the End of the Pentateuch are theſe Words;

Et abſolutum eſt opus miniſterii, viginti quatuor ſapiens ad docendum legem in Iſrael excellens & illuſtris Joſua Selomo *(videat ſemen, producat dies vitæ. amen.) filius illuſtris ſapientiſſimi* Iſrael Nathan, *feriâ tertiâ* xi *menſis Jiar ann* נמה *juxta minorem ſupputationem; manu minimi in familia ſua, fidelis chalcographi,* Abraham F. *illuſtris Rabbi* Hhajim *felicis memoriæ, ex viris piis terræ Piſauri Bononiæ, Impreſſum opus Soncini.*

Chevillier p. 80. mentions another Hebrew bible printed in fol. at *Bologna* in the ſame year 1488. It is in the Library of *C. Barberini* at *Paris*; the Catalogue of which gives us an account of it in the following Words, pag. 147. *Biblia Hebraica Bononiæ ab impreſſoribus Soncinenſibus apud Abrahamum Jarzium Piſaurenſem.* 1488. But it is a queſtion whether it be not the ſame with this of *Soncino.*

2 *Rambam* is an abbreviation of *Rabbi Moſe-Ben-Maimon*; as *Abenezra* is of *Abraham-Ben-Ezra,* &c.

2. GREGORY BOETICHER, 1 edit. 1493.

3. WOLFGANG MOLITOR *de Monaco*, 2 edit from 1495, to 1496

4. JAMES THANNER, 2 edit. from 1498, to 1499.

WITH about twenty more without Printers names.

5. ANDREW *Faijner*, a learned man, of whom we have given a full account under the article of *Nuremberg*, where he follow'd the Bufinefs of printing and correcting till the year 1478, after which he remov'd to *Leipfick*, and became *Rector magnificus* of that univerfity. The only book we find printed by him here is the *Hiftoria Longobardica*, but our *German* author not having given us the date of it, no proper rank could be affign'd to it in this lift.

Article III. VIENNA *and* URBINO, 1484.

§. 1. VIENNA (not the capital of *Auftria*, as *Orlandi* thought) but a city in *Dauphiny* had two Printers, *viz.*

1. PETER *Schenk* of whom we have only the following edition. *l'Abufe de Cour*, fol. *par Pierre Schenk.*

2. CONRARD *Celtis*, 1 edit. 1500.

§. 2. AT *Urbino* a city in *Italy* famous for being the native place of that excellent painter *Raphael Sancius*; firnam'd from it *Urbin*, was printed the following book without the Printer's name.

PAULI *Middleburgenfis Epifcopi Sempronienfis Practica de pravis conftellationibus, ad Maximilianum Cæfarem, Urbini,* 1484.

Article IV. ANTWERP, HEIDELBERGH, CREMONA *and* HARLEM. 1485.

§. 1. ANTWERP, a large, rich and populous city in *Flanders*, did not much fignalize itfelf in the art of printing in this 15*th.* century, but made ample amends for it in the two following, having produc'd fome of the fineft and largeft editions of any place in the world, and by the number of its Printers, among whom were the famous *Bellers, Raphelengius, Plantin, Morellus, Gumelers, Mevofius, Verdufen,* and
many

many more, all too well known to the learned, to need a digreſſion here in their praiſe. The firſt known Printer here was

1. GERARD LEU *or* de LEEU. 1485,

WHO printed firſt at *Goude* in 1480, whence he came to *Antwerp:* we have but four editions of his extant, from 1485 to 1491.

2. ADRIAN *de Liefvelt,* 1 edit. 1495.

3. NICOLAS *Keſler* of *Baſil,* where he wrought from 1486 to 1494, betwixt which times we find a *Latin* bible, fol. printed by him, in 1487.

WITH a few more without Printers names.

§ 2. HEIDELBERGH is a city and univerſity in the lower *Palatinat,* and feat of the elector *Palatine,* where we find 5 edit. from 1485 to 1489, all without Printers names.

§ 3. CREMONA is a city and univerſity in *Lombardy,* famous for the beſt violins, &c. the following edition was printed here in 1485.

HERMOLAI *Barbari Caſtigatio in Plinii Nat. Hiſt.* without the Printers name. Tho' this is all our annaliſts mention, yet a learned genleman aſſures me he has ſeen two editions more printed here, one was *Fracaſtorius* and the other *Vida.*

THE only Printers of this city as yet known are the two following, *viz.*

1. BERNARDINE *de Miſenti* of *Pavia,* and ⎱
2. CÆSAR *de Parma.* ⎰ 1 edit. 1492.

WE have ſeen *Miſenti* under the article of *Breſcia,* ann. 1495.

§ 4. HARLEM a city in *Holland,* ſufficiently known to thoſe who have read the firſt part of this hiſtory, for the great controverſy ſtarted in favour of it, and for the number of her champions, who have endeavour'd to deck her *COSTER*'s tomb with the trophies of this noble art, has produc'd ſo ſmall a number of works during this 15*th* century, if we allow it the *Donatus, Speculum,* &c. done upon wooden blocks ſo much boaſted of by the *Dutch* Writers (tho' their title even to theſe has been ſhewn to be as precarious as that of *Mentz* ;) that the reader no doubt will be ſurpriz'd, that we have not been able to find but one book printed there before 1500, *viz.*

DE

D E *Proprietatibus Rerum libri* xviii *Opus Theologicum & Philosophicum,* fol. 1485.

Article V. ABBEVILLE *and* TOLEDO, 1486.

§ 1. ABBEVILLE a city in *Picardy*, had two famous Printers and Bookfellers fettled there for a fmall fpace, *viz. John du Pré* and *Peter Gerard* of whom we have but one edition printed here; after which they remov'd to *Paris* as has been faid.

S. Auguftin de la Cité de Dieu, fol. *par Jean du Pré & Pierre Gerard* xxviii *Novem.* 1486.

§ 2. TOLEDO, in *Latin Toletum,* an archiepifcopal city of *Aragon* in *Spain* printed

PETRI *Ximenes Confutatorium errorum contra Claves ecclefiæ, nuper editorum Toleti,* without the Printers name, 1486.

PETER *Hugembach* reprinted by order of Cardinal *Ximenes.*

MISSALE *mixtum fecundum Regulam Beati Ifidori, dictum.*

MOZARABES fol. 1500.

TWO years after he was order'd by the fame Cardinal to print the breviary of the fame *St Ifidorus.*

THESE two Books are reckon'd very fcarce and valuable, efpecially by thofe of the Church of *Rome.*

§ 3. RIMINO, in *Latin Ariminum,* a city in *Romania,* had a Printer of the *Jewifh* family of *Soncino,* before mentioned, who printed

R. Jofeph Albo Philofophi, Arbor plantata, in *Hebrew* 4to 1486.

THIS book contains the fundamentals of the *Jewifh* religion, and is levelled.againft the *Chriftians.*

§ 4. AT *Munfter,* in *Latin Monafterium,* an epifcopal city, we meet with the following editions printed by *John Limburgh.*

RODOLPHI *Langii nobilis Weftphali & Monafterienfis Canonici Carmina,* 1486.

§ 5. AT *Meffina,* a famous city of *Sicily,* we find two books printed, one without Printers name, *viz.*

HISTORIA *præliorum Alexandri Magni Ducis Maced.* fol. 1486.

THE

THE other is printed by
WILLIAM *Schonberger* of *Frankford,* and is dated, 1498.

Article VI. 1. MODENA, 2. BOISLEDUC, 1487,
3. EYCHSTADT, 4. TÜBINGEN, 5. ROCCEN,
6. GAETA, *and* 7. THOLOUSE, 1488.

§ 1. MODENA, in *Latin Mutina,* is an ancient city in *Italy,* now
under the dominion of the houfe of *Efte* Duke of *Parma* and *Modena.*
The firft Printer we find here was

1. DOMINIC *Rocociola* of whom we have feven editions from 1487
1498.

2. DIONYS *Bertoch,* whom we have feen already under the articles of *Venice, Trevifo* and *Reggio,* and under feveral names, did at
length conclude the century at *Modena.* We have two editions left of
him from 1499 to 1500.

§. 2. AT *Boifleduc,* in *Latin Bofcum-Ducis,* a ftrong city in *Brabant*
was printed one edition, *viz.*

PRÆCEPTA XX. *Elegantiarum grammaticarum,* 4 to. 1487.

§. 3. AT *Eychftat* in *Upper Bavaria,* in *Latin Eifteta,* was printed
Obfequiale five Benedictionale Eiftetenfe per Michaelem Keifer, 1488.

§. 4. TUBINGEN a city in the duchy of *Wirtemberg,* and made
an univerfity in 1477. had a Printer nam'd.

FREDERIC *Meynberger,* who printed two editions of *Gabriel Biel's*
expofitio Canonis Miffæ, from 1488 to 1489. The laft of which was
revis'd by *Vendelin Stembach,* and is much more correct than the firft,
but has neither Printer nor places name.

§. 5. ROUEN in *Latin Rothomagum,* is an archiepifcopal fee, and
the capital of *Normandy,* whofe firft Printer was,

1. JOHN *le Bourgois* of whom we have 2 edit. from 1488 to 1498.

2. MARTIN *Morin,* 3 edit. from 1494 to 1500.

3. PETER *Regnault,* Printer and bookfeller, whom we have feen in
the article of *Caen,* 1 edit. 1500.

Ai

At this place was printed a book, on the subject of grammar, for Marti
Coeſtin *dwelling at* Exeter, *and the only one I ever met with, which is i*
the Earl of Pembroke's *library.*

§. 6. A t *Gaeta* an ancient city in that part of *Italy*, call'd *Latium*
was printed by,

M a s t e r *Juſtus*, 1 edit. *viz.*

D i a l o g o *de S. Gregorio Papa*, fol. 1488.

§. 7. T h o l o u s e is the capital city of *Gaſcony*, in which we read o
John James Colomiez with ſome more of his own family exerciſing th
Art of Printing before and after the year 1500, but can meet with onl
one edition before the cloſe of the century, *viz. Thomæ de Valois in D*
Auguſtini de Civitate Dei Commentarii, Tholouſe 1488, without Printer'
name.

Article VII. *The Cities of* SIENA *and* HAGENAW, 1489.

§. 1. S i e n a, an ancient city and univerſity in *Tuſcany*, had an emi
nent Printer nam'd *Sigiſmund Rot*, of whom we have two editions ſtill ex
tant, one without date, *viz. L. Florus de geſtis Romanorum*, and *Cicero'*
Clauſulæ Epiſtol. 1489 ; but whether he was the ſame with that *Sigiſmund*
who firnam'd himſelf *de Libris*, and for whom *Dominic de Lapis* printe
ſeveral books at *Bologna anno* 1476, or ſome other, is not eaſy to de
termine : theſe two are all the books which I could find printed at *Sien*
before the cloſe of the century.

§. 2. A t *Hagenaw*, a city in *Alſatia* in upper *Germany*, but now un
der the French king, we find the following edition dated 1489, but with
out Printer's name, *viz.*

J o h. *de Garlandia Cornutus, five Diſticha Exametra Moralia cum inter*
pretatione. Hagenoæ.

T h e two following Printers, *Joh. Ryman* and *Henry Gran*, did like
wiſe print in this city : we have two editions of theirs, one dated 1497
and the other 1500.

W e find likewiſe ſome other works done here without Printer's name
from 1493 to 1500.

Articl

Article VIII. *The Cities of* L I S B O N *and* S E V I L, 1491.

§. 1. L ISBON, in *Latin Ulyſſipo,* the metropolis of the kingdom of *Portugal,*did not ſignalize itſelf by any productions in this kind, if we except the two following ones, which being both in *Hebrew,* might be done by ſome of the family of *Soncino,* mention'd before. They are as follows,

P ENTATEUCHE *Hebraia cum Paraphraſ. Chald. & punctis, fol. Uliſſipone,* 1491.

I SAIÆ *& Hieremiæ lib. cum Comment. Rabbi David Kimchi, Hebraicé,. fol. Ulyſſipone,* 1497.

2. S EVIL, in *Latin Hiſpalis* and *Sevilia,* is an ancient archiepiſcopal city and univerſity in *Spain,* in which we find

P AUL *de Colonia, Joh. Pegniczer de Nuremberg, le Grand* and *Thomas,* flouriſhing *anno* 1491 ; in which they printed the two following works, after which we hear no more of them.

A LPHONS. *Teſt. Epiſc. Abulenſis opera, fol. Hiſpali.*

F LORETUM *S. Matthæi collectum a R. Præſule Caurienſ. Petro Praxano in ſacr. Scriptura Profeſſore Siciliæ,* both 1491.

B ESIDES theſe we meet with three other works printed by

M EYNARD U NGUT German, *and* S TANISLAUS Poloneſe, *Partners.*

T HEY are all three in *Spaniſh,* the firſt is dated 1494, and the other two 1495.

Article IX. D O L E *and* I N G O L D S T A D, 1492.

§. 1. A T *Dole,* a city in low *Britany,* was printed the following book, H ARNMUNDIENSIS *Lectio declarativa de Epidemio morbo, 4to,* per Johannem Hebertin, *Dolæ,* 1492.

§. 2. A T *Ingolſtad,* a city in *Bavaria,* was printed in the ſame year, *Porphyrii Iſagoge,* fol. *Ingolſtadii* 1492, without Printer's name.

Article

Article X. LUNEBURGH, MAGDEBURGH, THES-SALONICA, FRIBURGH *and* ANGOULESME, 1493.

§. 1. JOHN LUCE printed at *Luneburgh* in lower *Saxony*, *Tho. a Kemp. de Imitat. Chrifti*, *8vo*, *per* Jo. Luce, 1493.

§. 2. AT *Magdeburgh* in lower *Saxony* was printed *Vincentii* ——— *Ordin. præd. anno Chrifti* 1455, *canonizati contemplatio de Homine interiore*, without Printer's name, *Magdeburgi* 1493.

§. 3. AT *Theſſalonica*, an archiepiſcopal city in *Macedonia*, we find the following edition in *Hebrew* by one of the family of *Soncino*, as is ſuppos'd, tho' there is no Printer s name to it.

R. ISAAC ABARBANEI, *ſeu ut alii*, *Abravanel celebris Judæi*, *& magnæ æſtimationis, qui obiit* A M. 5269, *Commentarius in Prophetas priores, videlicet Jeſuæ, Judicum, Samuelis* I *&* II. *Regum* I *&* II. *Hæbraicé, fol.* Theſſalonicæ, 1493.

§. 4. AT *Friburg* in upper *Germany*, we find three editions printed by one *Kilian*, from 1493 to 1499.

§. 5. AT *Angouleſme* in *France* was printed the following work, *viz.* GRÆCISMUS *Angoliſmi.* without Printer's name.

Article XI. LYRIA, MADRID *and* BARCELONA, 1494.

§. 1. LYRIA is a caſtle in the kingdom of *Valentia* in *Spain*, where the following *Hebrew* work was printed by ſome of the *Soncino* family, *viz.*

PROPHETÆ *priores cum Com.* R. *David Kimchi, fol.* Leiriæ, 1494, without Printer's name.

§. 2. AT *Madrid* the capital of *Spain* was printed *Concilium Illiberitanum, fol.* Madrid 1494.

§. 3. AND at *Barcelona*, the capital of *Catalonia*, we find three editions from 1494 to 1500, without Printer's names.

Article XII. GRENADA, MONTFERRAT, MIRANDULA *and* PAMPELUNA, 1496.

WE have but one edition of each of theſe four places; the three firſt are inconſiderable, and without Printer's names: the laſt is printed by *William de Brocario.*

Article

Article XIII. AVIGNON, LEYDEN *and* PROVINS, *&c.* 1497.

1. A T *Avignon*, a city in the fouthern part of *France*, fubject to the
pope, we meet with a Printer nam'd *Nicolas Lepe*, a native of that city ;
we have but one edition of his before the clofe of the century, *viz. anno*
497.

2. A T *Leyden* in *Holland*, one edition in *low Dutch*.

3. A T *Provins* (not a province fo call'd in the fouth part of *France*,
as *Orlandi* and others have miftook it) but a town in the county of *Brie*
in the fame kingdom ; we have one fmall edition printed by one *William*
Tavernier, 1497.

4. A T *Bergamo*, we find one edition dated, *anno* 1498; and

5. A T *Bemberg* two, *anno* 1499 ; the former is without the Printer's
name, the laft by *John Pfeil.*

I M U S T not omit acquainting the reader that there are ftill above
twenty editions, which being without dates, places, or Printers names,
were not reducible to our former lifts, tho' they are fuppos'd to have
been printed before the clofe of the 15th century. The reader may find
them at the end of Mr. *Mattaire*'s annals, vol. 1. with fuch remarks as
that diligent author could make upon them.

I S H A L L conclude this chapter with this obfervation, that the Art of
cutting upon wooden blocks having paft from the Printers to the engravers of cuts, they began to interfperfe them among their works ; fo
that we find many hiftories, both facred and profane, adorn'd with wooden
cuts, which, tho' already mention'd in the lifts of impreffions under
every city, yet we fhall fubjoyn here altogether, at leaft the moft confiderable of them.

1. T H E *Speculum,* or mirrour of our falvation in *Latin,* and another
low Dutch.

2. T H E *Speculum morientium,* or mirrour of a dying perfon.

3. T H E hiftory of St. *John*'s Apocalypfe.

A L L thefe are challeng'd by the *Dutch* writers in favour of *Harlem.*

4. M E D I T A T I O N E S *in figuras, quas Romæ in templo S. Mariæ fupra*
Minervam pingere.   L l   5. C U-

5. C U R A V I T *Jo. de Turre cremata*, Romæ, *anno* 1467 *and* 1473, *fol.*

6. F A S C I C U L U S *temporum*, printed at *Louvain*, 1474, and afterwards both here and elfewhere, *fol.*

7. V A L T U R I U S *de re militari*, at *Verona*, 1472.

8. P A S S I O N A L E *van Jefu und. Mariæ Leben*. at *Strasburgh*, 1477; *Geneva*, 1490.

9. Æ S O P I *fabulæ, fol* at *Naples*, 1481, and elfewhere afterwards.

10. D I A L O G U S *creaturarum*, in *low Dutch*, at *Goude*, 1482.

11. T H E *Bible*, in *high Dutch*, fol. at *Nurembergh*, 1483.

12. L A *mer des hiftoires*, 1 vol. with 286 cuts, at *Paris*, 1485:

13. L E *proces de Belial*, &c. tranflated out of *Latin* into *French*, 4to, at *Lyons*, 1485, 1490.

14. A L B A M A S A R *Arab. aftrolog. flores aftrologiæ*, at *Ausburgh*, 1489, and elfewhere.

15. S E B A S T I A N B R A N T's *navis ftultifera*, at *Bafil*, 1491, 1496, and 1497.

16. H O R T U S *fanitatis*, at *Mentz*, 1491.

17. R E V E L A T I O N E S *S. Brigittæ*, fol. at *Lubeck*, 1492, and elfewhere.

18. T E R E N T I U S, 4to, at *Lyons*, 1493 ; *Strasburgh*, 1496.

19. O P U S *libri chronicon*. fol. at *Ausburgh*, 1497.

20. G U I L. C O U R S I N's fiege of *Rhodes* in *Latin*, at *Ulms*, 1497.

21. P O L I P H I L I *Hypnerolomachia*, fol. at *Venice*, 1499, and elfewhere.

I T muft be own'd, that the defign and performance of thefe, and many more of that fort, were very rude and uncouth, as all muft acknowledge, who have feen them ; which is rather owing to the covetoufnefs of the bookfellers, who chofe to employ the cheapeft hands, than to any want of excellent artifts in that kind. For foon after the very infancy of Printing we meet with a great number of thefe engravers, whofe performances were vaftly fuperior to the beft of thofe in the foregoing lift. Of this number were *Andreas Martegna* in *Mantua*, *Mafo Finiguerra* in *Florence*, *Bon Martin* in *Germany*, *Michael Volgemut* and *Albert Durer* at *Nurembergh*, *Ifrael Van-Mecheln* at *Mentz*, *Hans Schauflich* at *Nordeling*, and many more ; fome of whom, tho' they were excell'd by their fucceffors in the following century, yet were all excellent mafters, and whofe

names

names and works will be ftill valu'd by all fkilled in that Art. Engraving upon wood became afterwards no fmall ornament to the Art of
Printing, not only for the fine cuts with which the editions were inter-
fpers'd, but likewife for the front, head and tail-pieces, initial letters,
&c. which in time became in great vogue. It prov'd alfo of great ufe
in books of architecture, geometry, profpective, and others, which require a confiderable number of demonftrations, figures, &c. in all which
cafes the wooden ones are much more expeditious, being contriv'd of the
fame height with the letters, and fo impos'd, lock'd up and printed with
them at once; whereas the copper ones muft be printed off by themfelves,
and with a different prefs, which makes this method more tedious and expenfive.

C H A P. XIII.

Of fome eminent Printers from anno 1500 *to* 1520;
their Improvements to the Art; and their En-
couragement from the Great and Learned; with
a Catalogue of their moft confiderable Impreffions
in the Oriental Tongues, &c.

I HAVE, in the introduction to this fecond book, given the reader
my reafons for extending this hiftory fo far beyond the year 1500;
and I prefume that he is now fully fatisfied that it would have been imperfect, if I had ftopt there; fince the far greateft part of thofe Printers,
who fignaliz'd themfelves, either for their learning or their induftry, in improving every branch of Printing, appear'd not till the clofe of that century, or the beginning of the next; and confequently, he muft have
known little of thofe perfons, to whom the world is particularly oblig'd
for the vaft improvements to this Art. Upon this account I have continued, in the preceeding chapters, the hiftory of feveral famous Printers to the end of their lives, tho' fome of them furviv'd even this epocha
many years. But we omitted to give a lift of their works beyond 1500,

becaufe that would have fwell'd this volume exorbitantly, and thofe im-preffions are lefs fcarce than thofe of the former century. We fhall add nothing therefore to their hiftory, but proceed to do juftice to the merit of thofe, who tho' they enter'd not this province, till after the beginning of the 16th century, yet may be juftly efteem'd contemporaries with the former.

'T is not however to be expected that we fhould profecute the fame method, as in the former chapters, by fhewing the progrefs of the Art thro' every city, much lefs by giving an account of every particular Printer, and the number of their impreffions; fince fuch an hiftory, how fuccinct foever, would be too large for a fingle chapter. Our defign is therefore only to mention the moft confiderable Printers, and to point out the great improvements which each of them made to this Art, the encouragement they met with, and the noble impreffions in all languages, particularly the *Hebrew, Chaldee, Arabic,* &c. (the firft of which had been juftly effay'd, before 1500, but the other fcarce attempted) with an account of the undertakers and affiftants in that difficult province. For as to the beauty of the characters, whether Roman or Greek, they were brought to fuch a degree of perfection in the preceeding century by the *Italians* and *French,* as hardly admitted of much additional beauty.

T o proceed in order, we fhould begin with the Germans, to whom we owe the Art; tho' the Italians were the authors of thofe improvements, which the former were too indolent in imitating; for the oriental tongues, and even the Greek, which the Italians had made a very confiderable progrefs in, was ftill much neglected by them; fo that except *Amerbach* and *Froben* at *Bafil* in *Switzerland* (which can fcarce be call'd a part of *Germany*) who printed an *Hebrew* pfalter, and *Erafmus's Greek* teftament with his *Latin* verfion of it, *anno* 1586, we meet with but three eminent perfons, who attempted to print in the Eaftern languages. The firft is *John Schott* of *Strasburgh, anno* 1515, who printed *Lucian's* dialogues of the gods in *Greek* with the *Latin* verfion of *Othomar Nachtgall,* with the title page in red, and fome ornaments on the margin of the *Greek* text, and an *errata* at the end. By the compliments which the tranflator makes him in the preface, he feems to have been a very good Printer. He printed for

George

George Maxill about five years before. His rebus or mark is in the table at the end of this book. The fecond is *Eucharius Cervicorn* (*i. e.* Hartshorn) at *Cologn*, who printed fome *Greek* editions, the firft, *anno* 1517, is the *Hours of the bleffed Virgin Mary*, the *feven penitential Pfalms*, and fome litanies and prayers in *Greek*, with one or two more after. His types are tolerable, but the edition fomewhat faulty. The third is *John Potken* of the fame city, who publifh'd there a pfalter in *Hebrew*, *Greek*, *Latin* and *Æthiopic*, *anno* 1518, 4to This perfon travell'd into *India*, *Æthiopia*, *Ægypt*, &c. in order to become mafter of the *Chaldiac* or *Æthiopic*, and tranflated the pfalter into that language, and publifh'd it with the other verfions. He promis'd in his preface to perform fomething likewife in the *Arabick*, if he fhould meet with fufficient encouragement; but I do not find that he executed this. As for the Printer of this pfalter, his name is no where to be found in the book.

This is all I know of, that has been attempted by the Germans in that kind; tho' to do them juftice in another refpect, they were induftrious in printing *Latin* works that were very voluminous; particularly the *Decretum Gratiani*, printed by *Henry Eggeftein*, at *Strasburgh*, which exceeds all that have been fince printed for bulk; and *Vincentii Speculum*, by *John Mentel*, in ten large volumes, *fol.* In the following century they have been no lefs diligent, and publifh'd a very confiderable number of impreffions.

Italy follows in courfe; where, tho' great numbers of editions of the antient *Greek* and *Latin* writers, as well as of the modern, were publifh'd; yet the *Hebrew*, *Arabic*, &c. feem'd almoft wholly neglected. 'Tis true, that there had been, as we obferv'd, two *Hebrew* editions at *Lisbon* in *Portugal*, one *anno* 1491, and the other *anno* 1497; and that the Jews of *Soncino* had printed feveral *Hebrew* volumes there from 1485, to the clofe of the century; and, having difpers'd themfelves into other cities of *Italy*, continued printing their own books in that language. But with refpect to the Chriftians, no direct attempts were made that way, 'till *Daniel Bombergh*, an *Antwerpian*, fet up a Printing-houfe for *Hebrew* at *Venice*. His firft work was the *Hebrew* bible, *anno* 1511, 4to, reprinted by him feveral times, and particularly *anno* 1518; in which year he likewife printed

printed his *Bibliæ Hebræa Rabinica* in *fol.* containing the *Hebrew* text of the bible, the *Mafora* and *Targums* of *Onkelos*, *Jerufalem*, and *Jonathan*, *R. Jofeph*, firnam'd the *Blind*, and other *Rabbi*'s comments, *&c.* which he dedicated to *Leo* X. But tho' *Bombergh* took a great deal of pains in this impreffion, and was himfelf a good mafter of the *Hebrew*, which he had learn'd of *Fælix Pratenfis*, a learned *Italian*, who perfuaded him to undertake this edition, and affifted in correcting it; yet the Jews fet no value upon it; but *Rabbi Chajin* prevail'd on him to print another in 4 vol. in *fol.* which he did *anno* 1525; and which was reprinted *anno* 1548. 'Tis not my bufinefs to enquire into the merit of thofe editions; yet I cannot but obferve, after feveral great criticks, that the Jews have always fucceeded better in works of this kind than the Chriftians, as being more us'd to the niceties of the tongue, efpecially in its points and accents. *Bombergh* continued printing in *Hebrew* near forty years; and all his works were highly efteem'd on account of the beauty of the character and impreffion, their correctnefs, the finenefs of the paper, and the number that he printed, which *Jof. Scaliger* tells us amounted to above four millions of crowns of gold. He made ufe of the moft learned Jews for his correctors. His greateft work was the *Talmud* printed *anno* 1520 in xi vol. *fol.* *F. Bartolocci* obferv'd, that after his death *Hebrew-printing* declin'd exceedingly.

THE next improvement of this Art was by printing *Polyglot* works; and herein the city of *Genoa* firft oblig'd the world. *Peter Paul Porrus*, a native of *Milan*, but inhabitant of *Turin*, an eminent Printer, undertook to print the [1] Pentaglot pfalter of *Auguftin Juftinian*, bifhop of *Nebo*, *anno* 1516, in the houfe of *Nicholas Juftinian Paul*, at *Genoa*. It was in *Hebrew*, *Arabic*, *Chaldaic*, and *Greek*, with the *Latin* verfions, gloffes and Scholia, which laft made the 8th column, in *fol.*

SINCE I wrote this I have feen a fine copy of it upon vellum at my Lord *Pembroke*'s, on which I fhall venture to make the following obfervations, *viz.*

[1] Impreffit miro Ingenio, *Petrus Paulus Porrus*, genuæ in Ædibus *Nicolai Juftiniani Pauli* præfidente Reipub. genuenfi pro Sereniffimo Franc. Rege præftanti viro *Octaviano Fulgofo*, anno chriftianæ falutis millefimo quingentefimo fextodecimo menfe VIIIIbri. *Petrus Paulus Porrus Mediolanenfi*, *Taurini* degens.

THAT

THAT it is a compleat mafter-piece in that kind.

THE different difpofition of the columns are very regular and neat, and kept up to their exact proportions, nor having one double line in the *Latin* verfions, nor are any chafms or white lines feen throughout the work ; fo that I dare affirm that to this time I have never feen a work fo well contriv'd, and fo completely finifh'd. The *Hebrew* is printed with all the points, both orthographical and mufical, the *Greek* and *Roman* is very neat, but above all the *Arabic* (allowing for its antiquity) furpaffes all I have ever feen of the kind ; and, that nothing may be wanting to compleat the whole, the prefs-work and ink, both rubricks and black, excels any thing I have feen, except *Durand*'s *Rationale*, printed by the inventor, *Fauft*, in 1459, which book I have alfo feen in my Lord's library.

THE *Arabic* was the firft that was ever printed, and this the firft piece of the bible that ever appear'd in fo many languages ; for that of *Potken* at *Cologn* was not publifh'd till two years after, and wanted the *Arabic*. The reader might reafonably imagine, that this work met with deferv'd encouragement ; yet the reverfe appears from the juft complaints of the author. For *F. le Long* in his account of the po-lyglot bibles, p. 36, tells us, , that he (*Juftinian*) caus'd no lefs than , 2000 copies to be printed off, prefuming that fuch a work would , not only procure him a vaft reputation, but likewife prove very , gainful to him ; the profits of which he defign'd to beftow upon , fome of his family who were then in want.   He fancied that it , would infallibly meet with a kind reception, and that all rich prelates , and princes would think themfelves oblig'd to encourage it, and reim-, burfe and inable him to proceed with the other parts of the bible. ,, For this he promis'd in his preface to the pfalter ; and, about twenty years after, in his annals of the Republick of *Genoa*, he propos'd to add the whole old teftament in all thofe languages to the new one, which was preferv'd there, done after the fame manner ; and this he would un-doubtedly have perform'd, had he not been unfortunately drown'd in his paffage to the ifle of *Corfica* the following year. , But, continues , *Le Long*, he (*Juftinian*) was deceiv'd by his too great credulity ;
, every

, every body applauded the work, but few proceeded further than that ; , fcarce a fourth part of what he had printed was fold off. , He fays afterwards, , that, this pfalter being of no ufe to any except the learned, , he found it impoffible to reimburfe himfelf the expence he had been , at ; becaufe, befides the 2000 copies upon paper, he had about fifty , printed upon vellum, which he prefented to all the kings, whether , Chriftians or Infidels. *Vid. Matt. annal. Typ. Tom.* II. *par.* 1. *p.* 121. *fub not.* C.

'Tis well that the author's difappointment did not difcourage both him and others from attempting the like glorious performances : tho' we do not find any more works of that prelate in the oriental tongues, yet I have met with the following one printed at *Paris*, in 1516, which convinceth me, that he publifh'd more of them, and in particular that which is mention'd in it. It is entitl'd, *Liber Job ad Hebraicam veritatem reftitutus, duplici Latina verfione, una vulgata, altera ex Hebreo Auguftini Juftiniani*, 4to, *i. e.* the book of *Job* reftor'd to the *Hebrew* text, with a double verfion of it, *viz.* the vulgate, and another from the *Hebrew* by *Auguftin Juftinianus*, 4to. But when and where *Juftinian* printed the book of *Job* in *Hebrew* and *Latin*, I can no where find. As for *Porrus*, the Printer of the pfalter above mention'd, tho' he was paid by the Bifhop who employ'd him, yet 'tis probable he ventur'd no more upon that province ; for we do not find that ever he printed any thing more in thofe languages, tho' he return'd to *Turin*, and printed for feveral years after. His mark or rebus was a leak with a *P* on each fide, alluding to his name *Peter Paul Porrus*, as was the cuftom of that time to find fome beaft, bird, plant, *&c.* that had analogy to the perfon's firname, in order to form a rebus ; as appears from the table of them at the end of this book.

The next confiderable work is the bible of that great *Mecænas*, Cardinal *Ximenes*, archbifhop of *Toledo*, printed at *Alcala de Herares in Spain*, in *Latin Complutum*, from whence it is call'd the *Complutentian* bible. But before we leave *Italy*, I fhall juft mention fome other printers, who, tho' they did not excel in this kind, yet oblig'd the world with many noble volumes in *Latin* and *Greek*. Of this number was *Andreas Azulanus*, father-in-law to the great *Aldus* of *Venice*, who

fuc-

fucceeded him in that Printing-houfe, and kept up the credit of it for
feveral years. His acquaintance with the members of the learned af-
fembly at *Aldus's* houfe, as well as with his other foreign correfpondents,
and his own extraordinary learning enabled him to print many noble
editions, which it is not my defign to give an account of here, fince they
may be feen in Mr. *Mattaire's Annals,* vol. II.

T H E *Junta's* at *Florence,* a noble family of Printers, fome of whom
we have fpoken of under the heads of *Florence, Rome, Venice* and
Lyons, fignaliz'd themfelves in the preceeding and this century ; particularly thofe of *Florence* were famous for their beautiful and correct
editions in *Greek* and *Latin.*

T H E *Lilly* was their rebus, with this motto, *Nil candidius,* i. e. *nothing is
whiter* ; to which they fometimes added the initial Letters of their names,
and fometimes printed them at length. There were two of them at *Genoa,*
viz. *Philip,* who began to print in 1497, and continu'd till 1518,
about which time he is fuppos'd to have dy'd, and *Bernard Junta,* but
whether a brother or kinfman to him I cannot determine. The former having caufe to fufpect, that his works might be pirated, according
to the cuftom of thofe times, obtain'd a patent from pope *Leo* X. of
a ten years privilege for all the *Greek* and *Latin* editions, which he
fhould print from that time. As the former are all very curious and
highly efteem'd, I fhall give a lift of the moft confiderable of them,
which is as follows.

1. B A S I L I I *Magni liber de exercitatione grammatica.* 8vo, *ann,* 1515
2. A U S O N I I *fophiftæ præludia, & Hermogenis rhetorica,* 8vo, 1515
3. M U S Æ U S, *Batrachomyomachia, Oppiani Halieutica,* 8vo, 1515
4. N O V E M *comædiæ Ariftophanis,* 8vo, 1515
5. A P O L L O N *de conftructione,* 8vo, 1515
6. T H E O D O R. *Gazæ grammatices introductionis,* lib. 4, 8vo, 1515
7. D I O N. *Areopag. opera,* 8vo, 1516
8. X E N O P H O N T I S *opera,* fol, 1516
9. P L U T A R C H I *vitæ parallelæ Græc,* &c. fol, 1517
10. P H I L O S T R A T I *icones & heroie,* &c. fol, 1517
11. A R I S T I D I S *orationes,* fol, 1517
12. O P H O C L E S *cum fcholiis Græcis,* 8vo, 1518

M m

13. H O M E R I

13. HOMERI *opera.* 8vo.   1519

THIS is the laſt book which he printed; the next, *viz. Florilegium diverſorum epigrammatum,* &c. 8vo, being printed by his heirs.

I SHALL mention but one more Printing-houſe in *Italy, viz.* at the *Quirinal*-college at *Rome,* under the care of the famous *Angel Gallotius,* and protection of pope *Leo,* who was the founder of that college and Printing-houſe, and among other marks of his favour, gave them a privilege of ten years for all their impreſſions, ſome of which were extraordinary fine and correct, and revis'd by the learned *Conſtantine Laſcaris,* often mention'd in this book; of which number were the *Porphyri quæſtiones Homericæ & de nympharum antro,* &c. and a very antient *Latin* tranſlation of *Homer,* both printed in 15:7. *Sophocles*'s Scholiaſt, 1518, and others of great value.

I SHALL now return to that famous bible of cardinal *Ximenes,* as I hinted before, commonly call'd the *Complutenſian* bible, which 'is the only conſiderable one publiſh'd, either in *Spain* or any other part of *Europe* before that time. It conſiſts of ſix large volumes in fol. the firſt of which contains the new teſtament in *Greek* and *Latin,* finiſh'd in 1517; the ſecond is a *Hebrew* and *Chaldee* vocabulary of all the old teſtament with ſome other diſſertations, finiſh'd *May* 31, 1515; the third is the *Pentateuch* in *Hebrew, Greek* and *Chaldee,* with a *Latin* verſion of each; the fourth is a ſecond part of the old teſtament, and contains the books of *Joſhua, Judges* and *Ruth,* the two books of *Samuel,* of *Kings,* and of the *Chronicles,* with the prayer of *Manaſſeh,* in *Hebrew* and *Greek,* with their *Latin* verſion; the fifth is the third part of the old teſtament in *Hebrew* and *Greek,* with the *Latin* verſion, and contains the books of *Eſdras, Nehemiah, Heſter, Job,* the *Pſalms, Proverbs, Eccleſiaſtes, Canticles, Wiſdom of Solomon,* and *Eccleſiaſticus,* the Apocryphal part of *Heſter* only in *Greek;* the ſixth is the fourth and laſt part of the old teſtament in the ſame languages as the former, and contains the prophecies of *Iſaiah, Jeremiah,* with the *Lamentations* at the end, *Baruch, Ezekiel, Daniel* (with the hiſtory of *Suſannah,* and of *Bel* and the *Dragon) Hoſea, Joel, Amos, Obadiah, Jonah, Michah, Nahum, Habakkuk, Zephaniah, Haggai, Zachariah, Malachi,* with the three books of the *Maccabees;* theſe four laſt volumes were finiſh'd *ann.* 1517, *July* the

the 10th ; tho' Mr. *Mattaire* says, that the whole six volumes were not publish'd till the year 1520. Every page both of the old and new testament is divided into three columns : in the old, the first column contains the *Hebrew* text ; the middle the vulgate *Latin* ; and the third the *Greek* of the *Septuagint* : besides the *Chaldee,* which is plac'd in the inner margin with the version of it opposite to it. The vulgate is printed with *Gothic* letter.

T H E only objection against this work is, that the Printers made use of a sort of false letter to fill up the spaces, whenever any of the versions run to a greater length than the text ; that there might be no line sho ter than another, nor any blank spaces in the column. The new testament is in a very plain large character, without ligatures, abbreviations or accents ; tho' that of the *Septuagint* is different ; the reason of which they give in the preface, to the following purport ; that since all the ancient *Greek* authors, whether sacred or profane, were originally written without them, they were unwilling to introduce any thing into those holy books, which it is certain was neither originally in them, nor of any use towards the understanding of them ; but with respect to the *Septuagint,* which is but a translation, they thought it unnecessary to be too scrupulous about it.

T H I S work was printed by *Arnold William de Brocario,* in the university of *Alcala de Henares* in *Spain,* at the charges and under the direction of that learned prelate, whose merit in this respect can never be sufficiently extoll'd. *Alphonsus Zamora* tells us, that he gave no less than four thousand crowns of gold for seven *Hebrew* manuscripts ; and it would be difficult to determine the sums, which the *Greek, Chaldee* and *Latin* manuscripts cost him. As for the learned men, whom he sent for from all parts of *Europe* and *Asia* to assist him in this undertaking, *Malincrot* tells us they were very numerous, of whom we shall mention some. Among the *Greeks* were *Demetrius Cretensis, Antony Nebrissenus, Lopes de·Astuniga,* and *Terdianus Pintianus,* who were all professors of the *Greek* and *Latin* tongues, and famous for their works. Of the *Hebrew* professors were *Alphonsus Medicus,* a native of *Alcala, Paul Coronellus, Alphonsus Zamorali* and *John Vergera,* to the

last

laſt of whom was committed the tranſlation of ſeveral books, in which he reſtor'd a great number of texts, which were wholly unintelligible in the vulgate *Latin.* Theſe, with many of the moſt conſiderable men of the univerſity of *Alcala,* were engag'd by the Cardinal with very large ſalaries in this work, for the ſpace of 15 years, *viz.* from 1502 to 1517; ſoon after which he was prevented by death from executing ſeveral other glorious deſigns. A larger account of this work may be ſeen in *Malincrot,* p. 110. and Mr. *Mattaire's Annals,* p. 124, &c.

WHILE I am upon the ſubjeŧ of Polyglots, I muſt not omit one great advantage which the art receiv'd from it, and which it hitherto wanted, *viz.* that of printing in columns, by which the text and verſion are ſo eaſily diſpos'd, that the reader may at one view ſatisfy himſelf in any ſcruple, that may ariſe either from a word wrong printed, or miſunderſtood in the one, by caſting his eye immediately on the other. This is particularly neceſſary in *Greek* works and their verſions; in which when there happens to be ſome fault of impreſſion, as 'tis almoſt impoſſible both text and verſion ſhould be faulty in the ſame word, the one may be eaſily correŧed by the other. *Chevillier* gives us many remarkable inſtances of this, from pag. 240 to 243. I ſhall only mention one of them, in which the Printer or correŧor makes *Ælian* call all the greateſt and nobleſt men of *Greece* errant lyars thro' every part of their lives [*omnes Græcorum clariſſimi præſtantiſſimique viri per totam vitam in extrema mendacitate verſati ſunt*] a reproach which neither the author nor tranſlator ever dream'd of fixing upon that nation. But upon a careful examination of the *Greek* text, the word appears to be πενία, and conſequently it ſhould have been printed *mendicitate,* i. e. *poverty,* inſtead of *mendacitate* [lying] which eſcap'd the correŧor's obſervation.

THERE is another conveniency in this method, *viz.* that it obliges a tranſlator to be more conciſe, and to paraphraſe leſs, ſince the exorbitant length of his verſion would be viſible at firſt ſight. I have already taken notice of *Aldus's* method of Printing the text in one page, and the verſion in the other; but he was not follow'd in it by any Printer that I know of: whereas as ſoon as they had taken the hint of theſe columns from the Polyglot pſalter and bible, it was immediately

fol-

follow'd by moſt Printers ; and the famous *Badius,* in his edition of *Angelus Politianus*'s works, *anno* 1519, printed all the epigrams and verſions after this manner. How plain ſoever the advantages of this method may ſeem, yet ſeveral men of learning have decry'd it ; and particularly *Antony Muretus* and *Joſ. Scaliger* have complain'd, that this way of printing the *Greek* and the verſion in two columns had been the cauſe of the former being wholly neglected.

B e s i d e s books in two languages, the columns are very neceſſary in large folio's, and ſometimes in large quarto's, where the lines run to ſo great a length, that they puzzle the reader, who is apt to read the ſame line over again, or perhaps to ſkip the next, unleſs he conſtantly keep his finger moving from one to the other ; which is eaſily remedied by dividing the pages into two columns. This method has obtain'd almoſt from the middle of the 15th century, and is entirely owing to that of printing the ſacred books in ſeveral languages and columns. This ſhall ſuffice concerning this work printed in *Spain* ; in which I find but two Printers more of any note, *viz. John Peter Bonhomin* at *Lisbon, anno* 1514, where he printed a *Spaniſh* book, entitled *Ordinationes,* &c. fol. in *Gothic* ; and *John de Porris* at *Salamanca,* perhaps a relation of *Peter Paul Porrus,* who printed the pſalter at *Genoa,* mention'd before.

I c o m e now to ſpeak of the French Printers, whoſe merit, tho' late, became at leaſt equal with that of *Italy,* or any other kingdom, in all reſpects. *Henry Meibomius,* a German hiſtorian, owns[1], *that the Art of Printing, which was invented at* Mentz *in* Germany, *and improv'd in* Italy, *was at laſt perfected in* France : which is ſufficiently evident from the impreſſions of *Henry Stephens,* in *Hebrew, Greek* and *Latin,* were there no other Printers to be produc'd in favour of that kingdom. But this country has given greater encouragement, or abounded more in excellent Printers, than that ; and conſidering the care the univerſity of *Paris,* whoſe power and authority over Printers and bookſellers we have given an account of under the article of *Paris,* had continually over them, and the many ſignal marks of their favour, join'd to the genius of the nation, we ſhall not wonder at the perfection which they brought the

---

[1] —— quod ſcribendi genus ut *Moguntiæ* in *Germania* inventum, ita apud *Italos* excultum, & in *Gallia* demum perfectum eſt. *Riddagghuſenſ.* Tom. 3. p. 380. *Chronic.*

art to, tho' somewhat later than their neighbours. For we may remember that *Badius*, one of the first who signaliz'd himself in this province, did not begin to print till almost the close of the last century,
nor come to *Paris* till the beginning of this. Hitherto, tho' the *Roman*
character, and the elegant manner of printing introduc'd by the Italians, were here exactly imitated, and in some cases excell'd; yet with
respect to the learned languages, especially the Eastern, they were much
neglected throughout *France*; and tho' the noble *Greek* impressions of *Aldus*,
had rais'd an universal desire of reviving that tongue, yet the French
were backward in introducing it, till they began to be contemn'd by
the Italians, who were become every where masters of it. The only
pieces printed by them in that tongue till that time, were some quotations so wretchedly perform'd, that Mr. *Mattaire* tells us, they were rather to be guess'd at than read. The character was rude and uncooth,
without accents, *&c.* for which *Badius* makes an apology, and desires his
readers to impute those errors and omissions to the scarcity of types, and
want of compositors who understood in that language. *Franc. Tissard*, a
person compleatly skill'd in *Greek* and *Hebrew*, and qualify'd for such a task,
reviv'd those tongues, and prevail'd upon the Parisian Printers to introduce them, having printed several books in those languages : whereas
before this the expence of importing them from *Venice* was so great, that
it deterr'd many from the study of them. At first he address'd a pathe-
tic discourse to the scholars of *Paris* upon that subject ; in which he re-
presents how contemptible their neighbours in *Italy* thought them ; what
epithets they gave their nation, such as, barbarous, proud and ignorant,
who pretended to give laws to *Italy*, the most learned and polite nation
of the world, whilst themselves were not contented to despise the muses
at home, but must make excursions over the *Alps*, to disturb them in
their belov'd abodes there. He exhorted them to retrieve the honour of
their country, and to apply themselves immediately to the study of those
languages ; he promis'd them his own and other learned men's assistance ;
and tells them, that he had caus'd some *Greek* books to be printed, which,
tho' cheap, would be great helps to them in that study. In short, he
laid before them such powerful motives, and convincing arguments,
that he at length rais'd a desire in them of rivalling their neighbours for

learn-

learning. His extraordinary merit foon procur'd him the efteem and friendfhip of the great, who jointly affifted this noble defign; among whom was the duke *de Valois*, afterwards king of *France*, and fufficiently known by the name of *Francis* I. the great patron of learning, who receiv'd him into his family and protection.

THE firft *Greek* book which *Tiffard* caus'd to be printed at *Paris*, was entitled Βίβλος ἡ γνωμαγυρίκη, containing the fayings of the feven wife men of *Greece*, *Pythagoras*'s golden verfes, *Phocylides*'s ethic poem, and the verfes of the *Erithrean* fybil upon the laft day, with a *Greek* alphabet and fome other inconfiderable pieces. It was printed in 4to, *anno* 1507, by *Giles Gourmont*, and dedicated to the prince *de Valois* and the archbifhop of *Thouloufe*. This work was fo well receiv'd, that he caus'd the fame Printer to difpatch three more books in that language the fame year; *viz.* 1. *Homer*'s Βατραχομυομαχία, 4to, or *The battle of frogs and mice*. 2. *Hefiod*'s Ἔργα κ, ἡμέραι, 4to. 3. Ἐροτήματα Χρυσολώρα or *Chryfolaras*'s *Greek* grammar, 4to. This laft has a tetraftich written by *Ch. Roufeau*, to acquaint the world that *Francis Tiffard* caus'd the firft *Greek* editions to be printed at *Paris*; which *Tiffard* himfelf took care to tranfmit to pofterity in fome epiftles prefix'd to the books above-mention'd. In thefe he likewife informs us of the difficulties which he met with in procuring Printers, who would engage in this new province; that they all alledg'd there was neither a fufficient number of *Greek* matrices and characters in *Paris* for fuch a work, nor any compofitors that underftood or could read that language; that the expence of fetting up fuch a Printing-houfe muft be very great, as well as the danger of lofing both their labour and money[2]. Notwithftanding this, *Tiffard* ftopp'd not here, but refolv'd to bring the *Hebrew* into vogue; and to this end caus'd a font of *Hebrew* letters to be caft, and the following year printed an *Hebrew* alphabet and

---

[1] Primus Parrhafia Graiæ nova gloria linguæ
* Ambacus Argivum concinet urbe melos:
Quo duce morales Sophiæ amplexabere leges;
Hoc igitur ftabili pectore fige memor.

[2] Cum incufforum fibi hoc munus, hanc provinciam affumere vellet nemo nullus non id Labor s fubterfugeret — characteres præterea Græcos nobis hactenus defuiffe vidi; ad eorum quoque aliquot fcalpendos, & poftmodum liquefaciendos, & denique ad eos impreffioni aptandas tradendofque, ut aiebant, fumptibus — opus effe: ad hæc ea non intelligere, ne legere quidem, ejufque infolentes fateri.

* *Tiffard was a native of* Amboife, *in Latin* Ambaca: *for which reafon the poet calls him* bere Ambacus.

grammar with a *Greek* alphabet, and fome hymns in *Greek* and *Latin* at the end ; which book he dedicated to his great patron *Francis* prince de *Valois. Giles Gourmont,* who had printed his *Greek* works. likewife undertook the *Hebrew.* It is printed with his name ; and tho' there is no date to it, yet it is plain it was publifh'd in the year aforemention'd. However as he was the firft who merited the title of *Greek* and *Hebrew* printer to the city and univerfity of *Paris,* and has publifh'd feveral other *Greek* works after the year 1508, viz. the Idyls of *Theocritus,* fome of *Lucian*'s works, a fecond edition of *Chryfolaras*'s grammar in 1511, the *Gnomologia* and *Aldus*'s *Greek Lexicon* of 1497 much enlarg'd in 1512, the *Grammar* of *Theod. Gaza* in 1516, &c. I thought my felf oblig'd to do juftice to his merit. He us'd to put his coat of arms at the beginning or end of his books, and fometimes at both, with this French motto ; *Toft ou tard, pres ou loing, a le fort du foible befoing,* i. e. *fooner or later, far or near, the ftrong ftand in need of the weak,* with his name *Giles* or *Ægidius Gourmont.* His mark fometimes was the three crowns of the Kings of *Cologn* with the 25th verfe of the 37th pfalm ; *I have been young, and now am old,* &c. in *Hebrew* and *Greek,* under them. He liv'd overagainft the college of *Cambray,* in the fquare of that name ; and his books are much valu'd by the lovers of antiquity, efpecially at *Paris.* He continu'd printing till after the year 1527. As for the learned *Tiffard,* as we find nothing printed by him, after his *Hebrew* grammar, he is fuppos'd to have dy'd about that time.

However, he did not want a fucceffor of equal merit to carry on this work ; for *Jerom Aleander,* a perfon fo well fkill'd in *Hebrew, Greek* and *Latin,* as to fpeak them with as much fluency as his own language, was fent for by *Lewis* XII. from *Italy,* where he profefs'd the *Greek* and *Latin* tongues with univerfal applaufe. His reputation was fo great, that the elector *Palatine* fent his own brother *Wolfgang de Bavaria* to be inftructed by him, and the learned *Vatablus,* who had been formerly his fcholar, was proud to affift him in fome of his works, and take care of their correction, whenever *Aleander* was hinder'd by ficknefs or avocations. As foon as he came to *Paris,* he employ'd *Gourmont*'s preffes in printing thofe *Greek* works which we mention'd juft before in fpeaking of that Printer. The King fail'd not of giving

him

him immediate encouragement ; for he fettled on him a penfion of 500
crowns of gold, with many other marks of his favour ; fo that he was
chofen principal of the college of the *Lumbards*, and, in 1512, rector of
the unverfity, with general applaufe ; tho' he had not yet taken his doctor's degree there.   At laft he was made library-keeper to the pope, a bifhop and nuncio, and then cardinal, by *Clement* VII.   I fhall only add, that
he was one of *Aldus's* learned academy ; and that under his care the
Greek and *Hebrew* tongues were fo well fettled in *France,* as to flourifh
there ever fince.

But it muft be own'd, that thofe editions of *Gourmont* were very
far from perfection, fince the types were ill fhap'd, the punches ill finifh'd, and the matrices worfe funk ; befides which defects they had
not caft a fufficient font of types, and were for that reafon oblig'd fometimes to ftop till a form was work'd off and diftributed, before they
could go on.   Another defect in thofe types was, that the accents not
being caft to place between the letters as now, but by themfelves, and
fo compos'd in intermediate lines, as the *Hebrew* points are done at this
time, they were often plac'd over the wrong letters, and frequently
confounded one for another, thro' the unfkilfulnefs of their compofitors.   *Tiffard* complains of this more than once, but tells his readers,
that they were taking all proper means to remedy thofe defects ;
and hopes in time, that thofe characters would be brought to as great
a perfection there, as in *Italy.*   And indeed we find that the fuccefs
of *Gourmont's* impreffions, under all thefe difadvantages, excited other
printers in that city, to procure better types, workmen, correctors, *&c.*
(not to mention that beautiful font of fmall *Greek* which king
Francis I. caus'd to be caft at his own charge) in which they fucceeded
to admiration, and foon publifh'd much finer editions than thofe of
Gourmont.   We fhall only mention fome of the moft confiderable,
tho' they all came out later than 1520, except *Angelus Politianus's* epigrams, printed by *Badius* in 1519, already fpoken of in this chapter ;
and his edition of *Guillelmus Budæus's Greek* epiftles, 4to, in 1520.   After this, *Peter Vidoue,* or *Vidæus,* mafter of arts, and an eminent printer,
printed *Berault's Greek* lexicon in fol. and *Or. Apollo's Hieroglyphics,* 8vo,
in *Greek* and *Latin,* in 1521 and 1523.   *Gourmont* printed *Homer's* firft

and fecond *Iliad*, 4to, with *Wolmar*'s fhort notes ; and the *Greek* lexicon of *Magnus Chæredamus*; and in 1527, *Gwinler*'s *Greek* fyntax, 8vo. *Anno* 1528 *Simon Colinæus*, or *de Colines*, printed *Sophocles* tragedies, and in 1534, the new teftament. Thefe, with a few inconfiderable ones more, were all that came out in *Greek* during the fpace of 27 years, *viz.* from *Tiffard*'s firft impreffion in 1507 to 1534; which I have mention'd here, tho' they run beyond our period, to fhew how flow their firft progrefs was, tho' their advances afterwards were prodigious. *Chevilier*, from whofe lift I have extracted the beft part of thefe editions, has carry'd it on to the year 1560; and the reader will find, both in this piece and the remainder of it, feveral remarkable works omitted by *Mr. Mattaire* in his *Annals*, particularly the *Greek* lexicon and the new teftament above nam'd. However as *Chevilier* tells us, that he faw them all in the *Sorbon* library, I thought proper to mention them.

T HE reader perhaps will be furpriz'd to find nothing attempted by the Parifians in the polyglot way, whilft the Italians, Germans and Spaniards fet them fo fair an example. But, whatever be the reafon of this neglect, 'tis certain, that if we except the *Pfalterium quincuplex* of *Mr. Faber*, or *Fabry*, printed in fol. 1509, by *Henry Stephens*, in *Hebrew*, *Latin* and *French*, with the *Pfalterium vetus & conciliatum*, in five columns, and reprinted by him in 1513, and again at *Caen* [*Cadomi*] in *Normandy*, by *Peter Olivier*, in 1515, I can find nothing of that kind during the greateft part of this century. However, it muft be acknowledg'd they have made the world ample amends in the next, in which *Antony Vitré* printed that noble work, known by the name of *Monfieur le Jay*'s polyglot bible in 1657; which being of too late a date, and fo well known to the learned, I fhall only fay of it, that as far as relates to the Printing part, (for as to the author's merit with refpect to learning, 'tis not my province to enquire into) it has not yet been equall'd by any work publifh'd, in any nation, either for beauty of character or elegancy of difpofition, finenefs of paper or richnefs of embellifhment; in all which *Mr. le Jay*, who was at the charges of the impreffion, fpar'd neither coft nor labour, in order to render it a mafter.piece of that kind. Here I muft draw a veil over my own

coun-

country, which is greatly injur'd, if it did not contribute to the ruin of the undertaker of this glorious work.   An intimate friend at *Paris* fent me word, that the fheets of Mr. *le Jay*'s Polyglot was unfairly procur'd from the prefs at *Paris* before the work was publifh'd, and, by the editor's of the Englifh Polyglot, improv'd and publifh'd fo foon after, as to reduce Mr. *le Jay* almoft to want; after his having expended above 5000 *l.* fterling to compleat his work.   But, as 'tis unpleafant to relate, I fhall proceed.

As for the other printers who flourifh'd at *Paris* during this fpace of 20 years, fince my defign is only to mention thofe who were eminent for improvements, unattempted in the former century, I have but few to add to the preceeding.   The firft in rank and merit is *Henry Stephens,* the father of that numerous family of Printers, whofe learning and impreffions for near 200 years have been celebrated by much better pens, and particularly by *Mr. Bayle* and *Theod. Janfon* abroad, and by *Mr. Nichols, Collier,* but much more fully by the laborious and learned *Mr. Mattaire,* in his *Vitæ Stephanorum* and *Annales Typograph.* I fhall therefore content my felf with giving a fhort account of their great progenitor *Henry,* as far as relates to my prefent fubject.   He began to exercife the Art of Printing about 1502, in company with *Wolfgang Hopyl,* a noted *German* Printer at *Paris,* of whom we have given an account in the foregoing century.   He had afterwards feveral other partners, *viz. John Petit, Dennis Roce, John de Brié* and *John Hongel,* all eminent Printers.   We have already fpoken of his *Polyglot Pfalter,* which, for ought I find, was the only piece he did in that way.   As for the *Greek,* it was fo little in vogue in his time, that he printed but little in it.   He us'd two forts of characters for the *Latin,* viz. the *Gothic* and *Roman,* both good in their kind.   It were fuperfluous to tell the reader, that he was a man of great fkill in the learned languages, and wrote feveral curious pieces in elegant *Latin.*   He was extremely correct in his editions, fo that their faults are fo few, as fcarce to deferve an errata; yet he always readily acknowledg'd the fmalleft number of them, as appears from his edition of *Erafmus*'s apology againft *Latomus,* in which he confeffes,

* *that*

* *that fome faults efcap'd him thro' neglect* ; tho' the whole was but twenty. His chief correctors were *Peter Porta, Volgatius Pratenfis, John Solidus* of *Cracow* in *Poland,* and *Beatus Rhenanus.* As he wa fworn Printer of the city of *Paris,* inftead of a mark or rebus, he us'd to put the arms of that univerfity to his impreffions, which is the efcutcheon of *France,* with a hand from the clouds holding a book. Several other printers of that city follow'd his example in this. He dy'd in 1520, leaving among other children three fons, who became very eminent, *vid. Mattaire Vit. Steph.* the two firft *Robert* and *Francis* in printing, and *Charles* in phyfick.

His fucceffor was *Simon de Colines,* or *Colinæus,* who marry'd his relict, and educated his two fons before mention'd ; and with them rais'd the reputation of his Printing-houfe higher, than their father could, whilft the learned languages were in their infancy there. I fhall only add, that *Robert* became fo great a proficient under his father and father-in-law, that he was able to manage that great Printing-houfe at the age of 18 ; and that one of his editions of the new tefta-ment in 16º. *ann,* 1549, printed in a very fine *Greek* character, and ve-ry fcarce, is affirm'd to be without a fault. This deferves notice, becaufe there is another of his likewife in 16°, 1546, which has an errata at the end, and is frequently fold for the other. I cannot but obferve, that to this *Robert Stephens* we owe the invention of dividing the chapters of the bible into verfes, found out by him on a journey from *Paris* to *Lyons,* as we are inform'd by *Theod. Janfon de Vit. Stephanorum,* printed at *Amfterdam ann.* 1643, pag. 48 ; the great advantage of which is obvious to every perfon.

Before I difmifs the city of *Paris,* I cannot forbear mentioning a moft curious and elaborate work, which tho' not printed till the year 1529, yet, both for its fingularity and its having been begun many years before, ought by no means to be omitted, I mean the book entitled *Champ-Fleury,* written by the famous *Godfrey Tory,* printer and bookfeller of the city of *Bourges,* at the fign of the broken pitcher, and printed by *Giles Gourmont* likewife, Printer and bookfeller at *Paris,* under the following title ;

* Locis aliquot incuria noftra aberratum eft.

CHAM-

CHAM-FLEURY, *auquel eft contenu le Art & Science de la deue & vraye proportion des Lettres Attiques, qu'on dit autrement Lettres antiques & vulgairement Lettres Romaines, proportionees felon le corps & Vifage humain.*

THE author, who for his learning had been fome time before chofen prefident of a college in *Burgundy*, and had tranflated and publifh'd feveral learned works out of *Greek* and *Latin*, ever fince the year 1512, was afterwards admitted fworn Printer and bookfeller to the king, and to the univerfity of *Paris*; but became moft famous for the curious work abovemention'd; in which he endeavours to demonftrate the due proportion of letters from thofe of a human body and face, as appears by the title. As it would fpin this chapter to too great a length, were I to give the reader a more particular account of this fcarce and fingular piece, I fhall content my felf with referring him to Mr. *Mattaire's Annales Typogr.* vol. II. part 2. from page 550 to 559, where he will find fuch particularities both of the book and its author, as he will think worth reading, if he has any tafte in this way

I HAVE already dwelt fo long upon the fubject of Polyglots, the moft confiderable improvement of the Art in this century; and upon the city of *Paris*, the moft celebrated in *France* for productions of that kind; that I fhall fcarce have room to fpeak of *Lyons, Rouen, Tholoufe, Caen,* &c. which have produc'd many excellent works, if not in the Polyglot way, yet in all branches of the Art. I fhall confine my felf therefore to thofe Printers who have cultivated the *Greek* or Oriental tongues, and refer the reft to Mr. *Mattaire's Annals*, where the reader may fee their merit, and the lift of their impreffions.

THE city of *Lyons* has been always the next in rank to *Paris*, in every branch of Printing; and if we confider that it receiv'd lefs encouragement from their princes and the learned, the latter chufing to refide at *Paris*, where there was a greater probability of advancement, we fhall wonder that *Lyons* was fo little inferior to *Paris*; and may remember, that it produc'd many valuable impreffions during the laft century. However, the reader muft not expect any productions in *Greek*, much lefs in *Hebrew* and the Polyglot kind, during thefe 20 years, or long after, fince he has feen the flow progrefs of thofe languages at *Paris*; and with refpect to the *Latin* and modern tongues, they are foreign to our prefent

fent purpofe. I fhall therefore only fay, that the *Lyons* Printers publifh'd many editions of the claffics, &c. law-books, and efpecially *Latin* bibles, there being fcarce a year paft for a long time, in which they did not print two or three of them of different verfions, and fome with very fine rubricks and other curious embellifhments. The moft remarkable Printers of them were *James Sacon*, or *Sachon*, who printed fome works of the fathers, and one time two *Latin* bibles in one year; *James Marefchall*, *John Moylin* and *Nicholas de Benedictis*.

THE city of *Rouen*, in *Latin Rothomagium*, and *Caen* follow next: but their productions for thefe twenty years, and after, are fo inconfide-rable, if we except a *Latin* bible in 4to, *anno* 1511, and the *Pfalterium quincuplex* of *Faber* aforemention'd, which was printed in the latter *anno* 1515, both by *Peter Olivier*, and a *Latin* bible in the former; that I fhall infift no longer upon them. With refpect to the other cities of *France*, which receiv'd the Art either before or after the clofe of the laft century, their impreffions are ftill lefs confiderable. I now pafs therefore to *Holland* and *Flanders*, where the reader will be furpriz'd to fee the Art rather funk and loft than improv'd. In the preceeding century we find feveral cities in *Holland*, as *Utrecht* 1473, *Delfh* 1477, *Goude* 1479, *Harlem* 1485, and *Leyden* 1497, receiv'd and cultivated the Art; yet now we meet not with a fingle edition done in any of them; nor find that any other city receiv'd it during thofe twenty years. As for *Flanders* and *Brabant*, 'tis manifeft they have been lefs negligent than the *Dutch*; for the city of *Antwerp* entertain'd one or two Printers, who publifh'd three or four books during this fpace; the moft confiderable of which was the new Teftament in *Latin* and *Dutch*, in 4to, *anno* 1509; and the univerfity of *Louvain* had an eminent Printer, *Theodore Martin*, who, having printed at his own native town of *Aloft* 'till the end of the 15th century, remov'd to *Antwerp*, where he publifh'd fome *Latin* editions, and at length came hither and continued printing till 1528, or perhaps longer. His impreffions in this city are not indeed very remarkable for their bulk, beauty or number. I find but nine or ten, moft of which are fchool-books, either written or publifh'd by *Erafmus*; yet his moft confiderable work is the *Latin* teftament in 8vo, *anno* 1519, if it was printed by him, as is probable, fince we find

no

no other Printer here during this fpace, tho' *F. le Long* mentions not the Printer's name.

As for the other cities, which receiv'd the Art before 1500, as *Bruges, Aloft, Bruffels, Gaunt, Boifleduc,* &c. we find fo profound a filence among the ann lifts and hiftorians, as makes me fufpect that it either ceas'd entirely there, or that their produce was not worth preferving, unlefs we fuppofe that they were loft in the war, of which this country was the feat in thofe times; which is evidently the cafe of other countries, efpecially of thofe upon the *Rhine, Switzerland,* &c. Some eminent authors have told us, that they purchas'd fome of thofe valuable pieces, which had been plunder'd by the foldiers, during the wars, out of the libraries of the monks and others. If this be fact, 'tis ftrange that *Louvain,* which calls itfelf the *maiden city,* becaufe it was never taken by any foreign power, fhould not have preferv'd fome more valuable impreffions than thofe of *Theod. Martin,* juft mention'd. However, to do juftice to the *Low Countries,* and *Holland* efpecially, I muft fay, that how negligent foever they were at firft in this refpect, they have fufficiently oblig'd the world fince by their improvements to this Art; nor need I tell the reader how much they have excell'd the Englifh in the goodnefs of their paper, beauty and variety of characters, and in elegance and correctnefs of compofition; in fhort, how they have equall'd any nation of *Europe* in every branch of Printing fince. In the fecond volume we fhall fhew what improvements they have made to the mechanic part of it, and in particular to the Printing-prefs, chafes, &c. the former of which is fo compleat, as fcarce to admit a greater degree of perfection.

HERE I cannot but obferve the ftrange viciffitudes that have attended this Art fince its firft invention. We have feen how diligent the Italian nation has been in improving it, what quick progrefs they made in it, and to what a degree of perfection they brought it even before the clofe of the 15th century; whereas fcarce any nation in *Europe* has neglected it more within thefe hundred years, having fuffer'd their elegant Roman and Italick to degenerate, and are become very carelefs in their compofitions, ornaments, &c. fo that they are almoft inferior to any country in all the branches of Printing. The French, on the contrary, who did not introduce the fine *Venetian Roman,* *Italick,* and *Greek* 'till late in the

16th

16th century, have been allow'd the beft Printers, 'till *Elzevir* arofe; fince which time the Dutch, who were by far the lateft of any nation in *Europe* in bringing it to the perfection which their neighbours had, have been lately fuperior to all. I fhall fay but little of *England*, where every reader is already fenfible what rank our Printers here deferve with refpect to other countries; but 'tis with the utmoft regret that I obferve our nation, which took fo much pains to have the Art brought over in its earlieft days, and cultivated it with fo much application, fhould have been fo far excell'd by the French and Dutch Printers, and even by thofe of our own nation, who liv'd a century and a half ago. But were the reader confcious of the difadvantages we labour under, and the fmall Profit we reap from our labour, he would rather be apt to wonder that any of us have been able to keep it up to that degree of perfection it is ftill in. I could eafily make it appear from whence thefe difficulties arife. This complaint, which is far from being new, the *Latin* reader will find elegantly exprefs'd above 130 years ago by *Cornelius Kelian*, one of the great *Plantine*'s correctors, in an epigram of fixteen verfes, which I have fubjoin'd at the bottom of the page[1]. However, this I may modeftly fay for our felves, that, whenever we have met with fufficient encouragement, we have demonftrated our capacity by printing as beautiful and correct impreffions as any of our neighbours.

But to return from this digreffion, which I hope will merit the reader's pardon, I fhall now mention fome cities in other kingdoms, which receiv'd the Art after the 15th century, and conclude this chapter with fome remarks on the fuccefs of it in other parts of the world.

Hitherto we have not feen that any Printer ventur'd farther North than the empire of *Germany*. As for the kingdoms of *Poland, Sweden,*

[1] *Typographus Mercenarius.*

Arte mea varias excudo Typographus artes;
   Ars tamen hæc tenues artifici addit opes,
Rite characteres ad juftam redigo normam,
   Conftet ut ex æquis pagina verficulis.
Incifas nigra fuligine tingo figuras;
   Callofa prelum volvo trahoque manu.
Ecce iterum hefternus mihi adeft labor actus
   in orbem;
Quas ftruxi formas deftruo, & inde ftruo.

Diruo & ædifico; vigilatus tranfigo noctes;
   Sollicitum cruciat cura, premitque labor.
Verum quid profunt curæ durique labores,
   Cum mifero pateat femita nulla lucri?
Nofter alit fudor numatos & locupletes,
   Qui noftras redimunt, quique locant operas.
Nofter alit fudor te, Bipliopola, tuique
   Confimiles, quibus eft vile laboris opus.

Denmark,

Denmark, &c. they imported books from *Germany* and other countries, and tranfmitted any works thither, which they wanted to have printed. I can find no city in thofe parts, except *Cracow,* the metropolis of *Poland,* that receiv'd it fo foon as 1520; and even in this we have but one inconfiderable impreffion done in 1518, *viz.* a diary of *Sigifmund,* the king of *Poland*'s nuptials, printed by one *Jerom Victor,* in 4to. I fhall therefore pafs over to *Turky*; were we find fome of the difpers'd *Jews* of *Soncino,* and particularly Rabbi *Gerfon,* who, as we gave an account under the article of that place, brought the art to *Conftantinople*; whilft others fettled at *Theffalonica* and other parts, of which we have but a fmall account; and carry'd on the bufinefs of printing with good fuccefs. But it muft not be fuppos'd that the *Turks* invited them or any other Printers thither, much lefs that they gave them any other encouragement than a large toleration. On the contrary, we have fhewn in a former chapter, how Sultan *Bajazet* II. publifh'd an edict in 1483, againft the ufe of printed books under pain of death; which edict was afterwards confirm'd by *Selim* I. his fon. The encouragement therefore which they receiv'd was from the *Chriftians* and *Jews*; the latter undoubtedly were pleas'd to have their own books at a more moderate rate, than when they were only tranfcrib'd; and the former, being willing not only to have the old Teftament printed by them more correct than the editions of *Chriftian* Printers, but likewife to have it difpers'd among the *Turks, Indians,* &c. who were wholly ignorant of thofe important truths contain'd in it, fpar'd no coft to purchafe them. Befides this, their *Targums, Talmud,* and other *Rabbinical* learning were brought up by the *Chriftians* to furnifh themfelves with what arguments they cou'd, againft that poor infatuated people, out of their own books. And perhaps this might be the main motive which induc'd thofe two Sultans to publifh fo fevere an edict againft printing any books in the *Turkifh* language, fince the averfion of that nation to almoft every branch of learning, and efpecially the religious, is fufficiently known.

I FIND however but three editions of the facred books printed in that emperor's territories, during thefe twenty years, *viz.* at *Conftantinople.*

1. THE

1. T H E book of *Tobit* in *Hebrew*, without points, in 4to, in 1517.

2. T H E book of *Efther* in *Hebrew*, with the commentary of Rab. *Ifaac Armah*, 4to, 1518.

And at *Theffalonica*.

T H E book of *Pfalms*, *Proverbs*, *Job* and *Daniel* in *Hebrew*, with the commentary of R. *Rafi*, in fol. in 1500. Befides thefe three editions, which are all that Mr. *Mattaire* has given us out of father *Le Long's Bibliothec. facr. Chevilier*, pag. 266, mentions fome others which I fhall here fubjoin, viz.

1. O N E at *Conftantinople* in 1506. *Chevilier* does not tell us what it is.

2. *Jad Khafakkah*, fol. *ibid.* 1509.

3. *Jofippus Ben Gorion*, fol. 1510.

T H E two laft M. *Simon* tells us, he made ufe of in his *critical* hiftory of the Old Teftament.

4. *Berefcith Rabbah*, of Rab. *Bar. Nachman*, fol. *Conftantinople* 1512. T H I S book is now in the *Sorbon* library.

T H O' thefe be all that we can yet find to have been printed in *Turky* from 1500 to 1620; yet I cannot perfuade myfelf, that they were all which the *Jews* printed there, but am apt to believe, that they were bought up by the eaftern *Chriftians*, *Jews*, &c. and carried to the remote parts of *Afia* and *Africa*; whilft the *Jews* of *Soncino* and others were grown fo numerous as to fupply thofe countries with works of that kind. However that be, I do not find that this art made any further progrefs in thefe parts of the world during this fpace, or at leaft that thofe authors, who have reprefented its advances greater, have been much depended on by thofe that wrote after them; and therefore I think myfelf obliged to ftop here.

I H A V E already tranfgrefs'd my propos'd limits, as often as the life of any eminent Printer has extended beyond them, or any material occurrence happen'd worthy of the reader's notice. Agreeable to which liberty, I fhall now clofe this chapter with fome remarks on the fuccefs which attended the art, tho' at fome diftance of time from the year 1520. Firft 'tis obfervable, that it has extended itfelf to *Africa* and *America*; not indeed at the invitation of the natives, efpecially of

America,

America, but by means of the *Europeans,* and particularly of the *Spanish* miffionaries; who carry'd it to the latter for their ends, where it has throve, tho' not flourish'd ever since. The *Romish* fociety *de propagando fide,* gives us an account of printing-houfes being fet up in the cities of *Goa, Rachol,* in the country of *Salfetta, Manella,* the metropolis of the *Philippine* iflands, &c. in the firft of which were printed the two following works, *viz. Doctrina Chriftiana lingua Malabarica Tamul et litteris Malabaris in collegio Goano,* 1577. This edition was in *Scaliger's* poffeffion, and is now among thofe which he bequeath'd to the univerfity of *Leyden.* The other is part of *Confucius's* works printed likewife at *Goa* in 1569; a copy of which is now in the emperor's library at *Vienna.* We find alfo fome printing-houfes fet up about this time in the city of *Lima,* capital of the empire of *Peru,* and in feveral cities of the kingdom of *Mexico.* I fhall only add, that our honourable fociety for the propagation of the gofpel in foreign parts, having heard of the good fuccefs, which Mr. *Zidgenbalgh* and Mr. *Grundler,* two *Danifh* miffionaries, fent to the coaft of *Tanquebar* by his *Danifh* majefty, had in converting a great number of the natives of that country to the chriftian faith, were pleas'd to fend them the whole apparatus of a printing-houfe, with proper workmen and large quantities of paper, which they thankfully receiv'd, and immediately fet to work, having fince printed a fine quarto New Teftament, prayer-books, catechifms, &c. in *Portuguefe* and feveral eaftern languages and characters, for the promoting of their pious defign.

To return again to *Europe,* the Printers, who firft introduc'd the art into *Mufcovy* about 1560, were lefs fuccefsful. That nation was too little friendly to learning to give it any encourgement; and even fuffer'd both the printing-houfe and its whole apparatus to be burn'd and deftroy'd, without ever enquiring after the authors of the mifchief. The famous *Thevet,* hiftoriographer to *Henry* III. of *France,* and a great traveller, gives us the following account of it: , As for the Art of , Printing, they (the *Mufcovites*) had not the ufe of it till 1560; when , it was difcover'd to them by a *Ruffian* merchant, who bought a number , ber of types, &c. with which many neat editions were printed. Ne- , verthelefs, as they are a very fuperftitious nation, and apt to raife fcru-

' ples

, ples without any foundation, in which they imitate their followers of
, the *Greek* church ; fome of them hir'd feveral fellows privately to burn
, all their characters, apprehending that printing might make fome
, change or confufion in their religion. And yet not the leaft enquiry
, or profecution was made after this, either by the prince or his Subjects '.
But fince that time they have admitted it into their metropolis of *Mofcow*,
and elfewhere in the laft century, tho' they print but little, and fell
at exceffive rates.

I HAVE already hinted, that the emperor of *Ethiopia*, and monarch
of thofe chriftians, that are commonly known by the name of *Abyffines*,
who is falfly call'd by fome writers *Prefter John*, wrote a letter
in 1521, to Don *Manuel*, king of *Portugal*, and another in 1524 to his
fucceffor *John* III. (which letters are to be feen in the *Hifpania illuftrata*,
tranflated by *Paul Jovius*, tom. 2. p. 1293, 1297,) in which he defires
thofe princes to fend him fome of the moft curious artificers of *Europe* ;
and in the latter he fays thus : , I entreat you, my lord and brother, to
, fend me fome workmen to carve images, to caft books, make fwords
, and all forts of weapons ; likewife mafons, carpenters, phyficians, fur-
, geons, apothecaries, coiners of gold and filver, and perfons who un-
, derftand how to extract gold, filver, and copper out of the mines, to
, cover houfes with lead, to make fhields and muskets ; and in fhort,
, all forts of neceffary workmen '. What fuccefs thefe letters had, and
whether king *John* anfwer'd his requeft in any of thefe particulars, I
cannot determine. But the fecond tome of the *Abyffine* hiftory by *Job
Ludolph*, or rather the commentator upon it, informs us, that when
Abba Gregory Abyffin faw the library of father *Alphonfo Mendez* a jefuit,
whom the pope had fent into *Ethiopia* in quality of patriarch, in 1623,
he could not forbear extolling that art, which had produc'd fo many
books, and *efteeming it as a facred invention, worthy to be plac'd among
the regalia of the greateft princes* (*). By this it feems, that printing had
been wholly unknown to them at that time ; and confequently that it
was never fent thither by the king of *Portugal* or any other. However,
our knowledge is very imperfect of thofe remote parts of *Africa* ; and

* Exiftimaffe Typographiam, feu facrum   haberi. Vide *Chevil*. p. 274.
quoddam inventum, inter Regalia principum

even

even of thofe which are nearer, as *Morocco, Fez,* &c. we can only fay, that 'tis certain they receiv'd the art early from their neighbours, the *Spaniards* or *Portuguefe,* and encourag'd it for a confiderable time ; yet whatever be the reafon, fcarce any footfteps of it now remain, if we believe Mr. *S. Olon* the *French* king's embaffador to the king of *Morocco ;* who, in his prefent ftate of that empire, printed in 1694, affures us, that there is fcarce one printing-houfe left in it. He adds, that it is a piece of religion among them not to fuffer any corn, horfes or books to be exported ; and that their fondnefs for books is the greater, by reafon of their fcarcity, fince there is hardly a prefs in the whole empire.

We read of fome attempts made by the miffionaries in *Perfia* to introduce printing there ; which prov'd ineffectual. I fhall fay nothing here of the kingdoms of *China* and *Japan,* nor of their manner of printing, having already fpoken of it upon another account in the firft book of this hiftory.

CHAP VIII.

Of the Abuses of the Art *of* Printing.

IT would have been very wonderful, if the encouragement, which that art receiv'd from the great and learned, fhould not have induc'd at the fame time fome perfons, whofe ignorance and avarice would not permit them to aim at that degree of perfection ; which they faw others arrive at, to engage in bafe methods of enjoying the fruit of their ingenuity and diligence, without the trouble of imitating them in it. We have already given occafionally fome accounts of thefe practices, in counterfeiting the works, names and marks of the beft Printers, who have been oblig'd to remonftrate againft them to the world. For as foon as they had publifh'd a curious and correct edition, with prodigious charge and labour, fome of thefe pyrates immediately printed another after it, tho' in every refpect inferior to the former ; and either by underfelling, defrauded them of the reward of their care and expence, or by counterfeiting their names and marks, deftroy'd their reputation.

By thefe abufes, they were oblig'd to make many fruitlefs attempts in order to fupprefs thefe counterfeits, and at laft to have recourfe to the higher powers for priviledges and patents, the only effectual way to prevent fuch practices. We have likewife hinted, that fome of thefe pefts of learning have impos'd upon the world, by felling their impreffions as done at *Venice* or fome other famous place, or pretending they were printed *characteribus Venetianis*, with *Venetian* characters, &c. tho' they were the production of fome obfcure place and printer, whofe only aim was profit.

Another abufe confequent upon this, was the counterfeiting of dates. For when, by the care of a *Froben*, a *Badius*, or fome other eminent Printer, the world was fo far appriz'd of thefe counterfeits, that the authors of them could not vend their impreffions, they immediately reprinted the title page, perhaps with fome alteration, put a new date, and fometimes a new name to it, and fo pafs'd them off for new editions. To recommend them the more to the buyers, they generally afferted them to be newly revis'd, diligently compared with the beft MSS. corrected in above 500 places, and the like. It was with great difficulty that thefe abufes were detected in fuch a manner as to make the world aware of them. The complaints of the learned, and their vain efforts to remedy fuch inconveniences are too well known to be mention'd here. I fhal pafs to another equally fhameful and dangerous abufe, *viz.* printing of leud, infamous books, of which the learned *Gerfon*, among many others complains with great zeal ; and mentions particularly a romance, intitled the *Romance of the Rofe*, compos'd in 1300, of which he faid, that if he was the mafter of the laft copy, he would rather choofe to burn it than part with it at any price *. *Paftor fido*, is a poem almoft univerfally known, which, we are told by *J. Nicius Erith*, caus'd many virgin and marry'd women to proftitute their honour. Yet great numbers of a much more pernicious nature have been publifh'd in thofe times. fhall only mention one, which I efteem a mafter-piece in that kind heighten'd by the art of engraving, that it might be a confummate piece of the moft fcandalous lewdnefs in nature. *George Vafari*, in the live

* Si effet mihi Liber Romancii de Rofa, libras, comburerem potius quam venderem qui effet unicus, & valeret mille pecuniarum

o

of the *Italian* painters, gives us this fhort account of it ; that *Julius Romanus*, the moft celebrated painter of his age, invented above fourfcore defigns, which he caus'd to be engraven on wood, while *Peter Aretine*, a great Libertine and Atheift, compos'd a fonnet for each of the prints. This vile performance was publifhed about the year 1525. I fhall conlude with *Vafari*'s charaƈter of it, ✳ *that he knew not which was moft brutifh and fhocking, the defign of* Julius *to the eye, or the verfes of* Aretine *to the ear.* This fame avarice which prompted Printers to undertake fuch infamous works, as the foregoing, induc'd them to abufe their art in another refpeƈt, *viz.* in printing fcandalous and defamatory libels, to the fhame of their profeffion, and the regret of the virtuous. As printing and the reformation begun about the fame time, the former was proftituted by the meaner fort, who printed the vileft forgeries on each, tho' that which was uppermoft, aƈted moft flagrantly, when the other was oblig'd to work covertly. But as this and the laft do not fo properly fall within my province as a Printer, I fhall content myfelf with having juft mention'd them, with abhorrence of fuch praƈtices, and return to fome other abufes.

The next arofe from want of good correƈtors ; for perfons of that clafs were thought too chargeable by many Printers ; who therefore made ufe of illiterate fellows, whom they could hire much cheaper ; or, which often happen'd, us'd none at all. It will eafily be imagin'd, what a number of wretched editions the world muft have been pefter'd with by this fordid negleƈt. However, as books were not yet fo plentifully propagated, as to fuffice the number of ftudents, there wanted not perfons either dull or poor enough to purchafe them, efpecially upon a fmall abatement of the common price. This made fome Printers defignedly fupprefs the errata, which would have inevitably endanger'd the fale of fuch books ; tho' others were oblig'd by the authors or editors to print them at the end of their works. The reader will no doubt be furpriz'd to hear of fome of them fo prodigioufly large, as to be fcarce credible. We have a remarkable inftance in the works of *John Francis Picus de Mirandula*, printed at *Strasburgh* for the firft time in 1507, by *John Knob-*

✳ Iꝗ non fo qual fuffe piu o brutto le fpettacolo de i defegni di Giulo all' occhio, o le parole dell' Aretino a gl' erechi. *Vite del Pittori*, part 3. p. 302.

louch,

louch, a man of some note, and at the charges of *Matthias Schurrer,* another eminent Printer of that place, who ftyl'd himfelf mafter of arts. This edition was fo faulty, that the author was oblig'd to make an errata of fifteen pages in filio, tho' the book was but a thin fmall folio. Were I to trefpafs the bounds of this period, I could mention fome which amounted to fourfcore and eight pages, even in *Venice* itfelf, where *Bellarmin*, who had been very unfuccefsful in the former impreffions of his polemick works, fent them in order to have them more correctly printed ; tho' quite the reverfe happen'd. *Rome, Paris, Lyons,* &c. have been no lefs complain'd of upon this account. The learned *Mich. Fernus,* who with prodigious labour had collected, and revis'd the works of bifhop *Campanus,* was fo provok'd to fee them fo incorrect, that he put an errata in the edition of *Rome,* with this furprizing title at the head *✱ ; , If you have a mind to fhow yourfelf compleatly foolifh , and mad, print your books at *Rome* firft, *&c. Gaguinus* was not lefs difpleas'd to fee his *hiftory of France* printed at *Paris* with fuch a vaft number of faults, that he thought it impoffible to add an errata to it. He therefore fent it to *Lyons* to be reprinted, and tells the bifhop of *Mafcon*, to whom he intrufted the revifing of it, that he wifh'd he could get all the 500 copies of the firft, in order to burn them. The like complaints againft the Printers, he repeats in another edition at *Paris* in 1497, and wifhes thefe incorrect and mutilated editions could be condemn'd to perpetual oblivion. *Galatinus*'s book *De Arcanis Catholicae Veritatis,* printed at *Ortona,* by *Jerom Soncino* in 1518, was fo wretchedly maim'd by the Printer, that the author inveigh'd vehemently againft all Printers in general, accufing them, in his 12th book of *adulterating and corrupting the beft copies, tho' ever fo accurately written, in fuch a manner, that it is impoffible to mend them.* But the Printers fufficiently reveng'd themfelves on him, by reprinting, tho' long after his death, the *Pugio Fidei,* written by *Raymund Martin,* a *Dominican* fryer in 1280 againft the *Jews*; in which edition they unjuftly accufe *Galatinus* of having taken the beft part of his book out of this ; tho' *Galatinus* does ingenioufly own in his preface, that he had taken the greateft part of his book

---

* Vix ex ftulto demens, idemque ex de-   imprime. Corruptorum recognitio.
mente infanus fieri? Libros Romae primus

out of it. *Paul Middleburgh*, a learned Dutchman of the univerſity of *Louvain*, and afterwards biſhop of *Foſembrona* in *Italy*, having wrote a Treatiſe about keeping Eaſter, which he call'd *Paulina*, gave it to a Printer of his own metropolis, nam'd *Octaviano Petrucio*, to be printed; but he committed it to the care of an *Ethiopian* youth, wholly ignorant of the buſineſs, and who probably made his firſt tryal upon it; ſo that, in ſpite of all the accuracy of *Poſthumius* who corrected it, it was ſo maim'd and incorect, that the author was oblig'd to complain publickly againſt ſuch ignorant and careleſs Printers; who (ſays he) in the preface to the errata of that very book, invert the letters, change and tranſpoſe whole ſyllables from the end of one word to the beginning of another, and put one word in the text inſtead of another: he might have added, that they have ſometimes omitted not only words and lines, but whole paragraphs and chapters, or elſe miſplac'd them extremely. We have in the laſt chapter given an account of *Rob. Stephens*, who was certainly an excellent Printer; and yet, however it happen'd, M. *Le Clerc* tells us, *Bibl. An. & Mod. pag.* 415, that he has an edition of the bible in 8vo, printed by him in a ſmall character, containing the vulgate, and the verſion of *Leo Juda*, with *Vatablus*'s notes, in which there is a chaſm of one whole ſheet, tho' the figures of the pages follow each other exactly; ſo that there wants from part of the 2 to half of the 11th chapter of the prophet *Zachary*. If ſo great a man could over look ſo important a miſtake, what could be expected from thoſe who valued neither their own reputation, nor that of their authors, being actuated only by the views of gain. His ſon *Henry Stephens* afterwards wrote a poem of about 150 *Latin* verſes, entitled * *A complaint of the Art of Printing againſt ſome ignorant Printers, upon whoſe account it is fallen into contempt.* At the end of this, are ſome *Latin* and *Greek* epitaphs, in honour of the moſt learned Printers till that time. In this complaint he tells us, that the corruption of ſo many editions was entirely owing to the groſs ignorance of the Printers, ſome of whom he knew, that could not tell the letters of their names †. The reader would in all probability

---

* Querimonia Artis Typographicæ de illiteratis quibuſdam Typographis propter quos in contemptum venit.

† Proh pudor! haud rarus numero reperitur in illo, nominis ignorans prima elementa ſui.

be

be tir'd, if I fhould mention the tenth part of the complaints which we meet with in the writings of the greateft men of that time, againft the avarice, ignorance and negligence of the Printers; fome of which are fo fharp as to call them *beafts and drunkards, the offspring of wild centaurs and of* Vulcan's *untam'd* Cyclops; but I fhall choofe to give fome more diverting inftances of their own, and their corrector's ignorance and neglect.

John Chapius tells us of a change and tranfpofition of words, which render'd the fenfe wholly unintelligible, in his *Sext. Decret.* printed at *Paris* in 1510; where under the title *De dolo et contumacia,* he found thefe words; *Et nuntio ella cum creditur ex de appiurato parati;* inftead of, *Et nuncio jurato creditur ex De Apella cum parati.* *Henry Stephens,* in his preface to his *Querimonia* juft mentioned, tells us of an ignorant corrector whom he knew, who, wherever he met with the word *procos,* us'd to correct it *porcos,* and change the word *exanimare,* into *examinare.* He mentions others, who alter'd a word they underftood not, for one more common and known; thus in the fecond epiftle of the firft book, *Horace* fays, *Nunc adbibe puero pectore verba, puer;* but the word *adbibe* not being underftood by them, they fubftituted that of *adbibe,* which was more obvious to them; yet even this abfurd correction, is ftill retain'd in fome more modern editions. To this, I believe, we owe another correction in the fame poet, where they have chang'd *fectis unguibus,* into *ftrictis unguibus;* whereas, *Horace* only meant the kind fair ones par'd their nails clofe, when they encounter'd with the youths, leaft the fcratches which decency and formality oblig'd them to give them when they play'd too rudely, fhould enter deep enough to hurt them. *Chevilier* fpeaks of a book printed by *Guido Mercator* at *Paris,* in 1493, in which there is a flagrant error in the very frontifpiece, for the title is *Elegantiarum viginta præcepta.* It may be objected, that this was an overfight; but the contrary is plain, fince it is printed fo in the next leaf, and at the end of the book, *Expliciunt elegantiarum viginta præcepta Parifiis per Guidonem,* &c. fo that it evidently arofe from their ignorance of the *Latin* tongue. Nor is this to be wonder'd at, when *Erafmus* tells us, in his preface to the 4th edition of his *Adages* in 1525, that fome of the Printers of *Rome,*

Venice

Venice and *Germany*, scarce knew how to read. This same author likewise wrote 10 or 11 years before this to his friend *Schurrer*, a Printer of *Strasburgh*. *John de Savigny* had been so ill us'd by these drunken and ignorant Printers, as he styles them, in a work of the learned bishop of *Gaieta*, which he publish'd in 1520, that he took the most effectual way to make them trumpeters of their own ignorance, by couching his reproaches in such terms in *Greek* and *Latin*, as were not understood by either Printer or correctors. His words are these : *In istos haud abstemios* ὀινοφλύγας ἀμωσέστε βιβλιογράφως *a Clitorio fonte longe remotissimos cudatur faba.* Let the blame be laid upon those drunken and illiterate Printers, who are equally remote from learning and politeness. We shall conclude this subject with one instance more. After the bishop of *Aleria* had publish'd his edition of *Pliny's* natural history, in the dedication of which he tells the pope, *that he had spent nine whole years in correcting it, tho' he believ'd nine more would scarce suffice to make a perfect edition,* *Hermolaus Barbarus* corrected almost five thousand faults in it. Several other learned men engag'd in the same province, and in particular *John Cæsareus* corrected about four thousand faults in his edition printed at *Cologn*, by *Eucharius Cervicornus,* a famous Printer of that city, in 1524, as he acquaints us in the preface. But the composer and corrector suffer'd a prodigious blunder to go uncorrected in the frontispiece of that book, wherein the reader is told, that this new edition is corrected in no less than four hundred thousand places *. 'Tis surprising, that a book should be corrected in so many places since the last edition of it ; but when the reader comes to the preface, he finds but four thousand, and the Printer put *quadringentis millibus,* instead of *quatuor millibus.*

WHEN it was found, that neither the remonstrances of the learned, nor their sarcasms continually printed against such Printers, could prevail upon them to be more diligent, and procure better correctors ; several countries took methods of putting a stop to this growing evil. *Spain* was, I think, the first which shew'd the example, by a way to

---

* ———— opus hoc locis non paucioribus quam quadringentis millibus emaculatius atque olim, nunc demum in lucem prodire.

make

make the compofer and corrector more careful in their refpective provinces. It was order'd, that before a book could be fold, it fhould
be examin'd by cenfors appointed for that purpofe, and compar'd with
the manufcript; and that all the faults of the impreffion fhould be fet
down in the firft leaft; after which they were to write underneath, that
the book, the faults of the impreffion above noted excepted, was faithfully printed. This certificate had generally the following title in *Spanifh.*
Efta efte libro bien impreffo y corretto conforme a fu original de mano. En
Madrid, &c. fign'd N. N. It was fometimes printed in *Latin.* Where
they could not obtain fuch an order, they follow'd the *Spanifh* method as
far as they could. Thus *Jo. Ravifius Textor,* profeffor of rhetorick
at *Paris,* made a kind of affidavit, that he had corrected all the errata
of the dialogue of *Henry Hutten,* intitled *Aula,* printed at *Paris* in
1519, by *Antony Auffurd,* who put under the title-page. *Textor ema-*
culavit. The fame method was follow'd by *Henry Stephens,* who in
his edition of the *Pimander* of *Hermes Trifmegiftus,* printed in 1505,
publifh'd by *James Fabry d'Eftaples,* has fet down the names of the
correctors in thefe words; *Parifiis ex officinâ Henrici Stephani, recog-*
nitoribus mendafque ex officinâ eluentibus Jacobo folido Cracovienfi & Vol-
gatio Pratenfi, anno 1505. We could trace this method as far as the beginning of the 15th century; which had this good effect, that thofe
books, in which the correctors had put their names, were always preferr'd to thofe where no mention was made of any. There were afterwards better regulations obtain'd from the higher powers in every
kingdom, in order to abolifh thefe pernicious abufes; but as they do
not come within our epoch, we fhall forbear mentioning them.

T H E reader will excufe me, if I fo far digrefs from my fubject, as
to give an inftance or two of the dangerous confequences, which had
like to have happen'd to two eminent writers of that age, to the one
by the addition, and to the other by the fubftraction of a fingle letter.
The firft is of *Erafmus,* who in his paraphrafe on ch. 16, v.   of S.
Matthew, where S. *Peter* fays, *Tu es Chriftus Filius Dei vivi,* had written, *Non fufpicione proferens, fed certa & indubitata fcientia profitens,*
illum effe Meffiam a prophetis promiffum, fingulari more Filium Dei. &c.
by which laft words he only meant, as he afterwards explain'd it, that
Chrift

Chrift was the fon of God after a particular manner, different from that which was common to men. But it happen'd, that in his *Bafil* edition printed by *Froben*, the letter *a* being added to *more*, made it have a quite different fenfe. Hereupon *Noel Beda*, a famous divine of *Paris*, and enemy to *Erafmus*, fail'd not to take him to task for that expreffion, and charg'd him with having affirm'd, that Chrift was only the fon of God by adoption, and by a particular love of God towards him (*fingulari amore*) and not his eternal fon, *&c.* Soon after which, the divines of *Paris* publifh'd a cenfure of that propofition to the following tenour ; *That it gave a falfe fenfe to the words of the Evangelift, and a handle to men, to think wrong of the divinity of the Son of God, as* Neftorius *had done* ; *for that Chrift was not the Son of God* by any particular love of *God towards him, nor by any adoption or favour, but that he was originally and neceffarily fo. Erafmus* clear'd himfelf by faying, that it was a fault of the impreffion, and appeal'd to his original and former edition of the fame paraphrafe, in which they would find the word *more*, inftead of *amore* ; but he was too much fufpected by thofe gentlemen, to be eafily believ'd either in this, or any other cafe.

The other happen'd to the learned Dr. *Flavigny*, author of fome letters againft Mr. *Jay's* polyglot, in which two learned *Maronites* had been employ'd by Mr. *Jay*, viz. *Abraham Echellenfis*, Regius profeffor of *Syriac* and *Arabic*, who had given the text and *Latin* verfion of thofe two languages of the book of *Ruth* ; and *Gabriel Sionita*, profeffor of the fame languages. The former of thefe had committed a great many errors in his tranflation, as well as in the text of that book, neverthelefs he attack'd his brother *Maronite*, and charg'd him with fome miftakes in his part of the work. Hereupon Dr. *Flavigny*, who knew them both equally guilty, undertook to rebuke the aggreffor ; and in a letter to him *(Echellenfis)*, made ufe of thefe words of our Saviour ; *Quid vides feftucam in oculo fratris tui?* (why beholdeft thou the mote in thy brother's eye?) *&c.* It happen'd unfortunately, that the firft letter of the word *oculo* being either taken up by the balls, or dropt out of the form, or fome other way loft, after the firft proofs had been corrected, gave a very harfh found to it, and made it feem a profane jefting upon that facred book. *Echellenfis*, in his anfwer,

took

took notice of this, and calls him a facrilegious and *Jewish* perverter of the holy text; and, without acquainting him with his faults, tells him, that fuch an abominable correction of the text, was too foul for his pen, and only worthy the writings of a *Flavigny*; in fhort, he fpends near a whole page in the moft opprobrious language againft him, that the height of malice and refentment could infpire an inveterate antagonift with. Dr. *Flavigny* was a long time before he could difcover the caufe of this accufation, and in all probability might have been ftill longer ignorant of it, had not a friend of his fhew'd it to him in the printed copy; for in the two firft proofs the word was printed perfect. The refult was, that the author being recover'd of his furprize, threw the fault upon the corrector, appeal'd to his original, and to the two firft proofs, protefted his innocency and abhorrence of fuch an action, and took a folemn oath, in order to clear himfelf. *Chevilier*, who relates this ftory, tells us, that *Flavigny*, fome time before his death, happen'd to mention this; and tho' it was above 30 years after this tranfaction, he could not forbear expreffing the higheft indignation againft his Printer and corrector. Thefe inftances fufficiently demonftrate the dangerous confequences of neglect in correcting to the author of any book, efpecially in divinity.

BEFORE I difmifs this article of the incorrectnefs of the prefs, I cannot but mention fome of the greateft Printers; who, when any of their editions have happen'd to be incorrect, have made an ingenuous confeffion of, and apology for it, that the commonwealth of learning might not receive any difadvantage by it, nor the authors fuffer in their reputation thro' their neglect. I fhall begin with *Martin Schurrer*, of *Strasburgh*, allow'd by *Erafmus* to be a perfon of learning, who printed in 1500 the treatife *De Patientia* of *Bapt. Mantuanus*. But as he had committed the care of it to a negligent and ignorant corrector, he found himfelf oblig'd to add an errata of a page and half to it, which he prefaces in the humbleft terms imaginable *; I rather choofe, fays he, to take the fhame of them upon myfelf, by confeffing my fault, than to let the republick of learning fuffer by

---

* Maluimus potius pudore, noftro fatendo damno noftra peccata fint. plecti, quam tacendo refpublica literarai fuo

my

my concealment of it. Of this kind is the apology which the fame Printer makes for the errors of impreffion in an edition before mentioned, *viz.* the works of *Picus de Mirandula*; wherein he defires the reader, * that he would not attribute thofe errors to the author, but to the Printer, who frankly confeffes his fault. Such errata's not only make fome kind of reparations to the authors, but oblige likewife an honeft Printer to be more careful for the future. *Henry Stephens* hath often taken the fame method, and owns, that fome errors have crept unawares into fome of his editions †. I fhould digrefs too far, if I fhould inftance in all thofe Printers, who have follow'd fo good an example; 'tis fufficient to fay, that none of thofe eminent ones, of whom we have given an account in this whole book, have ever been afham'd of acknowledging the faults of their works, when they had any fhare in them. I fhall clofe this with a pleafant way, which the abovemention'd *Stephens* took to correct a fault in his edition *De præfagiis in morbis acutis* of *Hippocrates, anno* 1512. 'Tis obvious to every fcholar, that the firft fyllable in the word *Febris* (a fever or ague) may be either long or fhort; but he having thro' inadvertency fpelt the word with œ, which made it abfolutely long, he corrects himfelf for it, by faying, ‡ *That the Printer had foolifhly chofen a long fever, when a fhort one was much more eligible, as being lefs dangerous.*

But after all that hath been faid concerning the bafenefs, negligence, and ignorance of fome of the Printers of thofe times, it muft be own'd, that many a negligent and ignorant author, when he has been admonifh'd of his errors, hath not fcrupled to throw them upon the Printer and corrector; which I efteem another abufe of the Art of Printing. I could give many inftances of it, were I not apprehenfive of betraying too great a fondnefs for our profeffion. However, any judicious reader will eafily perceive by the largeft Errata's which we have mention'd, that the authors had as great a fhare in them as the

---

* Errores chalcographis, non authori adfcribito. Fatemur ingenuè culpam noftram.
† Locis aliquot incuria noftra aberrotum eft.

‡ Febrem longam fibi chalcographus delegit' tametfi febris correpta fit minus periculofa,

Printers.

Printers and correctors. *Chevilier*, who cannot be suspected of partiality to the latter, has excus'd them in many cases, and shewn that the fault was rather to be imputed to the former. But he has furnish'd me with an instance of this, which, I believe, he little thought of ; in the case of a learned divine of the university of *Paris*, whose works having been censur'd by that body, and he refusing to retract them, he was expell'd that university, but was afterwards prevail'd upon to recant. After his death a paper was publish'd in his name, in which the blame was laid upon the protestant Printers, to whom he had intrusted the work. I shall relate the story exactly after Chevilier, tho' somewhat abridg'd, and leave the reader to judge, whether the wrong persons were not unjustly blam'd. I hope the singularity of the fact will sufficiently excuse me, tho' it is of later date, than our prefix'd period.

René Benoist, D. D. curate of S. *Eustace* at *Paris*, made a *French* version of the bible, which he caus'd to be printed in fol. ann. 1566 by three eminent booksellers of that city. This book immediately met with many opposers, who censur'd it as heretical and erroneous, alledging, that it was only the *Geneva* translation; in which the author had soften'd those expressions which were most shocking to the Roman Catholicks. The divines of that university, having met several times, agreed to censure the book, which they did accordingly, *July* 15, 1567. The same censure was renew'd, and subscrib'd to, by seventy three doctors of that faculty, and approv'd *viva voce* by above one hundred and twenty more about 7 years after. *Gregory* XII. confirm'd the censure, and condemn'd the book, by a brief dated *Nov.* 3. 1475. During this, *Benoist* absolutely refused to submit, in spite of all the endeavours of that body to persuade him to it. At length they agreed upon expelling him that university as an obstinate heretick, and the sentence of his proscription was written in great letters, and set up in the common disputation-hall of the university, by which he was, as it were, executed *in effigie*. However, *Henry* IV. took him into favour, made him his confessor, and promoted him to a bishoprick ; but the Pope refus'd to grant him his bull. At last, his seniority entitling him to be chosen dean of the faculty, they all refus'd their votes, unless he would submit to their former censures, which he was at length oblig'd to do by a recantation,

in

in which he condemns his verſion, and rejects ſome parts of it as being falſly attributed to him. This was not done till the year 1598,
i. e. 32 years after the publication of it.

In 1608, a little before *Benoiſt's* death, came out a book in 8vo,
intitled, *A declaration of* René Benoiſt, *concerning his tranſlation of the
bible and annotations thereupon* ; in which he declares,

, That the ground of all his ſorrow was the treachery of the cor-
, rector, compoſer and preſs-man, who had been intruſted with the
, impreſſion of his bible ; that the copy which he had given them was a
, printed one (*here* Chevilier *notes, that it was a* Geneva *one*,) upon which
, he had made his corrections and eraſements, which were not ſo fully
, eras'd, but that they might be eaſily read :

, THAT ſome of the journeymen (*they did not dare publickly to at-
, tack their maſters, who would in all probability have clear'd themſelves*)
, were of the *Geneva* leaven, and printed nothing in the firſt and ſe-
, cond proofs but what was in his copy ; but when they came to the
, third, which he did not ſee, they ſubſtituted, inſtead of his corrections,
, the words or notes, which he had eras'd (*ſome inſtances of which the
, author of the book gives*), and which the compoſer and preſs-man in
, confederacy had maliciouſly falſify'd :

, That it were tedious to enumerate all ſuch pieces of treachery ;
, but that the reſult of it turn'd to his reputation, notwithſtanding his
, unſucceſsful attempts to bring thoſe journeymen to puniſhment:

, That his books had been ſold under his name, tho' he had diſown'd
, them :

, That the cenſure of the univerſity, and the confirmation of it by
, the court of *Rome*, which had condemn'd the work, and not the au-
, thor, was the conſequence of this impoſture, *&c.* '

I SHALL not enter into a detail of the reflections which *Chevilier*
makes upon the *Calviniſt* Printers, as he calls them, nor enquire whether this declamation was really penn'd by *Benoiſt*, or father'd upon
him ; or if the former, whether it might not be extorted from him, a
practice not unuſual with the divines of that church. I ſhall only obſerve, that, were the caſe as it is related in that pamphlet, 'tis ſcarce
credible, that the doctor could have been 30 years unappris'd of it,

Q q

eſpe-

especially when the censures and libels, continually publish'd against him, sufficiently pointed it out to him; and if he knew it, can it be imagin'd that he would have continued so long under all that scandal, and the persecution of his enemies, when he might have easily clear'd himself of the one, and so put a stop effectually to the other? Upon the whole, whoever the author of this declaration is, this story evidently confutes itself, and is no other than one of their pious frauds, on which 'tis not my province to animadvert, any further than the credit of our profession is concern'd.

BEFORE I close this chapter, it will be necessary to remind the reader, that this second book being wholly confin'd to the history of printing in other parts of *Europe,* (what relates to our nation being the subject of the next book,) I have given none but foreign instances of the corruptions and abuses introduced into this art.

'TIS not therefore to be concluded, that it hath been free in any case from them in *England*; since we have imitated our neighbours in these bad, as well as in their other good, examples; and therefore as these abuses have been equally common to us and them, I shall not repeat them in the *English* part, but only request the reader, once for all, to remember, that we have had our share as well in the disadvantages, under which our art has labour'd, as in the advantages and improvements, which it has receiv'd.

APPEN-

APPENDIX.

An Account of a newly difcover'd Edition, printed by John Guttenberg *at* Stratzburg *in* 1458, *communicated to me by, and now in the poffeffion of, the Right Honourable the Earl of* Pembroke.

THE reader may be pleafed to recollect that I have, throughout the firft book of this hiftory, conftantly endeavour'd to fix the glory of the invention of Printing upon *John Fauft*, and that of the improvements of it upon his worthy fon-in-law *Peter Scheoffer*, exclufive of *John Guttenberg*, notwithftanding the teftimony of fome few writers who have afcribed the firft difcoveries to the latter. I did likewife offer it as a probable conjecture of the ingenious Mr. *Maittair*, that *Guttenberg*, having been caft in a law-fuit at *Mentz* for non-folvency of his quota, might retire to *Stratzburgh*, and there teach *John Mentel*, what he had been able to learn of *Fauft*'s art. We had not till then the leaft ground to conjecture that he ever practifed it himfelf, no annalift that ever I could meet with ever mentioning, or perhaps dreaming of, any edition printed with his name. But fince then the noble lord abovemention'd, unwilling to reft fatisfy'd with conjectures, has fpared no pains or coft to inform himfelf whether there was any impreffion extant done by *Guttenberg*, and has at length procured this curious one, which his lordfhip has been pleafed to communicate to me. The reader, I doubt not, will be highly fatisfy'd to find that, inftead of contradicting any thing I have advanc'd upon that fubject, it rather confirms it all beyond any poffibility of doubting.

THE book is the dialogues of St. *Gregory* in *Latin*, it has no titlepage, but begins abruptly with the fubject itfelf, only at the end of it are thefe words ;

Explicit liber quartus
Dyalogor 4 Gregorii.

Q q 2

Then

Then follows in red letters,

Prefens hoc Op? factum eft per Johan.
Guttenbergium apud Argentinam,
Anno Millefimo c c c c l v i i j.

I sʜᴀʟʟ now beg leave to make a few remarks on this curious
piece, and to fhew how manifeftly it confirms all my former conjectures.

　　1. Iᴛ is very rude, and comes vaftly fhort of thofe of *Fauft* and
Scheoffer; and the great and almoft conftant difference of the fhapes
of the fame letters, fhews it to have been done upon wooden blocks,
after the manner of the *paginæ conglutinatæ* mention'd above, *pag.* 49 *&*
feq. there is, however, this difference and improvement in it, that it is
not printed with the fame (that is with the) common Ink, which made
them incapable of a reiteration, *i. e.* of being printed but upon one
fide, but with the new invented fort, which was a mixture of oil-var-
nifh and lamp-black, and will bear printing on both fides. This, therefore, fhews that he had only got an infight into the firft difcovery, but
was an utter ftranger to the laft and more ufeful one of feparate metal-
types, which *Fauft* had probably kept conceal'd from him.

　　2. Sᴜᴘᴘᴏsɪɴɢ it to be the firft piece that ever he did, as it probably was, if not the only one of that kind, it was printed in 1458,
i. e. about three years after the law-fuit and his falling out with *Fauft*;
fo that it took him up all that time in cutting his blocks, and getting
the reft of the apparatus of a Printing-prefs, making of tryals, maculatures, *&c.* after he was fettled at *Stratzburgh.*

　　3. Iᴛ is printed one year after the pfalter of *Mentz*, which was done
in feparate metal-types, and wherein *Fauft* and *Scheoffer* affume to themfelves the whole glory of the invention; fo that had *Guttenberg* had the
leaft pretenfion to it, he would not have fail'd doing himfelf juftice by
altering the ftyle of his colophon, and telling the world what fhare he
had borne in this noble difcovery, that his filence was not owing to
his honefty is plain from his refufing to pay his dividend of the charges,
much lefs to his being ignorant of the publication of *Fauft*'s pfalter, becaufe *Mentz* and *Stratzburgh* being both fituate upon the *Rhine,* and not
above 60 leagues afunder, it was morally impoffible he fhould not have
heard

heard of it. On the contrary, it is likely that, having feen it, and obferv'd it to be printed with fufile types, he might juft finifh this rude
edition of his, and then ftop his hand until *Mentel* and he had fallen
upon the fame way of cafting them.

4. THIS piece is printed upon the fame paper that *Fauft* did ufe,
which is mark'd with the heifer's head and horns, and might either be
his fhare of the paper-ftock which they divided at parting, and which
he took away with him, or elfe might be defignedly imitated by him,
to give a credit to his work. Upon the whole, its having neither title-
page, running title, fignature, nor direction-word, and being altogether
a rude piece of workmanfhip, doth plainly fhew it to have been of the
nature of the firft effays of *Fauft*, and that it is by no means antedated.

*A Catalogue of fome of the moft eminent Perfons, Authors
and Editors, &c. who condefcended to prepare MSS. and
to correct for the Prefs during the 15th Century, with the
Character of fome of the moft confiderable of them.*

At BASIL *for* JOHN AMERBACK.

1. JOHN CAPNIO, *alias Reuchlin,* an eminent lawyer, who had
ftudied at *Paris* under the famous *John de Lapide,* doctor of *Sorbonne,* at whofe requeft he wrote three books *de verbo mirifico.* He
wrote another treatife which he entitled *Oculare Speculum,* for which the
univerfities of *Cologn, Mentz, Louvain,* and *Erphord* condemn'd him of
Herefy and Judaifm, and made preffing inftances to that of *Paris* to
do the fame. To prevent which, *Reuchlin* wrote to the doctors of *Sorbonne,* and reminded them, that he had been *Lapidanus*'s difciple, and
that the univerfity of *Paris* was his dear mother : but, as all his rhetorick
could not prevent his book being cenfur'd by the *Paris* divines, he calls
her afterwards an unnatural ftep-mother. He was one of the moft diligent promoters of the ftudy of *Hebrew,* of which himfelf was a good
mafter, tho' he did not learn it of *Lapidanus,* as fome have imagin'd,
but

but from a *Jewiſh* rabbi, call'd *Jacob Jehiel Loans,* to whom therefore he directs a letter inſcrib'd as follows, *Johannes Reuchlin præceptori ſuo Jacobo Jehiel Loans Judæo, &c.* it is likely, therefore, that after his ſquabble with thoſe univerſities he retir'd to *Baſil,* where he became corrector to the great *Amerback,* who was himſelf a very learned man, and had taken his degrees of maſter of arts in the univerſity of *Paris. Vide pag.* 218.

2. JOHN CONN. CONUS, a native of *Nurembergh,* famous for his ſkill in the *Greek* and *Latin* tongues.

3. AUGUSTIN DODO, a learned canon of *Baſil,* who, dying of the plague in 1513, was ſucceeded by

4. FRANCIS WILER, a learned franciſcan.

5. CONRARD PELICAN, an eminent divine, and

6. BEATUS RHENANUS.

For JOHN FROBEN, *ibid.*

1 PETER CASTELLANUS.

2. SIGISMUND GELENIUS.

3. MARK HEILAND.

4. DES. ERASMUS of *Rotterdam.*

5. WOLFGANG MUSCULUS.

6. JOHN OECOLAMPADIUS.

7. WOLFGANG LACHNER.

ALL theſe are ſufficiently known to the learned, eſpecially the 4th, 5th, and 6th.

At BOLONIA.

BENEDICT HECTOR and both eminent and learned, who printed
PLATO DEI BENEDETI, $\}$ and corrected their own works.

At BRESCIA *for* BONINO DE BONINIS.

MARCUS SCARAMUCCINUS, a native of *Palazolo* in the territories of *Breſcia.*

For

For James *and* Angel Britannici, *ibid.*

Angelus de Montelmo, a learned francifcan.

At FLORENCE.

Demetrius Calcondilla, a native of *Milan*, printed and corrected that noble and beautiful edition of *Homer*'s works, fol. in 1480, of which I have given an account above, pag. 196. He corrected many other *Greek* and *Latin* works, and at length went and fet up a prefs in his own native city, where he continued printing and correcting for himfelf.

For Franc. Laurence *de* Alopa, *ibid.*

John Andreas Lascaris, a famous critick in the *Greek* and *Latin* tongues. He was defcended from an illuftrious family in *Greece*, which gave birth to three *Greek* emperors. After the taking of *Conftantinople* by the *Turks*, he retired into *Italy*, and fome time after went into *France*, whence he was fent embaffador to the republick of *Venice* by *Lewis* XII. As he was thoroughly verfed in all the antient authors of his own nation, he fpared no pains to procure the beft manufcripts from thence, to compare, correct, and fit them either for the Prefs, or for tranflating into *Latin.* He was in fuch credit with *Francis* I. that *Genebrard* tells us, that he and the great *Budæus* perfuaded that monarch to erect that noble library in his own palace of *Fontainbleau*, and to found a college at *Paris* for the royal profeffors in the learned languages. He is alfo fuppofed to have been the corrector, if not the editor, of that noble edition of *Avicen*, which was printed at *Lyons* by *Trechfel* and *Clean* in 1498, in 3 vol. fol. to which he prefixed a dedication to Dr. *Ponceau* the king's phyfician. *Erafmus* thinks it a kind of miracle that any *Greeks* fhould ever become fuch mafters of the *Latin* tongue as he and his two countrymen *Marcus Mufurus*, of whom we fhall fpeak by and by, and *Theodore Gaza* proved.

A

At LYONS *for* JOHN TRECHSEL.

THE famous *Jodocus Badius,* firnamed *Afcenfius,* who became afterwards one of the moft eminent Printers.

At MILAN *for* ANTONY ZAROT.

PETER JUSTINUS PHILELPHUS.

For LEONARD PACHEL, *ibid.*

BENEDICT, firnamed *Rhetoricus.*

At NAPLES *for* MATT. MORAVIUS.

JUNIANUS MAJO, profeffor of grammar and rhetorick.

At NUREMBERG *for* ANT. COBURGER.

THE learned *Frederick Piftorius.*

At PARIS *for* ULRICK GERING *and his two Affociates.*

JOHN LAPIDANUS, or *a Lapide,* doctor of *Sorbonne,* and a great promoter of learning. *Vide fupra pag.* 166, & *feq.*

WILLIAM FICHET, a native of *Aulney* in *Normandy* ; he was doctor of divinity, and fellow of the college of *Sorbonne. Vide fupra ib.*

ERHARD WINDSBERGH, doctor of phyfick in the univerfity of *Paris.*

For ULRICK GERING *and* BERTOLD REMBOLT, *ibid.*

THE learned *John Capuis,* editor of the *Corpus Juris Canonici,* with the glofs, fhort notes, index, &c. printed by *Gering* and his affociate in 3 vol. fol. in 1501. This was a moft elaborate and expenfive work, every page being charged with letters ranked in five or fix columns, and mix'd with red and black. This edition was fo highly liked, that it was prefently fold off, and a new one of a fmaller fize came out foon after.

At

At ROME *for* CONRARD SWEYNHEYM *and* ARNOLD PANNARTZ.

1. JOHN ANDREAS, bifhop of *Valeria*, and library-keeper to pope *Sixtus* IV. He wrote fome learned comments on the IVth, Vth, and VIth book of decretals, and gave the world the firft edition of *Pliny's* natural hiftory, in correcting of which he had fpent nine whole years. We have likewife a volume of his letters which are very curious, and the book itfelf fcarce. His province was to furnifh thefe two *German* Printers with the moft valuable manufcripts out of the *Vatican* and other libraries, to compare, correct, and prepare for the prefs, and then to revife the fheets as faft as they came out. All which he perform'd with indefatigable application. *Vide fupra pag.* 123, *&c.* He dy'd in 1470, and was fucceeded by

2. BARTHOLOMEW (by others call'd *Baptift*) *Platina*, famous for his hiftory of the popes.

For ULRICK HAN *or* GALLUS, *ibid.*

1. JOHN ANTONY CAMPANUS, bifhop of *Teramo*. This prelate undertook the fame province for *Han* that the bifhop of *Valeria* did for *Sweynheym* and *Pannartz, viz.* to procure, correct, and prepare for the prefs, and to revife the proofs. He was alfo at the pains and charges of collecting the *Latin* tranflations of *Plutarch's* lives, which till then did lay difpers'd, and by pieces among other manufcripts; and publifh'd the firft edition of it in two vol. fol. it has neither date, place, or Printer's name, and is dedicated by *Campanus* to Cardinal *Piccolomini*. In all thefe provinces he was fo diligent and affiduous that he fcarce allow'd himfelf time to eat, and not above three hours to fleep. He dy d in 1477, in the 50th year of his age, and was fucceeded by

2. CHARLES *de Alexandris.*

For Eucharius Silber, *ibid.*

1. Bartholomew *de Salicetis.*
2. Ludovicus *de Regiis.*
3. Michel Fern, firnamed *Archipoeta,* editor of bifhop *Campanus*'s works, and a fevere fatyrift againft carelefs and incorrect Printers, plagiaries, *&c.*

For George Laver, *ibid.*

1. Celestine Pulverinus.
2. Pomponius.

At TREVISO *for* Mich. Manzoli *al.* Manzolini.

Jerome Bonini.

For Bartholom. Consoloneri, *ibid.*

Bartholomew Perot.

At VENICE *for* Nicolas Jenson.

Omnibonus Laodicenus, a native of *Vincentia,* famous for his learned comments upon feveral antient authors. He revifed and corrected fome of *Cicero*'s works, as likewife *Quintiliani Oratoriarum Inftitutionum libri,* fol. which were printed by *Jenfon* in 1471, with this colophon, *Quintilianum Eloquentiæ fontem ab eruditiffimo Omnibono Laodiceno emendatum, M. Nicolaus Jenfon miro impreffit artificio, &c.*

For Vindelin *de* Spira, *ibid.*

Georgius Alexandrinus, *&*
Christophorus Berardus *de Pefauro.*

For

For Christopher Wardaffer, *ibid.*

The famous *Ludovicus Carbo,* who is said to have corrected his proofs with red ink, from which one might be led to conclude that they had not yet got the method of writing their corrections on the margin of the proof.

For Bernard Pictor *and* Erhard Radolt, *ibid.*

Peter Loslein *de Langencen,* who, from being their corrector, became their partner, and afterwards set up a Printing-house of his own.

For Antony *della* Strada, *ibid.*

Victor Pisanus.

For Peter Veronensis, *ibid.*

Jerome Centone of *Padua.*

For Philip Pinci, *ibid.*

Benedict Brugnoli, famed for his great skill in the *Greek* and *Latin* tongues.

For Ald. P. Manucius, *ibid.*

1. Peter Alcion.
2. Demetrius Calcondilla, mentioned above.
3. Alexander Bandinus.
4. Benedict Tyrenus, and
5. Marcus Musurus, who was a native of *Candia,* and became a famous professor of the *Greek* and *Latin* tongues in the university of *Padua,* and for his great learning and merit was afterwards made bishop of *Ragusium.* We have already mention'd what *Erasmus* said of him and his Countrymen *Lascaris* and *Theod. Gaza,* concerning their great skill in *Greek* and *Latin*; to which *Beat. Rhenanus* adds in his *Vita E-*

rafmi, that he was a man of fuch extenfive reading and profound erudition, that there was nothing fo obfcure and intricate which he could not render plain and eafy by his eloquence. *Ald. Manucius* doth likewife commend him very highly not only for his vaft learning, but alfo for his indefatigable diligence and accuracy in comparing and correcting antient manufcripts, both *Greek* and *Latin,* and fitting them for the prefs. Upon which account the care and correction of that noble edition of the *Etymologicon Magnum,* printed at *Venice* by *Zachary Caliergiu,* in 1499, was committed to him.

For B E N E T L O C A T E L L I, *ibid.*

M A U R I C I U S *de Hibernia,* afterwards bifhop of *Tuamo..*

At V I N C E N T I A, *for* H E R M A N L E V I L A P I S.

A E N E A S W O L P I U S, prior of the convent of the Holy Crofs.

I H A V E only mention'd fome of the moft famous for their learning and diligence, befides whom there were many more, who, tho' of an infe rior clafs, in comparifon of the former ; yet were all men of letters, and vaftly fuperior to thofe, which Printers have been forced to make ufe o in procefs of time. It muft be alfo remember'd, that many of thof Printers of the 15th, and part of the 16th century, were men of grea learning and parts, and indefatigable induftry, able to prepare thei manufcripts for the prefs, and to correct their own works : Such wer the great *Amerback* at *Bafil,* who was mafter of arts in the univerfity c *Paris, Froben* his worthy partner and fucceffor, *Ant. Coburger* at *Nurem bergh, Aldus Manucius* and *Azulanus* at *Venice, Jodocus Badius* at *Lyor* and *Paris,* and many more, of whom we have given an account in th hiftory. And yet it is obfervable from this table, that thofe, who wer the moft capable of correcting their own works, did ftill entertain th greateft number of correctors.

H O W E V E R, I muft not omit acquainting the readers, that tho great perfons whom we have mention'd in this lift, were not proper correctors in the fenfe we now underftand that word ; that is, men r

tain'

tain'd by a proper falary to perform that function, but editors or authors, and correctors only of their own works; or if at any time they
were prevail'd upon to overfee any curious edition, it was done rather
out of curiofity than for gain. For 'tis certain that every Printer had
befides a corrector of an inferior rank to revife and correct every proof,
if he did not do it himfelf, before they were fent to thofe great men,
whofe corrections were generally of a higher nature. What makes me
mention this diftinction, is the grief which the famous *Erafmus* conceiv'd
at his being upbraided by count *Carpi*, and more particularly by *Jul.*
Scaliger, with having ferv'd as corrector in *Aldus*'s Printing-houfe, and
the pains he took to clear himfelf from that imputation. Every body
knows that *Erafmus* had ventur'd to print a dialogue, entitled *Ciceronia-*
nus, in which he endeavour'd to fhew that *Cicero* was more cry'd up
than he deferv'd; at which *Scaliger* was fo enraged, that he wrote a vindication of that great mafter of eloquence in two different orations,
which he foon after printed. In the laft of which he addreffes himfelf
to *Erafmus* in words to this effect ; *Did not you get a livelihood by cor-*
recting Aldus's *proofs? and were not thofe errata we meet with in them*
more owing to your drunken careleffnefs than to the Printer? do they not
fmell ftronger of your drunken cups than of the compofer's dulnefs? He afterwards affirm'd that he met with *Aldus* one day at *Mantua*, who told
him that *Erafmus* was wont to difpatch as much bufinefs in one day as
other correctors did in two, and to folace himfelf the reft of the time
with drinking of good *Malmfy* wine. *Erafmus* was fo gall'd at this oration, that, as *Merula* tells us, he bought and burnt all the copies he could
poffibly get of it, and that he fucceeded fo well that there was not one
to be met with. However, in his anfwer to count *Carpi*, he fays that
he was fo far from correcting for *Aldus*, unlefs it were his own works,
that he refufed that office to fome eminent cardinals who defired him to
revife the laft proofs of fome works then printing : that if he took any
thing elfe in hand, whilft he ftaid at *Venice*, it was not for lucre, but
out of curiofity ; and acquaints us, that *Aldus* had a conftant corrector
to his prefs named *Seraphim*, and then adds, *Can he be call'd a fervant*
who revifes only his own works? for I never did any thing elfe for Aldus,
whofe Printing-houfe I ufed only for my conveniency. He has likewife been
fup-

fuppofed to have corrected for *Theodore Martin* at *Louvain*, but it is likely that it was in the fame manner, and on the fame foot as he did it at *Venice*. I had not dwelt fo long on this nice diftinction, were it not that thofe annalifts, who have mention'd thefe great and learned men as correctors, have not fufficiently taken notice of it. Befides, it ought to be confider'd that there is a vaft difference between Printing and correcting the works of antient authors after a number of manufcripts, which have been mutilated and fpoil'd by every hand through which they pafs'd ; and Printing the works of a modern author after his own manufcript-copy, who is at hand either to revife it, or to be confulted upon any difficulty. The former province requires perfons of the greateft learning, abilities, and moft indefatigable application, in reading and comparing their manufcripts, in order to diftinguifh between the genuine meaning of an author and the blunders of his tranfcribers ; whereas the latter may be fupply'd by a perfon of moderate parts and induftry. As therefore, they have been the greateft promoters of learning, I hope the reader will not blame me, if I have endeavour'd to do them all poffible juftice, and to diftinguifh them from thofe lazy and ignorant ones who have been, and are ftill, juftly reckon'd the common pefts of it.

The End of the Second Book.

The EDITOR to the READER.

SOON *after Mr.* Palmer's *death, I was defired to fee what was ftill wanting to compleat his* Hiftory *of* Printing, *according to his firft propofal, and what materials he had left behind. I found, upon enquiry, that five fheets of this laft Number were already printed off; but that the third fheet in courfe, viz.* Q q, *was left unfinifh'd, being partly compos'd, and partly in manufcript, moft likely in expectation of that curious edition which the R. H. the Earl of* Pembroke *was then in search after, which has been mention'd in the Appendix to this second Book ; and this seems to have been the cause of his delaying this last Number so long, that his last sickness prevented his publishing it.*

The reader will, no doubt, be as much surprised as I was myself, at finding the last page of the second book and the first of the third book so differently numbred ; and that there is a retrogression from 312 *to* 121 : *but, as the signatures of each sheet do follow in their regular course, I am fully persuaded that it must have been an oversight either of the compositor or of the author, which we hope the reader will easily forgive, especially considering that there is not any thing wanting to compleat this second book ; and that the materials he left behind do even exceed his computation for filling this suspended sheet. However, as there were but three sheets thus mis-number'd, having been printed off long before the author's death, I have ventured to set all the remaining ones in their due order, to avoid the confusion that would otherwise unavoidably happen in the Index ; and hope the reader will be kind enough to do the same with his pen to these three following sheets. Those, who know what a tedious sickness Mr.* Palmer *did labour under during the last two years of his life, will pass by so inconsiderable an oversight, in consideration of what he has done when he enjoy'd a better state of health. As for the rest of this History, we hope to find the materials in so good an order, that there will be little to do but to print after his manuscript, excepting where the noble Lord above-mention'd, or some of his learned correspondents, have communicated some new discoveries too curious to be passed by. And this furnishes me with an opportunity of adding a new authority to what has been before advanc'd, concerning the first invention of Printing by* John Fauft *at* Mentz, *omitted by Mr.* Palmer, *and since communicated to me by an ingenious friend of his. It is a paragraph extracted out of* Fox's *book of martyrs, printed in* 1537, *page* 837, *wherein that learned author gives an account of the first discovery of that art, in all the main particulars exactly agreeable to what has been advanc'd in the first part of this History, and is to this purpose ; That about the year* 1440, *or, as others affirm,* 1446 *and* 1450, *one* John Fauft *of* Strarzburg, *and since a citizen of* Mentz, *found out the way of Printing by engraving upon metals, and by degrees improv'd it to cutting of single words, and at length*
single

fingle letters: that, after fome effays, he communicated his difcovery to John
Guttenberg *and* Peter Scheoffer *; and thefe three, being firft fworn to in-
violable fecrecy, made fome confiderable improvements in it: that* Guttenberg *did at length, with* John Mentel, *publifh the art at* Stratzburg,
*which was foon after brought to greater perfeftion by fome eminent Printers
in other places; and in particular by* Ulrick Han, *or* Gallus, *at* Rome,
&c. *From this fhort account it is plain that our* Englifh *author had his
intelligence from much better hands than many of the writers that have been
quoted on that fubjeft; and it is no fmall pity that he, who has fo exaftly
informed himfelf with what had been done at* Mentz, *had not given us alfo
an account of the introduftion and progrefs of the art here in* England, *we
might then have found a much more fatisfaftory account of it, than the
reader will find in the next book from all that* Mr. Palmer *could poffibly
procure from other authors and records. However, as to this teftimony, I
doubt not but he would have been glad to have given it an honourable place
in his firft book, had he been apprifed of it; but it is not much to be wonder'd at, that a book of martyrs fhould be one of the laft pieces of hiftory
wherein one would have look'd for it. What Dr.* Fox *fays of their cutting
or engraving upon metal, and not upon wood, as Mr.* Palmer *and others
have fince more truly affirmed, can be only look'd upon as a pardonable
miftake in the former, who could not be expefted to be a judge of things of
this nature; whereas, what the latter advances may be furely rely'd on,
not only becaufe it was in his own province, and that he neither wanted
opportunities, nor fpared any pains to inform himfelf aright in all thofe
curious particulars, but alfo becaufe his modefty would not fuffer him to rely
upon his own judgment, till he had it confirm'd by other eminent mafters in
the art of* Printing, letter-cutting, &c.

G. P.

BOOK

BOOK III.

OF

ENGLISH PRINTING

AND

PRINTERS.

CHAP. I.

Of the Art's being firſt brought to England.

ALL our *Engliſh* hiſtorians and chroniclers, who have touch'd on this ſubjeƈt before *Richard Atkins*, viz. *Stowe, Baker, Howel*, &c. have proceeded only upon conjeƈture or common and fallacious reports ; or perhaps the firſt of theſe forementioned authors led the reſt into theſe miſtakes, that printing was not invented till the year 1459, nor brought into *England* till *anno*

1471 ; that at the *Abbey* of *Westminster* the first presses were set up ; that Dr *Islip*, *Abbot* of *Westminster*, first introduc'd the art into *England* ; and that *England* had it at least 10 years before any other city of *Europe*, except *Mentz* and *Harlem*. The falsity of several of these particulars, sufficiently appears from the first book of this history ; and the others are manifestly disprov'd since I have seen a book in the Earl of *Pembroke*'s library, printed at the university of *Oxford*, anno 1468. However, their mistakes were unavoidable in those times ; because they were ignorant of several material particulars, and of the first editions, which were absolutely necessary to determine the true periods of the invention and introduction of the art into *England*.

BUT in 1664, *Richard Atkins*, Esq; publish'd an account of the foremention'd edition and an old manuscript chronicle, preserv'd at *Lambeth* in the archbishop's palace, in his *Original and Growth of* Printing, printed by order of the right honourable Mr. *Morrice* secretary of state. The design of this book, which is little more than an invective against the *Company of Stationers*, is to prove that printing is a branch of the royal *Prerogative*, and a *flower* of the *English Crown*. This chronicle however, of which a friend of his, whom he does not name, sent him a copy, is far from being of undoubted authority, since it is liable to these exceptions. 1. That neither *Atkins* nor his nameless friend pretend to have seen the original, much less to have compar'd the copy with it. 2. They give no account when and by whom this chronicle was written, and how it was bequeath'd to the *Lambeth* library. 3. No author, that I know of, besides *Atkins*, mentions this chronicle in *Lambeth* library, except those who quote it from him ; tho' that author hop'd that his book would occasion the discovery and publication of it in time for publick satisfaction, p. 4. 4. It is not to be found there now ; for the Earl of *Pembroke* assur'd me, that he employ'd a person for some time to search for it, but in vain. 5. It gives an account of some particulars, altogether inconsistent with the more authentic accounts, which we are now masters of, with respect to the circumstances of the first discovery of the art ; so that we may suppose, that whoever the author was, he has taken some part of his account from common report, and from the *Dutch*, who have laid claim to this invention. I might add, that *Atkins* has so interspers'd terspers'd the chroniclers account with his own observations, that it is very difficult to distinguish them exactly. However, imperfect and precarious as it is, since it gives us the most probable and clear account of this important affair, I shall here set it down, as I find it in the author abovemention'd; after which I shall endeavour, by reconciling some inconsistencies in it, explaining several particulars, and adding some necessary remarks upon the whole, to lead the reader, if not to a certain, at least to the most probable account of this matter.

The chronicle is as follows.

Thomas Bourcher *archbishop of* Canterbury, *mov'd the then King* [Henry 6th.] *to use all possible means for procuring a mold (for so 'twas then call'd) to be brought into this kingdom; the king (a good man, and much given to works of this nature) readily hearken'd to the motion; and taking private advice, how to effect this design, concluded it could not be brought about without great secrecy, and a considerable sum of money given to such person or persons, as would draw off some of the workmen from* Harlem *in* Holland, *where* John Guthenberg *had newly invented it, and was himself personally at work. 'Twas resolv'd that less than one thousand marks would not produce the desir'd effect; towards which sum, the archbishop presented the king with three hundred marks. The money being now prepar'd, the management of the design was committed to* Mr. Robert Turnour, *who then was of the robes to the king, and a person most in favour with him, of any of his condition.* Mr. Turnour *took to his assistance Mr.* Caxton, *a citizen of good abilities, who trading much into* Holland, *might be a creditable pretence, as well for his going, as stay in the* Low Countries. *Mr.* Turnour *was in disguise (his beard and hair quite shaven off;) but Mr.* Caxton *appear'd known and publick. They having receiv'd the said sum of one thousand marks, went first to* Amsterdam, *then to* Leyden, *not daring to enter* Harlem *itself; for the town was very jealous, having imprison'd and apprehended divers persons, who came from other parts for the same purpose. They stay'd till they had spent the whole one thousand marks in gifts and expences; so as the king was fain to send five hundred marks more; Mr.* Turnour *having written to the king, that he had almost done his work; a bargain (as he said) being struck between him and two* Hollanders, *for bringing off one of the workmen, who should sufficiently discover and teach this new art. At last with much ado they got*

　off

off one of the under workmen, whose name was Frederick Corsells *(or rather* Corsellis), *who late one night stole from his fellows in disguise into a vessel, prepar'd before for that purpose, and so the wind (favouring the design) brought him safe to* London.

'Twas not thought so prudent to set him on work at London, *but by the archbishop's means, who had been vice-chancellor, and afterwards chancellor of the university of* Oxon, Corsellis *was carry'd with a strong guard to* Oxon ; *which guard constantly watch'd to prevent* Corsellis *from any possible escape, till he had made good his promise, in teaching how to print : so that at* Oxford, *printing was first set up in* England ; *which was before there was any printing-press or printer in* France, Spain, Italy *or* Germany, *except the city of* Mentz, *which claims seniority as to printing even of* Harlem *itself, calling herself* Urbem Moguntinam Artis Typographicæ inventricem primam ; *tho' 'tis known to be otherwise, that city gaining that art by the brother of one of the workmen of* Harlem, *who had learn'd it at home of his brother, and after set up for himself at* Mentz.

This press at Oxon *was at least ten years before there was any printing in* Europe, *(except at* Harlem *and* Mentz), *where also it was but new born. This press at* Oxford *was afterwards found inconvenient to be the sole printing place of* England, *as being too far from* London, *and the Sea : whereupon the king set up a press at* St. Albans, *and another in the Abby of* Westminster, *where they printed several books of divinity and Physick, for the King, for reasons best known to himself and council, permitted then no law-books to be printed, nor did any Printer exercise that art, but only such as were the king's sworn servants ; the king himself having the price and emolument for printing books.*

THUS far the chronicle, or our author's extract from it ; for, as I observ'd before, he distinguishes not his own from the chronicle, nor acquaints us whether it be literally copied from the chronicle, or an abstract of it ; nor whether it mentions any other transactions besides that of bringing printing to *England.* I shall therefore follow him no further, at present, but examine the truth of the several particulars of this account : yet previous to this, I shall observe, that we have the like account of this affair in Antony Wood's *History and Antiquities of the University of* Oxford, printed in 1674, *i. e.* ten years after *Atkins* had publish'd his piece ;

from

from which the foremention'd author feems to have taken his account wholly; in many particulars, of which he has been confuted by feveral writers, as fhall be fhewn immediately. To return to *Atkins's* book; which is unknown to foreigners, and feen but by few in *England*; the author of that chronicle is miftaken in feveral points; 1. in fuppofing *Harlem* or *Harlein*, as he calls it, to be the place from whence *Corfellis* came: It is not probable, that the art was invented there, efpecially by *Guttenbergh*, and in the year 1459, fince it appears, the pfalter was prin-at *Mentz* by *Fauft* two years before that, befides the feveral books printed on wooden blocks. Again, if the book mention'd by *Atkins* and *Wood* to have been printed at *Oxford, anno* 1468, be the firft book print-ted there, 'tis plain, that city had not the art ten years before any other; becaufe I have lately feen a book printed at *Strasburg* by *John Guttenberg*, in 1458, as I have already hinted in the poftcript of the foregoing number; befides *Strasburg*, it was at *Venice*, the monaftery of *Sublaco, Aufburgh, Rome* and *France* before 1468. If it be urg'd, that there might be other books printed before that at *Oxford*, or that it requir'd fome time to get all the neceffary materials of a printing-houfe; the fame pleas will equally ferve for thofe other places now mention'd. *Laftly*, if we admit *Guttenbergh* to have carried the art to *Holland*, which we fhall fhew hereafter to be extremely probable, it will be ftill falfe, that *Mentz* receiv'd it from the brother of one of his workmen. Thefe are the inconfiftencies and contradictions to plain facts, now certainly known, which derogate from the authority of this chronicle and of thofe that follow it. We fhall now endeavour to clear thefe inconfiftencies, or at leaft to fhew how the author of it was led into thefe palpable errors, and from thence to difcover the real truth of the whole tranfaction.

WE have already hinted at the probability, that he rather followed the reports fpread about from *Holland*, than made a ftrict enquiry into this fubject. This will appear more plain from the following confiderations. 1. We hinted in our 1ft book, that during the infancy of the art, *Fauft* and *Schoeffer*, and together with them *Guttenbergh*, carry'd on the bufinefs with all poffible fecrecy, till the former being oblig'd to difcover it at *Paris* for his own fafety, and the latter having broke the partnerfhip, and gone to fet up the art elfewhere; it was thought of no further uſe to conceal this invention. 2. The reader may call to mind that we advanc'd a probable conjecture of Mr. *Mattaire*'s, that *Guttenbergh* being caſt at law, and ſentenc'd to reimburſe his moiety, and pay the charges of the ſuit, went away to *Strasburgh* to evade the ſentence, which is now confirm'd by the book printed there juſt now mentioned; where not thinking himſelf ſafe from further proſecution, he might really come down to *Harlem*, and there inſtruct *Coſter*, or ſome others in the art. This ſeems to be more than probable, not only from the chronicle's mentioning *Guttenbergh*, and not *Coſter*, as inventor of the art, but likewiſe from his dating the invention nine years later than it was diſcover'd; which muſt be aſcrib'd to its not having been known at *Harlem* till the year 1459, tho' it had been practis'd at *Mentz* from the year 1450, or ſoon after, as has been ſufficiently ſhewn before.

Again, if we conſider that *Holland* and the *Low-Countries* were the only places of *Germany*, into which we traded, whereas the city of *Mentz*, which lies very far in the continent, was then little known to us, we ſhall not wonder, that our firſt accounts of the original of printing, ſhould be taken from the *Dutch*, agreeable to their violent claims to the invention of it, and their ſcandalous ſtories invented to deprive *Fauſt* of his diſcovery; for the chronicle acquaints us, that the city receiv'd it from a fugitive ſervant of *Guttenbergh*, who had learn'd it from his brother then working with him, and went to ſet it up there. There remains one ſingle difficulty ſtill; why the chronicle attributes the invention to *Guttenbergh*, when all their writers make no mention of him, but aſcribe it wholly to their countryman *Coſter*. To ſolve this, if we ſuppoſe this account given to the author by *Frederick Corſellis*, or even by Mr. *Caxton* or *Turnour*, which is very probable; we may juſtly preſume, that they ſpoke as they were inform'd on the ſpot, agreeably to the account which *Guttenbergh* gave of himſelf and of his invention, which the *Dutch* dar'd not to contradict, till after his death or departure from *Holland*, when they aſſum'd the whole diſcovery to themſelves, and repreſented *Coſter* as the ſole inventor, excluſive of every other pretenſion. I have dwelt longer on theſe circumſtances, becauſe they notoriouſly demonſtrate, that thoſe contradictions to plain facts, univerſally known and aſſented to by all but the *Dutch* writers, confirm the authority of the reſt

of

of the chronicle; fince they are exactly drawn from the legends of that nation, which were then generally believ'd over all the *Low-Countries,* and were the only accounts that our merchants, and particularly the two gentlemen employ'd by the king, could procure concerning the original of printing. And 'tis not improbable that what the chronicle mentions of the imprifonment of feveral perfons at *Harlem,* on fufpicion of a defign to fteal the art, might be done rather out of fear leaft any of thofe ftrangers fhould rob them of their honour by expofing the vantiy of their pretenfions; fince themfelves could not be ignorant of what was done at *Mentz* long before that time.

BEFORE I difmifs this chronicle,) which, as I obferv'd, was unknown till Mr. *Atkins* publifh'd it, I fhall give an account, which I found in a manufcript now in my poffeffion, which feems to be much older than the year 1664, when Mr. *Atkins* publifh'd his account, and which, a few Circumftances excepted, entirely agrees with that of the chronicle. The part relating to the introducing of printing into *England* being very fhort, I believe will be acceptable to the reader, and is as follows.

The rife and progrefs of printing in England.

The art of printing was firft brought into England *in the time of* Hen. vi. *at the charges of the archbifhop of* Canterbury (Bourchier,) *who employ'd one* Turner *mafter of the robes to the king, and one Mr.* Caxton *a mercer of* London, *but ufing the trade of a merchant, to go to* Harlem *to endeavour to bring over fome of the workmen, that had then newly practis'd the art there, who prevail'd upon fome of the under-workmen to come over with them into* England, *and to teach them their trade. As foon as they were landed, they were convey'd under a guard to the univerfity of* Oxford *for fear they fhould run back again; and there they fet up a prefs about the year* 1467, *as appears by feveral books that were printed there about that time. The names of thofe workmen were* Rood *an Almayn (or German) and* Winken de Worde; *and the charges of the journey coft the archbifhop* 1500 *marks, as appears by feveral papers and memorials relating to this matter, that are ftill extant in the library at* Lambeth. *Shortly after there was a prefs fet up at the Abbey of St.* Albans, *which continued till the diffolution,* &c.

THE remainder being foreign to this chapter, fhall be communicated in fome of the following, to which it more properly belongs. I need not obferve that this manufcript afcribes all the honour of this tranfaction to

the

the archbiſhoſhp ; whereas the chronicle aſſures us that the king contributed the greateſt ſum towards it, The date mention'd in my manuſcript
is a year before the *Oxford* edition came out.

It may be here objected that the year 1467 cannot bring it within the
reign of *Henry* VI. who had been depos'd ſix years before ; but I anſwer
that the manuſcript does not aſſert that the *Dutch* printers came not into
England till that year, but that their preſs was not ſet up till then ; and
tho' this happen'd in another reign, yet it will ſtill be true that king *Henry*
caus'd them to be brought over, whilſt he was upon the throne, tho' the
civil wars, and his being depos'd, put a ſtop to their proceedings for ſix or
ſeven years. We ſhall have occaſion to remark further upon this in the next
chapter. As for its complementing the archbiſhop with having been at
the whole expence of the journey ; it may be aſcrib'd to want of better
information, or partiality to that prelate, who might ſtill be in great
eſteem under king *Edward* ; whilſt the good king *Henry* was ſtrip'd of the
royal dignity and wholly neglected. With reſpect to the two printers mention'd there ; the firſt is probably the ſame, *Theodoric Rood*, who printed
afterwards by himſelf, and of whom we have but two editions printed at
Oxford in 1480, and 1481, of which we ſhall give a further account in the
next chapter. Whether he came along with *Corſellis* as an under-work-
man, is difficult to determine,

I am of opinion that *Winken de Worde* came not to *England* till ſome
years after ; tho' he might eaſily be confounded by the author of the M. S.
with the other, on account of his *Dutch* name, and of his having ſignaliz'd
himſe f afterwards by the number and elegance of his editions, which he
printed both under *Caxton* and by himſelf. Thus 'tis plain that the few records, which we have, agree in the following particulars ; that archbiſhop
Bourchier ſollicited king *Henry* VI. to procure the eſtabliſhment of the art
of printing in this kingdom ; that the king not only conſented, but contributed largely to it ; that *Turner* and *Caxton* were employ'd in this
deſign ; that it coſt 1500 marks to execute it ; that it was happily effected
during the reign of *Henry* VI. i. e. before the year 1461, ſince in the beginning of that year he was depos'd by *Edward* IV. and laſtly, that *Oxford* was fix'd upon by the king and Archbiſhop to ſet up the firſt preſs
in, and make the firſt eſſays of this art ; which city therefore ſhall be the
ſubject of our next chapter.   C H A P

C H A P. II.

Printing at Oxford *by* Frederic Corfellis.

SOME *English* authors, and particularly Mr. *Howel*, are of opinion, that the firſt trials of this art were made in the *Ambry* belonging to *Weſtminſter-Abby*, where Mr. *Caxton* afterwards carry'd on the buſineſs with good ſucceſs for a conſiderable time ; as ſhall be related in its place. But as they affirm this upon the ſuppoſition, that the Abbot of that place, [*Iſlip*], was the perſon, who procur'd the art to be brought to *England*; whereas the chronicle abovemention'd, which they knew nothing of, aſſerts the contrary ; in both theſe reſpects, I think it more reaſonable to follow it, than thoſe writers : nor indeed is it probable, that any but a crown'd head, or ſome perſons employ'd by him, would venture upon ſuch a dangerous project. Beſides, this account of the chronicle is confirm'd by the edition of 1468, mention'd in the preceding chapter, of which we ſhall ſpeak more fully hereafter : for tho' this comes ſhort in date of the laſt year of *Henry* VI, by ſeven or eight years, yet it is older by at leaſt as many, than any impreſſion of *Caxton*'s at *Weſtminſter*, as far as has been yet diſcover'd. Add to this, that according to their Suppoſition, that Mr. *Caxton* learn'd the art from the workman brought over from *Holland*, we muſt neceſſarily ſuppoſe the latter to have made ſeveral eſſays, and printed a volume or two at leaſt, before the former could be perfect enough in it to engage in that province. But I am far from thinking, that *Caxton* either learn'd the art from him, or even came over to *England* with him ; ſince 'tis much more probable, that he diſpatch'd Mr. *Turnour* with *Corſellis* thither, and carried on his commerce as well as his ſtudies beyond ſea. I am inclin'd to this opinion, by a paſſage in the preface to the ſecond book of his *hiſtory of Troy*, which he tells us he tranſlated from the *French* at the deſire of the *Dutcheſs of Burgundy*, the King's ſiſter ; which tranſlation, he ſays, he began at *Bruges*, anno 1468, continued at *Gaunt*, and finiſh'd at *Cologn*, anno *a thouſand four honderd* lxxi. Hence 'tis plain, that he was ſtill travelling in *Flanders* and *Germany*

S ſ

three years after the firft edition printed by *Corfellis* at *Oxford:* nor does it appear, that *Caxton* came prefently after to *England*, but ftay'd to write a third book in the laft mention'd place, *Cologn*, as he informs us in thefe words; ,, *The third book of the deftruction of* Troy ———— *I have now* ,, *good leyzer in* Cologn ———— *I have delibered in my felf beyng* ,, ———— *to take thislaboure in hand*". 'Tis unreafonable to ima-gine, that a man of his years, (of which he complains in the fame pre-face, faying, that *age crept on him daily and feebled all the body,*) fhould come along with the *Dutch* Printer, and learn the art from him, and then go travelling again, having one book to tranflate, and ano-ther to write, *viz.* his *Fruits of Time.* I am of opinion therefore, that he learn'd the art, at leaft got a good infight into it abroad, and per-haps at *Cologn*; tho' he might make himfelf mafter of the practical part of it after his return into *England.*

Thus far therefore 'tis plain, that *Caxton* had been on his travels fome time, when *Corfellis* printed that firft edition at *Oxford*; that the latter was the firft Printer in *England*; and that *Oxford* was the place, where the firft prefs was fet up. The chronicle gives thefe reafons why tha Printer was fent thither; 1. Becaufe it was an inland town, out of which it would be lefs poffible for him to efcape, than from *London* or any place near the fea; 2. Archbifhop *Bourchier*, who had been vice-chan cellor, and was then chancellor of that univerfity, may be fuppos'd to have had a more than ordinary regard for it, and, in confequence of that to have prevail'd upon the King to honour it with the firft prefs. To thefe we may add the two following, *viz.* 1. That an univerfity was th moft proper place for fuch a work; becaufe it would ftill be under th eye and direction of the learned men there, who could make choice c the beft works to be printed, the beft MSS. to print from, and the mot skilful perfons to correct them; 2. the city of *London*, and almoft th whole kingdom being difturb'd and divided by the *Earl of March*'s par ty, and the court engag'd in oppofing his meafures, an univerfity was much fafer and quieter place to lay the foundation of this art in, tha any other in the kingdom. *Corfellis* therefore, and thofe to whom l was to difcover the fecret, having fworn fidelity to the king and h fucceffors, and being admitted into the number of the king's fervants an

houfhold

houſhold, began to exerciſe this art as ſoon as they had got all things ready for it. How long they were thus employ'd in their preparations, and what progreſs they made after I ſhall next enquire.

The reader will have juſt cauſe to admire, that, if they began ſo ſoon as the latter end of *Henry* VI's reign, *viz.* before *anno* 1461, they ſhould have publiſh'd no work yet diſcover'd till ſeven years after, *viz.* 1468 ; and that there are but three editions extant between that time and the year 1481, the edition of 1468 included ; and, what is ſtill more admirable, that from that year to 1585, which is above 100 years, there is not one volume to be found printed at *Oxford*, tho' the art flouriſh'd in ſeveral other parts of *England*, as will appear in the progreſs of this hiſtory. This laſt particular I can by no means account for ; but the other, I mean their ſlow progreſs at firſt, is eaſily ſolv'd by what has been hinted before, *viz.* the troubles which were then breaking forth, and fell upon the king and court, as well as his depoſition, which happen'd immediately after their firſt ſettlement in that univerſity, together with the oppoſition made continually by his Queen and friends againſt his victorious rival. Beſides, if we conſider that the Printers were ſworn ſervants to the crown, and conſequently incapable to act without the king's ſpecial order, or at leaſt his licence, whilſt *Henry* their Patron was out of power, and the reigning monarch otherwiſe employ'd, it will be very eaſy to account for theſe delays, and the ſmall progreſs which they made in thoſe troubleſome times. We may likewiſe with great probability ſuppoſe, that moſt of their works were ſuch as were adapted to thoſe times of ſuperſtition, as prayer-books, manuals, legends, &c. which periſh'd ſoon after the reformation.

It muſt be own'd indeed, that the author of the chronicle, ſo often mention'd, tells us, that as ſoon as *Corſellis* had perform'd his promiſe, and inſtructed a ſufficient number of others in the art, it was thought proper to diſperſe them, ſome to *Weſtminſter*, others to *St. Albans*, &c. Yet it is ſtill very ſurprizing, that ſo conſiderable a place as *Oxford* could not detain one of them by a ſufficient encouragement. However, 'tis plain, that except *Theodoric Rood*, a *German*, and native of *Cologn*, who very probably came over with Mr. *Caxton* from thence, and of whom we have diſcover'd but two editions, there are no other footſteps of

printing

printing in this univerſity extant from that time to 1585, nor any tolerable account among the writers of thoſe times for ſuch a wonderful ſcarcity. But this is not the only thing which the reader will be ſurpriz'd at, with relation to the ſlow progreſs which printing made at *Oxford*.

I have, in the former book, given an account of vaſt improvements made to that art in foreign countries, and to what a degree of perfection the *Italians* and *French*, in particular, had brought it, not only with reſpect to the exquiſite beauty and variety of characters, richneſs and elegancy of compoſition, *&c.* but likewiſe by their introducing the learned and eaſtern languages, as *Greek*, *Hebrew*, *Arabic*, &c. into their printing-houſes, even before the year 1520, and printing ſeveral curious polyglot works in all theſe tongues, beſides the *Latin*. But tho' I have extended this *Engliſh* hiſtory thirty years further than theirs, *viz.* to the year 1550, yet the reader muſt not expect to find any thing of this nature done in *England* during that time. Our firſt Printers, tho' excellent men in their way, contented themſelves with printing in their own tongue ; and if they ventur'd ſometimes either upon *Latin* or *French*, their productions in thoſe languages were few and inconſiderable : but with reſpect to *Greek* and *Hebrew*, either thro' want of due encouragement from the learned, or of courage in them, 'tis certain they never attempted any thing of that kind till a long time after.

The reader may remember with what difficulty the *Pariſian* Printers were prevail'd upon to venture upon ſuch works ; what objections and obſtacles they rais'd againſt ſo expenſive and hazardous an undertaking : yet a learned *Frenchman* ſo far prevail'd with ſome of them, that he had the pleaſure of ſeeing ſeveral of his own works printed in thoſe languages ; the reception of which ſoon encourag'd them to proceed in ſeveral noble undertakings. But the caſe was far different in *England* : for the learned Dr. *Wakefield*, having made an oration in 1584, to recommend the ſtudy of the *Hebrew* and *Arabic* tongues, and ſhew the uſefulneſs and neceſſity of them, was oblig'd to publiſh it maim'd and imperfect, wanting near a third part, becauſe, as he tells us, the Printers of that time had no *Hebrew* types ; tho' it was printed by *Wynken de Worde*, one of the moſt eminent Printers in *Europe* of that age. Printing in *Greek* made no great figure in *England* before the 16th century,

tury ; and the moſt learned work, which we have to boaſt of, was the polyglot bible of Dr. *Walton*, mention'd at the latter end of the laſt book,
which was not printed till after the reſtoration by Mr. *Thomas Roycroft*,
of whom I ſhall ſay more hereafter.

E x c e p t this, I don't find any footſteps of any works in the polyglot kind, but what were ſmall and inconſiderable. However, we, like
the *Dutch*, have ſufficiently ſince atton'd for the ſlow progreſs which
our anceſtors made in thoſe noble branches of printing.

I ſhall now give an account of the editions before mention'd between
the years 1468 and 1585.

1. *SanEti Hieronymi expoſitio in Symbolum Apoſtolorum,* 4to, } Oxon, 1468.
    (without the Printer's name.)

T h i s antient piece begins with the following title. *Incipit Expoſitio
SanEti Jeronimi in Symbolum Apoſtolorum ad Papam Laurentium.* At the
end are the following words : *Explicit Expoſitio SanEti Jeronimi in Sym-
bolo Apoſtolorum ad Papam Laurentium, Impreſſus Oxonie & finita Anno
Domini* MCCCCLXVIII. xvii. *die Decembris.* There is one in the *Bod-
leian* library, given by the learned biſhop *Barlow*, who wrote with his
own hand, in the firſt page, that this *expoſition* was not St. *Jerom*'s, but
Rufinus's : *Rufini eſt hæc Expoſitio, non Hieronymi :* and in the laſt page
he wrote as follows,

Stephen Bateman *doEtor of divinity, and chaplain to* Hen. Cary *Ld.* Hunſ-
den *upon Bartholomæus de proprietatibus rerum* [*the book was writ in Latin
anno* 1366, *tranſlated into Engliſh in* 1397,] in the laſt he tells us, *that
Bartholomeus was firſt printed in Engliſh* in 1471, ·and then he adds,
——*at which time printing began firſt in* England, *the* 37*th year of* Hen. VI.
but he is manifeſtly miſtaken, for this foregoing book was printed in
1468 at *Oxford*, at leaſt two years before. This remark of Dr. *Bateman* has
another groſs miſtake, beſides that obſerv'd by biſhop *Barlow* ; which
is, that the year 1471 was far from being the 37th of *Henry* VI. who
had been depos'd 10 years before. The 37th year of that King's reign
was the year 1459 ; in which 'tis probable ſome foundations of printing
had been laid in *England*, tho', for the aforemention'd reaſons, we meet
with

with nothing done in that kind till eight or nine years after. We shall affirm nothing concerning this *English* edition of *Barth. de Propriet. Rer.* (tho' 'tis reasonable to suppose it printed at *Oxford*,) since we have no other account of it but this manuscript note of bishop *Barlow*.

2. *Leonardus Aretinus in Aristot. Ethic. Comment.*   Oxon, 1479.

I THINK 'twill not be amiss to insert here what is wrote before these two books, which are in the *Pembroke* library, 'tis as follows.
, Here are the only two books to be seen by *Corsellis*, the first Printer
, at *Oxford*; tho' there are other copies of the first, of the second we
, know of only this.   These are printed on the same shap'd letters as
, the *Rationale* and *Catholicon* by *Faust* (vulgarly doctor *Faustus*.) The
, civil wars in *Edward* IV's time might probably hinder the progress of
, the press; the third book, *viz.*

3. *Ægidius de Româ*, alias *Ægidius Columna Romanus Ar-*⎫
   chiep. Bituricens. Ord. Eremit. S. Aug. de Peccato Ori-⎬Oxon, 1479,
   ginali, 4to.   ⎭

, was printed about the time of the second, and, 'tis probable,
, this was printed by *Corsellis*, for the next Printer at *Oxford* was *Rood*,
, as appears by the following book.

4. The destruction of *Troy* in *Latin*, by *Guido de Colum-*⎱Oxon, 1480.
   na, by T. R.   ⎰

THERE is also·one more printed by *Rood* at *Oxford*, mention'd by *Orlandi*, viz.

5. *Alexandri ab Hales Angli Sententiosa, atque studio digna*⎫
   expositio super tertium Librum de Anima. Impressum⎪
   per me Theodoricum Rood [Road] *de Colonia* xi. *Octob.*⎬Oxon, 1481.
   in Alma Universitate.   ⎭

' Both

, Both *Corſellis* and *Rood* are mention'd by our hiſtorians, to have been
, brought over by *Caxton*. *Caxton* with Sir *Richard Whetehill* were ſent,
, after he brought *in the art*, by *Edward* IV. to ſettle a commerce
, with the *Dùke* of *Burgundy*, in 1464. *Vide Rymer's Fœdera.*
THUS much for *Oxford* in the infancy of the art.

C H A P. III.

Weſtminſter. MCCCCLXXIV.

WESTMINSTER being the moſt conſiderable place on ſeveral
accounts, and particularly for its productions, and the great applauſe with which Mr. *Caxton* carry'd on the buſineſs of printing there
for above 21 years; we have for this reaſon given it the priority; yet
hope I ſhall be excus'd for this digreſſion concerning St. *Albans*, which
has been far leſs eminent on this account, and as a hiſtory of the two
books printed there, I ſhall here relate as I found it wrote before the
Book of Miſcellanies, printed at St. *Albans*, in the *Pembroke* library.
'Tis as follows.

, IT is agreed, that *Corſellis* was the firſt who printed in *England*, and
, that *Oxford* and St. *Albans* were the two firſt places; the types, as may
, be ſeen in my Lord's books, at *Oxford* were like thoſe of *Fauſt*, the types
, of this at St. *Albans* are like the *Dutch Spieghel*. *Junius* argues for the
, firſt printing to be at *Harlem* from the *Dutch Spieghel*; but it appears
, from what is writ before the five books, call'd *Paginæ Conglutinatæ*,
, that the *Latin* one of this *Dutch* was before it, the which he had not
, ſeen, neither does it conclude where it was printed; however, this book
, of St. *Albans* affords an argument, which *Junius* could not then know
, of, that the *Dutch* letter might be before 1460, and it favours what *At-*
, *kins* ſays of a preſs brought over from *Harlem* in the time of *Henry* VI.
, who dy'd in 1460. This is the ſame letter, and we read that *Frederick*
, *Corſellis* did at St. *Albans* inſtruct an old learned ſchool-maſter to print,
, and *Corſellis* was of a conſiderable age when *Theodoric de Rood* of *Colen*
, ſucceeded him at *Oxford*, by whom we have two books printed; the firſt
, as old as 1480, already taken notice of. It has been a doubt, whether
, they

, they first printed at St. *Albans* or at *Oxford*, the oldest book of St. *Albans* with a date is here ; but we cannot prove this book of *Miscellanies* to be older than the diffolution of the Abbies by K. *Henry* VIII. 'till when a prefs remain'd, and the firft letter us'd as late as 1490, fuch a year appearing in this book. We know of but one more book at St. *Albans*, the which my Lord alfo has ; it difcovers that there was another prefs fet up at St. *Albans* after this, with the letter of the *Spieghel*, becaufe that is printed with *Caxton*'s types, and hath (as *Caxton*'s books have) the two improvements of indenting paragraphs, and dividing words by hyphens at the ends of the lines ; the Printers of this, with the letter of the *Spieghel*, continu'd to print as they began, without the two improvements, even after the prefs of *Caxton* ; tho' even here that prefs us'd his improvements. This other book is dated 1486 in words at length, at the end of the book of hunting, befides the arms of that monaftery, which are at the end of the whole book. *Spelman* in his *Afpilogia*, quotes the whole book, as wrote by *Juliana Barnes*, and is fo referr'd to by *Bale* in his *Scriptores*, tho' fhe appears to be the author only of the piece of hunting ; the treatife in that book of coat arms, is only a tranflation of *Upton de re Militari*. That printed by *Caxton* at *Weftminfter* in 1496, was a fecond edition of this book.

, O F this, with the types of the *Spieghel*, there is a fecond edition in 1529, printed by *Winken de Worde* ; it confifts of mifcellanies, and has fomething very remarkable, as the old tryal in K. *Henry* VI's time at *Leicefter*, (not taken notice of in our great collection of ftate-tryals) of the cardinal of *Winchefter*, impeach'd by the Duke of *Gloucefter* before the *Houfe of Lords*, in which appears the names of the mitred Abbots among the Lords fpiritual and temporal, and the form of the clerks entring as they came in, and at different times took the oaths. The names of the thirty fix churches in *London* and fuburbs that were not parochial ; alfo of the hundred and eighteen parifh churches and their patrons. In this is the *Nut brown maid*, fuppos'd by *Chaucer*, as *Skelton* confirms, by having had a copy given him by *Lidgate*, Monk of *Bury*. Mr. *Prior* has made a paraphrafe on it, and has alfo printed it from the old *English*, but knew not that it was by *Chaucer* ; befides, in his, each verfe is divided into two, as the firft verfe ends with *among*, and the fecond ends

, with

with *it is*, &c. Alſo in his, *Woman* and *Man*, is printed at the beginning of each Stanza [here they are ſuppos'd] as they ſpeak. Alſo the laſt Stanza (which makes twelve lines by his diviſion) is wanting.

THUS far we have copied from my Lord's manuſcript notes before his books of St. *Albans*. We now proceed to *Weſtminſter*; and here 'tis requiſite to obſerve, that Dr. *Iſlip*, abbot of *Weſtminſter*, having very liberally promoted this art, and encourag'd Mr. *Caxton*, to whom he aſſign'd that part of the Abby, ſuppos'd by ſome of our hiſtorians to be the Ambry or Eleemoſinary. As a confirmation of this opinion, Mr. *Newcourt* in his *Repertorium*, tom. i. pag. 721, has it thus : ' St. *Ann*'s, an
, old chappel, over againſt which the Lady *Margaret*, mother to king
, *Henry* VII, erected an alms-houſe for poor women, which is now turn-
, ed into lodgings for the ſinging-men of the college. The place, wherein.
, this chapel and alms-houſe ſtood, was called the Eleemoſinary or Al-
, monry, now corruptly the Ambry, [Aumbry] for that the alms of
, the Abby were there diſtributed to the poor ; in which *Iſlip*, abbot
, of *Weſtminſter* erected the firſt preſs for book-printing, that ever was in
, *England*, about the year of *Chriſt* 1471, and where *William Caxton*, citizen
, and mercer of *London*, who firſt brought it into *England*, practis'd it. '
This might occaſion the report, that this abbot firſt brought printing to *England* at his own charges. This notion of his introducing the art into our nation, which has prevail'd among ſeveral of our writers, is not only contradicted by the author of the chronicle, but ſeems to be groundleſs on this account, that if there had been any truth in it, Mr. *Caxton* would have been oblig'd in gratitude to have taken notice of this ſingular piece of merit of his friend and patron, in ſome of the prefaces to his works.

I HAVE follow'd the ſame method in this book, as I did in the former, dating the places according to the oldeſt edition extant, that bears any certain date ; tho' I am not ignorant that ſome of them may come ſhort of being the firſt that were printed there. Mr. *Bagford* (whoſe papers are now in the poſſeſſion of the right honourable the Earl of *Oxford*, at *Wimpole* in *Cambridgeſhire*) tells us, in a propoſal he publiſh'd for a Hiſtory of Printing, that *Caxton*'s firſt impreſſion ſeems to be that of

Game of Chefs, in 1474 ; becaufe it carries that date in the device, as the reader may fee under his picture at the front of the fecond volume, tho' he owns there was another impreffion of it without that device, as well as feveral other of his works without any date at all. However, the oldeft that has a certain date, ought in reafon to fix our epocha, according to our method.

WILLIAM CAXTON. 1474.

MR. *Caxton* was born, as he writes himfelf, in the *Weeld* of *Kent,* where the broadeft *English* is fpoken ; but as *Fuller,* in his *Eng-lifh Worthies* afferts, he was born at *Caxton* in *Hertfordfhire,* being per-haps lead into that error by his firname, fince it was the cuftom of that time for perfons to denominate themfelves from the place of their birth. I think it will be neceffary to fubjoin his own account of himfelf in this refpect, from his preface to the *Recule of the Hiftoryes of Troye,* tranflated by him out of the *French* of *Raoul le Fevre, Prieft.* —— , When I re-, member myfelf of my unperfitnefs in both languages. ——In *Fraunce* , was I never, and was born and lerned myne *English* in *Kente* in the , Weeld, where *English* is fpoken broad and rude. —— I have continu-, ed for the moft part in the countries of *Brabant, Flanders, Holland* and , *Zeland.* —— The Dutcheffe of Bourgogne fifter of the king of *Eng-*, *land,* when fhe had feen v or vi quairs, found default in myn *English,* , which fhe commaunded me to ammand, and to continue and make , an end of the refidue, — whofe commaund I durft not difobey. ' —— Thus far Mr. *Caxton:* and I can't but obferve, that the faults of his *Eng-lifh* are owing more to his long continuance abroad, than to the place of his birth; which will eafily appear from an accurate obfervation of his lan-guage and manner of fpelling, which difcover the foreigner more than a broad-fpoken *Kentish* man. His education was owing to his mother, and extended no farther than to read and write, which, he fays, procur'd him a good maintenance. Mr. *Bale* tells us indeed, that he underftood the *La-tin* tongue; which is plain, from his tranflations out of that language.

But

But, as he does not mention it as a part of his youthful education, 'tis very probable that he did not apply himself to the study of it till a long time after. He was bred a mercer of the city of *London*, and became a *Conjurys* thereof, * as he stiles himself in his preface to *Cato*, that is, a sworn member of that company, which in those days consisted of very considerable merchants, trading more particularly into the *Low-Countries*, and some of the maritime parts of *Germany*. To these he was frequently sent, but never had the fortune to visit *France*; tho' he became so good a master of that language, as to translate several volumes into *English*, of which we shall give an account hereafter. His travels likewise so well accomplish'd him in the *High* and *Low-Dutch*, that upon the account of this, and his knowledge of those countries and their trade, the king chose him as a fit person to undertake the bringing printing to *England*. This task, how difficult and hazardous soever, he acquitted himself with great integrity.

Mr. *Caxton*, besides his accomplishments as a merchant, acquired a great deal of politeness, partly by his travels for 30 years, and partly by his frequent residence at the court of the dutchess of *Burgundy*, sister to king *Edward* IV, who caress'd and patroniz'd him very much; for, in the preface abovemention'd, he tells us, that he was *a servant to her grace and received of her a yearly fee, and other many good and greate benefits*. He was likewise a favourite to several of our kings, particularly *Henry* VI, *Edward* IV, *Richard* III, and *Henry* VII; and highly esteem'd by the prime of our nobility, and especially by the duke of *Clarence*, the king's uncle, to whom he dedicated some of his works; the countess of *Derby*, king *Henry* VII's mother; the earl of *Rivers*, *Arundel*, with many others. As he was a person indefatigable and ambitious of applause, as well as earnest in promoting the glory of his own country, he read incessantly the

---

* I have indeed, thro' the favour of Mr. *Crump*, at *Mercer*'s hall, search'd their book of freemen, but could not find his name there. There was one *Richard Caxton* made free about that time, whether it was a relation of his, or a mistake in transcribing his christian name, I cannot be sure of; but however, as he calls himself a *Mercer* of *London*, we have no reason to doubt it.

history

hiftories of his own and other nations; which at proper times he digefted into order. At his return to *England,* he became acquainted with a learned fchoolmafter of *St. Albans,* fuppos'd by fome writers upon good grounds to have been the printer of *Juliana Barnes.* This perfon, having laid the foundation of a compleat body of *English* hiftory, kept a conftant correfpondence with Mr. *Caxton,* and was affifted by him in his tranflations; but, being prevented by death from finifhing his work, Mr. *Caxtom* procur'd his papers, examin'd, and reduc'd them to order, and compar'd them with the beft authors he could get, as *Livy, St. Auftin, Gildas, Beda, Ifidorus, Caffiodorus, Geoffrey of Monmouth, William of Malmefbury, Martin Canfulanus,* and others; from whom he alfo extracted many confiderable paffages, which he added to the hiftory. This work he entitled *Fructus temporum,* or the fruits of time, in feven books; to which he fubjoin'd a chronology. The hiftory begins with the giants, the firft fuppos'd inhabitants of this ifland, and concludes with the 23d year of *Edward* IV. viz. *ann.* 1483. What fhare our author had in this performance, and how great a part was done by the fchoolmafter, is impoffible to determine. This book was often reprinted and much valued at that time; yet, tho' it is the moft confiderable piece which Mr. *Caxton* publifh'd, we have feveral others written and printed by himfelf, which are as follow:

2. *An appendix to Trevifa's English tranflation of Randulph's polychronicon,* 1 book;

3. *The image of the world,* 1 book;

4. *The defcription of Great Britain,* 1 book;

5. *The life of Edward the Confeffor,* 1 book;

6. *The hiftory of king Arthur,* 21 books;

and fome others, all in *English.* The appendix to *Trevifa* is continued, from the year 1397, in which the fupplement of *Trevifa* to the *polychronicon* ends, to the year 1460, in which he wrote it. The learned Mr. *Selden* indeed afcribes the whole to *Trevifa*; but, befides that, *Caxton* takes the fupplement and other additions and interpretations to himfelf; but 'tis plain, as Dr. *Nicholfon* obferves, that *Trevifa,* according to that fuppofition, muft have wrote near a hundred years after his death. Thofe which he tranflated out of *Latin* and *French* are as follows:

Out

Out of *Latin*.

1. *Vegetius de re militari, or of the art of war,* 4 books ;
2. *Joannita of the game of chefs,* 4 books ;
3. *The hiftory of the deftruction of Troy,* 3 books ;
4. *Bonaventure of the Life of Chrift,* 1 book ;
5. *The hiftory of Lombardy,* 1 book ;
6. *John Tinmouth's Sanctilogium Britanniæ, epitomiz'd by Capgrave.*

From *French*.

1. *The fiege and conqueft of Jerufalem, by Geodfrey of Bologne,* dedicated to King *Edward* IV.

2. *The royal book, entitled in French le livre royal.*

BESIDES thefe, there are feveral others in the lift of his printed works fubjoin'd to the account of his life. He printed likewife fome books in *French*, as *La legende doree*, &c. and fome in *Latin*, as *Vita patruum* and *Boetius de confolatione philofophiæ*, &c. This catalogue of his works, as an author, I have taken from *Pitts* and *Bale* ; the latter of whom gives him the character of *vir non omnino ftupidus nec ignavia torpens*, neither a perfect dunce nor abandon'd to lazinefs : I fhall more readily affent to the judgment of a much later and more judicious writer, Dr. *Nicholfon* who fays of *Bale* (p. 177) that he gives the account of men and their labours at random ; and of *Caxton* (p. 190) that the opportunities he had, of being acquainted with the court-tranfactions of his own time, would encourage his reader to hope for greater matters from him ; but that his fancy feems to have lead him into an undertaking (with refpect to his *Fructus temporum*) above his ftrength. There is one thing very obfervable concerning this excellent Printer and author, that he tranflated, printed, corrected, illuminated and bound all his Books within his own office or printing-houfe. As he printed long before the method of adding the errata at the end of books was in ufe, fo his extraordinary exactnefs oblig'd him to a great deal more trouble than can eafily be imagin'd ; for he tells us, in the preface to fome of his books, that his chief care, after a work was printed off, was to revife it, and mend all the faults with his own hand with red ink ; which being done to one copy, he caus'd fome of his journey-men to do the fame throughout the whole impreffion ; which he afterwards compar'd with his firft fheet, to fee that

they

they had not omitted any of his corrections. 'Tis true, they did not print off so large a number of books as now ; for 250 or 300 were thought a large impression ; but even that number made it very tedious to correct throughout: tho' this was practis'd by several eminent Printers of other nations, 'till they found out the way of printing the errata in some blank leaves of the book.

M r. *Caxton* having made himself a perfect master of the Art of Printing (not at *Oxford* under *Fred. Corsellis,* as some authors imagine, but during his travels beyond sea, as will appear hereafter) came and settled at *Westminster,* where abbot *Islip* (as some say) his friend and patron, assign'd him one of the chapels belonging to the abby, as we have before quoted from *Newcourt,* as being retir'd and free from interruption ; and from this or some other chapel, 'tis suppos'd that the name of chapel has been given to all printing-houses in *England* ever since. And notwithstanding it is by some reported, that it was set up in the chapel there, I can trace no footsteps of its having been practis'd in that place. My manuscript beforemention'd says, , that a press was set up in *West-*, *minster* abby by abbot *Islip,* in the little ambry, where *William Cax-*, *ton* was master '. Mr. *Bagford* assigns the house in the ambry which was formerly the king's head, as the place where *Caxton* carried on his printing, but had I been early enough in my enquiry before 'twas pull'd down, as Mr. *Bagford* was, I flatter my self I could have found some remains. I have great reason to think it had been a printing-house, by having been inform'd, that some persons found among the rubbish some remains of printing materials ; but, thro' ignorance of the curiosity of them, they are either lost or destroy'd. As I have given my reasons against the arts being practis'd in the chapel at *Westminster,* I rather think, that our technical terms in printing, such as a printing-house being call'd a chapel ; and where printing is grey in one place, and too black in another, the grey is call'd a fryar, and the black a monk ; I think, I say, that these terms took their original from the art's being practis'd in other religious houses besides that at *Westminster :* for 'tis evident, by the book hereafter mention'd, printed in the exempt monastery of *Tavistock* in *Devonshire,* by *Dan Thomas Richard,* monk of the said monastery, that several of the religious orders exercis'd this art, perhaps in some

outer

outer chapel, which, being dedicated to fome faint, was only us'd once a year on the anniverfary of that faint.

T h e reader will find, that printing-houfes were fet up in feveral cities and towns in *England*, where they had any confiderable religious houfe. Thus we fee the abby of St. *Albans* had printing there very foon, as before notic'd. Nor was this the only religious houfe where printing was practis'd, and that very early; for time has difcover'd to us feveral others, fuch as *Taviftock*, as aforefaid, *Worcefter*, *Canterbury*, *Ipfwich*; which were chofen for that purpofe. We have already hinted, that the firft Printers were fworn fervants to the Crown; and in particular Mr. *Caxton* not only printed as fuch, but all his impreffions were recommended either by the king, or princes of the blood, or by fome eminent patron amongft the nobility, who bore the charges of the whole. The types with which he printed were peculiar to himfelf, and eafily diftinguifh'd from any other, being a mixture of fecretary and Gothic in fhape, the fize great primer. He had feveral eminent workmen under him; particularly *Winken de Worde*, a Dutchman, and *Rich. Pynfon*, a citizen of *London*, who afterwards printed for themfelves many valuable pieces, which fhall be mention'd in their proper place. They likewife us'd a letter peculiar to themfelves, which as I fhall take notice, differ'd from their mafter's, and was more refin'd and moderniz'd. Mr. *Caxton*, befides his other valuable qualifications, was a perfon of exemplary piety and ftrictnefs of life. He continu'd printing from before the year 1474 to 1495, as is evident from the end of the *Vita patrum* and *Hilton*'s *fcale*, printed, or rather finifh'd, in that year by *Winken de Worde*. Mr. auditor *Jett* deceas'd, affur'd me, that he was bury'd in St. *Margaret*'s church, *Weftminfter*; and that he faw the remains of his tomb-ftone, but I have not as yet been able to find it.

T h e lift of his works is as follows; in which I could not poffibly recover the right titles of each book; but fuch as I could meet with, I have fet down exactly as printed by him. Thofe which have no certain date are put at the end.

1. *The*

1. *The Game of chess*. fol. tranflated out of the Latin of *Joannita*, and by him dedicated to the duke of *Florence*, brother to king *Edward* IV, who was murther'd in the tower, *ann.* 1477. There are two editions of *Caxtons* of this book; one which has a kind of cypher or device, bearing the date of 74, and the other without both. The former therefore I fuppofe to be firft printed, which has the date, *VVeftminfter*, } 1474.

IT is now in the *Pembroke* library, nor do I know of one any where elfe.

2. *A book of fayings of the philofopher Socrates*, tranflated out of *Latin* into *French*, by *Johan. de Tronville*, provoft of *Paris*, and out of the *French* into *Englifh*, by *Wydewyll, Earl of Ryvers* ---- *emprinted by me William Caxton at Weftmeftre*. } 1477.

The work was by the Earl's defire overfeen by *Caxton*. *Caxton me fieri fecit*. This book is in the library of my worthy friend and promoter of this work Mr. *Granger*.

3. *Memorare noviffima*, which entreateth of the four laft things, the firft of death, the fecond of the laft judgment, the third of the pains of hell, the fourth of the joys of heaven; tranflated out of the *French* by *Antony, Earl of Rivers*, Lorde *Scales*, and of the *Ifle of Weight*, defenfor and dictator of the caufes apoftolique for our holy father the pope, uncle and governour to my lord, prince of *VVales* : printed by *VVillam Caxton*, in the year of *Edward* IV. 4*to*. Ibid. } 1478.

4. *Ovid's metamorphofis*. Ibid.   1479.

5. *Thymage or mirrour of the world, tranflated from the French into Englifh. ibid*. fol. } 1480.

BEGAN the fecond of *January*, 1480, and finifh'd it the 8th of *March* in the fame year. *Caxton me fieri fecit*.

6. *The*

6. *The history of England, together with the history of Ireland,* } 1480.
   taken out of the polychronicon. fol. ibid.

THERE are two editions of this book, both by *Caxton,* and since then it has been frequently reprinted by others till the year 1530.

7. *The life and history of king Arthur, &c. in 21 books, written* } 1480.
   and printed by Caxton. ibid.

8. *The history of the last siege and conquest of Jerusalem, trans-* } 1481.
   lated from the French of Godfrey of Bologn. [1] ibid.

9. *The history of Reynard the fox.* 4to. ibid.   1481.

10. *Tully of old-age and of friendship, in English.* fol.   1481.

11. *The continuation of Ranulph's polychronicon, English'd by Tre-* } 1482.
    visa. fol. *without the place's name. by W. Caxton.* [2]

12. *Bartholomeus de proprietatibus rerum Anglicé.* fol. ibid.

THIS was communicated to me whilst I was printing this list, so that I had not time to enquire after the English title of it.

13. *Cathone's exhortations or precepts, with comments,* fol. ibid. } 1483.
    [3] *december* xxiii.

14. *The history of the knights of the tower.* ibid.   1483.

---

[1] With many histories therein compriz'd translated, and reduc'd out of *French* into *English* by me simple person *William Caxton,* which book I present unto the most christian king *Edward* IV.———which book I began in *march* 7, and finish'd the 7th of *juin,* 1481. and the 21st year of king *Edward* IV. and in this month set in form and emprinted the 20th of *november* the year aforesaid in the abby of *Westminster* by the said *William Caxton.*

[2] First translated out of *Latin* by *John Trevisa,* chaplain to the lord *Berkley,* and then continued by me simple person *William Caxton,* &c. printed *july* 2.

[3] *At the end are these words :* Cathon translated out of *French* into *English* by *William Caxton,* in the abby of *Westmynstre,* 1483, first yere of our king *Richard* the thyrd, 23d of *decembre.*

15. *The*

15. *The pilgrimage of the soul, translated out of French into English with somewhat of additions.* fol. *emprinted by me William Caxton at Westmestre.* [1] } 1483.

16. *Cato Englished by Caxton.* fol. 1483.

17. *Confessio amantis, the confession of the lover made by Johan Gower, born in Walys, in the time of king Richard the second.* fol. *emprinted by me William Caxton at Westmestre.* [2] } 1483.

18. *The book of homilies in English.* fol. ibid. 1483.

19. *La legende dorée.* ibid. 1re *année de Richard* III. 1483.

20. *Directions for keeping the feasts of the whole year.* fol. ibid. *June the last.* } 1483.

21. *The lives of the saints.* ibid. 1484.

22. *The royal book, entitled in French,* Le livre royal. [3] fol. *translated and printed by William Caxton, in the second year of king Richard* III. *without the place's name.*

23. *Walter Hilton's scale of perfection.* ibid. 1484.

24. *The history of the noble and valiant knyght Paris, and the fair Vienne, the daughter of the doulphin of Viennes.* fol. ibid. [4] } 1485.

25. *The life of Charles the great.* ibid. 1485.

26. *Vita patrum.* ibid. 1485.

---

[1] Finish'd the sixth day of *juyn*, the first yere of king *Edward* the fifth.

[2] Finish'd the second of *september*, the first yere of *Richard* the 3d, in the yere a thousand CCCCXXXXIII. *In this date 'tis plain, by the king's reign, that the X's must be taken for twenties and not for tens.*

[3] A special book to know all vices and the branches of them, and also all virtues. This book sheweth and enseigneth it so subtilly, so shortly, so perceivingly, and so perfectly, that for so short comprehension of the noble cleargie, and of the right great substance that is therein compris'd, it may be call'd above other books, the royal book, or book for a king.

[4] Translated out of *French* into *English* by *William Caxton* of *Westminster*, finish'd the last of *august*, 1485, and emprinted the 19th of *december* the same year.

27. Mal-

27. *Malvire's hiftory of king Arthur.* ibid. *julii ult. in the year* 1485.

28. *The book of good manners.* ibid. [1] 1486.

29. *A treatife againft pride.* ibid. 1486.

30. *Dives and Lazarus, a dialogue on the decalogue.* fol. ibid. 1488.

31. *The book of* χριϛε, *(Chriftian) of Pyfedracon, out of Vegetius de re militari, and out of the arbre of battaile, with many other things fetten to the fame, requifite to warre and battailes; which book was delivered to tranflate and print, to William Caxton by king Henry the feventh, in the fourth year of his reign.* fol. ibid. [2] } 1489.

32. *The book of feats of arms.* ibid. 1489.

33. *Virgil's æneid tranflated, or rather epitomiz'd, from the French in profe by William Caxton:* printed by him. fol. ibid. } 1490.

34. *The hiftory of Jafon.* ibid. 1492.

35. *Confeffio amantis, or the confeffion of the lover, of Johan. Gower, &c.* ibid. This is the fecond edition, with the fame colophon as the former. } 1493.

36. *Vita patrum.* Second edition. ibid. 1495.

37. *Recueil of the hiftory of Troy, per Caxton.* 1502.

T H I S edition, with fome others, were communicated to me by a learned antiquary, in thofe very words, but whether he was really the Printer of it, or only the author, and the book Printed by fome other, is what I cannot determine, unlefs I could have feen the book.

[1] Compos'd by frere *Jacques le Graunt,* religious of the order of St. *Auguftin.*
[2] Which Tranflation was began the 23d of *january,* and finifhed the 7th of *july* the fame year, and emprinted the 14th of *july* next following.

Thofe

Thofe that follow are without date.

1. *Liber feftialis.*

THIS edition, though I have given it no higher rank, upon the account of its having no date, doth yet manifeftly appear to me to have been the firft book extant of *Caxton*'s Printing. I have feen it at my Lord *Pembroke*'s library, and compar'd it with thofe of the *Game of Chefs,* his three books of the hiftory of *Troy,* and his *Polychronicon*; all which have been feverally look'd upon as his oldeft edition by one an-nalift or other, and find in it thefe two unqueftionable marks of anti-quity above the other three, *viz* 1. The types on which it is printed appear to be entirely new, though they be the very fame which he ufed in all his other works; whereas, in the others they feem to be more ufed and worn. 2. This edition is the only one whofe lines are not fpaced out to the end; this being an improvement and elegancy introduced by him in imitation of foreign Printers; whereas all the firft editions had the fame defect with this.

As for the three books of the hiftory of *Troy,* the fecond is that which I imagine to have been printed firft. I have feen it very perfect in feveral libraries, but the firft and third I never could meet with any where, but in the noble library above mention'd. And even here they are fomewhat imperfect, the firft book wanting a few leaves at the be-ginning, and the third at the end. However, they all bear alike the mark of antiquity, and are unqueftionably done with *Caxton*'s types. The oldeft book I could ever meet with that bears a date is his fecond edition of the *Game at Chefs,* in 1474, as may be feen by the catalogue above; and what inclines me to believe it to have been the firft of that kind, is that the fame date 74 is continued in his following works that are dated, to which he fometimes added the two initial letters of his name, as in the mark or rebus here fubjoined.

N. B. W C *ftands for* William Caxton, *and the Figure between, for* 74, *i. e.* 1474; *the reader will plainly perceive the* 7, *and the other is a figure of* 4, *as made at that time.*

We

We have met with but five editions without date, though we have ventured to add several more upon the authority of Mr. *Maunsel* and other authors, who we think may be rely'd on.

2. *The game of Chess.* [1]

3. *The rule of the monks of St. Bennet.* fol. ibid.

4. *The life of our Lady.* fol. [2]

5. *The life of St. Winifred.* 4to. *translated and printed by* William Caxton.

6. *St. Austin raising two dead persons.* 4to.

7. *An exposition on the Lord's Prayer, Belief, Commandments, seven sacraments, seven virtues, seven deadly sins:* item, *the general sentence, or sentence of cursing,* modus fulminandi sententiam : *the beads on sonday.* fol. *Printed by* William Caxton *at* Westminster. [3]

8. *The fruit of time.* fol. *collected, compil'd, and Printed by* William Caxton. ibid.

9. *The spousage of a virgin.* 4to. ibid.

10. *The siege of Rhodes.* fol. ibid.

11. *Boetius de consolatione philosophiæ.* ibid.

12. *The mirrour of the blessed life of Jesus Christ, written in Latin by the worshipful Dr. Bonaventure ; translated into English in* 1410, *and brought to the reverend father Thomas Arundel, Archbishop of Caunterbury, who commanding and allowing the same, was afterwards printed by* William Caxton. ibid.

[1] Part of *Caxton's* Preface to the Game of Chess, in the hands of *Maurice Johnson,* Esq; is as follows ; ' And when I so had acheved ' the said Translacion I dyde do sette in em- ' prynte a certein nombre of theym whiche ' anone were depeshed and solde, and where- ' fore by cause thys sayd book is ful of holsom ' Wysedom and requysyte unto every astate ' and degree, I have purposed to emprynte ' it, shewing therein the figures of such per- ' sones as longen to the Playe.

[2] Written in verse by *John Lidgate,* monk of *Bury.*

[3] *This book begins thus ;* The maister of sentences in the second book and first distinct. saith, that the soveraigne cause why God made all creatures in heaven, earth, or water, was his own goodness.

13. *Chau-*

13. *Chaucer's Canterbury-tales, collected into one volume by Mr. Caxton.*.

14. *The book of arts and fciences by Mr. Caxton.*

15. *The Curiace of Mafter Alayn Charetier, tranflated by Caxton.* Belonging to *Maurice Johnfon,* Efq;

16. *Parvus chato ——— Cato's precepts in Latin and Englifh verfe.*

17. *De fide & cantû famule fue.*

II. WINKEN DE WORDE. MCCCCXCV.

WINKEN *de Worde,* the *Dutchman,* is fuppos'd to have come over with Mr. *Caxton,* and was his fervant and journey-man. He fucceeded him in his Printing-houfe, as appears from fome of his firft impreffions done by him, as he tells us, *in the houfe of Mr. Caxton.* It's difficult to affign the exact time when he came to *England*; whether with *Frederick Corfellis,* as my manufcript affirms, or fome years after, which is more probable. After Mr. *Caxton's* death, he carry'd on the bufinefs, and finifh'd fome volumes begun by his mafter, as the *Canterbury-tales* and *Hilton's fcale of perfection.* This laft Mr. *Mattaire* dates in the year 1494, and Mr. *Bagford* 1465, who gives it as the firft impreffion done in *Winken de Worde's* name. I have chofen to follow Mr. *Bagford,* who was very exact, as far as he could procure materials ; for I have not yet met with the book my felf. Though the lift of this Printer's works is very large, yet I am certain there are many more either loft or ftill latent in fome libraries; for he was a perfon of vaft induftry, and receiv'd all imaginable encouragement ; fo that he publifh'd feveral volumes in one year, though we meet with fome confiderable chafms in others, during which time we cannot fuppofe him idle. He left *Weftminfter,* and fet up his Printing-houfe in *Fleet-ftreet,* at the fign of the *Sun,* in the parifh of *St Bride.* I cannot determine the year of his removal ; though his firft impreffion there was done, *anno* 1503. He printed feveral *Latin,* as well as *Englifh* volumes, but no *Greek,* as I can find. He continued Printing with great applaufe till the year 1533,

if

if not beyond that time. At his death he left a fum of money for an annual *obiit* for his foul to the parifh of *St. Bride's*, of which he was an inhabitant. He was a perfon of great accomplifhments in learning, as well as ftrictnefs of morals ; and though he was the immediate fucceffor of *Caxton*, yet he improv'd the art to a very great perfection. At his firft fetting up for himfelf, his firft care was to cut a new fett of puncheons, which he funk into matrices, and caft feveral forts of Printing-letter, which he afterwards us'd. As *Caxton* us'd but two fizes, *Double Pica* and *Great Primmer*, viz.

Begun and finifhed by me fimple Man, W. C.

Begun and finifhed by me fimple Man, W. C.

Winken de Worde gave a greater fcope to his fancy, and form'd fuch a variety of forts and fizes of letter, that for feveral years after him, none of his fucceffors attempted to imitate him therein. If he was the manual operator in cutting and cafting in his own founding-houfe, 'tis an incredible improvement which he made to the art ; but, if he had his letter from any other Printer abroad, though it robs him of this glory, yet his excellent method of difpofition, compofition, and prefswork, fhews him to have far excell'd his mafter, and even to rival any of of his contemporaries abroad. There is one circumftance that induces me to think that he was his own letter-founder ; which is, that in fome of his firft Printed books, the very letter he made ufe of, is the fame us'd by all the Printers in *London* to this day ; and I believe were ftruck from his puncheons.

The firft is the two lin'd *Great Primmer* black,

by me Winken de Wozde

The next is the *Great Primmer* black,

This Wozk was finifhed by me, Winken de Wozde.

He

He is the firſt *Englijh* Printer, who introduc'd the *Roman* letter in *England*, which he us'd with his *Gothic* or black letter, to diſtinguiſh any thing remarkable, as we do the *Italic* with the *Roman* at this time. His letter is different from moſt other Printers, and is caſt ſo true, and ſtands ſo well in line, as not to be excell'd by any ever ſince : in his *Gothic* and *Roman* letter he fell in with the cuſtom of thoſe times by uſing abbreviations, even in his ſmall ſiz'd letters. One circumſtance I would obſerve is, that he is the only Printer I can find in *England* that us'd very ſmall body'd letters in the infancy of the art, and he was fond even to the very laſt of uſing his maſter *Caxton*'s rebus, of which we have given a ſpecimen at the bottom of page 340. Upon the whole, he was a very curious, laborious, and indefatigable Printer ; and I doubt not but time will add to his character, by bringing to light ſome noble teſtimonies of ſo great a man, which for want of, I am obliged to ſay ſo little here. He is the firſt Printer I have yet diſcover'd who began to print the year-books. [1]

The Liſt of his Works, as far as I have been able to collect them, are as follows.

1. *Polychronicon.*　　　　　　　　　　　　　　　　1495.

2. *Chaucer's Canterbury-tales collected by William Caxton, and printed by Wynken de Worde at Weſtmeſtre.* fol. ⎱ 1495.

3. *The lives of the holy faders hermits, tranſlated by Caxton, with cuts,* 10. *Hen.* 7. *Weſtmynſtre.* ⎱ 1495.

4. *Walter Hylton's ſcale of perfection, printed in William Caxton's houſe.* ⎱ 1495.

5. *Meditations of St. Bernard, tranſlated from Latin into Englijh by a devout ſtudent of the univerſity of Cambridge, and has been put to be imprynted by W. de W.* 4to. *Weſtmynſter the* ix. *of March.* ⎱ 1496.

[1] He and his Succeſſor *Richard Pinſon* printed above 40 year-books, which are in Lincoln's-Inn Manuſcript-library, being inſcrib'd *Libri manuſcripti.*

5. *A*

5. *A compendyouse treatife, dialogue of Dives and Pauper, viz. the ryche and the poore, fruƈtuoufly treatynge upon the tenne com-maundements, emprynted at* WeƗmonƗre, 111. *Decembre.* } 1496.

6. *Treatyfes pertaynynge to hawkynge and huntynge, and a trea-tyfe of cotarmours.* ibid. } 1496.

7. *Nicholas* Uptonus Sarisberienƒis *canonicus, & fcriptor haraldicus : de re haraldica Anglicé.* WeƗmynƗer. } 1496.

8. *Frute of tymes, compyled and emprynted by one fomctyme Schole-mayƗer of Saynt Albons ; and in* 1497 *emprinted at* WeƗ-meƗre. } 1497.

9. *Contemplation of finners, for every day in the week, a fingular meditation, compyled at the requeƗ of Richard Lord Bifhop of* DurefmeƗ, *Lord Privie feal of England, by dit.* ib. 4to. *July* 10. } 1499.

10. *Jo. Gubriand. finonima.* 4to. 1500.

11. *The Hill of perfeƈtion intituled in Latin, Mons PerfeƈƗionis, writen by John Alcocke, Bifhop of Ely, by ditto,* ibid. 4to. } 1501.

12. *Vobabula MagiƗri Stanbrigi.* 1501.

13. *The Ordinary of ChriƗen men.* 4to. 1502.

14. *Hore Beate Marie Virginis, cum fig.* printed upon Vellum. 1502.

15. *John Gerfon's three books of the Imitation of ChriƗ, tranflated into Englifh, by Will. Atkinfon,* DD. *at King Henry* VIItb's *Mother's defire.* } 1502.

16. *Aefopi fabulæ, cum comm.* 1503.

18. *The boke of the Recules of the fiege of Troy, emprynted in Lon-don in FleetƗreet, at the fign of the Sonne, with figures.* } 1503.

19. *Garlandia vocabulorum interpretatio.* 1505.

20. *The Ordinarye of ChriƗen men.* 1506.

X x

21. *Ars*

21. *Ars moriendi, that is the craft to dye, for the health of man's foul, by ditto.* 4to. } 1506.

22. *The caftle of honour, a poem.* 1506.

23. *The Feftival, or fermons on fondays and holidais, taken out of the Golden Legende,* 4to. } 1508.

24. *The book of carving.* 1508.

25. *The golden legende, reprinted.* 4to. 1508.

26. *The parliament of devils.* 1509.

27. *The court of fapience, a poem.* 1510.

28. *Demands joyous.* 1511.

29. *Promptuarium parvul. clericor.* 4to. 1512.

30. *Hiftory of Hilyas, knight of the fwans, with figures, on parchment.* 4to. } 1512.

31. *Bucolica Virgilii.* 1512.

32. *The long Accydence.* 1513.

33. *The fruit of redemption. Approved by Richard, bifhop of London.* 1514.

34. *Liber Theodeli, cum comm.* 4to. 1515.

35 *Expofitio Sequentiarum fecundum ufum Sarum.* 1515.

36. *The Chronicle of the world, or the fruit of time, in 7 books.* 1515.

37. *Virgilii bucolica, cum comm.* 2d. *edition.* 1516.

38. *Seneca de 4 virtutibus cardinalibus.* 1516.

39. *Ortus vocabulorum alphabetico ordine ferè omnia quæ in catholicon, Breviloquio, cornucopia, gemma vocabulorum atque medullâ grammaticæ ponuntur ; cum vernaculæ linguæ Anglicanæ expofitione continens, impreffus per Wincandum de Worde, ac in urbe in parochia Sanctæ Brigidæ* (de Fleteftrete) *ad fignum folis moram trahentem,* 4to. } 1516.

40. *Fa-*

40. *Fabulæ Æſopi, cum comm. 4to.* 1516.

41. *Rob. Whittintoni Litchfield. gramm. lucub. 4to.* 1517.

42. *Parabole Alami, cum comm.* 1517.

43. *Sulpitius Verulamus de moribus puerorum.* 1518.

44. *Whittintonus de concin. gram. conſtruƐt.* 1518.

45. ———— *de 8 partibus orat. 4to.* 1519.

46. *Familiaria colloquia Eraſmi.* 1519.

47. *The Orcharde of Syon, with the revelations of Saynt Catherine of Sene, tranſlated by Dane James, at the coſt of maſter Richard Sutton* [1] *, Steward of the monaſtery of Sion.* } 1519.

48. *The paſſion of our Lord, tranſlated from the French, by Andrew Chertſey, Gent.* } 1519.

49. *The dietary of ghoſtly health.* 1520.

50. *Hiſtory of England. fol.* 1520.

51. *Vocabula Magiſtri Stanbrigi (2d Edition)* 1521.

52. *Whittintonus de nominum generibus.* 1521.

53. *Vulgaria Rob. Whittintoni Lichfeldienſis.* 1521.

54. *The mirrour of the Church of St. Edmond of Abyndon.* 1521.

55. *The flower of the commaundments of God, with many examples and authorities drawn out of the holy ſcriptures and ancient Doctors, tranſlated out of French. fol.* } 1521.

56. *Whittintonus de ſyllabarum quantitate.* 1522.

57. ———— *lucubrationes.* 1523.

58. ———— *Verborum præterita & ſupina.* 1524.

[1] Founder of the *Charter-houſe.*

59.

59. ———— *Declinationes nominum.* 1524.

60. *Roberti Wakefeldi oratio de utilitate ling. Arabicæ & Hebra-*
icæ. 4to. [1] } 1524.

61. *Vulgaria Rob. Whitintoni.* (2d Edition) 1525.

62. *The image of love.* 1525.

63. *Whitintonus de heteroclitis nominibus.* 1526.

64. *The lives of the three kings of Colein,* 4to. 1526.

65. *The mirrour of gold for a sinful soul, translated out of the*
French by the ryght excellent Princesse Margaret Mother to } 1526.
King Hen. 7. Countess of Richmond and Derbie. 4to.

66. *The golden legende, wherein beene contayned all the high feasts*
of our Lord, and of our Ladie, the lives, passions, and many
other miracles of many other saintes histories, finished the 27th } 1527.
of August. fol.

67. *Whitintoni vulgaria, & de instit. gram.* 4to. 1527.

68. ———— *de syllabarum quantitate.* 1528.

69. ———— *lucubrationes.* 2d. edit. 1529.

70. ———— *syntaxis.* 1529.

71. ———— *de partibus orationum.* 1529

72. *Constitutiones Othonis.* 8vo. 1529.

73. *The miracles of our Ladie.* 4to. 1530

74. *Grad. Comparat. cum verb. anomal.* 1530

75. *Parvulorum. inst. ex Stranbrig. collect.* 1530

[1] The Author excuses himself to the king [*Hen.* VIII.] to whom he dedicates this speech, that he is forced to omit one third part of it for want of *Hebrew* types, which he says his Printer had none of; and it is very probable that there were none as yet in *England,* since nothing of that nature had been attempted, that ever I could hear of no doubt the Author made enquiry whethe any such types were in *England,* before h resolv'd to let it go maim'd of its best an most curious part. I have seen this book and find the *Arabic* and *Hebrew* types cu on wood.

76. Th

76. *The pilgrimage of perfection.* fol. 1531.

77. *The plowman's prayer and complaint.* 1531.

78. *Abby of the Holy Ghost.* 4to. 1531.

79. *Bonaventure's leſſons.* 4to. 1532.

80 *Life of Edward the confeſſor.* 4to. 1533.

81. *Virgil's Bucolica, Lat.* 4to. 1533.

82. *Whitintoni ſynta is.* 8vo. 1533.

83. ———— *de Heteroclitis.* 4to. 1533.

84. *A work for houſholders and governours of families, &c.* 4to. 1533.

85. *Life of Hildebrande.* 1534.

86. *The Roſary of our Saviour Jeſus.* 4to. 1536.

Books Printed by W. de WORDE. without dates.

1. *The life of Johan Picus, earl of Myrandula.*

2. *Bartholom. de proprietatibus, or the proprieties of things.*

3. *Donatus minor ad Anglican. ſcholar. uſum.*

4. *The roſe and mirrour of conſolation and comfort.* 4to.

5. *Vulgaria Stanbrigi.*

6. *Whitinton. de 8 partib. orat.* 4to.

7. *Quæſtiones magiſtri Alberti de modis ſignificandi, by W. de Worde in Fleet-ſtreet.*

8. *Nichodemus's goſpel, with other tra{c}ts,* 4to.

9. *Gradus comparationis, &c.* 8vo.

10. *The book named the Royal, Engliſh'd by Caxton.*

11. *Sermones declamati coram Univer. Cantab. per Steph. Baron.*

12. A treatiſe call'd *Parvula* in *Caxton's* houſe.

13. *Ac-*

13. *Accidence. Weſtmuſtre.* ibid. in *Caxton*'s houſe. *Remov'd into Fleet-ſtreet at the Sun.*

14. *A morning remembrance had at the month-mind of the noble Princeſs Margareth, Counteſs of Richmond and Derby, Mother to King Henry VII. To which is added a funeral ſermon to King Henry VII. his body being preſent, preached May* 10, 1509, *by John Lord biſhop of Rocheſter, and printed at the ſpecial requeſt of the Counteſs of Richmond, the mother of the deceaſed.*

15. *A ſhort treatiſe of contemplation taught by our Lord Jeſus Chriſt, or taken out of Margery Kempe of Lynn.*

16. *The life of Joſeph of Arimathy, taken out of a book found by Theodoſius the Emperor in Jeruſalem, in the pretory of Pilate.*

17. *The comfort againſt tribulations.*

18. *Richard Rolle, hermit, of Hampull's contemplation of the dread and love of God ; with other divers titles.*

19. *The meditations of St. Bernard.*

20. *A little inſtruction out of St. Jerom, drawn by Tho. Botton.*

21. *Hornodeus, or the remorſe of conſcience, a poem.*

22. *The Abbaye of the Holy Ghoſt, with* 29 *ghoſtly ladies in it.* [i. e. *a good conſcience*] *printed at Weſtminſter.*

23. *The lamentation of our Lady.*

24. *A collection from Gerſon and ſeveral authors, by Tho. Botton.*

25. *The Bewge of court, a poem.*

26. *Againſt peſtilence, and of infirmities.*

27. *Stans puer ad menſam.*

28. *Biſhop Groſshead's treatiſe of husbandry, or rather a tranſlation of his out of the French.*

29. *The life of Robert the devil, afterwards called the ſervant of the Lord.*

30. *The*

30. *The hiſtory of Jacob and his twelve ſons.*

31. *The proverbs of Lydgate, a poem upon the fall of princes.*

32. *King Edward, and Robin Hoode, and Little John.*

33. *The aſſembly of the gods.*

34. *The merry jeſt of the Fryer and the Boy.*

35 *How the plowman learn'd his Paternoſter, a poem.*

36. *The Churl and the Bird, a poem.*

37. *The Horſe, and Sheep, and the Gooſe, a poem.*

38. *The governal of health.*

39. *The eleven grammars by Winken de Worde.*

THIS curious piece is in the Lord *Pembroke*'s library, and has ſome obſervations written on a blank page at the beginning, which are to this effect; , The eleven grammars printed by *Winken de Worde*, who , was the 2d Printer in *Weſtminſter*, he lived afterwards within the walls , of *London*, at the ſign of the *Sun* in *Fleet-ſtreet*. *Richard Pinſon*, af- , terwards his worthy ſucceſſor, and he printed above 40 year books , which are in *Lincoln's Inn* Manuſcript library; they being inſcribed , *Libri Manuſcripti*. He was ſon-in-law to *Caxton*, who firſt printed , at *Weſtminſter* in the Almonry beyond *Weſtminſter*-School. Theſe , eleven grammars were all printed above 100 years before *Lily*'s gram- , mar, and appear to be the foundation of his.

WE ſhall have occaſion to give a further account of theſe year-books, when we come to ſpeak of *R. Pinſon*, who continued printing them a con- ſiderable time after *Winken de Worde*'s death. As for the eleven gram- mars they are in one volume in the form of a very ſmall quarto and neatly printed, and it is judiciouſly obſerved that they were printed above a century before that famous one of *Lylly*, which has been thought (and is ſtill, by thoſe who never heard of this edition,) to be the firſt grammar that ever was printed in *England*.

FROM

FROM this large catalogue of *Winken de Worde*'s works, it is plain that he must have been an indefatigable Printer; and that the chasms that frequently happen in some years must be owing to the books being either lost, or as yet undiscover'd; but more probably the former: and whoever considers that the greatest part of them were either school-books, classics, prayer-books, &c. (besides a vast number of popish ones, which might daily perish soon after the Reformation) and of how short duration the former are in the hands of school-boys and devotees such as that age abounded with, will rather wonder that so great a number of them have escaped the common fate of such performances. So that we may justly conclude, that the preservation of these books is more owing to the character and excellency of the Printer than of the authors, and to the neatness and correctness of the work, rather than the goodness or usefulness of the subject. After he was removed from *Westminster* to *London*, we do not hear of any other Printers at the former; if there were any, they were such whose works and memory in all probability died with, or soon after them.

The City of LONDON, MCCCCLXXXI.

THO' *Richard Pinson* be the first known Printer that set up his Press in this famous city, and all former annalists have ranked it in their list from his first edition, 1493; yet father *Orlandi* has since discover'd to us a much more antient one which was printed in *London*, *anno* 1481, that is 12 years before the former; which makes me hope that time may still discover more, if not of older date, yet at least to fill up the chasm between this and the first of *Pinson*. For it is scarce to be supposed that *Westminster* should begin so soon to encourage the art, as we have seen in the last article, and that *London* should wholly neglect it. However, be that how it will, it is certain that if it was but slow in receiving it, it made ample amends for it afterwards, and that *Pinson* and *De Worde*, when he removed thither, gave a new life to it; so that in a little time there were several considerable Printing-houses set up in the most convenient parts of this large metropolis,

wherein

wherein it has flourished and improved ever since. Some of those eminent Printers received likewise great encouragement from the Crown, particularly by patents for printing of Bibles, and other works, of which I shall give an account under the names of the Printers to whom they were granted.

N.B. As *Caxton* printed all his works in the old letter, and *W. de Worde* in a mix'd character of Roman and Black, we have distinguish'd their works in the two former catalogues, from those that follow, by printing them in Italic: but, as the Roman types became by this time more common, we shall give the list of the following Printers works in that character.

THIS antient and curious edition above mention'd is as follows;
Valdesius super Psalterium Londini. 1481.

I. RICHARD PINSON. Anno MCCCCXCIII.

RICHARD PINSON, *alias* PYNSON, is the first known Printer in the city of *London,* no edition having been hitherto discover'd, except that anonymous one mention'd above, of older date than his dialogue of *Dives* and *Pauper* in 1493. Besides, as we have about 15 editions of his that are without date, we may more reasonably suppose that they were printed before than after this year, in which he began to put a date. He was brought up under Mr. *Caxton,* as well as *Winken de Worde,* and being become a thorough master of the art, went and set up a Press of his own at *Temple-bar,* as the inscription of his first edition shews. The friendship which he had contracted with *De Worde,* whilst these two wrought under *Caxton,* was so far from being disturb'd by any mutual emulation or rivalship, that it continued to their death; and it is thought that after their master's death, *Pynson* prevail'd upon him to leave *Westminster,* and to come and settle nearer to him, which he accordingly did. What makes this more than probable is, that the last edition of *Caxton* is dated, as we have shewn, *anno* 1502, and the first that *De Worde* printed in *London,* as far as we have been able to discover, is dated 1503. These two were joined in

Y y

the

the Printing of the king's year-books, as long as *De Worde* lived, which were afterwards continued by *Pinson*; and this is a sufficient testimony of his having been an excellent Printer, were there nothing else to assure us of it: for it is not to be suppos'd that he would have associated himself to any other. *Pynson* stiles himself Printer to the king in some of his editions, probably from a grant he had for the printing of those year-books above mention'd. For we neither find that he printed any bibles, or other books, for which patents were granted by the crown. I don't find that he used any rebus, but he either printed his name at length, or else only the two initial letters R. P. The list of his works is nothing so copious as those of his associate, tho' he continued Printing at least 34 years, as appears from the dates of his first and last edition, which makes me conclude that a great part of them are lost. Those I have been able to recover are as follow;

1. Dialogue of *Dives* and *Pauper* upon the X Commandements, emprinted by *Richard Pynson* at *Temple-bar* of *London*, V. day of *July*. } 1493.

2. Sulpitii Verulami opus grammaticum. *4to.*   1494.

3. *Boetius*'s Fall of Princes, *&c.* by *John Lydgate*, Monk of *St. Edmund's Bury:* } 1494.

4. *Gerson*'s Imitation of Xt. *English'd* by *Atkinson*. 4to.   1503.

5. *Navis stultifera*, or the ship of fools; done into *English* by *Barclay*. fol. } 1509.

6. Liber intrationum.   1510.

7. An Exposition of the 7 penitential Psalms, compyled by the Ryghte Reverende Fader in God *Johan. Fysser* D. D. *&c.* Bp. of *Rochester*, at the Exortation and Storyinge of the most Excellente Pryncesse *Margaret*, Countesse of *Rychemont* and *Darby*, and Moder to our Soveraigne Lord King *Henry* the Seventh, on whose Soule Jesu have Mercy. } 1510.

8. *John Beckham*, Arch. *Cant. de summa Trinitat. & Fide Cathol.* 1510.

9. *Colet,*

9 *Colet*, Dean of *Paul*'s Sermon to the Convocation. *Lat. 8vo.* 1511.

10. The Hift. Siege & Deftruction of *Troy*, *Englifh'd* by *J. Lid-*
gate, with Cuts. } 1513.

11. Textus Alexandri, *&c.*   1516.

12. The Kalendre of the newe Legende of *Englande*, compyled
by Mafter *Walter Hylton*, emprynted at *London* in *Flete-*
ftrete, at the figne of the *George*, by *Richard Pinfon*,
Prynter unto the King's Noble Grace, in the Yere of } 1516.
our Lorde God 1516, and endy'd in the laft Day of *Fe-*
bruary.

13. Guil. Hormain. Vulgaria. 4to.   1519.

14. The Life of St. *Verburge*. *Virg.* 4to.   1521.

15. Affertio Septem Sacramentorum adverfus *Martin. Luther.*
edita ab invictiffimo *Anglia* & *Francia* Rege, & de *Hy-*
bernia Henrico hujus Nominis octavo. Apud inclytam urbem *Londinum* in ædibus *Pinfonianis*, an. M. D. XXI. } 1521.
quarto Idus *Julii*, Cum privilegio a rege indulto. Editio prima.

16. *Cutberd.* Tonftalis Ars fupputandi. 4to.   1522.

17. *Froiffard*'s firft Volume. 4to.   1523.

18. *Powel*'s Propugnaculum fummi Sacerdotii contra *Lutherum.*
4to. } 1523.

19. *Tho. Linacr.* de emendata Latini Sermonis ftructura. 4to.   1524.

20. *Froiffard*'s fecond Volume. 4to.   1525.

21. *Whittintoni* Vulgaria & de Inftitutione partium. 4to.   1525.

22. Olde Tenurs newly corrected.   1525.

23. Accidence.   1526.

24. Magna Charta. 8vo.   1527.

25. The Book of *John Bochas* on the Fall of Princes, *Englifh'd.* 1527.

Y y 2   26. Li-

26. Literarum quibus, &c. or K. *Henry* VIII's Epiftolary An-} *1527*.
fwers to *Luther*. 8vo.

Thofe that follow are without date.

1. *Saluft* tranflated by Syr *Alexander Barclay*, Prieft, at the Commaundement of *Thomas* Duke of *Norfolke*.

2. *Littleton*'s Teners newe correated.

3. Natura Brevium.

4. *Tonney*'s Rules of Grammar, *&c.*

5. How yong Scholers now adays emboldened in the Flyblown Blaft of the moch vayne glorious pipplying Wind, whan they have delectably lycked a lytell of the lycorous Electurry of lufty Lernyng, in the moche ftudious Scole Houfe of fcrupulous Philology, countyng themfelfs Clerkes excellently informed, & tranfcendingly fped in moche high conyng, & whan they have ones fupercilioufly caught. By *Skelton* Poets Laureat. By *R. Pynfon*.

6. *Littleton*'s Tenures. *French*.

7. *Barclay*'s Figure of Mother Church opprefs'd by the *Fr.* King. 4to.

8. The Ch. of Evil Men, where Lucifer is head, *&c.* 8vo.

9. *Henry* VIII's Anfwer to *M. Luther*. 8vo.

10. *Bonaventure*'s Life of J. Chrift, tranflat. by *Caxton*, & reprinted. fol.

11. The Life of St. *Alborow Virg*. 4to.

12. A Sermon preach'd long ago at *Paul's Crofs*, *He that hath Ears to hear*, &c. 4to.

13. The Mirrour of good Manners, *&c.* fol.

14. Speculum Vitæ Chrifti, or Mirrour of the Life of Chrift.

15. The Deftruction of *Hierufalem* by *Vefpatian* and *Titus*. Printed by *Richd. Pinfon* the King's Printer.

Be-

Besides thefe he printed a confiderable number of Year, or Law-Books that pafs'd under feveral Kings Reigns, as was hinted before; fome with *Winken de Worde*, and others after his death; fome with the dates of the Year and Month in which they were printed, and his name at the end, and fome without either. However, it muft be ob-ferved that a great part of the oldeft of them have the name Γουλιελ-μος Ραστελ (*Guilelmus Raftell*) written at the head, by which we con-jecture that they only printed them for him. For *Raftel* was Printer to the King, and a very confiderable perfon at that time, and in great credit at Court upon the account of his having m rry'd Sir *Thomas More*'s Sifter. So that it is very likely he had the Privilege of printing all thefe Royal Books, and gave them a fanction by prefixing his name to them, whilft the others only acted under him. What feems to con-firm it, is that thofe earlier ones with *Pynfon*'s name mention only *Ex Officinâ Pynfonianâ*; whereas in thofe of later date he calls himfelf Printer to his Majefty, in which Office he probably fucceeded *Raftell*, who died according to Dr. *Nicholfon, an.* 1536. Thus at the end of the 2d Edition of that of the 2 of *Edward* IV. We find this Colophon, *Explicit annus 2dus* Ed. iiij. *Townfend de novo impreffus in Academia, &c. ac Impenfis honefti viri* Richardi Pynfon *Regii Imprefforis.* Thefe Year-Books were of different Bulks, tho' all Folio's, fome of them containing but 4 or 5, others 10, 20, 50, and even as far as 90 Sheets. They are as follows;

Years of *Edward* III. 7th, 21, 38, 40, 41, 42, 43. 2d Edition, ditto 44, 45, 46, 47, 48, 49, 50.
——— *Henry* VI. 2, 8, 9, 10, 12, 20, 21, &c.
——— *Edward* IV. 1, 2, 3, &c.
——— *Edward* V. 1.
——— *Richard* III. 2.
——— *Henry* VII. 9.
——— *Henry* VIII. 14.

Whether thofe that are wanting in the Lift are loft, or were printed by others, we cannot affirm, but more probably the latter; becaufe

caufe we find fome few printed by *Grafton*, *&c*. But, as thefe are only of ufe to the Lawyers, this Specimen fhall fuffice. Thofe who want a more particular account of them, may have recourfe to the *Lincoln's-Inn*-Library, where they are carefully preferv'd in a large wooden Cheft.

II. WILLIAM FANQUE. MDIV.

William Fanque ftiles himfelf the King's Printer in the only Edition I have been able to find of his, *viz*.

Pfalterium ex mandato victoriofiffimi *Angliæ* Regis *Henrici* Septimi.

Per *Guillelmum Fanque*, Imprefforem regium anno M D IIII. feptimo *Februarii*.

III. JULIAN NOTARY. MDXV.

We have two Editions of the fame work printed by him, *viz*.

1. The Chronicle of *England*, with the fruit of Tymes, *newly imprinted by me* Julian Notary, *dwelling in St*. Powlis *Church-yard*, *befyde the West-dore by the Lordes Palyefe*. fol. .in the yere M CCCCC & XV. } 1515.

2. The fame with Cuts, *&c*. reprinted an.   1537.

IV. HENRY PEPWELL. MDXXI.

The Dietary of ghoftly health divided into twenty four Con-fiderations. 4to. *London*, by *Henry Pepwel*. } 1521.

V. PETER TREVERIS. MDXXV.

Who lived in *Southwark*, and fubfcribed the place of his abode as follows; Dwelling in the fign of the Wodow's in *Southwark*. We have but the three following Editions of his.

1. *Jherom* of *Brunfwick*'s Surgery. fol.   1525.

2. The *Polichronicon* corrected by *Winken de Worde*. fol.   1527.

3. The great Hearbal, with Cuts. fol.   1527.

VI, THO-

VI. THOMAS BERTHELET. MDXXX.

T. B ERTHELE T was Printer and Bookfeller to K. *Henry* VIII. had a Patent for printing the *Englifh* Bible, and fome other Books relating to the King's Divorce; the firft of which has the following pompous Title.

1. Graviffimæ atque exactiffimæ illuftriffimarum totius *Italiæ* & *Galliæ* Academiarum Cenfuræ, efficaciffimis etiam quo- rundam Doctiffimorum Virorum Argumentationibus ex- plicatæ, de Veritate illius propofitionis, *videlicet* ; quod ducere Relictam Fratris mortui fine liberis ita fit de Jure Divino & Naturali prohibitum, ut nullus Pontifex fuper hujufmodi Matrimoniis contractis five contrahendis dif- penfare poffit. 1530,

   In Officina Thomæ Berthleti *Impefforis Regii.* 4to. Lon- dini, *menfe* Aprili, An.

2, The fame in *Englifh*, tranflated and publifhed by the King's Command, & printed by *T. Berthlet.* 1531.

3. The fame in *L on* and *Englifh.* 8vo. by ditto. 1531,

4. The New Additions, by ditto. 1531,

5. *Salem* and *Bizance*, a Dialogue againft Sir *Tho. Moore's* A- pology. 8vo. 1533,

6. A Treatife written by *Johan. Valerian*, a greatte Clerke of *Italy*, which is intitled in *Latin*, *pro Sacerdotum Barbis*, tranflated into *Englyfhe*, with a Preface of the Tranfla- tour to the Reader. 8vo. 1533,

   Londin. in Ædibus *Tho. Berthleti.*

This is a fcarce and curious Piece. [1]

[1] At the End of the Book is the Picture of *Lucrece*, with thefe Words in Capitals, L U C R E T I A R O M A N A. T H O M A S B E R T H E L E T U S. Then follow thefe Words; *Endlofs Grace, Blyffe, Thankyng and Prayfing unto our Lord God Omnipotent, by whofe Ayde and Helpe this Tranflation was ended at* Ber- keley, the vi daye of Feverer, the yere of *our Lorde*, M CCC LXXXXVII. *the yere of Kyng* Richard *the Second after the Conqueft* XXII. *the yere of My Lordes Age Syre* Tho- mas Berkeley, that made me make this Tranf- lation XLVII.

7. De

7. De Contemptu Mundi, or Contempt of the World. 8vo.　1533.

8. Sir *Thomas Knight*'s Tranflation of *Cyprian*'s Sermon on Mortality. 8vo. } 1534.

9. Additions to *Salem* & *Bizance.* 8vo.　1534.

10. *Matthews*'s Sermon at St. *Paul*'s 8vo.　1535.

11. Barthol. de Proprietatibus Rerum. Cum Privilegio a Rege indulto. Tranflated into *English.* fol. } 1535.

12. Dives & Pauper, a Dialogue on the 10 Comm. reprinted. 8vo. } 1536.

13. Comparifon of a Virgin and a Marry'd Woman. 8vo.　1537.

14. Sturmius's Epiftle to the Cardinals and Bifhops of *Rome*. 8vo. 1538.

15. A Treatife, that by the King's Laws the Bifhops of *Rome* have no Supremacy in *England*. 8vo. } 1538.

16. The Moft Sacred Byble, which is the holy Scripture, conteyning the Old and New Teftament, tranflated into *English*, and newly recognifed with great diligence after moft faithful Exemplars by *Richard Taverner. Dedicated to* K. Henry VIII. *with decent Humility.* Prynted at *London* in *Fleet ftreet* at the fygne of the *Sonne*, by *John Byddel* for *Thomas Barthlet.* } 1539.

　　　At the End are thefe Words;
To the honour and praife of God was this Byble prynted and fynifhed in the yere of our Lorde God. M D XXXIX.

　　　A very fcarce Edition.

17. St. *Cyprian*'s Expofition of the Lord's Prayer, &c. 8vo.　1539.

18. *Henry* Ld. *Parker*'s Declaration of the 94th Pfalm. 8vo.　1539.

19. *Tonftal*, Bifhop of *Durefin*'s Sermons. 8vo.　1539.

20 Of *Guaccum* Wood againft the *French* Pox, Stone, and Gout, 8vo. } 1539.

21. *Ri-*

21. *R. Taverner's* Recognition of the Bible. fol.   1539.

22. *Frontine's* Stratagems of War, *English'd*. 8vo.   1539.

23. The neceffary Erudition of a Chriften Man, &c.   1543.

24. *Cope's* Hiftory of *Hannibal* and *Scipio*. 4to.   1544.

25. St. *Tho. Eliot's* Banquet of Sapience. 8vo.   1545.

26. *Ant. Gisbie's* Anfwer to *Steph. Gardiner*, Bp. of *Winchefter*. 8vo. 1547.

27. *Erafmus's* Sermon on God's Mercy. 8vo.   1547.

The following are without date.

1. Dean *Colet's* Sermon to the Convocation. 8vo.

2. *Tho. Starkey's* Exhortation to the People to Unity, *&c.*

3. A Dialogue between a Knight and a Clarck about Power.

4. *Erafmus's* treatife on *Pater Nofter.* *English'd by a Young Wm.* 19 Years old. 4to.

5. *Ricardi Sampfonis* Regii Sacelli Decani Oratio contra Papam. 4to. in Pergam.

VII. W I L L I A M R A S T E L, Printer to the King, as was mention'd before, was an eminent Citizen of *London*, and a good Hiftorian. We find an *English* Chronicle of his quoted by *Athen. Oxonienf. John Petit*, and other antient Hiftorians, but now loft, in Dr. *Nicholfon's* Opinion. He liv'd in St. *Bride's* Church-Yard, *Fleet-ftreet.* M D XXX.

1. A Dialogue of Sir *Tho. More* touching the peftilent doctrine of *Luther* and *Tyndal.* Prented by *Willyam Raftel.* fol. *Lond.* } 1530.

2. Regiftrum Omnium brevium tam Originalium quam judicialium. *Londini* apud *Guillelmum Raftel.* Cum privilegio. } 1531.

Z z   *At*

At the Beginning of the Book are thefe Words printed in Capitals;

Hunc librum Regiis litteris ne quis alius in hoc Regno impune im-primat infra feptennium cautum eft.

At the End of the Book thus;

Thus endyth thys Book callyd the Regyfter of the Wrytyngs orygynal and judycyal. Prentyd at *London* by *Wyllyam Raftell,* and it is to fell in *Fleet ftreet,* at the houfe of the fayde *Wyllyam,* or in *Poulys* Chyrch yarde, or els at *Temple-bar,* at the houfe of *Robert Redman.* Cum privilegio.

3. The fecond part of the Confutation of *Tyndal*'s Anfwer by } 1533. Sir *Tho. More.* Prentyd by *W. Raftel.* fol.

4. *Fabyan*'s Chronycle newly prentyd. Cum privilegio.   1533.

5. A merry Play between the Pardoner and the Frere, the Cu- } 1533. rate and Neighbour *Patte.* 4to.

6. The Apologye of Syr *Thomas More* Knyght.   1533.

Without date.

1. *German Gardiner*'s Letter againft *John Fryth* lately burnt. 8vo.

2. A New Commodye in *Englyfh,* in manner of an interlude, ryght ele-gant and full of Craft and Rethoryke, wherein is fhew'd and de-fcrybed as well the Bewte and good properties of Women as their Vices.

VIII. R O B E R T   R E D M A N, againft St. *Dunftan*'s Church in *Fleet-ftreet.* M D XXX III.

1. A playne and godly Expofition or Declaration of the Crede,] (which in the *Latin* tongue is called *Symbolum Apoftolorum*) | and of the X Commandementes of Goddes Law,

Newly

Newly made and put forth by the famoufe Clerke May-
fter E R A S M U S of *Roterdame.* At the Requefte of the
mofte honorable Lorde, *Thomas* Erle of *Wyltfhyre:* Father to ⎱ 1533.
the moft gratious and vertuous Quene *Anne,* Wyf to our
moft gratyous Lorde Kinge *Henry* the viii. *Cum privilegio.*

At the End thus;

Imprinted at *London* in *Flete ftrete* by me *Robert Redman,*
dwellynge at the figne of the *George,* next to Saynt *Dun-*
ftone's Churche. *Cum privilegio Regali.* ⎰

2. *Otho* and *Othobone's* Provincial Conftitutions. 8vo.　　1534.

3. Mirrour of Xt's Paffion, tranflated by *John Fruterer.* fol.　1534.

4. Sum of Xtianity out of the Scriptures. 8vo.　　　　　1536.

5. *Erafmus* in *Latin* and *Englifh.* 4to.　　　　　　　1538.

6. *Magna Carta* in *French,* whereunto is added more Statuts ⎤
than ever was imprynted in any one Boke before this tyme: ⎪
with an Alminacke & a Calender to know the Mootes. ⎪
Neceffarye for all young Studiers of the Lawe. ⎪
⎬ 1539.
At the End thus, ⎪
Here endeth *Magna Charta,* and divers other Statutes. ⎪
Imprynted at *London* in *Fleetftreet* by me *Robert Redman* ⎪
dwellynge at the fygne of the *George* next to Saynt *Dun-* ⎪
ftones Church. 1539. in 12mo. in the Front 1529. ⎦

7. *John Standifh* againft the Proteftation of *Robert Barnes* at ⎱ 1540.
the time of his Death, by the Widow of *Robert Redman.* ⎰

Without date.

1. Confeffion exhibited by the *Germans* to the Emperor *Charles* V.
with *Milington's* Apology for it. 8vo.

2. Of the Lives of Priefts, Canons, Clerks, and Church-Minifters. 8vo.

Z z　　　　　　　　　　　　　3. Ser-

3. Sermon on the Child Jeſus. 8vo.

4. Lantorn of Light. 8vo.

5. A Book of Medicine of King *Boetius.* 4to.

6. *Littletons* Tenures.

7. The Paradox of *Marcus Tullius Cicero,* tranſlated lately out of the *Latin* Tongue into *Engliſh* by *Robert Whittinton* Poet Laureat.

8. *Tho. Moulton* Doctoure of Dyvynyte, of the Order of *Frere-Prea-chours* Myrrour or Glaſſe of Helthe, neceſſary for every perſone to look in that will kepe theyr body frome Syckneſs of the Peſti-lence. 8vo.

The Author tells us that he wrote this Treatiſe whilſt the plague raged.

9. Returna Brevium, vel ſi mavis, Reſcripta Vice Comitum eum aliis ſcitû digniorib⁹. 8vo.

　　　　　At the End, *Rob. Redman me fecit.*

10. *Littleton*'s Tenures.

11. A Work for Houſholders, by *Rich. Whitford.*

12. The Year-Books printed by him are as follows,

　　　　　24 of *Edward* III.　25 Sheets ½
　　　　　40 ——————— 26
　　　　And above 30 more.

At the End are the Words following;

Imprimé a *Londres* par moy *Robert Redman* le X. jour de *Marche* l'an de grace M CCCCC XXXIII. Cum privilegio Regali.

IX.　J O H N　B Y D D E L.　M D XXXIV.

Jонn Biddel is the Printer mention'd above, p. 360. who printed the great *Engliſh* Bible for *Berthelet*; his Printing-houſe was at the ſign of our Lady of *Piſe* next to *Fleet-bridge:* his *Rebus* was a Heart pierc'd
　　　　　　　　　　　　　　　　　　　　with

with a double Crofs, on each fide of which within were the
two initial letters of his name I. B. to which he fometimes
added his name at length, J O H N B I D D E L.

1. Of the olde God and the new, of the olde Fayth and the
   newe, of the olde Doctryne and the newe, or the original Begyning of Idolatry ; imprinted at *London* by *John*
   Byddle, at the Sign of our Lady of *Pife*, &c. M VC XXXIIIJ.
   the XX day of *June*.   } 1534.

2. *Rob. Whittingtonus* de nominum Gener. 4to.   1536.

3. A Bible in *Engl.* fol. Printed by him for *Berthelet*.   1539.

4. Of the olde and new God, olde and new Fayth, &c. 8vo. 1539.

5. *Cupito*'s Prayers and Meditations on the *Pfalms, Eng.* 8vo.   1539.

6. A Chronicle of Yeres from the beginning of the World,
   wherein ye fhall find of al the Kinges of *England*, of the
   Mayrs & Shiriffs of the Citie of *London*, & briefly of many
   notable Actes done in & fith the reigne of Kyng *Henry*
   the fourth newly augmented & corrected, *Anno Domini*,
   M VC XLII. by *John Biddle*.   } 1542.

Without date.

1. *John Roberts* Mafter of Schifmatick Bps. of *Rome.* 8vo.

2. A Book of Feafts Royal and Cookery for Princes. 4to.

3. Accidentia ex Stanbrigiana Editione nuper recognita a *Whittingtono*
   Laureato.

4. A Seraphick Dirige of 7 Secrets granted to St. *Francis.* 8vo.

5. The Lives of Pope *Hildebrand* and *Henry* IV. Emperour of *Ger-*
   many. 8vo.

X. R O-

X. ROBERT WYRE. MDXXXV.

He lived at the fign of Saynt *John the Evangelyfte* in Seynt *Martyn*'s Paryfhe in the Filds befyde *Charynge-Crofs*, in the Byfhop of *Norwytche*'s Rents, as he fays himfelf, and ufed to fubfcribe fome of his Works, efpecially the Year-Books, with his name in large Capitals thus, R O B E R T   W Y R E.

WE have but one Piece of his that bears a fure Date, which is as follows ;

1. The Deffence of Peace, lately tranflated out of *Latin* into
Englyfhe : with the Kynges mofte gracious priviledge. *The*
Author, Marfilius of *Padway. Imprynted and publifhed, and*
fet forth abrode in the Englifhe *tonge by* Wylliam Marfhal,
who prays for our Soveragne Lorde Kynge Henry the Eight,
of his moft vertuous Lady Quene Anne, *and of the Lady Pryn-*
cefs Elyzabeth, *Daughter and Heyre to them both.*   1535.

   N. B. *This Book appears by its date to have been publifhed*
   about the time when King Henry 8. *had refolv'd to break*
   with the Court of Rome. *At the End are thefe Words* ;

   Prynted by me *Robert Wyer* for *Wylliam Marfhal,* &c.
   with the King's priviledge for 6. years.

2. The Debates between the Heralds of *England* and *Fraunce,*
compyled by *Jn. Coke,* Clarke of the Kynge's Recogny-
fances, or vulgarly called Clarke of the Statutes of the
Staple of *Weftmynfter,* and finifhed in the year of our
Lorde M D L.   *At the End as follows* ;   1550.

   Finifhed by me *John Coke le dernier jour Doctobre den*
   yaer ons here duiffent venf hundred negen en viertick (that is
   thoufand five hundred and fourty nine.) Finis Laudat opus.
   Imprinted by me *R. Wyer, &c.*

With

Without date.

3. Ten Places of Scripture againſt the Traditions of Men. 8vo.

4. Wm. Hunnis Abridgement of Meditat. on certain Pſalms in meter. 8vo.

5. *Antitheſis* comparing the Word of God and Mens Inventions by *Th. Beacon.* 8vo.

6. *Antidotarius* or the way of making Salves, Ointments, &c. 8vo.

7. *Macer's* Herbal. 8vo.

8. *Th. Linacre.* M. D. Compend. regimen of Health uſed at *Montpelier.*

9. The Caſtle of Love, tranſlated out of *Spanyſhe* into *Englyſhe*, by *John Bowrchier* Knyght, Lord *Bernes*, at the Inſtance of the Lady *Elyzabeth Carew*, which book treateth of Love betwene *Leriano* and *Laureola* Daughter to the Kinge of *Maſedonia.*

10. The Breviary of Healthe.

11. The Signs in the Zodiac.

12. Erra Pater.

13. A Piece of *Tycho Brahe* upon the Heavens.

14. A Year-Book for the 9th of *Henry* IV. printed by *Robert Wyre* dwellynge at the ſygne of St. *John* the Evangelyſt, &c.

XI. THOMAS GIBSON. MDXXXVI.

A Treatiſe againſt the Peſtilence, written by a *Daniſh* Bp. & } 1536. Phiſician. 4to.

XII. JAMES NICHOLSON, at *Southwark.* MDXXX.

1. Expoſition on the 1. 2. & 3 Canonical Epiſtles of St. *John.* } 1537. 8vo.

2. The

2. The New Teftament both in *Latin* and *Englyfhe*, eche cor-⎫
refpondente to the other after the Vulgare Texte communely ⎬ 1538.
called St. *Jerome*'s, faithfully tranflated by *Johan. Hollybufhe*. ⎪
By *James Nicholfon* dwellyng in *Southwarke*. ⎭

3. Invectives againft Cardinal *Wolfey*, by *L. R.* at *Wefel*.   1546.

   N. B. *Maunfel* affirms it to have been printed by *Nicholfon* ; no
doubt but he compar'd it with fome other of his Works, and it is
certain that nothing was more common in thofe ticklifh times than
to date any dangerous Book from fome place abroad, or to in
fcribe it printed ——————— beyond Sea.

4. A Treatife of Meafuring, without date.

                 The Title runs thus,

   This Book fheweth the manner of Meafurynge of all manner of
Land, as well of Woodlande, as of Land in the Felde, and compt-
ynge the true Nombre of Acres of the fame, By Syr *Richard Be-
nefe*, Chanon of *Marton Abbay* befyde *London*.

            Printed in *Southwarke* by *James Nicholfon*.

XIII. T H O M A S P E T I T. M D XXX VIII.

1. *Longland* Bp. of *Lincoln*'s Sermon before the King. 4to.   1538.

2. Treafure of poor men, a Book of good Medicine 8vo.   1540.

3. St. *Bernard*'s fruitful Treatife of living well.   Tranflated by *Th.
   Paynel.* 8vo.

4. *Chaucer*'s Works dedicated to *Henry* VIII. no date.

XIV. J O H N W A Y L A N D. M D XXX VIII.

1. *Nicholas Wife*'s Chryftian Confolation. 8vo.   1538.

2. *James Chanceller*'s Path to Obedience. ⎫
                                          ⎬ without date.
3. The Tragedies of *John Bochas*, tranflated into *En-* ⎪
   gl fhe by *John Lydgate*, Monke of *Bury*.   ⎭

                                                  XV.

XV. RICHARD GRAFTON. MDXXXIX.

RICHARD GRAFTON, Citizen of *London*, from an indifferent Author and Hiftorian, became a famous and eminent Printer. Among other of his works under the former charaçter, we have his Abridgement of the Chronicle of *England*, in which he is a conftant borrower from the bulkier work of *Edward Hall* Recorder of *London*, who wrote the Hiftory of the Wars between the Houfes of *York* and *Lancafter*, wherein the Reader will find little worth notice, if we may believe Dr. *Nicholfon*, than the fafhions and changes of Drefs in each King's Reign. As *Grafton* was not over judicious in the choice of this Author, fo neither was he in the compiling of his Abridgement; in fo much that the learned *Buchanan*, in his Hiftory of *Scotland*, doth not fcruple to call him *a very headlefs and unskilful Writer*, tho' he has had the honour of being quoted by *Stow*, and other Hiftorians.

THE occafion of his turning Printer was his being pitch'd upon to procure an Edition of *William Tyndal*, alias *Hickins* Verfion of the New Teftament, and afterwards of his Bible revifed and correçted by *Myles Coverdal*, a learned *Francifcan* Fryar, well learned in the *Hebrew, Greek* and *Latin* tongues. Some impreffions of the former had already been difperfed about *England* and elfewhere, but were bought up by *Tonftal* Bifhop of *London*, and Sir *Thomas More*, and been burnt at St. *Paul's Crofs*; and it was very dangerous to undertake the reprinting of fuch a work in *London* upon that account. This made *Grafton* and his affociate *Edward Whitchurch* refolve to get it done at *Hamburgh*, whither they likewife fent *Coverdal* to correçt the Prefs. This proved a very expenfive work, and the impreffion of the Bible alone coft them 500 *l.* a great fum in thofe days. When it was brought over into *England*, it met with great oppofition from the *Romifh* Priefts, they having fome time before obtain'd a Royal Proclamation, to prohibit and abolifh that among other heretical books; and, had not *Bonner* Bifhop of *Hereford* bought up the greateft part of the Copies in order to deftroy them, the undertakers muft have been infallibly ruin'd. This Edition is fuppos'd to have been printed *anno* 1535.

A a a

HIS

His New Teftament met with worfe fate, of which we have an authentick teftimony extant in the Library of the Honourable Earl of *Pembroke, viz.* two Editions of it printed at *Antwerp* in the fame year, *viz. anno* 1434, one of which has a Preface prefix'd to it, to juftify that Edition, from the other of the fame year printed under his name, but ftrangely mutilated and mifprinted. A more particular account of which is given in the Introduction to *Wickliff*'s Bible lately publifh'd.

Finding that a verfion of the Bible was as much defir'd by the favourers of the Reformation, as it was cry'd down by the enemies of it, they ventur'd to print a fecond edition of it under the patronage of Archbifhop *Cranmer* and the Lord *Cromwell.* But *Tyndal* having been by that time burnt as a heretick in *Flanders,* and his name growing then fomewhat ignominious, they thought fit to publifh it under the name of *Matthews*'s Bible, tho' *Tyndal* is affirm'd to have finifh'd all but the *Apocrypha* as fome, or as far as *Nehemiah,* as others affirm. *Grafton* having finifh'd the printing of it prefented it to his two great Patrons, by whom, at his requeft, it was likewife prefented to the King to whom it was dedicated. It had thefe words in red letters printed at the bottom of the title-page *fet forth with the King's moft gracious licence.* But, as they were fufpected to have been foifted in, *Grafton* obtain'd leave to have it further licenfed under the privy feal. Soon after this it being obferved how acceptable an *English* Bible was to the people, fome perfons form'd a defign to print it in a fmaller volume, in order to underfell *Grafton*'s, which obliged him to apply to *Cromwell,* and to obtain a patent from the King, that none fhould print it for three years; and for the better fale of this, that noble man did likewife procure him an order that every Curate of a parifh fhould be obliged to have one, and every Abby fix of them; fo that this fecond impreffion, wherever printed, was very foon bought up.

Grafton and his partners in the work obferving that there was ftill a call for them, refolved to reprint it a third time, and in a larger volume, but without thefe notes and prologues which they obferv'd had given fome offence. *Paris* was the place pitch'd upon to print it at, and *Cromwell,* who favour'd the enterprize, procured letters from King *Henry* to the *French* King, *to permit a fubject of his to print the* Englifh
Bible

Bible in the univerſity of Paris, *becauſe of the goodneſs of the* French *paper and workmen.* Bonner, then Ambaſſador from *England* to the Court, had likewiſe orders *to aſſiſt the undertakers of that good work in all reaſonable ſuits.* Bonner obtain'd not only the deſir'd licence, but likewiſe letters patents for printing this Bible, and for conveying it ſafe over to *England.* This edition, being thus encourag'd, went briſkly on to the end; but *Bonner,* who never liked the work, and did only promote it to make his court to *Cromwell,* found means to obſtruct it privately, notwithſtanding the King's patents.

ACCORDINGLY, *anno* 1438, the Printers were taken up, and charged with hereſy, by order of the Faculty, and *Coverdale* the corrector, *Grafton* the Head Printer, and other *Engliſhmen,* who contributed to the charges of the impreſſion, were ſent for ; but they foreſeeing the conſequences, fled away as faſt as they could, and left the whole impreſſion which was juſt finiſh'd, and conſiſted of 2500 Copies, behind them. This was immediately ſeiz'd by the Lieutenant Criminal, and order'd to be burnt, except ſome few which he'ſold, through covetouſneſs, for waſte-paper, which were afterwards bought up again, being about four fats or cheſts full.

My Lord *Pembroke* favour'd me with the ſight of an *Engliſh* Bible printed in *Gothic* characters, *an.* 1537. without place or Printer's name, with theſe words at the end ;

The end of the New Teſtament, and of the whole Byble.

❡ To the Honoure and Prayſe of Gode was this Byble prynted and fyneſhed in the yere of oure Lorde Gode. a M D XXXVII.

BUT whether this is one of them that were printed at *Paris,* or one of the former edition I cannot determine ; but it is more probable to be the latter, becauſe it has a Concordance of the moſt remarkable texts of Scripture againſt the errors of Popery : whereas, as I obſerv'd before, they had ſuppreſs'd moſt things of that nature in the *Paris* one. But let this be of what edition it will, it is very probable that the Concordance proved the cauſe of the almoſt total deſtruction of it, in ſo much that I queſtion whether there be any other copy of it left except this above mention'd. However, *Grafton* and his aſſociates, by *Crom-*

A a a 2 *well's*

well's encouragement, went foon after to *Paris*, and got the preffes, letters and workmen, and brought them over to *London*, and fo fet up for Printers themfelves, which they never intended before, and began to reprint the fame Bible, which they finifh'd in 1537; an account of which you'll find in the following lift of *Grafton*'s works.

We find a patent in *Rymer's fœdera*, vol. 17. p. 766. from King *Henry* VIII. appointing him and his partner *Whitchurch* to print the Book of divine fervice; but, as I have not been able to meet with the Book, I have not inferted it in the lift. The patent is dated *Jan.* 3. 1543. *Grafton* ftyled himfelf *Typographus Regius*. His mark or fign was an Apple-

 tree fpringing up out of a Tun, or Ton, as they fpell'd it then, alluding to his name *Graft-ton*, with this motto *fufcipite infitum verbum*, Jacob. 1. He had likewife a Cypher over the Tun, with the two initials of his name one in another thus.

His works are as follows.

1. The New Teftament in *English* and *Latin*. 8vo. *London,* printed by *Rich. Grafton* and *Ed. Whitchurch.* } 1439.

2. The Bible in *English*, that is to fay, the contents of all the holy fcripture, both of the Old and New Teftament, truly tranflated out of the veryty of the *Hebrew* and *Greke textes*, by the dylygent ftudye of dyvers excellent learned men, expert in the forefayd tongues. Printed by *Richard Grafton* and *Edward Whitchurch.* Cum privilegio ad imprimendum folum. fol. *At the end is as follows*;

Fynifhed in *Apryll, Anno* M CCCC XXXIX. } 1539.

The Title is adorn'd with a noble piece of Hiftory, fuppofed to be done by *Holbein*, of King *Henry* 8. Archbifhop *Cranmer*, and Vicar-general *Cromwell*, with their Coats of Arms.

3. The Primmer in *Latin* and *English*. 4to. Printed in the precinct of the diffolved houfe of Grey Fryars, by *Richard Grafton*, Printer to the Prince's Grace the VI. day of *Septemb.* M D XLIII. Cum privilegio ad imprimendum folum. } 1543.

4. *Plu-*

4. *Plutarch*'s Precepts for the prefervation of health. 8vo.   1543.

5. The Chronicle of *John Hardyng, &c.* with a Supplement in profe. *Londini ex officina* Ric. Graftoni, *menfe Januario.* } 1543.

6. The Anfwer of *Charles fift, Emperour,* ever more *Auguft,* unto the Letters Convocatory of *Paule the thyrde bifhop of Rome,* concerning a general Councel to be celebrated at *Trident.* 1543. *Ex officina* Rich. Graftoni 8vo. } 1543.

   With a remarkable Preface to the Reader.

7. The Primer in *Englifh* and *Latin.* 4to. Printed in the precincte of the diffolved houfe of Grey Fryars, by *Richard Grafton,* Printer to the Prince's Grace the VI. day of *Sept.* MDXLV. Cum privilegio ad imprimendum folum. } 1545.

8. An Abridgement of *Polidore Virgil* of the Divifers, *&c.* of Artes, by *T. Langley.* } 1546.

9. *Philip Gerard*'s Invective againft ftopping the free paffage of the *Englifh* Bible. 8vo. } 1547.

10. Certain Homilies or Sermons appoynted by the King's Majefty to be redde by all Perfons, Vicars, or Curates, every Sondaye in their Churches where they have Cure. 4to. } 1543.

11. Articles to be enquired into in the Vifitation to be had within the Diocefe of *Canterbury,* in the fecond yere of the Reign of our moft dred Sovereigne Lord *Edward* VI. by the Grace of God King of *England, Fraunce* and *Ireland,* Deffender of the Faith, and in the Yearth of the Church of *England,* and alfo of *Ireland* the fupreme Hedde. 4to. } 1548.

12. Expedition into *Scotland* of the moft worthy fortunate Prince *Edward* Duke of *Somerfet,* Uncle to our moft noble Sovereign Lord *Edward* VI. *&c.* by way of Diarie, by *W. Paten.* } 1548.

13. Alcoran of the Barefoot-Fryars. 8vo.   1550.

14. *John*

14. *John Marbeck's* Concordance of the Bible. fol.   1550.

15. *Hall* 's Chronicle. fol.   1550.

     Befides a number of Year-Books.

XVI. EDWARD WHITCHURCH. MDXXXIX.

He was alſo one of the King's Printers, and a famous one. We have mention'd him already in the laſt article, as having printed,

1. *Coverdale's* New Teſtament *Lat.* & *Engl.*

2. The *English* Bible. fol. with *Rich. Grafton.*

    The reſt of his Works are as follows;

3. Earl of *Purlilia's* Precepts of War. *English'd* by *Philip Be-* } 1544.
   tham. 8vo.

4. A Treatiſe of Moral Philoſophy, containing the Sayings of the Wiſe, gathered and *Englyſhed* by *Wylliam Baldwyn. London,* Imprinted by *Edward Whitchurch,* the 10 day of *January.* 8vo. } 1547.

5. *Chriſt. Langton's* Treatiſe of Naturals and Non-naturals, *&c.* 8vo. } 1547.

6. *Melanɛton* upon weighing & conſidering the Interim. *Eng-liſh'd* by *John Rogers.* 8vo. } 1548.

7. Paraphraſe on St. *Paul's* Epiſtles and *Revelations,* by ſeve-ral hands. fol. } 1549.

8. The Booke of the Common Prayer and adminiſtration of the Sacraments, and other rites and ceremonies of the Church; after the uſe of the Church of *England. Londini* in Officina *Edouardi Whitchurch,* cum privilegio ad imprimendum ſolum. Anno Do. 1549, *Menſe Junii.* } 1549.

                                           The

The King's Majeſtie by
the adviſe of his moſt dear Uncle the Lord Pro-
tector, & other his highneſs's Counſel, ſtrictly
chargeth & commaundeth, that no manner
of Perſon do ſell this preſent booke
bounde, above the price of ii Shyl-
lynges & ii pence the piece.   And
the ſame bounde in paſte or
in boordes, not above the
price of three Shyl-
lynges & viii
pence the
piece.
God ſave the King.

Imprinted at *London* in *Fleet-ſtreet*, at the
ſigne of the Sunne over againſt
the Conduyte by *Edward Whitchurch*,
the xxvi daye of *June*, the year of our Lord
1549.

9. Epiſtle of Conſolation and Advertiſement to the Duke of *Somerſet* before his troubles, and tranſlated by him in his Impriſonment. 8vo. } 1550.

10. *Edmund Allen*'s Catechiſm. 8vo.   1550.

11. Form of Common Prayer uſed at *Geneva*, with *Calvin's* Catechiſm. 8vo. } 1550.

12. Paraphraſe on the Goſpels and Acts. *Engliſh'd* by *N. Udal.* fol. } 1550.

XVII. WILLIAM MIDDLETON. MDXXXIXI.

Richard Whitford, a Brother of *Sion*, his Treatiſe on Patience, and the Lets and Impediments to Perfection. 4to. } 1541.
Imprinted at *London* by me *Wylliam Middleton.*

XVIII.

XVIII. JOHN MAYLER. MDXXXIXII.

1. A Sermon, that no Man can be hurt but by himfelf. 8vo.   1542.

2. Neceffary Doctrine & Erudition for a Chriften Man. By } 1543.
the King. 8vo.

XIX. JOHN DAY. MDXXXIXVI.

He was a curious and diligent Printer ; how foon he began to print is not eafy to guefs, becaufe I find feveral of his editions without date. He continued printing till the year 1575 ; however, I fhall carry the lift of his works no farther than 1550.

1. R. *Crowley's* Confutation of *Nich. Saxton,* Bifhop of *Sarum.* } 1546.
8vo. *London*

2. A godly Meditation upon xx felect and chofen Pfalms of } 1547.
the Prophet *David, &c.* 4to. By Sir *Ant. Cope.* Dedicated
to Quene *Catherine.*

3. Heavenly Acts of Parliament made by Father, Son and } 1547.
Holy Ghoft, how Men ought to live. 8vo.

4. *John Bancroft's* tranflation of the *Bafil* Preacher's Anfwer. } 1548.
By *J. Day* and *W. Seres.*

5. Confutation of *Miles Hoggard's* Ballads in defence of Tran- } 1548.
fubftantiation. 8vo. by *J. Day* and *W. Seres.*

6. A fimple and religous Confultation about making a prefent } 1548.
Reformation till God fend a better by a general Council, *&c.*

7. *Fr. Lambert's* Judgment againft the Freedom of Man's } 1548.
Will. 8vo.

8. *Rob. Hutton's* Sum of Divinitie.   1548.

9. A Warning againft the Anabaptifts. 8vo. by *J. Day* and } 1549.
W. Seres.

10. St. *Auftin's* 12 Steps to Abufes, by *J. Day* and *W. Seres.*   1550.

11. An

11. An Apology of *Johan. Bale* agaynfte a rank Papiſt, anſwering both him and his Doctors, that neyther their Wowes, nor yet their Prieſthood, are of the Goſpel but of Antichriſt. 8vo. } 1550.

12. Homilies on the 6th of St. *John*. 8vo.　　　1550.

13. Confeſſion of the Chriſtian Faith, with reſpect to God, the King, *&c.* 4to. } 1550.

14. Expoſition of *Daniel's* Prophecies out of *Melangton*, *&c.*　1550.

Without date.

1. Expoſtulation againſt a phrentic Papiſt of *Hamſhire*. 8vo.

2. *Baſil* the Great to *Gregory Nazianzen* about a Monaſtic Life.

3. 25 Sermons on Predeſtination. *Engliſh'd* by a Gentlewoman. 8vo.

4. Communication between a poor Man and his Wife, *&c.* 8vo.

5. Brief Exhortation in the time of Viſitation.

6. Auncient Teſtimonies about the Faith of the Church of *England* about the Sacrament. 8vo.

7. A verie, familiare and fruitefull Expoſition of the Apoſtles Crede, made in Dialogues, wherein thou maiſte learne all Things neceſſarie to be beleved, Compyled by *Peter Viret* a *Frenchman*, and tranſlated into *Engliſhe*. 8vo.

8. *Thomas Norton's* Warning againſt the dangerous practices of Papiſts, and ſpecially the Parteners of the late Rebellion. *Lond.* by *John Day*, no date, but ſuppoſed to be printed about the year 1549. 4to.

XX. JOHN HERTFORD. MD XXXIXVI.
at St. *Alban's*.

He printed at firſt at St. *Alban's*, and we have two editions of his printed there, one without date, and the other done in 1538, of which

B b b

we need not give any further account here. What I have been able
to recover of his Works, after he removed to *London*, is as follows;

1. *Richard Smith*, D. D. Defence of the Sacrament of the Mass.
   8vo. *London.* } 1546.

2. *Stephen Gardner* Byffhoppe of *Wynchefter*'s Declaration of
   fuch true Articles as *George Joye* has gone about to confute } 1546.
   as falfe. 4to.

Without date.

1. St. *Jerom*'s Expofition. Printed at *London* in *Alderfgate-ftreet*, by
   John Hertforde for *Robert Toy.*

2. The Epiftles and Gofpels, in 4to. by *John Hertforde* in *Alderfgate-
   ftreet.*

The following was printed by his Widdow.

The Cenfure and judgement of the famous Clark *Erafmus* of *Rote-
rodam* ; whyther Dyvourfemente betwene Man and Wyfe ftondeth
with the law of God, with dyvers Caufes wherefore it is permitted ;
with the mynde of the olde Doctours, *&c.* *London*, Prynted by
the Wydowe of *John Hertforde* for *Robert Stoughton*, without date.
8vo.

XXI. ROBERT TOY. MDXXXIXVI.

1. *Stephen Gardner* Bifhop of *Winchefter*'s Declaration of fuch
   true Articles as *George Joy* hath gone about to confute as } 1546.
   falfe. 4to.

2. Detection of the Devil's Sophiftry, *&c.* 8vo.   1546.

3. Of the Refurrection of the Dead, and laft Judgment, by
   John Clarke. 4to. } 1547.

Without date.

4. The Workes of *Geffray Chaucer* newly printed, with dyvers workes
   whiche were never in Print before.
   Imprinted at *London* by *Robert Toy.* fol.

N. B.

N.B. There was afterwards a much fuller Edition of Chaucer's *Works publish'd by* John Stowe, *and printed by* John Kyngston *for* John Wight, *in* 1561. *fol.*

XXII. NICHOLAS HILL. MDXLVI.

John Clark's Declaration of certain Articles and capital Errors, &c. 8vo. } 1546.

XXIII. WILLIAM SERES. MDXLVI.

WILLIAM SERES was a very eminent Printer, curious and correct; but he was much excell'd by his Succeffor and Affignee *Henry Denham*, who kept the fign of the *Star* in *Pater-Nofter-Row*, and became an extraordinary Mafter of his Art, not only for his wonderful Correctnefs, but for the beauty of his Types, whether *Greek, Roman, Italic,* or *Gothic,* of which he had a great variety of fizes as neat and beautiful as any now in ufe. I have feen a Dictionary of his printed in 1580, under the title of An Alviarie (Beehive) or a quadruple Dictionarie in *Greek, Latin, French,* and *Englifh*; which I think a mafterpiece of art for beauty and correctnefs, as well as great rarity for its order, method, and difpofition, it being the only one of that kind I ever met with.

As for *William Seres* he lived without *Alderfgate,* and went partner in fome works with *John Day,* and in fome with *Ant. Scholoker*; as the lift of his works doth fhew, which is as follows.

1. *Robert Crowley*'s Confutation of *Shaxton*'s Recantation. Printed oy *W. Seres* & *J. Day.* } 1546.

2. *Bancroft*'s Tranflation of the *Bafil* Divines on the Lord's Supper. By ditto } 1548.

3. Confutation of *Miles Hoggard*'s Ballad in defence of Tranfubftantiation. By ditto. } 1548.

4. *Peter Viret*'s Collection of Scriptures which explain the Lord's Prayer. 8vo. By *Seres* & *A. Scholoker.* } 1548.

5. A

5. A Warning againſt the Anabaptiſts 8vo. with *Day*.   1549.

6. St. *Auſtin*'s 12 Steps to Abuſes, &c. 8vo. ditto.   1550.

Without date.

7. The Tryal, Examination, & Death of Sir *John Oldcaſtle*. 8vo. with *A. Scholoker*.

8. Private Prayers for every Day of the Week, firſt printed in King *Edward*'s days. 8vo.

9. The right Inſtitution of Baptiſm, by *Herman* Archbp. of *Cologne*. By *Anthony Scholoker* & *Wyllyam Seres*, dwelling wythout *Alderſgate*.

XXIV. REYNOLD WOLF. MDXLVII.

HE was choſen Printer to the King (*Edward* IV.) for the *Hebrew*, *Greek* and *Latin* tongues. His Patent, which is extant in *Rymer's Fœdera*, 15 Vol. p. 150, is dated from *Weſtminſter April* 19, 1547. But I have not been able to meet with any thing done by him in any of thoſe learned languages. His other works are as follows.

1. Dr. *Smith*'s Declaration upon his Retraction at St. *Paul's Croſs*. 8vo.   } 1547.

2. A Deffence for Marriage of Prieſts by Scripture and auncient Writers, *before the* Biſhop of Rome *by his wicked decrees ordeined the contrary*; made by *John Pouel*, Doctour of Divinite. Imprinted at *London*, by *Reynold Wolf*. Cum fereniſſimi Regis privilegio. 8vo.   } 1549.

3. Ant. Corvinus's Poſtils on the Goſpels of Sundays & Holydays. 4to.   } 1550.

4. *Coverdale*'s New Teſtament conferr'd with that of *W. Tindal*. 8vo.   } 1550.

5. Defence of the Catholick Doctrine of the Sacrament of the Body and Blood, &c. 4to.   } 1550.

6. Injunctions of *Nicholas Ridley* Biſhop of *London* to his Diocefe. 4to.   } 1550.

With-

Without date.

1. Advertifements partly for the order of publick prayer, and partly for regulating the Minifters apparel. 4to.

2. An Anfwer to Doctour *Smith*'s Calumnyes in his confutation of the faid book. 8vo.

XXV. W I L L I A M   P O W E L.   M D XLVII.

At the fygne of the *George*, next to St. *Dunftan*'s Church, in Fleet-ftreet.

1. A Treatife of Juftification by Faith, tranflated by *Nich. Leffe*. 8vo. } 1547,

2. The Fall of the late *Arrian*. 8vo.   1549.

3. The Voice of the People againft fuch Parfons, as fly away from their Cures. 8vo. } 1549,

4. St. *Auguftin* to *Pollentius* againft adulterous Marriages. 8vo.   1550,

5. *Anto. Afcham*'s Treatife of Aftronomy, and of Medicines under each planet. 8vo. } 1550,

6. Proverbs or Adagies gathered out of the *Chiliades* of *E-rafmus*, by *Richard Taverner*, as well *Latyn* proverbs as *Englyfhe. London*, Imprinted by *Willyam Powel* XX day of *April. anno* M D L. } 1550.

7. The A B C fet forth by the King's Majefty (*Hen.* viij) & his Clergy, & commanded to be taught out all his Realm, and all other utterly fet apart, as the Teachers thereof tender his Grace's favour. 8vo. *London*, by *Willyam Powell*. without date.

XXVI. H U M P H R E Y   P O W E L.   M D XLVIII.

1. The Harveft is at hand. By *John Champneis*. 8vo.   1548.

2. The Sin & abominable Blafphemy of the Mafs. 8vo,   1548,

3. *John*

3. *John Proctor's* Fall of the late *Arrian.* 8vo.   1549.

4. The ordinary fashion of good living. 8vo. no date.

XXVII. GUALTER LINNE. MDLXVIII.

1. *Richard Bonner's* Treatise of worshipping Christ in the Sacrament. 8vo.   } 1548.

2. Archbp. *Cranmer's* Catechism. 8vo.   1548.

3. *Urban. Regis* Epistle to his friend about the causes of Church Controversy. 8vo.   } 1548.

4. *Bern. Ochinus's* Dialogue of the unjust Supremacy of the Pope. 4to.   } 1549.

5. *Peter Martyr's* Epistle to the Duke of *Somerset.* 8vo.   1550.

6. *John Ponet's* Sermon before the King. 8vo.   1550.

XXVIII. WILLIAM HILL. MDXLVIII.

1. *Heron. Bodin's* Collection out of St. *Austin* de Essent. Divinitatis. 8vo.   } 1548.

2. The Endightement of Mother Mass, by way of Dialogue. 8vo.   } 1548.

3. The Soul's solace against Sickness & Death. 8vo.   1548.

4. Sum of the H. Scripture about Xtian Faith, Baptism, & gospel-life. 8vo.   } 1548.

XXIX. THOMAS RAYNOLD. MDXLVIII

1. Declaration of God's power in the Sacrament against the Mass. 8vo.   } 1548.

2. Lesson of the Incarnation of J. Christ. 8vo.   1549.

3. The Bible translated by *Tho. Mathews,* anno 1537, & new imprinted by *Tho. Raynold* & *Will. Hyll.*   } 1549.

4. *John Mardey's* Instructions to the Rich and Covetous. 8vo.

Ad-

Addenda to the Article of GRAFTON.

We are fince inform'd that the Edition of the New Teftament *againft whih* Tyndal *juftifyes himfelf in the reface mentioned* pag 370. *was a third Edition privately printed undr his name in the fame year and place by* Joyce, *ard defignedly corrupted, in order to make him pafs for a Heretick, as h fhows in that Prefac, which was the occafion of his publifhing this fecond Edition in the fame year.*

XXX. ANTHONY SCHOLOKER. MDXLVIII.

1. Sermon on the Keys & Abfolution. *Englifh'd* at *Ipfwich.* 8vo. 1548.

2. *Zuingliu 's* Inftructions of Youth. ibid. 8vo. 1548.

3. *Scholoker's* Tranflation of *Peter Viret's* Collection of Scripture-places explaining the Lord's Prayer. 8vo. with *W Seres.* } 1548.

4. *John Olde* of the old Faith of *Great Britain.* 8vo.

5. *Pyor's* Plowmn's Exhortation unto the Lordes, Knightes & Burgoyffes of the Parlyment-houfe. *Lond. temp. Ed.* VI.

XXXI. ROBERT STOUGHTON. MDXLVIII.

1. Two Epiftles of *Henry Bullinger,* and two of *Calvin* about affifting at the Mafs. 8vo. } 1548.

2. *Urban. Regius's* Comparifon between old and new Learning. 8vo. } 1548.

3. The Cenfure and Judgement of the famous Clark *Erafmus* of *Roterdam*; whyther Dyvourfement betwene Man and Wyfe ftondeth with the law of God, with dyvers Caufes wherefore it is permitted; with the mynde of the olde Doctoures, *&c.*

4. *Peter Martyr's* Judgment of the Lord's Supper. 4to.

XXXII. RO-

XXXII. ROBERT CROWLEY. MDXLIX.
an Author and Printer.

1. Voice of the Trumpet, containing 12 Leſſons for 12 ſeveral eſtates in meter. } 1549.

2. A New Year's Gift, wherein is taught the knowledge of God, of our ſelf, and the fear of God, worthy to be geven and thankefully receyved by all Chriſten men. } 1549.

3. Pſalter of *David.* 1549.

4. Voice of the Trumpet, *&c.* 1550.

5. Battery of the Pope's Boteveux, or the high Altar. 8vo. 1550.

6. The Way to Wealth, teaching a moſt preſent remedy for ſedition. Wrytten and imprinted by *R. Crowley. Lond.* } 1550.

7. Lady *Eliz. Fane's* Pſalms and goodly Meditations, with 102 Proverbs. } 1550.

8. Prologue for the underſtanding of the Bible. *It is by Crowley intitled the Pathway to Knowledge.* 8vo. } 1550.

9. An Information and Petition againſt the Oppreſſion of the pore Commons of this Realme, *&c.* to the Parliament. no date.

XXXIII. WILLIAM TILLY. MDXLIX.

Coverdale's Teſtament. By *Wylliam Tilly*, dwellynge in St. *Anne & Agnes* Pariſhe at *Aldriſhgate* } 1549.

XXXIV. RICHARD KELE. MDXLVX.

1. Tranſlation of a *Dutch* Prognoſtication out of the Script. and Proph. 8vo. *London, Rycharde Kele.* } 1549.

2. Image of Both Paſtors, by *Zuinglius.* 8vo. By *Richard Kele & W. Seres.* } 1550.

3. Expoſition on the Epiſtle of St. *Jude.* 8vo.

4. Mir-

4. Mirrour or glafs of Helth, 8vo. nedeful for every perfon to loke in that wyll kepe their Body from the Sykeneffe of the Peftylence, and it fhoweth how the planets do raygne.

XXXV. ANDREW HESTER. MDL.

The *Englifh* Bible corrected and revifed by *Miles Coverdale.* 4to. 1550.

XXXVI. JOHN CAWOOD. MDL.

John Cawode or *Cawood.*———— I can find but one of his works extant, tho' he was appointed by the King to print the Patents. His Patent is in *Rymer's Fœdera,* and the Book is,

A fpiritual and moft precious perle, *&c.* Dedicated to *Edward* Duke of *Somerfet.* A moft fruitfull Treatife of behaviour in the danger of Death. *Somerfet-Place,* 6 *May,* 1550.

XXXVII. RICHARD JUGGE. MDL.

1. *Tertullian's* 2d. Book to his Wife about the choice of a Husband and Wife. 8vo. } 1550.

2. The New Teftament of King *Edward* VI.

3. Whether it be mortal fin to tranfgrefs the Civil Laws, with the judgement of *Melangton* and other Divines thereupon. 8vo.

XXXVIII. RICHARD CHARLTON. MDL.

A Treatife of all the Arguments of the Old and New Tefta- ment. 8vo. } 1550.

XXXIX. STEPHEN MIERMAN. MDL.

The Market or Fair of Ufurers, a new Pafquil or Dialogue againft Ufury, *&c.* 8vo. *Lond.* by *Steph. Mierman.* } 1550.

XL. JOHN

XL. JOHN TISDALE.

Sermons on *Jonas.* 8vo.
Abridgment of *Polydore Virgil.* } 1550.

BESIDES thefe we meet with a Patent in *Rymer's Fœdera,* Vol. XIV. pag. 745, granted to *Stephen Merlar* for the fole printing the *Englijh* Bible. It is dated at *Weftminfter, March* 12. *an.* 1542. but I never could meet with this Bible, nor any other of his works. I found moreover about half a fcore more who printed for, or under fome of the more eminent mafters above mentioned, fome of whofe works have dates, and others not, befide a very confiderable number of other anonymous editions, not worth fwelling this lift with.

The City of *YORK.* MDXVI.

I have feen in the late Mr. *Rawlinfon's* library the following edition printed at *York,* viz.

Whyttintonus de Concinnat. Grammat. & Conftruct. 4to. *Eboraci* 1516.

THIS is the only one I have feen or heard of printed there fo early, and did not the Types convince me of its being an ancient piece, I fhould have thought that the date had been mifprinted, *i. e.* 1516 for 1616.

At *CAMBRIDGE.* MDXXI.

THIS Univerfity feems to have given but fmall encouragement to the Art of Printing, either by the earlinefs of its reception, or the continuance of it there. Mr. *Maittaire* tells us that he has not been able to meet with any thing printed there of earlier date than 1521, and all that either he, the late Mr. *Bagford,* or any of my correfpondents from thence have been able to procure, is only four editions, all printed in the fame year, by *John Siberch,* and one in 1522 without Printer's name, though probably done by him. This *Siberch* ufed to put the King's-arms to the title of his books, and to ftyle himfelf in fome of them, *Primus utriufq; linguæ in* Anglia *impreffor,* meaning *Greek* and *Latin.*

Thefe

Thefe Editions are as follows;

1. Libellus de confcribendis Epiftolis Autore *D. Erafmo* opus olim ab eodem cæptum, fed primâ manu, mox expoliri cæptum fed intermiffum, Nunc primum prodit in lucem.

Apud præclaram *Cantabrigienfem* Academiam.

Cum gratiâ & privilegio.

At the End,

Impreffum Cantabrigiæ *per* Joannem Siberch, *Anno* M D XXI. *menfe* Octobri.

It is dedicated by *J. Siberch, Cantabrigienfis Typographus* to *J. Fifher,* Bifhop of *Rochefter.*

1521.

2. *Henry Bullock*'s Oration againft Cardinal *Wolfey,* by ditto. ib. 1521.

3. Lepidiffimum.
Luciani opufculum περὶ διψάδων
Henrico Bulloco interprete
Oratio ejufdem cum annotationibus marginalibus
Ex præclara Academiâ *Cantabrigienfi* An. M D XXI.

At the End,

Impreffum eft hoc opufculum Cantabrigiæ *per* Joannem Siberch, *&c.*

4. Galeni de temperamentis & de inequali intemperie libri tres. Thoma Linacro Anglo interprete. 4to. *per* Jo. Siberch, *apud præclaram* Cantabrigiam.

1521.

5. Papyrii Gemini *Eleatis* Hermathena, feu de Eloquentiæ victoria. 4to. ex præclara *Cantabrigiâ.*

1522.

Taviftock in *Devonfhire.* M D XXV.

The Boke of Confort called in laten *Boetius* de confolatione philofophie. Tranflated into *Engleffe* tonge.

At the End thus,

Here endeth the boke of Confort called in latyn *Boecius* de confolatione phil. Emprented in the exempt Monaftery of *Taveftok* in *Denfhyre*

by

by me *Thomas Rychard* Monk of the ſaid Monaſtery. To the inſtant deſyre of the ryght worſhypful Eſquyer Mayſter *Robert Langdon*, Anno D' MDXXV.

Deo gratias

Robertus *Langdon.*

This is ſuppoſed to have been Eſq; *Langdon*'s Mark.

JOHN OSWIN at *Ipſwich* and *Worceſter*. MDXLVIII.

1. Mind or Opinion what a Xtian ought to do that duells with the Papiſts. 8vo. By *John Oſwin* at *Ipſwich*. 1548.
2. *Chriſtopher Hegendorphine*'s houſhold Sermons. *Engliſh'd* at *Ipſwich*. 8vo. 1548.
3. Of the true Authority of the Church. ibid. 16°. 1548.
4. *John Ecolampadius*'s Epiſtle againſt reſpect to perſons. 16°. ibid. 1548.
5. Invective againſt Drunkenneſs. ibid. no date.
6. *Hegendorphine*'s houſhold Sermons. 8vo. at *Worceſter*. 1549.
7. The Book of Common Prayer, *&c.* fol. ibid. 1549.
8. Spiritual Matrimony between Xt and his Church. 16°. ibid. 1549.
9. Conſolatory for all Xtians. 8vo. ibid. 1549.
10. Dialogue between the ſeditious Anabaptiſt and the true Xtian about Obedience to Magiſtrates, *&c.* 8vo. ibid. 1550.
11. Short Pathway to underſtand the Scriptures. *Engliſh'd* by *John Vernon*. 8vo. ibid. 1550.
12. St. *Ambroſe* of Oppreſſion. Tranſlated by *John Oſwin*; intitled Poor *Naboth* oppreſſed by rich *Ahab*. no place's name.

JOHN

J O H N   M Y C H E L.

THOUGH this Printer put no dates to thefe few Editions of his I have been able to meet with, yet they feem both by the language, types, &c. to be older by much than 1550.

1. Two Dialogues of *Erafmus* in *Englifh*. Tranflated by *Ed. Beke*. 8vo. Emprynted by me *John Mychel*, dwellynge in St. *Paules* Paryfh in *Canterbury*. 8vo.

2. *Randal Hurlefton*'s Dialogue againft the Papifts. 8vo. at *Canterbury*.

3. *Lan. Ridley* of *Canterbury*'s Expofition of the Epiftle to the *Philippians*. 8vo.

N. B. I defigned to have enlarged this Catalogue with the compleat lift of all the curious editions of the moft ancient Print rs, fuch as printed only from Manufcripts as I have feen in my Lord *Pembroke*'s library, &c. but am glad to find that Mr. *Maittaire* has been beforehand with me in favouring the world with it in his *Annales Typographici*.

IN the conclufion of the fecond book of this Hiftory, pag. 257. I ventur'd to affirm after *Orlandi* and other Annalifts, that the invention of ingraving began much about the fame time with that of Printing; but I have been fince convinced, that the former began much earlier, from a curious collection which my Lord *Pembroke* was pleafed to fhow me, in which the whole progrefs of that invention is fet down in writing under each print. Having therefore obtain'd his Lordfhip's leave to copy it from his own book, and to give it a place in this work, I think I cannot better conclude this Hiftory than by obliging the curious with this valuable collection.

A N

AN

APPENDIX

To the GENERAL HISTORY of

PRINTING of BOOKS:

BEING AN

ADDITIONAL HISTORY

OF THE

RISE and PROGRESS of *PRINTS*,

Which are Incus'd.

Exactly copy'd from the R. H. the Earl of *Pembroke*'s curious Book of thofe P R I N T S, in which each Piece hath its own particular account of its manner, &c. in Manufcript, in a right progreffive order, as follows.

1. A NTONIO POLLAIOLOLO nat. 1426. ob. 1498. *Bal-dinucci* fays that he engraved the Battle at *Florence* about 1460, and that *Andrea Montegna* graved his Triumph at *Rome* foon after his being there. They both graved upon Pewter. The former printed his name on it thus, *Opus Antonij Pollaiololo Florentini.*

2. *Ifrael van Meckenem* his own Effigies.

3. This

3. This *Israel van Meckenem* is by some authors called *Van Mecklin* & *Mentz* & *Moguntin.* *Lomazero* says he was the first that engraved; he was Master to *Bon Martino*, who was Master to *Albert Durer*, whose first Print was a Copy after this of *Israel*'s *an.* 1497. and as *Baldinucci* says *Israel* did not engrave till he had seen the Triumph of *Ant. Montegno*, *anno* 1467, which is the oldest date that any author has mention'd, and the termination being *Spanish*, shows that the art spread very soon.

4. *A. M.* was, as is supposed, *Andrea de Murano* 1412. This Print is upon that mixt metal on which Goldsmiths used to engrave their first proofs. It is now likewise used by other artists. Founders call it the hard metal, and Printers the Type-metal, tho' the latter has a greater proportion of Iron. The other materials are Lead, Block-tin, and Regulus of Antimony. *Albert Durer* began by copying of old Prints, as you will see when you come to him ; this Print is older than that of 1467, which stands by it, which was taken to be the oldest of any one with a date by the author, who mentions this for want of knowing of that. As for the year 1412 above-mention'd it agrees with the time in which *A. de Murano* flourish'd ; and *Baldinucci* speaks in one place as if other authors were uncertain how near 1400 the invention of Prints was. Yet he seems to say that *Maso Finiguerri* was not long before *Pollaiololo*, who follow'd *Baccio Baldini*, who imitated *Maso* the inventor of Prints, by taking off some from engraved silver work to see the impression : but, unless he did so some years before, this Print must be older.

5. *Andrea Montegna* N. 1431. *an.* 1517. The next after *Pollaiololo* who engraved in *Italy.* His best works were after the Antique. But this first is none of the nine which he composed from the Antiques.

6. The sixth in order of his painting. This is his original Print; they have since finished (within these outlines) the Prints that are commonly sold for it.

7. This was printed when they used the smoke of a candle instead of
mp-black ink.

8. *Mich.*

8. *Mich. Angelo* on filk. This is only from a drawing, the painting of which has much more in it, and is to be feen in my Lord's Gallery. This is the firft Print that is not upon Paper.

9. The *Suavius* was the firft Print done on two Copper-plates This Print, befides the blue ground, has the figure of old *Time* clipping *Cupid's* wings After this *Perrier* did engrave this, and then the five more on three Copper-plates, as *Carpi* did upon wood.

10. The Head of *Lutma* the Father, done with the hammer; the black and white difpofed contrary to Mezotinto. *Per Janum Lutma.*

11. In this *John Lutma* has added graving to the hammering.

12. *Jacobus Lutma* mixed etching with engraving.

13. *Venus* and *Mavors* (*Mars*) by *Joannes Collaert*.
This is the only Print that ever was graved on Steel.

14. *Dominico Campagnola*, the firft that printed with red on a black ground.

15. This manner, which was invented in *Germany*, differs from all Prints, becaufe the ink rifes upon the paper.

16. This, done by *J. S.* (as in the fhield) came from *Venice* ; the lines are not engraved, but made by Points.

17. Four Mezotino's varying from the common manner of thofe Prints. In this the figure (our Saviour on the Crofs) is engraved, the reft is done in Mezotinto, the other three are each in a different colour.

18. Mr. *Tayler* a Painter, who improved the printing of Stuffs in *Holland*, he invented this Art of printing in colours ; and Mr. *Le Blond* (though he might take the hint from this has further improved it by printing his pieces fo as to look like painting ; the firft that he did in this kind was after the *Baroccio* in my Lord *Pembroke's* gallery.

19. The firft Print of *Martin Schön*, *al. Chon*, as the *French* write and pronounce it) and called *Bon Martino* by the *Italians*, *Bon* being a kind of a tranflation of *Schön*; which in the *High-German* fignifies *fine*

beau-

beautiful. *Martin* was Mafter to *Albert Durer,* but learned his Art at firft by copying after the Print next to it of *Ifrael van Meckenem.*

20. *Ifrael van Meckenem.* This is the only one of his that has the place's name, *viz. Tzù* (at) *Boackholt.*

21. The firft Print of *Albert Durer* 1497, which is a Copy after *Ifrael's.* He engraved this alfo upon Pewter.

Albert Durer nat. 1470, *ob.* 1528, was famous for cutting on Wood, and all other manners of ingraving, as may be feen by thefe four that follow, *viz.*

1ft. Engraved on Pewter, which was his firft manner.

2d. Cut on Wood, and on three planches.

3d. Engraved on Copper, in which he was the firft and the beft, and was imitated by *Mark Antonio.*

4th. Etched, being the firft of that kind.

22. *Mafo Finiguerra,* a Goldfmith at *Florence,* the inventer of Prints, tho' he made no Print till after *A. Pollaiololo.* *Albert Durer* copy'd this fo as to ftand the fame way as the Original. They ftand each by the other in the book.

23. *Albert Durer* made this piece in imitation of the oldeft Print, which was graved, *anno* 1412.

24. This bears the oldeft date of all his, whether on Wood or Copper

This is alfo dated 1502, but the mark differs from his ufual mark.

25. If *Hugo Carpi* was the inventor of Printing upon three planches, he muft have been very young ; for he was but 18 years old when *A. Durer* did this in 1522, which is the Head of *Ulricus Varnbuler* very large from three planches, with his own name to it *Albert Durer.*

26. The firft Print etch'd upon Iron by *A. Durer:*

27. Another of his of *anno* 1518, in which he perfected the Art of etching on Iron, even before *Parmigiano* ; tho' this laft in *Italy* is af firmed to have been the firft Etcher.

D d d

28. *Albert Durer* before his he ufed a mark, the manner of this is that of his Mafter.

29. The firft Print on Copper by *A. Durer*, with his mark before he began to date ; this is his firft manner.

30. This is without crofs-ftrokes ; *Melaine*'s manner is a fine improvement of this.

31. This piece is dated 1502, and bears the oldeft date either on Copper or Wood.

32. One of 1504. This *Adam* and *Eve* were the chief of his laft manner, vaftly neat, and imitated by *Marc Antonio* in *Germany*. This is reckoned more fcarce than his St. *Jerom*.

33. The St. *Jerom*. This the *Bolonia* edition of *Vafari* calls *La Maraviglia*, or the prodigy of Art.

34. The laft piece that *Durer* engrav'd. It is the head of *Erafmus*, and is dated 1526.

35. A Crucifix engraved on a golden head of the Emperor's Cane. It was fold for 150 Gilders, and is the only Print taken from Gold ; that of *An. Caracci* is only from a filver falver. My Lord has it : there is but this one Print of it, which he took off as a proof before it was gilt.

36. The famous Bag-piper by *Lucas van Leyden*. This is the Original, which was fold for 60 Duccatoons. The Copy, which ftands next to it, is pretty fcarce. Thefe two, and that on the gold cane, were on one Cartoon in the *Arundel* Collection.

N. B. Incufed is the proper term to fignify thofe plates which bear the ink between the lines of the graving, as *excufed* is of thofe that have it on the face of the line. Thus the prints in the *Paginæ Conglutinatæ* were *excufed*, but thofe of *Albert Durer incufed*, he being the firft inventor of this manner, as being cheaper, and eafier cut than upon copper.

The

The following is a Lift of XVI Volumes of D R A W I N G S
and P R I N T S in the fame Library relating to the fame
fubject as the former, and copy'd from the Manufcript-Titles
of the Books themfelves.

THESE Drawings and Prints confift but of a very few,
in comparifon of many numerous collections ; for here are chiefly
Italian defigns, and only one of each mafter, to fee the variety of manners, except of the moft noted *Italian* mafters a pretty many, and all
of fuch *Italian* Painters, as alfo themfelves graved, etched, or cut in
Wood : of original Drawings here are but two volumes of 220 ; *Italian*
Painters (except a few who were alfo efteem'd in *Italy*) in a chronological order. The 1ft Vol. has 200 Painters, one of each ; the 2d Vol·
has 20 of the chief Painters, of each five, but of *Rafael Urbin* and
Correggio 20 of each. As to Prints, *Marolles* had more than 50 times
as many. In his 1ft book he fays he had above 120,000 ; and in his
2d he added about 50,000 more. (The King of *France* has fince bought
them). But he gathered all, and of all forts that he could find, well or
ill preferv'd : as for intire books graved, there are very many, but here
are only thofe of *Italian* Painters, antiquities excepted ; as for loofe
Prints, only 14 volumes, as follows.

IN the firft 4 volumes of Prints are above 1500, each by a different
mafter, ending with *Edelinck, Andran,* and their difciples, engraving
and etching being brought to perfection by them.

Vol. III. but the firft of P R I N T S.

Part I. The Introduction comprehends the firft inventors of all the different manners, many of them now difus'd, or the Art loft.

Part II. Gravers, all of *Italian* Pictures.

Vol. IV.

Part 1. Etchers,
2. Cut on Wood, } all of *Italian* Pictures,
3. Mezotinto,

Vol.

Vol. V.

Gravers by Pictures of other nations not *Italian*.

Vol. VI.

Part 1. Etchers,
    2. Cut in Wood, } by Pictures of other nations not *Italian*.
    3. Mezotinto,

Vol. VII.

The 17 chief Gravers, their principal Prints all after *Italian* Paintings of *Rafael Urbin*, and all that they graved.

Vol. VIII.

23 Etchers, who were also Painters; and at the end are all that *Ang. Caracci* graved, the other two *Caracci's* being in this book.

Vol. IX.

12 More noted Etchers who were also Painters; most of these are famous for Landskips, and some also for little figures.

Vol. X.

The 5 chief Artists who cut in Wood, and only after great *Italian* Painters, all that they did both single, and as intire books.

Vol. XI.

All these are after *Rafael Urbin* by many Gravers and Etchers, different from those before-mention'd, at the end of which are many Drawings by *Santo Bartholi*, after such of *Rafael's* Pictures as were never graved, he intending, had he liv'd, to have graved them, they were sold by his Widow. Of *Raphael* and the following three, here are collections of single Prints also, the other great Painters have been graved chiefly in entire books.

Vol.

Vol. XII.

All thefe are after *Correggio*, both fingle Prints, and as entire books.

Vol. XIII.

All thefe are after *Guido Rheni* of fingle Prints.

Vol. XIV.

All thefe are after *Barocci :* but the 2d part is of the *Arundel* collection, only of the *Italian* hiftorical Pictures or Drawings.

Vol. XV. in two parts.

The heads of *Vandyke*, both thofe which he etched himfelf, and that were done by others, of which here are above 300. Part I. hath 100 of them, 19 of which are etched by *Vandyke*, the reft of the 100 are of M. *Vander Enden*.

Vol. XVI.

Single Prints of Antiquities, and chiefly thofe by *Lafreri*, being by the largeft fcale, as well as before they were mended, and fome are alfo as mended, by which one may compare what parts were truly antique ; I have alfo the book of *Lafreri* with the Title-page, but tho' fcarce, and of an old date, yet after thefe, fome body got an imperfect collection of fome of his Plates, and mix'd them with others of lefs value.

Thefe Volumes of DRAWINGS and PRINTS my Lord tells me were collected by his Father, except fome few, agreeable to his defign, which were afterwards added by my Lord himfelf, efpecially fuch as related to the origine of Prints.

AN

AN
ALPHABETICAL and CHRONOLOGICAL
TABLE

Of all the CITIES and PLACES in which the

ART of PRINTING

Began to be exercifed before the Year 1500,
and in ENGLAND to 1550.

*The firft Number is the Date of their firft known Edition,
and the fecond is the Page in which they are mention'd.*

A.

	an.	pag.
ABBEVILLE	1486	252
Alban St.	1486	327
Aloft	1487	215
Amberg	1471	191
Angoulefme	1493	256
Antwerp	1485	250
Aquila	1482	245
Argentina, al. *Stratzburg & Argentoratum*	1458	183 / 299
Augufta Vindelicorum, alias *Ausburgh*	1466	121
Avignon	1497	257

B.

	an.	pag.
BAMBERG	1499	257
Barcelona	1494	256
Bafil	1475	216
Bergamo	1498	257
Boifleduc	1487	253
Bolonia	1471	186
Brefcia	1474	214
Brudges	1477	231
Bruffels	1478	242

C.

F I N I S.